Children's Phobias:
A Behavioural Perspective

Children's Phobias:
A Behavioural
Perspective

NEVILLE J. KING
*Monash University
Melbourne, Victoria, Australia*

DAVID I. HAMILTON
*Deakin University,
Melbourne, Victoria, Australia*

and

THOMAS H. OLLENDICK
*Virginia Polytechnic Institute & State University
Blacksburg, Virginia, USA*

JOHN WILEY & SONS
Chichester · New York · Brisbane · Toronto · Singapore

Copyright © 1988, 1994 by John Wiley & Sons Ltd,
Baffins Lane, Chichester,
West Sussex PO19 1UD, England
Telephone (+44) 243 779777

Reprinted March 1994 (pbk)

Other Wiley Editorial Offices

John Wiley & Sons, Inc., 605 Third Avenue,
New York, NY 10158-0012, USA

Jacaranda Wiley Ltd, 33 Park Road, Milton,
Queensland 4064, Australia

John Wiley & Sons (Canada) Ltd, 22 Worcester Road,
Rexdale, Ontario M9W 1L1, Canada

John Wiley & Sons (SEA) Pte Ltd, 37 Jalan Pemimpin #05-04,
Block B, Union Industrial Building, Sinapore 2057

Library of Congress Cataloging-in-Publication Data

King, Neville J.
    Children's phobias.

    Bibliography: p.
    Includes index
    1. Phobias in children.   2. Behavior therapy.
I. Hamilton, David I.   II. Ollendick, Thomas H.
III. Title.   [DNLM: 1. Behavior Therapy—in infancy
& childhood.   2. Phobic Disorders—in infancy &
childhood. WM   178 K53c]
RJ506.P38K56   1987   618.92'85225   87-18894
ISBN 0-471-95139-0

British Library Cataloguing in Publication Data

A catalogue record for this book is available from the British Library

ISBN 0-471-95139-0 (pbk)

Typeset in 10/12pt Times by Thomson Press (India) Limited, New Delhi
Printed and bound in Great Britain by Redwood Books,
Trowbridge, Wiltshire, England

Contents

SECTION 3: CONCEPTUAL ISSUES

Preface

The clinical and educational problems of children have been subject to intensive research from a behavioural standpoint since the early 1960s. Despite advances in the behavioural treatment of adult phobics with Wolpe's (1958) *Psychotherapy by Reciprocal Inhibition*, the fears and phobias of children were somewhat neglected during the 1960s. Recent years have witnessed the publication of many case reports and experimental studies on children's phobias. This is welcomed as there is a definite need for clinical services to help parents with children who are 'too afraid' about certain things, 'nervous' about starting school, and so forth. Through the Psychology Centre at the Phillip Institute of Technology (NJK and DIH) and the Psychological Services Center at Virginia Polytechnic Institute & State University (THO), we have been fortunate to offer clinical services to parents seeking help for their children with problems of this nature. Consistent with the findings of other clinicians and researchers, we have been impressed with the potency of behavioural procedures and their acceptance on the part of children and their care providers.

Clinical experience and research findings indicate that the automatic extension of adult behavioural assessment and intervention procedures to childhood disorders is highly dubious. This is true for the behavioural management of children's phobias in several ways. First, a decision as to whether the child's fear is a clinical problem must be made with reference to the normal developmental fear pattern. Second, behavioural assessment and intervention must be cognizant of the child's age-related abilities lest there be unrealistic expectations of the child. Exposure is as critical with children as it is with adults, but the *application* of the principle to children requires skills and expertise of a different kind. Third, care providers are very important as sources of vital clinical information, and for their efforts and responsibility regarding the implementation of behavioural programmes. We hope that our concern for children as a special population and these particular issues are evident in the book.

In writing *Children's Phobias*, we have attempted to provide a systematic and evaluative account of the behavioural approach. Our aim is to provide a useful book in so far as the assessment, treatment and prevention of children's phobias is concerned. Literature reviews serve a vital function in the organization of research studies, case reports and theoretical dissertations. There is also a need for behavioural texts to provide detailed guidelines and practical points on the use of behavioural techniques. In our opinion, this is essential to the development of clinical expertise and effective intervention. Thus, we have been conscious of the need to strike a balance between literature review and practical guidelines for professionals employed in psychiatric, educational and health-care settings.

Our research and clinical services have been funded by the William Buckland Foundation and Research and Development Grants awarded by Phillip Institute of Technology, for which we are extremely grateful. We would like to express our gratitude to the many people that have assisted us over the journey with *Children's Phobias*. Thanks are due to our colleagues—especially Alan Hudson and Gregory Murphy—in the Department of Psychology at the Phillip Institute of Technology, for their comments and encouragement on various parts of the book. We are grateful to Henry Jackson, Clinical Psychology Department, Royal Park Psychiatric Hospital, for his advice and assistance on several issues related to phobia reduction. We are honoured to have the comments of the late Mary Cover Jones, University of California, Berkeley, a great pioneer of the behavioural approach with children. We would like to thank Rosalynn Wright for the typing of the manuscript, Eleonora Gullone for her assistance on the draft and proofs, Julie Plateo for her secretarial assistance at the Phillip Institute of Technology, and Cynthia Koziol for her efforts at Virginia Polytechnic Institute & State University. Above all, our warmest appreciation to our spouses and children—Judith-Anne and Melanie King; Jenny, Robert, Stephen, Katherine and Michael Hamilton; and Mary, Laurie and Katie Ollendick—without whose personal encouragement and patience the book would not have been written.

Finally, we dedicate the book to Mary Cover Jones (1897–1987).

NEVILLE J. KING
DAVID I. HAMILTON
THOMAS H. OLLENDICK

Foreword

This book needs no introduction. The authors speak for themselves and for children with problems, forcefully, clearly, comprehensively and under-standingly. I do have the pleasure of highlighting the fact that this is an excellent book, and that I am sympathetic to the behavioural approach which the authors promote. Joseph Wolpe once pointed out to me that I had neglected to align myself with innovators in the field of 'behaviour therapy'. My satisfaction in writing a foreword to this book may have set me on the proper path!

Within the behavioural framework the authors are eclectic and inclusive as well as evaluative (classical conditioning and sub-types, operant conditioning and sub-types, and vicarious conditioning). Some early writers would under-standably be impressed with the wealth of information presented in this book. How would G. Stanley Hall—who in the 1890s (e.g. Hall, 1897; Hall & Allin, 1897) used 'questionnaires' to obtain data on childrens' anger, humour and fears—view today's elaboration of emotional assessment measures? They are no longer described as the 'underworld of science'. The authors point out that although self-report measures have traditionally been down-graded in behavioural assessment because of their dubious validity, in recent years they have gained acceptability owing, to a certain extent, to 'consumer satisfaction'.

Behaviourism has come a long way since John B. Watson's 'behaviourist manifesto' in 1913 (Woodworth, 1958). The field of behaviour therapy has developed, as the authors explain, since the early studies of individual childrens' emotions, including Watson and Raynor's (1920) case of 'Albert', and my 'Peter'. In a lecture included in his book, *Behaviorism*, Watson (1924) stated: 'Finding that emotional responses could be built in with great readiness (Albert) we were all the more eager to see whether they could be broken down and by what methods' (p. 132). Watson and Watson (1921) were not able to continue their work with Albert. This brings up to Peter. The patient, meticulous, painstaking procedures used in the experiments with Peter reflected the methodological style of John B. Watson, who faithfully followed Peter's progress. I saw Peter in his home only once, several months after treatment. The authors of this book, in evaluating procedures, impress us with the fact that now follow-up is practically mandatory to good procedural design and beneficial outcome.

On a personal note, I entered Vassar College in 1915. Although I had no way of knowing it that time, it was the outcome of this event which led to my professional association with John B. Watson five years later. Rosalie Raynor Watson and I were classmates at Vassar College. It was through our association, which continued after our graduation in 1919, that I had the opportunity to work with John B. Watson. Watson paid us professional visits on many Saturday afternoons during the conduct of the therapeutic sessions with Peter. This was at the Hechscher Foundation ('for the protection and welfare of children'), Fifth Avenue, New York City. During my year of research, my husband, Harold E. Jones, and myself and our daughter, Barbara, lived there with some 30 children. Over the entrance was engraved 'The Childrens' Home for Happiness', but we sometimes wondered! Further reflections on these years and the work of John B. Watson can be found in other articles that I have written (Jones, 1974, 1975).

There are readers with many different backgrounds who will find the book profitable as well as pleasurable. Clinicians, medical and dental personnel, paediatricians, teachers, school administrators, care providers, and parents, will want to cooperate to facilitate the removal, reduction and prevention of childrens' problems. Otto Klineberg in his foreword to Stone and Church, *Childhood and Adolescence* (1957), rather humorously described Americans as eager disciples of the so-called experts: 'Our comic magazines are filled with flattering references to the "techniques" of the child psychologist'. However, Murphy, Hudson and King (1982) found that the parents of Australian school children would either prefer to consult an alternative professional to a child psychologist, or would not seek any professional advice. This book will induce many parents and other care providers to become partners with specialists in the prevention and treatment of children's problems. For me, *Childrens' Phobias* is an outstanding contribution to the field.

MARY COVER JONES

Section 1
Phenomenology, Aetiology and Assessment

CHAPTER 1

Childhood fears and phobias

INTRODUCTION

The meanings of, and relationships between, constructs such as *anxiety*, *fear* and *phobia* need to be carefully examined. In its traditional usage, the word 'anxiety' refers to an aversive or unpleasant emotional state involving subjective apprehension and physiological arousal of a diffuse nature. Miller (1983) writes: 'Anxiety is defined as a dysphoric, aversive feeling similar to fear that arises *without* an obvious external threat' (p. 338). Similarly, Johnson and Melamed (1979) state: 'Anxiety is a more diffuse, less focused response, perhaps best described as apprehension without apparent cause' (p. 107). Sometimes the term *free-floating* anxiety is used to describe feelings of anxiety that cannot be related to any particular situation (Lader & Marks, 1971). At other times anxiety is depicted as being either *state* anxiety or *trait* anxiety. On the basis of their factor analysis research, Cattell and Scheier (1958, 1961) define state (or acute) anxiety as a transitory condition which varies from moment to moment and from day to day, whilst trait (or chronic) anxiety is defined as a relatively permanent and stable characteristic. Spielberger (1972) defines state and trait anxiety in the following way:

> State anxiety (A-State) may be conceptualized as a transitory emotional state or condition of the human organism that varies in intensity and fluctuates over time. This condition is characterized by subjective, consciously perceived feelings of tension and apprehension, and activation of the autonomic nervous system.... Trait anxiety (A-Trait) refers to relatively stable individual differences in anxiety proneness, that is, to differences in the disposition to perceive a wide range of stimulus situations as dangerous or threatening, and in the tendency to respond to such threats with A-State reactions. (p. 39).

As we shall see, the distinction between state and trait anxiety has a bearing on the instruments and measures that are chosen in working with children.

Fears are usually described as normal reactions to real or imagined situations. According to Marks (1969): 'Fear is a normal response to active or imagined threat in higher animals, and comprises an outer behavioural expression, an inner feeling, and accompanying physiological changes' (p. 1). Ollendick (1979b) states:

'Nearly every child experiences some degree of fear during his emergence from childhood to adulthood. While such fears vary in intensity and duration, they are usually mild, age-specific, and transitory' (p. 127). Typically, children display these reactions towards stimuli such as darkness, animals, dentists, and imaginary creatures at some point in their development. These fears are relatively short-lived, tend to reflect the age of the individual, and do not involve extremely intense reactions.

A phobia, on the other hand, is regarded as a special form of fear. In differentiating phobias from fears, Marks (1969) points out that a phobia:

(1) is out of proportion to the demands of the situation;
(2) cannot be explained or reasoned away;
(3) is beyond voluntary control;
(4) leads to avoidance of the feared situation.

Each of these points deserves elaboration in relation to children's phobias. The first point highlights the fact that children's phobic reactions are extreme, given the reality of the situation. For example, the sight of a dog does not warrant a near panic reaction as displayed by children with such a phobia. The second point informs us that providing children with a verbal explanation of the phobia has no impact on their phobic behaviour. Stressing the illogical or silly nature of the phobia also does not help to relieve the problem. The third point suggests that children may attempt to overcome the phobia, to 'will' it away, but are often unable to do so. Several approaches or interactions with the feared situation may be attempted, but for various reasons the children remain afraid. Hence efforts at voluntary control are unsuccessful. The fourth point refers to the most significant characteristic of phobic behaviour. Typically, children (as well as adults) deliberately avoid the feared object or situation. Rather than confront feared situations, phobic children pursue various means of avoidance. If unexpectedly confronted with the fear stimulus, an immediate escape from the situation is usually evident. Avoidance and escape behaviour become the typical ways of coping with the phobia in everyday life.

In a similar vein to the definition presented by Marks, the American Psychiatric Association (1987) describes a phobia as a

> ...persistent and irrational fear of a specific object, activity, or situation that results in a compelling desire to avoid the dreaded object, activity, or situation (the phobic stimulus). More commonly, the person does actually avoid the feared situation or object, though he or she recognizes that the fear is unreasonable and unwarranted by the actual dangerousness of the object, activity, or situation. (p. 403)

The above definitions of a phobia do not explicitly rule out the possibility of the fear reaction being part and parcel of normal child development. As just noted, children become afraid of many things in their development. Most of these fears are transient and age-related and should not be regarded as phobias. In response to these issues, Miller, Barrett and Hampe (1974) have elaborated upon the definition provided by Marks. According to Miller *et al.*, a phobia is a special form of fear which:

(1) is out of proportion to the demands of the situation;
(2) cannot be explained or reasoned away;
(3) is beyond voluntary control;
(4) leads to avoidance of the feared situation;
(5) persists over an extended period of time;
(6) is unadaptive;
(7) is not age or stage specific. (p. 90)

Because of its attention to the transient nature of fears and their developmental course, this is probably the most widely accepted definition of a phobia by those working with children (Morris & Kratochwill, 1983; Ollendick, 1979b). Hence phobias are differentiated from fears on the basis of their magnitude, persistence and maladaptiveness (Barrios, Hartmann & Shigetomi, 1981; Graziano, DeGiovanni & Garcia, 1979; Marks, 1969; Morris & Kratochwill, 1983; Miller *et al.*, 1974). Graziano, DeGiovanni & Garcia further attempt to operationalize clinical fears or phobias. According to these authors: 'Intensity and duration might be important defining characteristics, and we suggest that clinical fears be defined as those with a duration of over 2 years or an intensity that is debilitating to the client's routine life-style' (p. 805). A period of 2 years is specified on the grounds that Hampe, Noble, Miller and Barrett (1973) found that most children, even those with intense fears, overcame these fears within 2 years. A 2-year period may have some merit from a research viewpoint, but would be problematic as a criteria for therapy in a clinical setting (Miller, 1983) and pays little attention to the discomfort experienced by the child during that interval of time (Ollendick, 1979b).

When the above terms are examined more closely, we become less certain about their meanings and relationships. Berecz (1968) has identified some of the sources of confusion. Theoretical bias is frequently evident in definitions of phobias. Psychoanalysts often define phobias as displaced fears; hence description is confounded with theory. The word 'phobia' has been used to describe such a variety of conditions that it might be seen to lose its communicative value (some political leaders are considered to have a phobia of communism!). The terms anxiety and phobia have carried different meanings in different periods of history (consider the development of terms such as *anxiety neurosis, anxiety hysteria, anxiety reaction,* and *phobic reaction*). These problems are accentuated in the study of children's phobias, according to Berecz, if childhood psychopathology is regarded as a 'miniature replica' of what is found in adults. Problems with definitions do not rest here, with much debate about the nature of anxiety. Anxiety is defined as a diffuse entity, but it is not uncommon to speak of *phobic anxiety.* It can be argued that anxiety is a construct that has been reified (i.e. given concrete existence) in clinical psychology and psychiatry. According to Borkovec, Weerts and Bernstein (1977), anxiety itself has developed a 'multiple personality':

> It has been viewed as transient emotional/physiological *behavior* (i.e., 'He is anxious today'), a dispositional *trait* ('She is an anxious person'), and a cause or *explanation* of behavior (i.e., 'He overeats because of anxiety'). (p. 368)

Also, the distinction between fear and phobia on the basis of the intensity or magnitude of the individual's reaction is sometimes questioned. An individual may react with the same degree of physiological and behavioral distress to a harmless stimulus (e.g. the sight of a bird) as to a life-threatening event (e.g. an earthquake), yet one instance may be judged 'pathological' and the other 'normal'. Carr (1979) argues that pathology lies in the degree to which the individual's reaction disrupts the processes that are functionally important. The disruption may be in the cognitive/verbal, physiological or motor areas. Thus pathology arises when the reaction interferes with the lifestyle of the individual or family. Despite any apparent precision, the terms anxiety, fear and phobia are employed very loosely, and sometimes treated as being virtually synonymous.

Other writers on children's fears and phobias have been forced to the same conclusion regarding these terms and concepts. Bamber (1979) states: 'There appears to be little agreement either to what is meant by "fear" or to the precise relation between the concepts of "fear", "anxiety" and "phobia"' (p. 11). For Morris and Kratochwill (1983):

> Problems of definition are somewhat of an understatement in the literature on childhood fears. Such terms as 'fear', 'anxiety', 'phobia', 'avoidance behavior', are used somewhat differently and sometimes interchangeably within and among different theoretical positions.' (p. 28).

Morris and Kratochwill maintain that an analysis of these states in terms of the individual's cognitive, physiological and motor systems should help operationalize these labels and advance knowledge in the field independent of theoretical position. Leaving theoretical problems and language nuances aside, we shall now review the basic research on childhood fears, and then focus on the clinical fears or phobias of childhood. Fortunately, semantic problems have not impeded the assessment, treatment and prevention of children's phobias.

CHILDREN'S FEARS

The fears of children have been studied by numerous investigators for many decades. Towards the end of the nineteenth century, G. Stanley Hall (1897) published a lengthy article on a study of children's fears. Hall accumulated data and impressions on the fears of over 1500 people mostly under 23 years of age. Special groups of fears were studied in considerable detail (e.g. fear of high places and falling, fear of losing orientation; fear of closeness; fear of water, fear of wind). Interestingly, Hall noted the frustrations of questionnaire research in this area:

> Some merely list the objects they fear, and others give copious details of a single fear or even fright; some report half a dozen fears of their own and add others of their friends, sometimes omitting not only age, but sex. Thus the problem of statistics was rendered exceedingly difficult, and each table is based upon only those returns which yield its data, so that everything had to be gone over independently for each table. (p. 151)

There appear to be several reasons for research on children's fears. Most researchers have been concerned with the identification of these fears and how they develop and are related to demographic variables. Thus, children's fears have been seen as an important area of developmental psychology. Other investigators have taken an interest in this area because of the clinical implications of such findings. In the 1930s, this research raised the question of how parents manage the excessive fears of their children (Jersild & Holmes, 1935b). The research on children's fears has been reviewed extensively by Berecz (1968), Bamber (1979), Graziano, DeGiovanni, & Garcia (1979), Johnson and Melamed (1979), Miller (1983), Miller et al., (1974), Miller (1979) and Ollendick (1979b). In the present discussion, the research on children's fears will be reviewed in terms of its findings and methodological and theoretical issues related to those findings.

Findings

Childhood fears have been investigated in various ways, depending upon the purpose of the research as well as the age and number of children being studied. Some researchers have asked parents or children to verbally describe or write down the fear stimuli. Fear survey schedules provide a more structured means of identifying the specific stimuli that elicit fear in children. Typically, the child is required to provide a self-rating of the level of fear experienced for each item listed on the survey. Representative of these instruments are the Fear Survey Schedule for Children (Scherer & Nakamura, 1968), the Louisville Fear Survey for Children (Miller, Barrett, Hampe & Noble, 1972b) and the Children's Fear Survey Schedule (Ryall & Dietiker, 1979). A revised version of the Scherer and Nakamura scale has been reported in recent years (Ollendick, 1983b).

Anxiety scales and other instruments have at times been used in conjunction with the fear survey schedules. Of particular note are the State Trait Anxiety Inventory for Children (Spielberger, 1973) and the Children's Manifest Anxiety Scale (Castaneda, McCandless & Palermo, 1956) with the latter scale also being revised in recent years (Reynolds & Richmond, 1978, 1979).

As well as being designed for research purposes, these scales are utilized in clinical settings (see Chapter 3). Here, a summary of the research findings on children's fears is given in relation to frequency, content, age, sex differences, socioeconomic class, pathological behaviour and special populations.

Frequency

As would be anticipated, the research evidence indicates that childhood fears are common. In a very early study, Hagman (1932) interviewed the mothers of pre-school children and concluded that the average number of fears for the group was 2.7. Jersild and Holmes (1935a) found that children aged 2 to 6 years had an average of 4.6 fears, and displayed a fear reaction every $4\frac{1}{2}$ days. Pratt (1945) studied rural children and found the average number of fears to be 7.5. In a longitudinal investigation, MacFarlane, Allen and Honzik (1954) found that 90% of children in their sample had a specific fear at least once during the first 14 years of their lives. In a study of 482 children, Lapouse and Monk (1959) found that 43% of the mothers reported having children with seven or more fears.

Using a self-report fear survey schedule, Ollendick (1983b) found an average of 11 fears for children aged 8 to 11 years. In another study of 126 children and adolescents between 7 and 18 years of age, Ollendick, Matson and Helsel (1985a) found the average number of fears across age and gender to be about 13. It will be noted that the two most recent studies are fairly similar in the average number of children's fears, at least as reported by children themselves.

In conclusion, it appears that childhood fears are very common and that children report experiencing multiple fears.

Content

In relation to what elicits fear in children, Hall (1897) noted thunder and lightning, reptiles, darkness, strange persons, fire, death, disease, insects, wild animals, ghosts, water, and other stimuli. Hagman (1932) found that the things most feared in rank order were dogs, doctors, storms, deep water and darkness. In this study, there was a tendency for the child to have fears corresponding to those of the mother. Jersild, Markey and Jersild (1933) reported the following rank order of fears: supernatural agents (ghosts, witches, corpses, mysterious events); being alone, in the dark, in a strange place, being lost; attack or danger of attack by animals; bodily injury, falling, illness, traffic accidents and operations.

More recently, Scherer and Nakamura (1968) administered two self-report instruments (the Fear Survey Schedule for Children and Children's Manifest Anxiety Scale) to a group of children aged 9 to 12 years. A factor analysis was performed on each scale yielding eight factored subscales: fear of failure or criticism (e.g. by parents, teachers), major fears (e.g. fire, being hit by a truck), minor fears (travel—e.g. riding in the car or bus), medical fears (e.g. sharp objects, doctors), fear of death (e.g. death or dead people, getting sick at school), fear of the dark (e.g. ghosts or spooky things, being alone), home–school fears (e.g. being tested, getting poor grades), and miscellaneous fears (e.g. bats or birds, loud sirens). The 10 most prominent fears to emerge from this study were being sent to the principal, fire (being burned), being hit by a car or a truck, germs or getting a serious illness, not being able to breathe, death or dead people, bombing attacks or being invaded, getting poor grades, failing a test, and arguing parents.

Miller *et al.* (1972b) used the Louisville Fear Survey for Children to identify what children fear. The survey was administered to the parents of a group of children aged 6 to 16 years. In carrying out a factor analysis of the parent ratings, the researchers extracted 'three primary' dimensions, including: (a) fear of physical injury, (b) fear of natural and supernatural dangers, and (c) fear of psychic stress (e.g. social events, examinations). In comparing parent-rating factors obtained in their study with the child-rating factors reported by Scherer and Nakamura (1968), Miller *et al.* noted 'remarkable similarities' despite the methodological differences between the two studies. According to Miller *et al.* (1972b):

> Scherer and Nakamura report eight factors, two of which (medical and miscellaneous) grouped items which factored out in the present study. Three factors (major fears, minor fears, and death) fall clearly within the domain of Factor I (physical injury), two Scherer and Nakamura factors (criticism and home/school) represent Louisville Factor III (psychic stress), and Scherer and Nakamura Factor VIII is one component of the present Factor II (natural events). (p. 267)

Thus, the factor structure of fears reported by children appear to be similar to those reported by parents. But as Miller *et al.* also point out:

> Confirmation of observed similarities between parent and child ratings, however, can occur only when both samples are given the same inventory and both sets of data are subjected to the same statistical procedures. (p. 267)

In examining the factor studies of adult fears (e.g. Dixon, Monchaux & Sandler, 1957), Miller *et al.* conclude that fear of physical injury and psychic stress carry through much of the life span, while fear of natural events mitigates with age.

Recent research on what children fear has involved a revision of the Fear Survey Schedule for Children. Ollendick (1983b) performed a factor analysis on the responses of two normal samples of children that had been administered the revised scale. A 5-factor solution was obtained which accounted for 77% of the variance. The factor structure described by Ollendick is as follows:

Factor 1: Fear of failure and criticism
Factor 2: Fear of the unknown
Factor 3: Fear of injury and small animals
Factor 4: Fear of danger and death
Factor 5: Medical fears

While only five factors were retained in the solution, Ollendick noted that they were conceptually similar to those found by Scherer and Nakamura (1968) and Miller *et al.* (1972b). Ollendick also observed: 'items occasionally appear together without having an easily discernible logical relationship' (p. 688). For example, Factor 5 includes 'riding in the car' and 'talking on the telephone as well as medical items like 'having to go to hospital' and 'going to the doctor'. Children may have both kinds of fear (perhaps fearing the car because it might be transport to the doctor). Ollendick maintains: 'These possible relationships await empirical verification through cross validation of the factor structure of the FSSC-R and through intensive individual interviews of children in future research' (p. 688). Seven of the 10 most prominent fears were identical for girls and boys (a burglar breaking into our house, being sent to the principal, bombing attacks, being hit by a car or truck, falling from high places, earthquakes and not being able to breathe). Also, 8 of the 10 most prominent fears for boys and girls belong to Factor 4 and are remarkably similar to those reported by Scherer and Nakamura (1968).

Ollendick *et al.* (1985a) obtained very similar results in another investigation on the fears of 126 children aged 7 to 18 years. In this study the percentage of children and adolescents endorsing the 10 most common fears was as follows: being hit by a car or truck (42%); not being able to breathe (38%); fire—getting burned (38%); death or dead people (36%); bombing attacks—being invaded (34%); getting poor grades (34%); a burglar breaking into our house (33%); having my parents argue (33%); looking foolish (31%); falling from high places (30%); and being sent to the principal (30%). Of the 11 fears (two were tied for tenth place), 8 belong to Factor 4 while the other 3 belong to Factor 1. Looking over the results of the factor analysis studies, one is immediately struck by the similarity of the findings. A definite theme in children's responses concerns safety and danger. For Ollendick (1983b) it is understandable that fears of physical danger should continue, but alarming to see that children are still afraid of being sent to the principal.

Age

The relationship between age and fear has been of interest to many researchers. In the early months it is difficult to judge what is fearful behaviour and what is non-fearful behaviour. Watson believed that diffuse responses in the infant are indicative of fear (Watson, 1928; Watson & Watson, 1921). Jersild and Holmes (1935a) also concluded that sudden movement, loud noises and loss of support elicited fear responses in infants. Their findings on the relationship between age and fear are reproduced in Fig. 1.1. However, not all researchers are prepared to identify fear behaviour in the young infant so readily (Bronson, 1968).

Towards the end of the first year there is an increase in fear of strange persons, strange objects and heights (Levy, 1951; Scarr & Salapatek, 1970). Around 1 and 2 years of age, children are also afraid of the toilet (Miller *et al.*, 1974). At about 2 to 4 years, children develop fears of being alone, darkness, dogs and snakes (Jersild & Holmes, 1935a; MacFarlane *et al.*, 1954; Pratt, 1945). Fear of ghosts, monsters, spooks, bogeymen, robbers and kidnappers (depicted in stories and television programmes) become predominant in 4–6 year olds (Bowlby, 1973). Between 7 and 10 years, children develop fears of bodily injury, death and school (Bauer, 1976; Croake & Knox, 1973; Mauerer, 1965). Economic-political, social and personal conduct fears increase during later childhood and remain important concerns (Angelino, Dollins & Mech, 1956; Croake, 1969; Miller *et al.*, 1972b; Pratt, 1945). Generally, there is an age-related decline in fears of animals, darkness and imaginary creatures, but an age-related increase in school and social fears (Graziano, DeGiovanni & Garcia, 1979).

An important age-related fear that has received much attention on the part of developmental psychologists is fear of strangers or 'eight-month anxiety'. Many studies have shown an accentuation of negative responses to strangers in infants between 7 and 9 months (see reviews by Smith, 1979; Sroufe, 1977). Numerous theories have been offered in explanation of this phenomenon. For example, it has been theorized that fear of strangers may be innate (comparable

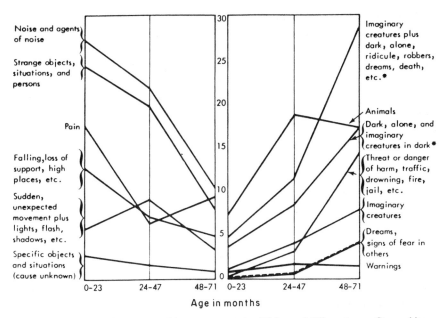

Fig. 1.1 The relative frequency of fear responses in children of different ages. Starred items represent a cumulative tally of two or more categories that are also depicted separately. Reproduced from Jersild and Holmes (1935b) by permission of Columbia University Press.

to innate flight mechanisms in animals), or due to the infant's increasing social and cognitive discrimination capacities, or related to fear of separation from the mother, or stimulus incongruity between the stimulus properties of the stranger and the infant's mental representational structure of familiar humans (Horner, 1980).

The most interesting development in the literature is the more conservative stance that is now being taken with respect to the universality of fear of strangers. Rheingold and Eckerman (1973) state that 'only the rare baby has shown any behavior that resembles fear of the stranger' (p. 118). Smith (1979) agrees that not all infants show fear of strangers, but maintains that if low-intensity fear (gaze aversion, heart-rate acceleration) is monitored as well as 'frank' fear (overt crying or flight) about 60% of infants may be expected to show signs of fear they would not have shown in a similar situation before. According to Horner (1980), the two basic methods of confronting infants with unfamiliar adults (i.e. stranger-controlled and infant-controlled confrontations) elicit different responses. Sroufe (1977) argues that stranger wariness is moderated if the stranger approaches gradually, the child feels some control of the situation, and the mother is present and the setting is familiar. Sroufe also notes stable individual differences in the fear of stranger phenomena.

Age-related fears tend to be viewed as being fairly transient and of short duration (Morris & Kratchowill, 1983). In support of this hypothesis, Jersild and Holmes (1935a) found that three-quarters of the fears of 2–5 year old children did not last a 3-week reporting period. However, not all researchers have found children's fears to be this transient. In an investigation of the stability of fears in 4th-grade children, Eme and Schmidt (1978) found 83% of the fears initially reported by the children to be expressed 1 year later. In a study of fears in children and adolescents, Ollendick *et al.* (1985a) were surprised at their findings on this issue. Although it appeared that younger children have more fears than older children and adolescents, clear age differences in the quantity and pattern of fears were not observed. In fact, fears of injury, natural events and social fears were characteristic of all ages. The researchers emphasized that children's fears may be more stable and durable than indicated in the literature.

Sex differences

A fairly consistent finding is that girls report more fears than boys (Angelino *et al.*, 1956; Bamber, 1974; Croake, 1969; Croake & Knox, 1973; Cummings, 1944, 1946; Hall, 1897; Lapouse & Monk, 1959; Ollendick, 1983b; Ollendick *et al.*, 1985a; Pratt, 1945; Russell, 1967; Scherer & Nakamura, 1968; Spiegler & Liebert, 1970). It also appears that there are sex differences in terms of fear objects and fear intensity, although this is a less certain finding. In the study by Lapouse and Monk (1959), mothers of children aged 6 to 12 years reported a significantly higher percentage of girls as having fears and worries about snakes, strangers, dirt, animals and bugs than boys. In their study of children aged 7 to 18 years, Ollendick *et al.* (1985a) found that girls reported more fears and an overall higher intensity of fears compared with boys. The findings applied across a wide range of children and adolescents. Girls reported an average of 16 fears, while boys reported an average of 8 fears. Girls also scored significantly higher than boys on all five factors (failure and criticism, fear of the unknown, fear of injury and small animals, fear of danger and death, and medical fears). Greater fear intensity in girls than in boys has been shown in other studies as well (Bamber, 1974; Ollendick, 1983b; Russell, 1967; Scherer & Nakamura, 1968).

Interestingly, Morris and Kratochwill (1983) have expressed concern about the reliability of the findings on sex differences. They believe that studies based on self-report or teacher ratings are more likely to show significant sex differences than observational studies (see, for example, MacCoby & Jacklin, 1974). Furthermore, they point out that that some studies do not find sex differences (e.g. Miller, Barrett, Hampe & Noble, 1971; Nalven, 1970). Nevertheless, it is difficult to escape the overall conclusion that sex differences do exist in relation to children's fears. However, an obvious area of concern regarding sex differences is the extent to which sex role expectations (according to which girls are less able to cope than boys) may affect the reporting of fear either by children or their parents (Graziano, DeGiovanni & Garcia, 1979, Ollendick *et al.*, 1985a).

Measuring the physiological responses (e.g. heart rate, GSR) of girls and boys during a slide presentation of neutral stimuli (e.g. landscape) and common fear stimuli (e.g. snakes) may help yield useful information on this issue. If girls are 'really' more afraid than boys, greater physiological changes should occur for girls. A similar experiment on adult phobics was conducted by Wilson (1966). In this experiment there was no significant difference between males and females in terms of physiological responses. Such a study is yet to be conducted with boys and girls.

Socio-economic class

Socio-economic class (SEC) also appears to be an important variable in children's fears, particularly on the type or content of fears. Lower-SEC children seem to have more fears of specific events or things. An often cited study which illustrates the importance of socio-economic class is that of Angelino *et al.* (1956). In this study, a large number of children were grouped into upper- or lower-class. Lower-class boys were found to fear switchblades, whippings, robbers, killers, guns and matters of violence, whereas upper-class boys feared car accidents, getting killed, juvenile delinquents, disaster, and other more nebulous events. Lower-class girls feared animals, strangers and acts of violence, whereas upper-class girls feared kidnappers, heights, and a variety of things not mentioned by lower-class girls, such as train crashes and shipwrecks. Support for SEC differences in type or content of fears, and sometimes number of fears (lower-SEC children having more fears), has been provided by several other studies (Bamber, 1974; Jersild & Holmes, 1935a; Nalven, 1970; Newstatter, 1938).

The interpretation of these findings deserves comment. It is possible that the differences in fear content (if not number of fears) between lower- and higher-SEC children may be a function of quite different environmental experiences (consider parental values, standard of living and dangers). As noted by Graziano, DeGiovanni and Garcia (1979):

> The fears of lower SEC children ('ghetto' children in Nalven's, 1970, study) strongly suggest the socially determined nature of fear content and an immediacy and reality basis for the expressed fears of the lower SEC children. The data suggest that these children may perceive their immediate environments as far more hostile than do higher SEC children. This is a hypothesis well worth testing, but it has not been investigated within the scope of the fear literature. (p. 810)

However, it is possible that differences in education and understanding may also account for the findings. In relation to this point, Nalven (1970) found that lower-SEC children tended to list specific animal fears (rats and cockroaches) rather than generic groupings (dangerous animals or poisonous insects). This problem would be especially significant for those studies that rely upon children listing their fears. Finally, it should be noted that comparing the outcome of studies to ascertain differences in fear between SEC groups is difficult because of the lack of standardization as to how SEC is defined (Morris & Kratochwill, 1983).

Pathological behaviour

The relationship between fear and pathological behaviour in children has not been subject to much systematic research. There is weak evidence of a relationship between fear and manifest anxiety (Scherer & Nakamura, 1968) and between fear and neuroticism (Bamber, 1974). McFarlane *et al.* (1954) reported correlations between children's fears and a variety of problems including general anxiety, irritability and timidity. However, the correlations were low and not consistent across age groups.

Whether there is a relationship between fears and specific behavioural problems is an interesting question. In their extensive study, Lapouse and Monk (1959) found no significant correlations between fears and other behaviours (e.g. bedwetting, nightmares, stuttering, tics), as reported by mothers. A subsample of children were interviewed, but again no significant relationship between fear and pathological behaviour emerged. As noted by Morris and Kratochwill (1983), there is a paucity of data on this issue, thus making it difficult to draw any definite conclusions. Graziano, DeGiovanni and Garcia (1979) suggest that intensity of fear may be the critical factor in the attempt to relate children's fears to behaviour pathology. Bearing in mind that clinical fears or phobias sometimes present together with other behavioural problems, their hypothesis is quite reasonable and should be researched more fully.

Special populations

Fear in intellectually and physically handicapped children has not been extensively researched. Prima facie, it would not be surprising if certain handicaps produced concerns and fears that are less apparent in normal children. Hence there may be quantitative and qualitative differences in fears between normal and special children. For example, Derevensky (1979) examined the fears of exceptional and normal children. Three groups of exceptional children were studied; that is, educable mentally retarded children, trainable mentally retarded children, and specific learning disabled children. The children in each of these groups were 6–12 years of age. The children were interviewed individually, and asked 'What are the things to be afraid of?' followed by 'And what else?' Eight categories of responses were analysed (i.e. animals, people, dark, spooks, natural hazards, machinery, death and injury, and miscellaneous). In general, exceptional children were found to have a wider range and greater number of fears than normal children. The percentages of responses within categories were quite similar across student populations. Similar developmental trends were found in all groups, with younger children reporting more unrealistic fears than older children. There were no appreciatable differences between males and females concerning the number of fears.

Ollendick, Matson and Helsel (1985b) examined the level and structure of fear on the revised fear survey schedule in visually impaired and normally sighted children and adolescents. The visually impaired were given various forms of assistance (magnifying aid, large print, braille, taped explanation) to ensure that they understood the stimulus items and response alternatives. The visually impaired group had significantly higher total fear scores than the sighted group, suggesting quantitative differences with respect to overall levels of fear. Important qualitative differences were also apparent. Visually impaired youths showed greater fear on items depicting potentially physically dangerous and harmful situations (e.g. burglar breaking into the house), while normally sighted youths were more fearful about psychologically harmful situations (e.g. getting a report card). As the researchers comment, such results are not surprising. A visually impaired person is likely to be fearful of situations in which vision is useful or imperative to their well-being. It appears from these two studies that children with intellectual and physical handicaps may have more fears than normal children, and tend to fear different events or situations.

Methodological and theoretical issues

There are several theoretical and methodological issues associated with the research on children's fears that should be emphasized. The first issue concerns sampling. Because of research costs and the limited availability of subjects, researchers have examined fear in limited segments of the child population. For example, most samples have been drawn from psychiatric populations (Marks & Gelder, 1966; Poznanski, 1973), children referred to school psychologists (Maurer, 1965), and rural children (Pratt, 1945). Obviously greater attention should be given by researchers to diverse groups (by sex, age, race, socio-economic level, and geographical location) if samples are to be representative of the general child population. One of the few attempts at random sampling was carried out by Lapouse and Monk (1959). According to the researchers:

> ... the 482 children admitted to the sample were found by approaching 1600 addresses systematically from the 1955 Buffalo City Directory. In each household having more than one child in the age range 6 to 12, the sample child was chosen by the use of a selection table specially devised to meet such a problem. (p. 804)

Of course, relying upon a telephone directory is questionable in terms of the representative nature of the sample. A reasonable compromise for researchers would be carefully selected samples of school children. Schools are a convenient source and location for the study of children's fears (Ollendick, 1983b; Ollendick et al., 1985a). With more attention being given to the demographic characteristics of school-based samples, it will be possible to extrapolate to the general child population with a greater degree of confidence.

The second issue concerns the reliability and validity of the fear assessment procedures employed in the research investigations. Many studies (e.g. Angelino et al., 1956; Croake, 1969; Derevensky, 1979; Maurer, 1965; Nalven, 1970; Pratt, 1945) have relied upon asking children or parents to 'write down' or 'tell me' the things they are afraid of. Such data-gathering procedures are highly questionable in terms of reliability and validity. Comparing the separate interview data of children and their mothers, Lapouse and Monk (1959) found that mothers underestimated their children's assessment by 41.9%. With the advent of the fear survey schedules for children, research has become increasingly sophisticated. The advantages over earlier methods reside in better standardization and more comprehensive assessment, and hence potentially greater reliability and validity.

In terms of the reliability of the fear survey instruments, Scherer and Nakamura (1968) report a very high split-half reliability coefficient (0.96) for the Fear Survey Schedule for Children. Miller *et al.* (1972b) also report a very high split-half reliability coefficient (0.96) for the Louisville Fear Survey for Children, and Ryall and Dietiker (1979) report a satisfactory test–retest reliability coefficient (0.85) for the Children's Fear Survey Schedule. In the absence of hard data, the validity of nearly all of the fear survey schedules is questionable, however. Interestingly, Scherer and Nakamura found a modest correlation (0.49) between the Fear Survey Schedule for Children and the Children's Manifest Anxiety Scale. Scherer and Nakamura (1968) note that the correlation between the two instruments is similar to that obtained in adult studies, and is due to differences in theoretical rationales (and hence item content) between the scales. Obviously, more research is required on reliability (split-half and test–retest reliability) and concurrent validity (data gleaned on a fear survey schedule needs to correlate highly with the child's behaviour when encountering fear-arousing stimuli in the natural environment).

Recent years have seen further research on the psychometric properties of the fear survey schedules for children. Ollendick (1983b) reports high internal consistency, and high test–retest reliability over one week, and moderate long-term stability, for the revised fear survey schedule. The validity of the scale was supported through factor analysis, a comparison of scores with four related psychometric instruments (including the State Trait Anxiety Inventory for Children), and adequate discrimination between a sample of school-phobic children and matched controls. Further support for the validity of children's self-reports comes from a study by Bondy, Sheslow and Garcia (1985) in which the same fear survey schedule was administered to a group of children and their parents. From this investigation, it appears that children's self-reports correlate with their mothers' estimates of the highest rated fears. However, mothers' overall estimates of their children's general fearfulness were significantly correlated only with their daughters' fearfulness, not with their sons'. Perhaps the next step is to determine how well children's fear scores correlate with laboratory measures of the child's physiological reactivity to fear stimuli and the child's fear behaviour in the natural setting. Although reliability and validity are still major concerns, it appears that significant methodological advances have been made in the study of children's fears.

The third issue concerns the questions that are traditionally addressed in the research on children's fears. As would be appreciated from the above review of children's fears, a great deal of research has examined the frequency of childhood fears, what children fear, and how children's fears relate to demographic variables. Graziano, DeGiovanni & Garcia (1979) have questioned the value of pursuing these areas further. According to these authors:

> The type of identification and tracking of fear stimuli that has been done could probably be continued indefinitely. However, the question must be raised as to the point of such an enterprise. In an area as broad and important as fear in children one must ask oneself what kind of research is worth doing and what kind of knowledge is worth having. (pp. 812–813)

From a clinical viewpoint, however, it is important that research addresses the frequency, intensity and stability of children's fears. Such research-based information is useful in counselling parents and children and in determining whether intervention is warranted. Nevertheless, the scope of the research needs to be broadened. There has been a plea for research on the processes involved in children's fears. Graziano, DeGiovanni and Garcia (1979) state:

> It seems reasonable to assume that children's fears, like other human reactions, proceed through complex paradigms—from fear stimuli that vary in number, type, and intensity and that may be internal, external, or both; through emotional and cognitive operations within the child; through overt fear responses that may act upon and modify both the social and physical environment and that themselves, by means of feedback loops and chaining, may occasion variations in any part of the process. The processes themselves may further vary with developmental factors. (p. 813)

As yet little has been written on how these processes and their interaction should be investigated. In the meantime other issues of practical interest can be studied, including the duration of childhood fear and the manner in which children and parents deal with them in the natural setting. Given the current concern for implementing programmes that are acceptable to consumers, research of this nature would be very appropriate.

CHILDREN'S PHOBIAS

Attention is now turned to clinical fears or phobias. As previously stated, these reactions represent a special form of fear that are of clinical interest because of their magnitude, persistence and maladaptiveness (Barrios et al., 1981; Graziano DeGiovanni & Garcia, 1979; Morris & Kratochwill, 1983; Miller et al., 1974). Children's phobias are a challenge to care providers and professionals in terms of their assessment, treatment and prevention. Prior to discussion of assessment and intervention, however, it is necessary to consider such fundamental issues as the incidence, seriousness, classification and natural history of children's phobias.

Incidence and seriousness

Determining an accurate estimate of the incidence of phobias in children is confounded by methodological problems (sampling and assessment). On the basis of test questionnaires, observations and interviews, Agras, Sylvester and Oliveau (1969) classified the fears of children and adults as common fears, intense fears, or phobias. The rate of intense fears was approximately 8%, whilst the rate of phobias that warranted treatment was considerably lower at 2.2%. In an extensive survey of children 9 to 11 years old on the Isle of Wight, Rutter, Tizard and Whitmore (1970) found fewer than 1% of the children to have clinically significant phobias. However, this may be a conservative estimate, since they omitted children with monosymptomatic phobias. In a study of children aged 7 to 12 years, Miller et al. (1974) rated the fears of the children at three intensity levels: no fear, normal or expected fear, and excessive or unrealistic fear. Excessive or unrealistic fear was evoked in about 5% of the sample. Ollendick (1979b) estimated that excessive fears are probably present in about 3–8% of the population.

Children's phobias may be quite debilitating and create serious living problems for the child and parents or other care providers. For example, a child's phobia of darkness often manifests itself in tantrums and panic at bedtime. Such children may also refuse to stay overnight with relatives because of embarrassment about their phobia (Graziano, Mooney, Huber & Ignasiak, 1979). A child's phobia of a medical procedure may be so intense that it is impossible to conduct a routine diagnostic or treatment procedure which may be vital to the health of the child. The severity of children's phobic reactions to dental procedures is well known, and accounts for a considerable amount of uncooperative behaviour in dental surgeries. A child's phobia of school, especially if involving prolonged absenteeism, may impede the child's social and academic development (Hersov, 1960a). Phobic reactions to specific activities or events within school, such as tests, can also interfere with optimal performance. A child's phobia of dogs may be so extreme that the child takes an enormous amount of time to get from home to school and back again (Lazarus & Abramovitz, 1962). In fact, the parents may have to drive the child to school in order to avoid the fear stimulus (MacDonald, 1975). On a family outing, the dog-phobic child may become panic-stricken at the sight of an oncoming dog and possibly run in any direction (even on to a busy road) to avoid the dog. Unfortunately, some dog-phobic children have been involved in fatal car accidents as a result of their panic reaction. Thus, childhood phobic conditions produce a great deal of personal anguish and unhappiness on the part of the child, possibly impede general social and educational development, at times create danger for the child, and can be very disruptive for the child's parents and family. These factors prompt many parents into seeking professional assistance.

In view of the incidence and seriousness of excessive fears, the amount of contact therapists have with phobic children is an intriguing question. Graziano and DeGiovanni (1979) obtained questionnaire data from 19 'behaviour therapists' on this issue. Of 547 children referred within the previous 6 months, 37 (6.8%) were referred for treatment of phobic problems. In proportion to the overall number of children referred for treatment, a higher percentage of girls as compared with boys were referred for fear treatment. Graziano and

DeGiovanni noted that the number of fear cases was not a large proportion of the clinical sample, which is surprising in view of the amount of time and clinical expertise devoted to the phobias of adults. As well as children referred specifically for fear problems, other clinic-referred children sometimes evince phobias. Poznanksi's (1973) study of children with excessive fears chosen from an outpatient psychiatric population illustrates this point. Diagnostically, most of the children (about 80%) were categorized in the neurotic or personality sub-classification of the American Psychiatric Association's (1968) *Diagnostic and Statistic Manual of Mental Disorders* (DSM-II). As a general comment, the actual referral rate is probably due to an interaction between the availability of clinical services in the community, and how well informed parents and professionals are of these services. In the experience of the authors, there is a dramatic increase in the number of phobic child referrals as the existence of clinical services for such problems become known to parents and professionals in the community. Thus, the statistics on the incidence and referral rate of children's phobias need to be interpreted cautiously.

Classification

The classification of children's phobias is of interest to clinicians and researchers. The best known clinically derived classification system is the *Diagnostic and Statistical Manual of Mental Disorders* (DSM-III-R) developed by the American Psychiatric Association (APA, 1987). By way of background, DSM-III-R involves a multiaxial diagnostic system which encompasses mental, medical and psychosocial information. Five axes are entailed in diagnosis:

Axis I: Clinical syndromes
Conditions not attributable to a mental disorder that are a focus of attention or treatment

Axis II: Developmental disorders and personality disorders

Axis III: Physical disorders and conditions

Axes IV and V are available for use in special clinical and research settings and provide information supplementing the official DSM-III-R diagnoses (Axes I, II and III) that may be useful for planning treatment and predicting outcome:

Axis IV: Severity of psychosocial stressors

Axis V: Global assessment of functioning

The first major diagnostic class of the DSM-III-R classification is 'disorders usually first evident in infancy, childhood, or adolescence'. Within this section is the sub-class 'anxiety disorders of childhood or adolescence' which encompasses 'separation anxiety disorder' (essential feature is excessive anxiety concerning separation from major attachment figures), 'avoidant disorder of childhood or

Table 1.1 Phobic disorders and diagnostic criteria in the DSM-III-R classification

AGORAPHOBIA WITHOUT HISTORY OF PANIC DISORDER

A. Agoraphobia: Fear of being in places or situations from which escape might be difficult (or embarrassing) or in which help might not be available in the event of suddenly developing a symptom(s) that could be incapacitating or extremely embarrassing. Examples include: dizziness or falling, depersonalization or derealization, loss of bladder or bowel control, vomiting, or cardiac distress. As a result of this fear, the person either restricts travel or needs a companion when away from home, or else endures agoraphobic situations despite intense anxiety. Common agoraphobic situations include being outside the home alone, being in a crowd or standing in a line, being on a bridge, and traveling in a bus, train, or car.

B. Has never met the criteria for Panic Disorder.

Specify with or without limited symptom attacks (p. 241).

SOCIAL PHOBIA

A. A persistent fear of one or more situations (the social phobic situations) in which the person is exposed to possible scrutiny by others and fears that he or she may do something or act in a way that will be humiliating or embarrassing. Examples include: being unable to continue talking while speaking in public, choking on food when eating in front of others, being unable to urinate in a public lavatory, hand-trembling when writing in the presence of others, and saying foolish things or not being able to answer questions in social situations.

B. If an Axis III or another Axis I disorder is present, the fear in A is unrelated to it, e.g., the fear is not of having a panic attack (Panic Disorder), stuttering (Stuttering), trembling (Parkinson's disease), or exhibiting abnormal eating behavior (Anorexia Nervosa or Bulimia Nervosa).

C. During some phase of the disturbance, exposure to the specific phobic stimulus (or stimuli) almost invariably provokes an immediate anxiety response.

D. The phobic situation(s) is avoided, or is endured with intense anxiety.

E. The avoidant behavior interferes with occupational functioning or with usual social activities or relationships with others, or there is marked distress about having the fear.

F. The person recognizes that his or her fear is excessive or unreasonable.

G. If the person is under 18, the disturbance does not meet the criteria for Avoidant Disorder of Childhood or Adolescence.

Specify generalized type if the phobic situation includes most social situations, and also consider the additional diagnosis of Avoidant Personality Disorder (p. 243).

SIMPLE PHOBIA

A. A persistent fear of a circumscribed stimulus (object or situation) other than fear of having a panic attack (as in Panic Disorder) or of humiliation or embarrassment in certain social situations (as in Social Phobia).
   Note: Do not include fears that are part of Panic Disorder with Agoraphobia or Agoraphobia without History of Panic Disorder.

B. During some phase of the disturbance, exposure to the specific phobic stimulus (or stimuli) almost invariably provokes an immediate anxiety response.

C. The object or situation is avoided, or endured with intense anxiety.

D. The fear or the avoidant behavior significantly interferes with the person's normal routine or with usual social activities or relationships with others, or there is marked distress about having the fear.

E. The person recognizes that his or her fear is excessive or unreasonable.

F. The phobic stimulus is unrelated to the content of the obsessions of Obsessive Compulsive Disorder or the trauma of Post-traumatic Stress Disorder (pp. 244–245).

adolescence' (essential feature is excessive shyness with unfamiliar people) and 'overanxious disorder' (essential feature is excessive or unrealistic worry). Whereas anxiety is focused on specific situations in separation anxiety disorder and avoidant disorder of childhood or adolescence, anxiety is generalized to a variety of situations in overanxious disorder. Phobias are omitted from 'disorders usually first evident in infancy, childhood or adolescence', although it appears that phobic reactions are being described in separation anxiety disorder and avoidant disorder of childhood or adolescence.

In the DSM-III-R classification, phobias are included in the 'anxiety disorders'. This group of disorders subsumes 'panic disorder with agoraphobia', 'panic disorder without agoraphobia', 'agoraphobia without history of panic disorder', 'social phobia', 'simple phobia', 'obsessive–compulsive disorder', 'post-traumatic stress disorder', 'generalized anxiety disorder', and 'anxiety disorder not otherwise specified'. All of the aforementioned disorders involve anxiety and avoidance behaviour; in the phobic disorders anxiety is experienced when the person confronts the feared object or situation. The diagnostic criteria for the phobic disorders—agoraphobia without history of panic disorder, social phobia and simple phobia—are presented in Table 1.1. *Prima facie*, these appear to be disorders of adults rather than of children and adolescents. Using the DSM-III-R, however, a child or adolescent may be diagnosed as having a phobic disorder provided the diagnostic criteria are fulfilled. In addition, more than one diagnosis may be applied as studies on the anxiety disorders of children and adolescents are beginning to show (Last *et al.*, 1987; Ollendick, 1983a).

The relationship of phobic disorders to children and adolescents can be gauged from the comments on age at onset and predisposing factors given in the DSM-III-R. Agoraphobia without history of panic disorder is rare in clinical samples although it may be more common in the general population. The age at onset is variable and no information is given on predisposing factors. According to DSM-III-R it is unclear whether agoraphobia with limited symptom attacks is a variation of panic disorder with agoraphobia which is more prevalent clinically. However, for panic disorder with agoraphobia: 'The average age at onset is in the late 20s' (APA, 1987, p. 236). On predisposing factors: 'Separation Anxiety Disorder in childhood and sudden loss of social supports or disruption of important interpersonal relationships apparently predispose to the development of this disorder' (APA, 1987, p. 237). Certainly we need more information on agoraphobia and panic disorder in children and adolescents as some findings suggest. In a study of agoraphobics, for example, Thorpe and Burns (1983) found that 9.3% of the sample claimed that the agoraphobia developed before 16 years of age. With respect to the age at onset of social phobia: 'The disorder often begins in late childhood or early adolescence' (APA, 1987, p. 242). This is consistent with the observation that there is an age-related increase in school and social fears among children (Angelino *et al.*, 1956; Lapouse & Monk, 1959). With simple phobias: 'Age at onset varies, but animal phobias nearly always begin in childhood' (APA, 1987, p. 244). Hence, simple phobia and social phobia can be expected to be seen in children and adolescents. As would be evident at this stage, 'school phobia' does not appear as a disorder within the DSM-III-R classification. From the viewpoint of the DSM-III-R, school phobia is a behaviour and not a diagnosis. The multiplicity of factors in 'school phobia' are encompassed by the aforementioned phobic disorders and anxiety disorders of childhood or adolescence. Finally, there is a continuing debate about such classifications in relation to their reliance on the medical model, reliability and validity of diagnoses, dehumanizing effects and relevance to treatment (see reviews by Harris, 1979; Kazdin, 1983; Spitzer & Cantwell, 1980).

In the absence of a generally accepted nosology of children's phobias, Miller *et al.* (1974) proposed a tentative classification drawn from research and clinical experience: 'The criterion governing its construction was that it be clinically usable, that is, points to different treatments, yields prognoses, and shows the limit of current knowledge' (p. 91). Upon comparing their work with other studies (Lapouse & Monk, 1959; Scherer & Nakamura, 1968), these researchers emphasized how fears cluster around particular sets of objects, and the implication of this for their nosology:

> This tendency suggests an underlying dimensionality, which, in turn, suggests that phobic objects do not occur randomly, but many are interrelated. For a given patient, treatment of one phobia within a dimension should reduce the aversiveness connected with other stimuli within that dimension. In addition, if factor analysis yields anything more than just phenotypes, the same treatment should be applicable to all phobics within a given dimension. For these reasons, we decided to use the three primary factors of physical injury, natural events, and social anxiety as the major categories of child phobia. (p. 93)

Their classification of children's phobias is given in Table 1.2. It will be noted that there are actually four categories: physical injury, natural events, social anxiety and miscellaneous. The latter category was reserved for items (e.g. dirt, furry toys, sirens) about which little is known. The researchers expressed the hope that as evidence accumulated these items would be placed within the three major categories. School phobia is included in the social anxiety category, and further divided in terms of age and the Type I and II distinction (Coolidge, Hahn & Peck, 1957; Kennedy, 1965). More information on the classification of school phobia can be found in Chapter 6.

Miller *et al.* (1974) maintain that any clinician using the classification must decide whether the phobia is the primary problem ('phobic trait') or secondary to a more pervasive condition such as aggression and hyperactivity ('phobic state'). The proposed classification is addressed to those phobias that constitute the primary treatment focus, and excludes phobic state conditions. In outlining their nosology, Miller *et al.* discuss each of the categories and sub-categories in relation to assessment and treatment. For example, the physical injury category is divided into concrete and abstract objects. The researchers suggest that concrete objects can be made available for *in vivo* therapy while abstract objects must be dealt with conceptually. It is also pointed out that the prognosis for phobias of concrete objects may be better. Thus different classes of phobias may require different assessment and treatment procedures. As Miller *et al.* explain:

> The main point is that the categories should be functional, and only research can determine whether the categories suggested in this scheme have utility for prognosis, treatment or assessment. We hope that eventually, the scheme could incorporate such information. (p. 95)

Overall, the classification is of interest and has attracted support in terms of its heuristic value (Ollendick, 1979b). Of course, a classification system of this nature can always be criticized on the grounds that in grouping problems the uniqueness of the individual tends to be overlooked. For any group of phobias that children experience it can be argued that there is considerable diversity in terms of the antecedent stimuli that elicit the phobia, the consequential variables that maintain the phobia, the general family situation, and related factors. In clinical practice the use of the classification would always have to be supplemented with other forms of assessment information. Miller *et al.* concur with this point:

> In addition the age of the child, the chronicity of the phobia, the severity of the child's and family's disturbance, the conditioning history, and the reinforcements that maintain the phobia need to be taken into consideration. (p. 91)

The classification was proposed in a very tentative and arbitrary manner, it being argued that this would be improved by future research. However, the claims that the different classes of phobia may be associated with different assessment and treatment strategies, and that treatment generalizations should occur within a dimension, have yet to be validated. At the moment the classification scheme offered by Miller *et al.* has not progressed beyond its descriptive merits.

The place of anxiety, fears and phobias within empirically based classifications of child psychopathology is another point of interest. Multivariate procedures (factor analysis and cluster analysis) have been used to identify which behaviours tend to occur together in data derived from rating scales and checklists. In his research, Achenbach (1966) found two general clusters or 'broad-band' factors which he labelled 'internalizing' and 'externalizing' or 'personality' problems and 'conduct problems'. The internalizing symptoms include, for example, phobias, insomnia, stomach upsets and shyness. Some of the externalizing symptoms include destructiveness, stealing and running away. More-specific 'narrow-band' dimensions have also been identified—academic disability, aggressiveness, anxiousness, deliquency, depression, hyperactivity, immaturity, obsessive–compulsive behaviour, schizoid behaviour, sexual problems, sleep problems, social withdrawal, somatic complaints, and uncommunicativeness (Achenbach & Edelbrock, 1978). It may be that internalizing children are more inclined to stay longer in 'psychotherapy' and improve with treatment

Table 1.2 Proposed nosology for children's phobias

I. Physical injury	II. Natural events	III. Social anxiety	IV. Miscellaneous
A. *Abstract*	A. *Storms*	A. *School*	1. Dirt
1. War	1. Tornadoes, floods, earthquakes	1. Young (ages 3–10)	2. Furry toys
2. Riots	2. Lightning	(a) Type I	3. Sirens
3. Poisoned food	3. Thunder	(b) Type II	4. People who are old
4. Specific foods		2. Old (ages 11–22)	5. Crossing a street
5. Dying	B. *Dark*	(a) Type I	6. People who are ugly
6. Someone in family dying		(b) Type II	7. Loud sounds, as caps, firecrackers, explosions
7. Seeing someone wounded	C. *Enclosed places*	B. *Separation*	8. People in uniforms, a policeman, mailmen, etc.
8. Being wounded	1. Bathrooms	1. Separation from parents	9. People of the opposite sex
9. Someone in family getting ill	2. Closets	2. Parts of house	10. Having bowel movements
10. Becoming ill	3. Elevators	3. Going to sleep at night	11. Members of another race
11. Germs	4. Confined or locked up		
12. Choking	5. Strange rooms	C. *Performance*	
13. Having an operation		1. Tests or examinations	
14. Hospitals	D. *Animals*	2. Being criticized	
15. Hell	1. Snakes	3. Making mistakes	
16. The devil	2. Insects, spiders	4. Reciting in class	
17. Breaking a religious law	3. Rats or mice		
18. Being kidnapped	4. Frogs or lizards	D. *Social interactions*	
19. Getting lost	5. Dogs or cats	1. Attending social events	
20. Being adopted	6. Horses or cows	2. Making another person angry	
21. Parents getting a divorce			
22. Going crazy			

B. *Concrete*
1. Flying in airplane
2. High places
3. Deep water
4. Strangers
5. Being seen naked

E. *Other*
1. Fire
2. Frightening thoughts or daydreams
3. Ghosts
4. Being alone
5. Nightmares
6. Space creatures or monsters
7. Faces at window
8. Masks or puppets
9. Sight of blood
10. People with deformities
11. Toilets

3. Crowds
4. Being touched by others

E. *Medical procedures*
1. Doctors or dentists
2. Getting a shot

F. *Other*
1. Riding in a car or bus

SOURCE: Miller, Barrett and Hampe (1974). Reproduced by permission of John Wiley & Sons Ltd.

Table 1.3 Frequently found characteristics defining four behavioural dimensions

Conduct disorder	Anxiety-withdrawal
Fighting, hitting, assaultive	Anxious, fearful, tense
Temper tantrums	Shy, timid, bashful
Disobedient, defiant	Withdrawn, seclusive, friendless
Destructiveness of own or other's property	Depressed, sad, disturbed
Impertinent, 'smart', impudent	Hypersensitive, easily hurt
Uncooperative, resistive, inconsiderate	Self-conscious, easily embarrassed
Disruptive, interrupts, disturbs	Feels inferior, worthless
Negative, refuses direction	Lacks self-confidence
Restless	Easily flustered
Boisterous, noisy	Aloof
Irritability, 'blows-up' easily	Cries frequently
Attention-seeking, 'show-off'	Reticent, secretive
Dominates others, bullies, threatens	
Hyperactivity	*Immaturity*
Untrustworthy, dishonest, lies	
Profanity, abusive language	Short attention span, poor concentration
Jealousy	Daydreaming
Quarrelsome, argues	Clumsy, poor coordination
Irresponsible, undependable	Preoccupied, stares into space, absent-minded
Inattentive	
Steals	Passive, lacks initiative, easily led
Distractibility	Sluggish
Teases	Inattentive
Denies mistakes, blames others	Drowsy
Pouts and sulks	Lack of interest, bored
Selfish	Lacks perseverance, fails to finish things
	Messy, sloppy

Socialized-aggression

Has 'bad companions'
Steals in company with others
Loyal to delinquent friends
Belongs to a gang
Stays out late at night
Truant from school
Truant from home

SOURCE: Quay (1979). Reproduced by permission of John Wiley & Sons Ltd.

(Achenbach & Lewis, 1971). Thus at a general level, children's phobias should be fairly responsive to therapy.

Of course, the final cluster of symptoms derived from the data in factor analysis research will depend largely upon the nature and character of the items on which the child is rated. Given differences between research investigations in relation to items and sampling, there is likely to be some variation in factor analytic classifications. Quay and his colleagues (Quay, 1975, 1979; Von Isser, Quay & Love, 1980) have identified four dimensions, namely 'conduct disorder' (e.g. overt aggression, disruptiveness, negativism) 'anxiety-withdrawal' (e.g. over-anxiety, social withdrawal, shyness, sensitivity), 'immaturity' (e.g. short

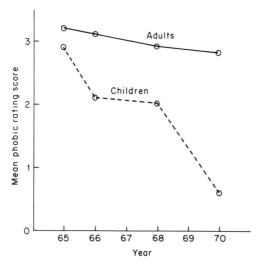

Fig. 1.2 Mean phobic rating scores. Reproduced
from Agras, Chapin and Oliveau (1972).

attention span, passivity, daydreaming) and 'socialized aggression' (e.g. gang
activities, cooperative stealing, truancy). A more detailed listing of the
characteristics associated with the four dimensions can be found in Table 1.3.
Comparing the classification systems, it will be noted that Achenbach's
'internalizing' syndrome is similar to Quay's dimensions of 'anxiety-withdrawal'
and 'immaturity', while the 'externalizing' syndrome approximates the
dimensions of 'conduct disorder' or 'socialized-aggression' (Kauffman, 1985).
Although the multivariate approach holds considerable promise in terms of the
development of parsimonious, reliable and valid classifications of child
psychopathology, the clinical usefulness of the taxonomies in individual
assessment and treatment is not apparent (Mash & Terdal, 1981).

Natural history

An impression appears to be building up in the literature that children's phobias
have a good prognosis with or without treatment, despite the fact that there is
very little hard data on the natural history of children's phobias. In a 5-year
follow-up of untreated phobic children and adults originally identified in a
population survey, Agras, Chapin and Oliveau (1972) concluded that untreated
phobias tend to improve over time (see Fig. 1.2). Children's phobias improved
quickly, 100% being improved or recovered at the end of 5 years. The phobias
of adults improved more slowly, 43% being improved or recovered, 20%
unchanged, and 33% worse at the end of 5 years. However, the 100% figure of
recovery or improvement on the part of the children should not lead to a casual
dismissal of children's phobias on the grounds that they will improve as a result
of their natural history. Ollendick (1979b) points out that although 100% of

the phobics under 20 years 'improved' in 5 years, considerable discomfort was experienced in the first 3 years of the follow-up. In view of the fact that the phobias must have existed for some time before their identification, the duration of the phobias was at least several years and presumably accounted for considerable distress in that time for the children.

Hampe *et al.* (1973) conducted 1- and 2-year follow-ups on children who had participated in an earlier therapeutic study (Miller, Barrett, Hampe & Noble, 1972a). The target phobias were school phobia, and excessive fears of storms, darkness and domestic animals. Since the original study involved a waiting-list control group as well as treatment groups (reciprocal inhibition and psychotherapy), the follow-up data would seem to have implications for the natural history and prognosis of children's phobias. Assessment procedures used in the 1- and 2-year follow-up studies for determining phobias were identical to those reported in the original study: (a) a clinician's rating, (b) parent ratings of the severity of each child's target phobia, (c) the Fear scale, and (d) the Total Disability scale of the Louisville Behavior Check List. As initially reported, the findings suggest that childhood phobias may disappear over time without treatment. Hampe *et al.* point out that: 'The justification for treatment comes from the fact that treatment greatly hastens recovery' (p. 451). It should be emphasized, however, that treatment was offered to a large proportion of the children on the waiting list within the 2-year period! As Hampe *et al.* state:

> During the two years following the completion of the project, 35% of the children received some form of psychological treatment. This was due in part to our offering treatment to children on the waiting list who still manifested phobic behaviour (53%). (p. 448)

Thus, the data may underestimate the natural durability of childhood phobias.

In conclusion, the small amount of data available on this issue suggests at first glance that the natural history and prognosis of children's phobias is quite favourable. However, closer examination of the studies (Agras *et al.*, 1972; Hampe *et al.*, 1973) upon which this impression is based does not support the conclusion that children's phobias are short-lived. For an individual child it is difficult to state the time period for a natural recovery—is it one, two, three, four, or more, years? In their study of different ages of onset of phobias in adult phobics, Marks and Gelder (1966) found that most animal phobias started by 5 years of age and none started in adult life. This suggests that animal phobias, at least, may be extremely durable in certain children. In view of the uncertainty of natural recovery for the individual phobic child and the debilitating nature of the problem for the child and family, caution should be observed about withholding therapeutic intervention on the grounds that the child will 'naturally' outgrow the phobia.

SUMMARY

In this chapter we have examined what is meant by anxiety, fear and phobias. Following the conventional definitions in the literature, anxiety entails an aversive emotional state (subjective discomfort and physiological arousal) with no specific focus or external trigger. In contrast, fears and phobias are more specific in their focus. Fear is a normal reaction to a real or perceived threat. Fears are usually mild, age-specific and transitory. A phobia has been described as a special form of fear which:

(1) is out of proportion to the demands of the situation;
(2) cannot be explained or reasoned away;
(3) is beyond voluntary control;
(4) leads to avoidance of the feared situation;
(5) persists over an extended period of time;
(6) is unadaptive;
(7) is not age- or stage-specific.

Thus, phobias are differentiated from fears on the basis of their magnitude, persistence and maladaptiveness. However, the literature is by no means clear-cut in the usage of these terms. Sometimes their meaning is clouded by theoretical orientation, while at other times the terms tend to be used interchangeably.

The normative and developmental aspects of childhood fears have been examined in considerable detail. Generally, there is an age-related decline in fears of animals, darkness and imaginary creatures, but an age-related increase in school and social fears. Recent findings suggest that children's fears may be more stable and durable than usually thought. Girls have more fears than boys, and lower-SEC children have more fears than upper-SEC children. Children with intellectual and physical handicaps seem to have more fears than normal children, and tend to fear different events or situations than normal children. Methodological concerns about the studies on children's fears include the unrepresentative nature of samples and the questionable reliability and validity of the assessment procedures. Although the usefulness of research on children's fears has been questioned, we believe that normative data are important for work in clinical settings.

The incidence of children's phobias is difficult to estimate, but it is thought to be about 3–8% of the population. The seriousness of children's phobias was emphasized bearing in mind the personal distress and danger experienced by the child, as well as disruption to family life. In the DSM-III-R classification phobias are included in the anxiety disorders. Agoraphobia, social phobia and simple phobia were described with particular reference to children and adolescents. L. C. Miller's classification of children's phobias was examined in which four categories of phobias are proposed, including physical injury, natural event, social anxiety and miscellaneous. Although the classification is interesting and comprehensive, the claims regarding its usefulness on assessment and treatment matters have not been validated. The natural history of children's phobias has been discussed, it being noted that childhood phobias are more durable than is generally believed.

CHAPTER 2

Aetiology of children's phobias

INTRODUCTION

Just how children acquire phobias is an intriguing question, about which there has been much controversy, but little empirical data. Most attempts to account for children's phobias have relied upon psychoanalytic and behavioural models. Historically, psychoanalysis has wielded the greatest influence. According to psychoanalytic theory, phobias are symptomatic of underlying disturbances as exemplified in the legendary case of little Hans (Freud, 1909/1963). Other sources have examined the psychoanalytic model of phobia acquisition (e.g. Brown, 1961; Buss, 1966; Costin, 1976; Hall, 1954; Stafford-Clark, 1965) and have reviewed its limitations (e.g. Bandura, 1969; Eysenck, 1965; Rachman & Costello, 1961; Wolpe & Rachman, 1960).

Contrary to opinion that is often expressed, however, the psychoanalytic model and its variations continue to flourish in clinical practice and prestigious teaching facilities throughout the world. Fiery debates frequently occur between protagonists of the psychoanalytic and behavioural schools. Interestingly, the case of little Hans has been 'reopened' in recent years (Cheshire, 1979, 1980; Conway, 1978; Thorpe, 1979). According to psychoanalysts, the behavioural critique of little Hans is a clever 'hatchet-job' involving intellectual double standards. It seems to us that arguments and counter-arguments between psychoanalysts and behaviourists could continue indefinitely. In our view there is nothing to be gained from continuing the debate; neither side is likely to budge from its position. Perhaps the healthiest outcome of the controversy would be for both schools of thought to agree on their disagreements. Hence the development of the behavioural model of psychopathology does not depend upon the invalidity of psychoanalysis. This point has been cogently argued by Franks (1982):

> Behavior therapy and psychoanalysis are conceptually, methodologically, and technically incompatible and an integration of the two at any level will probably be to the disadvantage of both. We therefore suggest that the systems remain incompatible, occupy different worlds, and go about their respective business constructively but independently. (p. 7)

In advancing the behavioural model, we argue that children's phobias are *learned* behaviours. The challenge is to understand the processes by which they become established. In broad terms, we maintain that childhood phobias result from traumatic and/or non-traumatic experiences in the environment. Initially, we examine the conditioning theory of childhood phobias, and review the evidence drawn from animal and human studies, as well as clinical case reports. The growth or incubation of children's phobias is also discussed. In a re-evaluation of conditioning theory, we posit additional mechanisms or pathways by which children may develop phobias, including modelling, fear messages and reinforcement. Social learning theory is presented as a means of integrating the various pathways of fear and phobia acquisition in children. A critical issue is why some children develop phobias and not others, as well as the apparent selectivity of childhood fears and phobias.

CONDITIONING THEORY

Development of conditioning theory

The conditioning theory of childhood phobias is based on the assumption that phobias have traumatic or sub-traumatic origins. The classical aversive conditioning paradigm is highly pertinent to this conceptualization. In classical conditioning terminology, the traumatic event that elicits a negative emotional reaction is referred to as the 'unconditioned stimulus' (UCS). The negative emotional reaction to the UCS is referred to as the 'unconditioned response' (UCR). In classical conditioning, the UCS is paired with a neutral stimulus over a number of trials. As a result of the association with the UCS, the neutral stimulus alone is sufficient to elicit the negative emotional reaction. At this stage the neutral stimulus is referred to as the 'conditioned stimulus' (CS) and the negative emotional reaction as the 'conditioned response' (CR). Stimuli similar to the original CS may elicit the CR. This is referred to as 'stimulus generalization'. The magnitude of the CR is related to how closely the stimuli resemble the original CS. Another important principle is that of extinction, which entails the continuous presentation of the CS in the absence of the UCS with the eventual disappearance of the CR. More detail on classical conditioning theory can be found in Kimble (1961), Mackintosh (1974) and Rachlin (1976).

In order to illustrate the relevance of the classical conditioning paradigm to the acquisition of children's phobias, a child's trauma-induced dog phobia will be discussed. In this example, a child has become extremely upset and frightened at the sight of large dogs and their barking. Over the last few years, the child has been bitten on three different occasions by large dogs in his neighbourhood. On each occasion, the child screamed and cried. In the classical conditioning framework, the attacks by the dogs constitute the UCS, whilst the child's screaming and crying are the UCR. The size and bark of the dogs impinged upon the child during these attacks. Subsequently the sight of large dogs and their barking alone (CS) are sufficient to elicit screaming and crying

(CR). Furthermore, the child becomes upset when in contact with smaller dogs that bark a great deal (stimulus generalization). Extinction might be expected to occur if the child were to have contact with dogs similar to those that attacked him but in the absence of trauma.

The conditioning theory of children's phobias is more elaborate than classial aversive conditioning. A problem that had to be overcome in the development of conditioning theory concerned the fact that extinction does not always occur in the natural environment. Very often, phobic children engage in escape/avoidance behaviour, thus preventing extinction from occurring. Consequently, conditioning theory evolved as a 'two-factor' or 'two-stage' theory which was able to address both the acquisition and maintenance of phobias. The two-factor theory had its historical antecedents in the writings of Mowrer (1939). Mowrer's first factor addressed the origin of the phobia and was consistent with the classical aversive conditioning model. Mowrer wrote: 'anxiety is a learned response, occurring to 'signals' (conditioned stimuli) that are premonitory of (i.e. have in the past been followed by) situations of injury or pain (unconditioned stimuli)' (p. 563). The second factor of his theory addressed the maintenance of escape/avoidance behaviour which Mowrer conceptualized in terms of anxiety reduction. According to Mowrer: 'reduction of anxiety may serve powerfully to reinforce behavior that brings about such a state of "relief" or "security"' (p. 564).

Further to these historical foundations, Eysenck and Rachman (1965) set out the essentials of the two-factor conditioning theory in the following manner:

(1) Phobias are learned responses.
(2) Stimuli develop phobic(-producing) qualities when they are associated temporally and spatially with a fear-producing state of affairs.
(3) Neutral stimuli which are of relevance in the fear-producing situation and/or make an impact on the person in the situation, are more likely to develop phobic qualities than weak or irrelevant stimuli.
(4) Repetition of association between the fear situation and the new phobic stimuli will strengthen the phobia.
(5) Associations between high-intensity fear situations and neutral stimuli are more likely to produce phobic reactions.
(6) Generalization from the original phobic stimulus to stimuli of a similar nature will occur.
(7) Noxious experiences which occur under conditions of excessive confinement are more likely to produce phobic reactions.
(8) Neutral stimuli which are associated with a noxious experience(s) may develop (secondary) motivating properties. This acquired drive is termed the 'fear drive'.
(9) Responses (such as avoidance) which reduce the fear drive are reinforced.

It was also implied (a) that fears are due to conditioning, either through single-trial or many-trial sub-traumatic learning; and (b) spontaneous remission of such reactions can be due to extinction (repeated exposure to the CS in the absence of the UCS).

An important assumption in the conditioning theory of phobias is the premise of 'equal conditionability' or 'equipotentiality' that dates back to Pavlov (1927). Given comparable exposures, all stimuli are seen to have roughly an equal chance of being transformed into fear signals. For Pavlov the choice of conditioned stimulus was of no consequence in terms of conditionability. Pavlov wrote: 'Any natural phenomenon chosen at will may be converted into a conditioned stimulus... any visual stimulus, any desired sound...' (p. 86). Similarly, in their critique of little Hans, Wolpe and Rachman (1960) stated: 'Any "neutral" stimulus, simple or complex, that happens to make an impact on an individual at about the time a fear reaction is evoked acquires the ability to evoke fear subsequently' (p. 145). The premise of equipotentiality remained unchallenged in the conditioning theory of phobias for many years.

The number of trials necessary to produce a phobia in children depends upon many variables (e.g. the strength of the unconditioned stimulus, the physiological state of the child). In the animal and human learning theory literature, there are examples of what is called 'one-trial learning'. For example, Sanderson, Campbell and Laverty (1962) were able to produce an intense fear reaction in their human subjects on the basis of one harrowing experience. The occurrence of one-trial learning in children is supported by Woodward's (1959) findings that 81% of 198 children who had suffered severe burns showed 'fear and anxiety' from 2 to 5 years after the accident. On the other hand, an argument can be mounted for multiple traumatic or sub-traumatic trials. As will be seen in the discussion of evidence for the conditioning theory, Watson and Rayner (1920) carried out repeated trials before the subject displayed a conditioned fear of the white rat. Also, several animal experiments have shown that prior exposure to fear-producing stimulation tends to weaken the animals' resistance to later stress (Kurtz & Walters, 1962; Walters, 1963). Eysenck and Rachman (1965) concluded that: 'it is likely that the great majority of phobias develop after cumulative traumatic or subtraumatic experiences' (p. 83).

Great variation exists in the magnitude of phobias observed in children. Hence a conditioning model must be able to explain individual variations in the intensity of phobic reactions. Basing their argument on some earlier work reported by Miller (1951), Eysenck and Rachman (1965) proposed that five major determinants contribute to the magnitude of fear:

(1) Repetition of exposures to the fear-inducing situation will increase the strength of the fear.
(2) Strong noxious stimuli will produce strong fears (e.g. a powerful shock will produce a greater fear than a weak one).
(3) Stimuli which are closely associated, temporally and spatially, with a noxious experience will produce strong fears.

(4) Generalized fear stimuli which resemble the original stimuli closely will produce strong fears.

(5) The summation of fear-inducing stimuli will increase the strength of the fear.

Evidence for conditioning theory

The conditioning theory of phobia acquisition was believed to be very strongly supported by scientific evidence. Eysenck and Rachman (1965) asserted that all nine of the aforementioned statements 'are supported by the full weight of almost all the evidence accumulated in research on the learning process' (p. 92). Consequently, the two-factor theory of phobia acquisition came to be widely accepted. Practitioners employing systematic desensitization in the treatment of phobias accepted this theoretical account, and assumed that phobias were analogous to experimentally established conditioned avoidance responses. In the present discussion of the evidence for the conditioning theory of children's phobias, we shall focus upon clinical observations of phobic children, and the fear-induction studies on children and animals. The reader is referred to other sources (Eysenck & Rachman, 1965; Rachman, 1976, 1977) for more comprehensive reviews.

Case histories of phobic children

Sometimes case histories of phobic children and adults support the conditioning theory of phobia acquisition and its corollaries. Monosymptomatic or specific phobias frequently date back to a traumatic event or series of traumatic events that can be conceptualized within the conditioning model. For example, MacDonald (1975) reports the following historical information on a dog-phobic child:

> Historically, the acquisition of the fear was related quite clearly to three separate incidents. The first, occurring when the child was 3 yr old, involved his being frightened by a stray dog's running through his yard. His fear of dogs following this episode was extreme but began to diminish with reasoning and repeated, parentally-structured exposures to neighbourhood dogs. Unfortunately, it was within the context of one of the parentally-guided exposures that the second incident occurred, less than a year after the first episode. While father and son were sitting together on their back porch, a neighbourhood dog wandered by; the father, seizing the opportunity for a natural desensitizing event, called him over. After patting the dog himself, the father coaxed the son to touch the animal. Just as the child reached out to do so, the dog nipped his arm. As a result, the child's earlier extreme fear was reinstated and extended to include anticipatory situations. ... The final incident occurred nearly a year later. While the child and the father were playing ball in their front yard, 'a dog burst through the opening in the bushes and viciously attacked' the child, who was knocked down by the animal, but not injured. (pp. 317–18; reproduced by permission of Pergamon Press).

Bentler's (1962) observations of an infant with a water phobia illustrate how a conditioned phobic reaction may generalize to a wide variety of similar stimuli:

During the first few moments of the bath, Margaret was happy. She tried to stand up in the bathtub, slipped, and began screaming. She refused further bathing with violent screams and had to be removed from the tub.

Testing during the next few days indicated that Margaret reacted with violent emotion not only to the bathtub, the faucet, and water in the tub, but also to being washed in the handbasin, to faucets or water at any part of the house, and to the wading pool. It is clear that slipping in the tub plus other possible unknown prior circumstances (e.g. at the baby-sitter's) or concomitant events (e.g. soap in the face) caused a great change in Margaret's emotional responsiveness to a wide range of situations.

During the next week it became apparent that Margaret would continue this behaviour unless systematic steps were taken to overcome her fear. Being cleaned in the washbasin brought only further screams and Margaret refused to play with water. (pp. 186–7)

The importance of traumatic experience in the acquisition of dental phobias is highlighted in a study by Lautch (1971). In 34 cases of dental phobia, traumatic dental experience in childhood was reported in every case. Four of these people avoided further dental treatment until the time of the study, while the remaining 30 patients reported traumatic experiences during subsequent dental treatments. Of the 34 matched control patients, 10 reported traumatic experiences. In this study, the phobic patients scored slightly but significantly higher on Eysenck's neuroticism scale and lower on the extraversion scale than the non-phobic patients. Along with other factors, painful dental experiences have been found to account for adverse dental reactions in other studies (Kleinknecht, Klepac & Alexander, 1973; Shoben & Borland, 1954).

Fear-induction research with children

The research on fear induction with children that can be cited as evidence for the conditioning theory of childhood phobias is very limited. Watson and Rayner's (1920) classic demonstration of fear induction is usually reported in this respect (Ollendick & Cerny, 1981). The study has become known as the case of 'little Albert', and is often referred to as the behavioural counterpart to little Hans (Eysenck, 1965; Lazarus, 1971). Because of the historical importance of the study, the case of little Albert will be described in detail. According to Watson and Rayner, the experimental study was undertaken to answer three questions:

(1) Can an infant be conditioned to fear an animal that appears simultaneously with a loud, fear-arousing sound?
(2) Would such fear transfer to other animals or to inanimate objects?
(3) How long would such fears persist?

In attempting to answer these questions, Watson and Rayner selected an infant named Albert B, whom they described as 'healthy' and 'stolid and unemotional' (p. 1). At approximately 9 months of age, Albert was tested and was judged to show no fear when successively observing a number of live animals (e.g. a rat, a rabbit, a dog and a monkey), and various inanimate objects (e.g. cotton, human masks, a burning newspaper). However, he displayed fear whenever a long steel bar was unexpectedly struck with a claw hammer just behind him. Two weeks later Watson and Rayner attempted to condition Albert to fear a white rat. After presenting a white rat to Albert, a loud clanging sound was made (with a hammer and steel bar) whenever Albert touched the rat. After seven pairings of the rat and noise (in two sessions, one week apart), Albert reacted with crying and avoidance when the rat was presented without the loud noise. In order to answer the question of generalization, Albert was presented with a range of stimuli five days after the conditioning trials. Albert seemed to show a strong fear response to a rat, a rabbit, a dog and a sealskin coat; a 'negative' response to a Santa Claus mask and Watson's hair; and a mild response to white cotton. However, Albert played freely with the wooden blocks and the hair of Watson's assistants.

After an additional five days, Watson reconditioned Albert to the rat (one trial, rat paired with noise). Watson also attempted to condition Albert to fear the previously presented rabbit and dog. When the effects of this procedure were tested in a larger room, it was found that Albert showed only a slight reaction to the rat, dog and rabbit. Consequently, Watson attempted 'to freshen the reaction to the rat' by presenting it with the loud noise. Soon after this, the dog began to bark loudly at Albert, scaring him and the experimenters, and further confounding the experimental demonstration. Concerning the permanence of conditioned responses over time, Watson and Rayner conducted a final series of tests on Albert after 31 days of neither conditioning nor extinction trials. In these tests, Albert showed fear when touching the Santa Claus mask, the sealskin coat, the rat and the rabbit, showing 'strife between withdrawal and the tendency to manipulate'. Following these final tests, Albert's mother removed him from the hospital where the experiment had been conducted.

Although not often referred to in the literature, another 'successful' fear induction experiment involving an infant was conducted by Jones (1931). The subject in this experiment was a 15-month-old boy (Robert). According to Jones, the subject was 'of a markedly stolid and apathetic disposition, able to walk, and possessing a speaking vocabulary limited to fewer than five words' (p. 127). The conditioning was carried out in a laboratory that included a one-way vision screen for two observers to record Robert's behaviour. The 'primary stimulus' (unconditioned stimulus) was a mild electric shock applied to the hand or foot, or both. The primary stimulus was associated with a bell, that together produced a startle reaction and whimpering in Robert. After three associations with the primary stimulus, the bell was sounded alone. For the five 'stimulations' that ensued, startle reactions were recorded that were indistinguishable from those elicited by the primary stimulus. Two stimulations by a buzzer also produced the startle response, but with some delay. A small hand-bell, quite different in sound to the conditioned stimulus, failed to elicit any reaction. In subsequent trials, 'extinctive inhibition' was established to the bell. Further conditioning was instigated over five trials that was successful in reinstating the power of the bell as a conditioned stimulus. After 24 hours, Robert was returned to the laboratory. The bell-produced reactions gradually built up in magnitude (summation) to that resembling the reaction elicited by the primary stimulus. A less marked disturbance was registered to the buzzer, while only an attention response was recorded by the hand-bell. Temporary external inhibition of the conditioned response was observed when Robert was given some food. Although the bell produced the conditioned overt emotional response for another three trials, extinctive inhibition followed over the next three trials ('implicit' responses like pupillary dilation still occurred). After 72 hours, further testing was carried out. Applications of the bell resulted in progressively stronger conditioned reactions culminating in a 'generalized bodily startle reaction'. Since these were the most marked responses obtained in the whole series, the experiment was discontinued in order to avoid further emotional disturbance. Jones predicted that Robert's CR would be short-lived with the effect of telephones and bells.

Fear-induction research with animals

Fear-induction experiments with animals have been the strongest source of evidence for the conditioning theory of phobias. In such experiments, the unconditioned stimulus is usually electric shock. The shock is paired with a neutral stimulus which eventually becomes the conditioned stimulus. Conditioned fear is inferred from physiological disturbance (e.g. defecation) and unusual behaviour (e.g. rushing about the cage). Escape and avoidance behaviour can also be produced in animals that have undergone aversive conditioning. Although working with animals, researchers (e.g. Wolpe, 1958) emphasize the marked physiological and behavioural similarities between animal and human fear reactions. Since the early work of Pavlov (1927), 'experimental neuroses' have been demonstrated by many researchers (Masserman, 1943; Gantt, 1944; Liddell, 1944). Because of their particular relevance to the conditioning account of fear acquisition and generalization, the experiments conducted by Miller (1948) and Wolpe (1958) will be described.

In Miller's experiment, albino rats were placed in a simple apparatus consisting of two compartments separated by an open door. One compartment was painted white and contained a grid floor through which an electric shock could be administered. The other compartment was painted black and was not designed for the administration of electric shocks. The animals showed no marked preference or negative reaction to either compartment before training. The animals were then placed in the white compartment and administered an electric shock. Typical responses included jumping, quivering, defecating and running. Eventually, the rat would escape through the open door into the black compartment. After a number of trials, the animal would quickly run out of the white compartment to the black compartment. When the shock was withdrawn, the rats still continued to run to the black compartment. The experiment continued in order to demonstrate the power of fear as an acquired drive and fear reduction as reinforcement. On additional non-shock trials, the door was closed in front of the animals. After some random behaviour, the animals learned a new response (turning a wheel) which opened the door and allowed for their escape into the black box.

In Wolpe's (1958) experiment, fear was induced in domestic cats. Six cats in an experimental cage were given electric shock that was preceded by a hooter (schedule I). Another six cats were given shocks in the experimental cage until they ceased to make their previously conditioned foot-approach response to a buzzer (schedule II). The latter schedule corresponds to the method for producing neuroses described earlier by Masserman (1943). When returned to the experimental cage, the cats displayed neurotic symptoms even though the shock had been withdrawn. The cats resisted being placed in the cage, displayed anxiety symptoms when inside the cage (especially muscle tension and mydriasis), and refused to eat pellets in the cage, despite 1–3 days of starvation. Whatever symptoms an animal showed in the experimental cage were exacerbated by the sound of the hooter that had preceded the shock. Stimulus generalization of neurotic responses was also evident. Half of the cats displayed neurotic symptoms in rooms that resembled the original laboratory.

Incubation

An important modification to the conditioning theory of phobias has centred upon the principle of extinction. Theoretically, the presentation of the CS without the UCS should result eventually in the extinction of the CR. According to Eysenck (1967a), however, presentation of the CS can result in the maintenance and enhancement of the CR in certain phobics:

> Occasionally phobic patients are found in which the original traumatic event is not immediately followed by a strong conditioned fear of the CS, but where this fear seems to grow in time, so that exposure to the unreinforced CS does not seem to lead to extinction, but rather to an increase in the severity of the conditioned response. Again not all patients show spontaneous remission; a fair proportion either remain ill or even get worse with time, in spite of the fact that no further reinforcement (pairing of CS and UCS) occurs. (p. 63)

The extent to which this applies to phobic children is difficult to estimate, although clinical observations suggest that the phenomenon may be present in a number of cases. For example, parents sometimes report an exacerbation of their child's dental phobia even though subsequent visits to the dentist have been free of trauma. Eysenck has drawn attention to the similarity between these observations of human phobias and certain laboratory findings, particularly the 'Napalkov phenomenon' (Napalkov, 1963). As a result of inflicting dogs with various noxious stimuli (electric shocks, flashing lights, firing of toy pistols), Napalkov noted an increase in blood pressure between 30 and 50 mmHg, lasting for about 10 to 15 minutes. After 20 to 30 applications, the dogs adapted to the stimuli. However, no such adaptation occurred in another experiment in which the noxious stimulus was administered only once with subsequent presentations of the conditioned stimuli without any reinforcement.

The intensity of the dog's fear reaction seemed to grow over time, and blood pressure did not fall after the dogs had been excluded from the experiments and kept in kennels for five months. Consistent with these findings are a number of experiments on human subjects (Campbell, Sanderson & Laverty, 1964; Sanderson *et al.*, 1962) and animals (Dykman, Mack & Ackerman, 1965; Lichtenstein, 1950), in which the power of the conditioned stimulus appears to have been maintained or increased, despite 'extinction'. This spontaneous growth of fear over time following an aversive stimulus has been termed 'incubation' (McAllister & McAllister, 1967).

A complex theory designed to account for the incubation phenomenon has been advanced by Eysenck (1968, 1979). Basic to Eysenck's theory of incubation is the distinction between Pavlovian A conditioning and Pavlovian B conditioning. Pavlovian A conditioning involves the familiar bell–salivation experiments. Usually involving appetitive unconditioned stimuli (e.g. food), the conditioned stimulus has no motivational properties and is subject to the law of extinction. Typically, the drive state is already present in the hungry dog when the experiment begins. However, it is Pavlovian B conditioning that is more relevant to an understanding of phobias and incubation—a point that has not been fully realized in the literature according to Eysenck. Type B conditioning involves classic aversive conditioning in which the UCS may be an electric shock. It is argued that the UCS produces the drive, and that the drive properties of UCR can be transferred to the CR, thus making it possible for the CR to act as reinforcement for the CS–CR link. The CS acquires the function of signalling danger and coming pain, discomfort, fear and annoyance. These 'nocive' responses (NR) always occur to some extent, and are seen to reinforce the CS. According to Eysenck (1979):

> What is being suggested, in other words, is that conditioning sets in motion a positive feedback cycle in which the CR provides reinforcement for the CS. Usually the extinction process will be stronger than this form of reinforcement, leading to overall extinction, and making the action of CS/NR reinforcement unobservable, but under certain circumstances (e.g. when the UCS is exceptionally strong) the extinction process may be weaker than the CS/NR reinforcement process and observable incubation will result' (p. 160).

In Eysenck's opinion, the major parameters that facilitate incubation include (1) a potent conditioned response of the Pavlovian B conditioning type, (2) a strong unconditioned stimulus, (3) very short exposures to the conditioned stimulus, and (4) certain genetically determined personality characteristics that make the individual susceptible to fear arousal.

In a critical review of the incubation hypothesis, Bersh (1980) questioned the validity of the incubation phenomenon and Eysenck's theoretical analysis. According to Bersh, the incubation hypothesis has little experimental support. It is claimed that most of the studies cited in support of incubation are poorly reported and difficult to replicate, particularly Napalkov's (1963). Also, it is maintained that the findings can be partially explained in terms of an operant analysis. Assuming the validity of the incubation phenomenon, Bersh argues that Eysenck's theory is in doubt in relation to several assumptions (e.g. CR strength as a function of UCS intensity). Most problematic for the theory is its lack of predictive power at its present stage of development. Bersh concludes his critical analysis of Eysenck's theory of incubation:

> At best, the theory suggests qualitative guidelines for arranging conditions under which incubation may be more or less likely to occur. Accordingly, its potential for contribution to an understanding of 'paradoxical' failures of extinction, the etiology of neurosis or the effectiveness of therapeutic procedures must remain in doubt. (p. 16)

The reader interested in the incubation problem should also consult the open peer review of Eysenck's thesis and his replies (Eysenck, 1979).

RE-EVALUATION OF CONDITIONING THEORY

Criticisms of conditioning theory

Despite his important contribution to the development of the conditioning theory of trauma-induced phobias, Rachman (1977) now believes the theory to be unsatisfactory as a comprehensive account of the genesis of phobias. Rachman advances six arguments against acceptance of the conditioning theory of fear acquisition, most of them challenging the equipotentiality premise:

First argument. People fail to acquire conditioned fears in what are undoubtedly fear-evoking situations. For example, during the Second World War people appear to have adapted fairly well to air raids even as the raids became progressively heavier (Janis, 1951). More recently, children living in Israel in an area under frequent bombardment were found to be no different on self-ratings of anxiety than children from peaceful areas (Ziv & Israeli, 1973). With regard to the affect of natural disasters, an Australian study found that new fears were relatively infrequent among children following a cyclone (Milne, 1977).

Second argument. It is difficult to produce conditioned fear reactions in human subjects, even under controlled laboratory conditions. Here it is noted that patients undergoing aversion therapy rarely develop conditioned fear reactions (Hallam & Rachman, 1976; Marks & Gelder, 1967). Also, several experimenters have been unsuccessful in conditioning fear in infants (e.g. Bregman, 1934).

Third argument. The premise of equipotentiality has now been recognized as untenable. Generally speaking, there appears to be a bias towards biologically significant stimuli becoming conditioned (Seligman, 1971; Seligman & Hager, 1972). Attempts to condition fear reactions in infants and children to geometrically shaped wooden objects, curtains and opera glasses, for example, have all been unsuccessful (e.g. Bregman, 1934; Valentine, 1946).

Fourth argument. The distribution of fears in normal and neurotic populations is difficult to reconcile with the conditioning theory. Given the equipotentiality premise, the corollary for fear acquisition would be that all stimuli have an equal chance of being transformed into fear signals. However, this is not supported by survey data on the distribution of fears, either in a general population or in psychiatric samples (Rachman, 1974).

Fifth argument. A significant number of phobic patients, psychiatric and military, recount histories that cannot be accommodated by the conditioning theory. The aetiology of many clinical phobias is difficult to determine (Rachman, 1968), and cannot always be traced back to a traumatic learning incident (Marks, 1969).

Sixth argument. Fears can be reduced by vicarious processes and it seems highly likely that they can be acquired by similar processes.

Pathways of phobia acquisition

An important feature of the re-evaluation of the conditioning theory of phobias is the recognition that phobias can have non-traumatic origins. Bearing in mind that behavioural theorists and clinicians have adhered very strongly to the notion of trauma-induced phobias and conditioning theory, acceptance of other means of phobic acquisition has been very slow. Rachman (1977) identifies 'three major pathways' to the acquisition of fears and phobias that are particularly relevant to children. In addition to direct conditioning, Rachman emphasizes vicarious acquisition and transmission of information and/or instruction. The reinforcement of children's phobias on the part of care providers is another factor. Ollendick (1979b) proposes that most fears and phobias are multiply determined and, perhaps, overdetermined.

The vicarious acquisition of phobias involves what is customarily referred to as 'observational learning' or 'modelling'. For example, having been exposed to the fearful or phobic behaviour of parents, siblings and peers at the sight of spiders, a child may imitate these reactions on future occasions when the individual is confronted with the relevant stimulus. The precise manner by which children acquire phobias through observational learning in the natural environment is unknown, although arousal level, attention to the model, identification with the model, and possible consequences of such behaviour, seem to be important considerations (Bandura, 1969).

Although the power of observational learning in the genesis of childhood phobias has not been subject to direct experimental evaluation, various sources of data support the hypothesis that modelling is a factor in phobia acquisition. Some laboratory research with animals and humans is worthy of mention. Miller, Murphy and Mirsky (1959) demonstrated that fear can be transmitted from a fearful monkey to an observer monkey. Adult human subjects display fear responses after observing a model supposedly receive electric shock in an aversive conditioning procedure (Berger, 1962). Responses acquired through vicarious conditioning in the laboratory are probably fairly mild, and more readily extinguishable, compared with phobic reactions due to the same mechanism (Rimm & Lefebvre, 1981). Of greater relevance to the issue, children with fears and phobias often have parents with similar fears. In an early study, Hagman (1932) reported a correlation of 0.67 between similar fears of mothers and their children. Bandura and Menlove (1968) found that the parents of dog-phobic children had a higher incidence of these fears than the parents of children free of dog phobia. Windheuser (1977) compared phobic children and their mothers with non-phobic children and their mothers. The mothers of the phobic children exceeded the mothers of the non-phobic children in relation to general anxiety as measured by the Manifest Anxiety Scale (Taylor, 1953). Furthermore, the mothers of phobic children tended to fear the same kinds of objects and situations as did their children. Phobias of animals, medical or dental treatment, and social situations were the most common. While Bondy et al. (1985) found little correspondence between the self-reports of school children and their mothers on overall fearfulness, the pattern of fears reported by mothers was similar to the pattern reported by sons and daughters. However, there was no significant correspondence between the peak fears reported by the mothers and those reported by their children. Finally, it has been argued that the therapeutic effectiveness of modelling with phobic children supports the notion of phobias being acquired through the same mechanism (Rachman, 1977).

Although a child could observe a family member display poor coping behaviour and fearful behaviours if present at the critical moment, it seems more likely that the individual's distress will be conveyed to the child at other times. In other words, the opportunities for immediate observation are far more limited than are exposures to experiences and attitudes on the part of the family member. For example, Emmelkamp (1982) suggests that information on dental procedures is probably more potent than modelling so far as the development of dental phobias is concerned. The transmission of fear-inducing information by parents and others may be quite significant in the acquisition of children's phobias. Everyday observations suggest that children's fears and phobias of spiders and dentists are to some extent due to the expectation of danger or pain conveyed in conversation and jokes by parents. As Rachman (1977) states:

Although I am unaware of any conventionally acceptable evidence that fear can be acquired through the transmission of information (and particularly, by instruction), it seems to be undeniable. Information-giving is an inherent part of child-rearing and is carried on by parents and peers in an almost unceasing fashion, particularly in the child's earliest years. It is probable that informational and instructional processes provide the basis for most of our commonly encountered fears of everyday life. Fears acquired informationally are more likely to be mild than severe. Like the acquisition of fear by vicarious experience, informational and instructional processes have no difficulty in coping with the fact that people display fears of situations and objects which they have never encountered. Acceptance of the notion that fears can be acquired by informational processes, also enables us to explain some but by no means all of the failures to acquire fear in situations where it might, on the conditioning theory, have been expected to arise. Not only do we learn by information and instruction which situations to fear, we also learn to distinguish those situations and objects which are not dangerous and therefore not to be feared. We also learn and are taught to cope with dangers and to endure the accompanying discomfort or pain. (p. 384)

From the viewpoint of operant conditioning, positive reinforcement would be expected to play a significant role in the development of children's phobias. Perhaps surprisingly, theoretical accounts of phobias have given little attention to reinforcement as a means of phobia acquisition. It should be emphasized, however, that an operant approach is compatible with the indirect pathways of phobia acquisition proposed by Rachman (1977). An operant conditioning account of children's phobias has been provided by Miller *et al.* (1974):

Operant theory postulates that behavior that is rewarded will tend to reoccur while behavior that is not rewarded will extinguish. This theory would assume that avoidance behavior observed in phobias, as well as many of the accompanying behaviors such as temper tantrums are positively and systematically reinforced. The primary reinforcers are social rewards dispensed by significant persons in the immediate environment, primarily members of the family. Attention, whether affectionate or punitive, seems to serve equally well as a reinforcer. Parents and other significant persons teach children to be afraid by selectively attending and rewarding fearful and avoidant behaviors. Thus children are taught fear of the dark, death, dogs, separation, school, and such, by parents' and age-mates' responding with affection, anger, or reassurance to the child's fear, cautious approaches, and avoidance of these situations. The child, in turn, learns that parents are sensitive to such behaviors and respond with much attention and preoccupation so that a little fear evokes intense and frequent responses from significant others. Thus the more fear and avoidance behavior that a child evokes, the more attention he will receive from significant others. Since fear and avoidance rather than coping responses are consistently rewarded by significant others, the child fails to develop adaptive responses to aversive stimuli. (p. 115)

Phobic behaviour in children may be established on a gradual basis through inadvertent or deliberate reinforcement (shaping) on the part of parents and others. Intermittent reinforcement would be expected to be very powerful in the maintenance of such behaviour once acquired.

The relative importance of these 'pathways' is unknown, although most authorities believe that vicarious mechanisms are of greater significance in the development of everyday fears than clinical fears or phobias. Rachman (1977) states; 'The common everyday fears are probably acquired by the indirect and socially transmitted processes of the information-giving type and by vicarious exposure' (p. 385). On the basis of his clinical experience with phobics, Emmelkamp (1982) argues that modelling and informational processes are relatively small factors in the development of phobias. Certainly, a number of studies (e.g. Lautch, 1971; Öst & Hugdahl, 1981; Rimm, Janda, Lancaster, Nahl & Dittmar, 1977) on adult phobics suggest direct conditioning is far more common than vicarious conditioning. However, children's phobias may need to be viewed differently. A wide variety of behaviours and attitudes are taught to children by their parents and other care providers. The barrage of expectations and teachings is impossible to avoid in these formative years, in which children attain their physical and psychological independence fairly gradually. Thus vicarious exposure and the transmission of information regarding feared situations are more likely to have a greater impact than the manner in which they are processed in adult years. To wit, a recent telephone survey of parents of 30 phobic children on a waiting list revealed that trauma and frightening experiences accounted for 26.7% of the cases (Clowes-Hollins & King, 1981). Interestingly, in the opinion of the parents, modelling the fearful behaviour of family members was the most significant aetiological determinant (53.3% of cases where classified accordingly). Of course, it should also be understood that the various mechanisms (direct and indirect) of phobia acquisition are not mutually exclusive (Ollendick, 1979b). For example, a child's phobia of darkness may have been caused by a traumatic incident in the dark (direct conditioning) as well as by having a parent who is 'still a little afraid of darkness' and who inadvertently reinforces such behaviour. Hence, the indirect pathways of phobia acquisition should not be overlooked.

Whether the expression of childhood phobias is determined by their aetiological processes is an intriguing question. Perhaps children with animal phobias who have been severely frightened or attacked by dogs are more inclined to display a different reaction from children who have acquired their excessive fear of animals through listening to exaggerated stories about the dangers of animals or by being exposed to animal-fearful parents. In a critical examination of conditioning theory, Rachman (1977) has considered the manner in which fear/phobia acquisition may differentially affect the various response components. For phobias acquired through direct conditioning, it is speculated that the physiological and behavioural components are predominant while the subjective aspect plays a minor role. When phobias are acquired through indirect means—observational learning and information—it is speculated that the subjective aspect will be predominant with minor effects in the physiological and behavioural spheres. Inherent in this theorizing is an assumption concerning the one-to-one correspondence that exists between the causal pathways and components of phobic reactions. Such an isomorphic relationship may not be valid at all. Furthermore, it must be remembered that aetiological processes are confounded with numerous maintenance factors which may affect the form of the phobic reaction.

Integration

From the preceding discussion it is clear that the behavioural model of children's phobias does not involve a unified theory of phobia acquisition and maintenance. The behavioural model of children's phobias has a variegated conceptual basis drawing upon classical, vicarious and operant conditioning paradigms. However, no single paradigm appears to be an adequate explanation. A comprehensive behavioural model is required that integrates the 'major pathways' of phobia acquisition (i.e. direct conditioning, modelling, instruction and reinforcement). Social learning theory allows for the integration of the mechanisms that are responsible for children's phobias.

According to social learning theory, cognitive processes mediate the influence of environmental events upon the acquisition and regulation of behaviours (Bandura, 1977; Wilson & O'Leary, 1980). The emphasis upon cognitive mediation is important in view of the fact that behavioural accounts of children's phobias have been criticized for their disregard of cognitive processes (Graziano, De Giovanni & Garcia, 1979). An illustration of cognitive mediation has been provided by Ollendick and Cerny (1981):

> ... a child exhibiting intense fear of failure might think, 'If I make a mistake, no one will like me' and 'I'm no good if I fail'. When the child is in an evaluative situation, these thoughts quite naturally lead to expectancies of failure, thoughts of self-depreciation, and eventual withdrawal and avoidance of the situation. When queried as to avoidance behavior, the child replies that he/she can't do anything right, knows that he/she is a failure, and that there is no use in trying. The child feels justified in maintaining these inappropriate cognitions since they are congruent with previous experiences in similar situations (p. 221).

From a social learning theory perspective, children's phobias can be due to traumatic experiences, modelling, instruction, or reinforcement; but the final 'common pathway' entails the learned expectations children have about their inability to cope with frightening events and situations. Once established, these 'efficacy-expectations' can be self-initiated or activated by the environment, producing autonomic arousal and/or escape/avoidance behaviour. A major attraction of social learning theory is the emphasis upon the reciprocity between the individual and the environment. Unlike traditional conditioning theories that assume unidirectional causality (i.e. the environment acting upon the individual), social learning theory acknowledges the interaction between behaviour, cognitive and other internal events, and the external environment. It is to be hoped that more attention will be given to social learning theory by those interested in the development of an integrated model of children's phobias.

INDIVIDUAL DIFFERENCES IN PHOBIA ACQUISITION

It is generally agreed that some children are more susceptible to the development of phobias than others, despite similar circumstances regarding traumatic experiences and other learning histories. The most popular explanation of individual differences in phobia acquisition highlights organismic variables, particularly the lability of the autonomic nervous system (Davison & Neale, 1974). Consistent with this theory, Wolpe (1958) maintains that people differ in emotional reactivity, and that highly reactive individuals are at risk in terms of conditioned anxiety. According to Wolpe (1958):

> It is likely that individuals differ in general emotional reactivity because of maturationally established physiological differences. Observations in infants (e.g. Shirley, 1933) uniformly indicate the presence of such differences. A highly reactive individual exposed to given anxiety-evoking conditions would obviously have a greater intensity of conditionable anxiety evoked in him than an individual whose reactivity was low. (p. 76)

However, the most comprehensive theoretical attempt to deal with the individual difference problem in psychopathology is Eysenck's two-dimensional model of personality (Eysenck, 1957, 1967b; Eysenck & Rachman, 1965). Eysenck posits that personality consists of two bipolar dimensions, extraversion–introversion and neuroticism. Looking at the extraversion–introversion dimension, it will be recalled that the 'typical extravert' is outgoing, sociable and impulsive, whilst the 'typical introvert' is quiet, cautious and serious. Introverts are more readily conditioned than extraverts. Neuroticism is more akin to the description given by many authors (e.g. Wolpe, 1958) of emotional stability or instability, and relates to the lability of the autonomic nervous system. On the one hand, there are individuals whose emotional reactions are labile, intense and easily aroused; on the other hand, there are individuals whose emotional reactions are stable, weaker and more difficult to arouse. Phobias are thought to be part of the so-called 'dysthymic neurotic disorders' that are found predominantly in people who are introverted and high on neuroticism. Working from Eysenck's model, Rachman (1968) summarized the explanation of individual differences in this way:

> Phobias are most likely to develop in people who are innately predisposed towards introverted patterns of behavior, and are at the same time endowed with a labile autonomic nervous system. It can be expected that people who have this constitution will develop phobias earlier and/or more readily than either extroverts or people who are low on the neuroticism factor. (pp. 11–12)

Although Eysenck's model has varying degrees of support in accounting for the question of individual differences in conditionability and psychopathology (Eysenck, 1971; Yates, 1970), no empirical research has tested the adequacy of the model in relation to the genesis of phobias in children and adolescents.

Individual differences in phobia acquisition may also be explained in terms of non-constitutional factors. Previously acquired maladaptive anxiety may in fact 'sensitize' the individual, thus potentiating the development of excessive fears. Wolpe (1958) states: 'a severe neurosis is more likely to develop in a person who already has many unadaptive anxieties conditioned in him than in a relatively "nonneurotic" person' (pp. 76–7). Lovibond (1966) argues that there are a significant number of phobics for whom intense arousal-eliciting psychological stresses of a continuing nature may 'disinhibit and potentiate mild fear states and lead to the development of conditioned fear of the situation in question' (p. 99). According to Lovibond, phobias that develop in this fashion have three components: disinhibited inherent fear, a potentiating component of pervasive anxiety, and a super-added conditioning component.

In examining the role of disinhibition in the aetiology and maintenance of phobias, Farmer (1971) makes several observations of the literature supporting Lovibond's (1966) model. For example, a number of phobias seem to have been precipitated by stress. On this point, Davidson (1960) found that a high incidence of deaths or threatened death preceded the onset of school phobia. Poznanski (1973) makes an observation in her study of phobic children that supports the disinhibition model:

A subjective impression from perusing the charts was that the children with excessive fears tended to have the onset of their fears associated with a definite historical event. For example, one child witnessed the slaughtering of a pet cow, another child connected the onset of fears with watching the Kennedy funeral on TV, while a third child's fears were associated with a brother's being sent to Vietnam. The children in the control group lacked specific anxiety-producing events followed by behavioral symptoms, and their fears generally had a more insidious onset. Most of the children who were excessively fearful seemed to have more than the usual amount of anxiety prior to the onset of the excessive fears, and a mild situational stress precipitated a more open display of fears and anxiety. (p. 432)

In addition, Lovibond's model appears to have considerable support in the psychophysiological and neurophysiological literature (Eccles, 1953; Pavlov, 1927; Rachman, 1962; Razran, 1939). The therapeutic implications of the disinhibition model are quite profound, a point to which we shall return in subsequent chapters. Farmer recommends that for those cases where the phobic intensity does fluctuate markedly and/or pervasive anxiety is present in other areas, therapy should primarily focus on reducing the level of arousal or anxiety elicited by factors in the person's life situation other than the phobic stimuli themselves.

SELECTIVITY OF CHILDREN'S PHOBIAS

An issue which has already been anticipated is the highly selective nature of stimuli that elicit fear and phobic reactions. Examples of the most common childhood phobias include excessive fear of the dark, water, animals and school. On the other hand, the idea of a toothbrush or pyjama phobia seems absurd, and the reader would be struggling to find a report of such a phobia in the literature. Looking at this phenomenon in strict learning theory terms, it may be argued that this is due to the fact that the mechanisms of phobia acquisition very rarely operate under those circumstances in which a toothbrush phobia, for example, could be acquired. Taking a broader perspective in which learning plays still an important but limited role, it may be argued that certain stimuli are more easily transformed into phobic stimuli than others, owing to selective processes. Given the similarity of children's fears and the fact that they are age-related, it would appear *prima facie* that a biological mechanism may operate to determine the conditionability of potential phobic stimuli. Consistent with this viewpoint, Marks (1969) has emphasized the 'prepotency' of certain stimuli to trigger off phobias. However, the most influential theorist in this respect is Seligman (1971). According to Seligman, an association which is readily acquired is defined as *prepared* and one which is acquired with difficulty is *unprepared*. In relation to phobias, Seligman (1971) argues: 'Phobias are highly prepared to be learned by humans, and, like other highly prepared relationships, they are selective and resistant to extinction, learned even with degraded input, and probably are non-cognitive' (p. 312). The critical consideration here is that most phobias are of biological significance, which seems to be borne out by the fact that human phobias are largely restricted to objects and situations that are survival threats—including potential predators, unfamiliar places and the dark (Seligman & Hager, 1972).

In support of the preparedness theory, it will be recalled that learning theorists have an unsuccessful history of attempts at conditioning fear in children to neutral stimuli. For example, English (1929) was unsuccessful in his attempt to condition a fear response to a toy duck in a 14-month-old infant. Working with 15 infants aged 8 to 16 months, Bregman (1934) was unable to condition a fear reaction to a wooden rectangular block and wooden triangle. Also supportive of the preparedness theory is Valentine's (1946) study on a 1-year-old infant. Using a loud whistle as the UCS, Valentine was unable to induce a conditioned fear response to an old pair of opera glasses, but successfully induced an intense fear reaction to a caterpillar with the same loud whistle.

More recently, Öhman and his colleagues (review by Öhman, 1979) have conducted a series of well-controlled experiments on non-phobic college students addressed to the preparedness theory. In these experiments, the subjects were conditioned to slides by means of an aversive UCS (mild electric shock or loud noises) while autonomic activity such as skin conductance or vasomotor responses were monitored. The slides were grouped as fear-relevant (e.g. pictures of snakes and spiders) or fear-irrelevant (e.g. pictures of flowers and mushrooms). In support of the preparedness theory, the basic finding was that fear-relevant stimuli were more resistant to extinction than fear-irrelevant stimuli. Consequently, it has been suggested that the preparedness concept should replace the premise of equipotentiality which assumes the equal conditionability of all stimuli in conditioning situations (Rachman, 1976, 1977; Rachman & Seligman, 1976; Seligman, 1971; Seligman & Hager, 1972).

However, the notion that fears and phobias are to some extent biologically preprogrammed has not gone unchallenged. On the basis of an intensive review of many related areas of research, Delprato (1980) concludes that no body of research conclusively supports the evolutionary hypothesis. According to Delprato, attempts to fit the ontogeny of fear into the traditional 'innate versus learned' framework may hamper identification of development factors underlying fear behaviour that go beyond concepts of heredity and learning. In a clinical test of the preparedness hypothesis, de Silva, Rachman and Seligman (1977) rated phobic and obsessional clients for the 'preparedness' or evolutionary significance of their fears, and related these measures to therapeutic outcome. Contrary to the preparedness hypothesis, the preparedness ratings failed to predict treatment outcome and related considerations.

SUMMARY

From a behavioural perspective, childhood phobias are regarded as learned behaviours. Conditioning theory has been developed to account for the acquisition and maintenance of phobias. Traumatic experience has been seen to be the cause of many children's phobias. Evidence for conditioning theory is found in animal and human studies, as well as in clinical case reports. The case of little Albert provided an illustration of a trauma-induced phobia and conditioning theory principles. Albert was a 9-month-old boy who, prior to the study, did not fear rats. As a result of pairing an aversive sound with the presentation of a white rat, he became afraid of white rats after a number of conditioning trials. Generalization of the fear response to other stimuli (e.g. rabbit, dog and sealskin coat) was evident. Another 'successful' fear-induction experiment involving an infant was conducted by H.E. Jones. The 15-month-old infant was conditioned to fear the sound of a bell with mild electric shock as the unconditioned stimulus.

Whether childhood phobias grow or intensify with time in the absence of further traumatic experience is an interesting question. Eysenck argues that incubation of this kind does occur, and that it is facilitated by several factors, including short exposures to the conditioned stimulus. Many criticisms have been made of conditioning theory, including the observation that it is difficult to produce conditioned fear reactions in human subjects. Another criticism involves the fact that many case histories of children with phobias are not consistent with conditioning theory.

In addition to direct conditioning, we now recognize the importance of modelling, instruction, and positive reinforcement, in the acquisition of children's phobias. The relative importance of these pathways is difficult to establish, although they should not be regarded as being mutually exclusive. On a speculative note, we question whether the different pathways of phobia acquisition have different effects on the three response systems. Social learning theory is a useful means of integrating these pathways, with the child developing low efficacy expectations about his or her ability to cope with the frightening object or situation.

Finally, two general issues have been examined. The first concerned the question of individual differences in phobia acquisition. Several explanations were offered as to why some children are more prone than others to develop phobias, including varying levels of emotional reactivity, Eysenck's two-dimensional model of psychopathology, and a disinhibition model emphasizing the role of stress. The second issue concerned the highly selective nature of stimuli that elicit fear and phobic reactions. The concept of preparedness has been advanced to explain the selective nature of children's phobias, it being hypothesized that phobias are highly prepared to be learned by humans and resistant to extinction. However, the clinical significance of preparedness theory appears dubious at the moment.

CHAPTER 3

Behavioural assessment of children's phobias

INTRODUCTION

Although somewhat elusive to define, behavioural assessment exemplifies the empirical nature of the behavioural approach to child and adult problems. Of course, the full impact of behavioural assessment on diagnosis, treatment design and evaluation is beyond the scope of this chapter. Hence the reader is referred to other sources (Ciminero, Calhoun & Adams, 1977; Cone & Hawkins, 1977; Gelfand & Hartmann, 1984; Haynes, 1978; Haynes & Wilson, 1979; Hersen & Bellack, 1976; Keefe, Kopel & Gordon, 1978; Mash & Terdal, 1981; Ollendick & Hersen, 1984) for more detailed theoretical and practical information on behavioural assessment. Similarly, the use of experimental designs (e.g. reversal designs, multiple baseline designs, alternative treatments design) in clinical practice will not be discussed here (see Barlow, Hayes & Nelson, 1984; Hersen & Barlow, 1976).

As has been recognized for many years, behavioural assessment has several purposes in its function as preintervention assessment (Cautela & Upper, 1977):

(1) to identify behaviours to be modified and their maintaining stimuli;
(2) to assess functional relationships among response classes and among discriminative and reinforcing stimuli;
(3) to determine available social resources, personal assets and skills for use in a therapeutic programme, as well as limitations and obstacles in the person and in the environment;
(4) to provide specific therapeutic techniques which are most compatible with the personal and environmental factors in the patient's life situation.

However, behavioural assessment is more than a systematic analysis of the presenting problem and its situational determinants in order to decide the most appropriate form of treatment. Behavioural assessment should be approached as a process of hypothesis testing regarding the nature of the behavioural

50

problem and likely treatment effects. This notion is reflected in current definitions of child behavioural assessment. According to Mash and Terdal (1981):

> ...the behavioral assessment of children involves a process of hypothesis testing regarding the nature of the problem, its causes, and the likely effects of various treatments. Such hypothesis testing proceeds from a particular assumptive base and is carried out in relation to existing data, with specific methodologies and purposes. (p. 8)

Similarly, Ollendick and Hersen (1984) define child behavioural assessment as:

> ...an exploratory, hypothesis testing process in which a range of specific procedures is used in order to understand a given child, group, or social ecology and to formulate and evaluate specific intervention strategies. (p. ix)

Ollendick and Hersen note that three primary characteristics guide the selection of specific procedures in child behavioural assessment: (1) the multimethod approach which yields the best 'picture of the child', (2) the selection of procedures which have been empirically validated, and (3) the sensitivity of the procedures to developmental processes.

DEVELOPMENTAL AND NORMATIVE ISSUES

Although it is readily acknowledged that children should not be viewed as miniature adults, this stricture is especially true in child behavioural assessment. We must remember that children are characterized by rapid and uneven developmental change in many areas of functioning (perceptual-motor, cognitive, language, social, sexual and moral). Hence child behavioural assessment should be developmentally sensitive and reflect the cognitive and verbal abilities of children. This was elucidated by Ollendick and Hersen (1984):

> ...age-related constraints are numerous and await clearer articulation and categorization. Until such time, it is imperative that child behavioral assessors be aware of developmental considerations and constraints when selecting specific methods of assessment. Certain procedures are more appropriate for age specific groups and ability levels than others. The continued and indiscriminate use of developmentally sensitive instruments will fail to advance our understanding and subsequent modification of child behavior disorders. (p. 13)

Our concern for the use of developmentally sensitive methods has direct implications for the behavioural assessment of childhood fears and phobias. An obvious example is the behavioural interview. Although we depend upon care providers for much information, children are not passive recipients in the interview. The age of the child will influence the manner in which questions are framed, and the extent to which the child and parents are interviewed separately and together (Gross, 1984; Kanfer, Eyberg & Krahn, 1983). Self-monitoring is an assessment strategy that requires children to record their fear behaviour (e.g. test anxiety). Older children and adolescents are able to provide useful assessment information through self-monitoring. In our experience, young children lack the requisite abilities for self-monitoring. In fact, confusion and impaired performance has resulted from self-monitoring in children under 6 years of age (e.g. Higa, Tharp & Calkins, 1978; Ollendick & Cerny, 1981). A self-report instrument that has proved useful for older children is the Fear Survey Schedule for Children (Scherer & Nakamura, 1968). However, it has been found to be less applicable to children under 8 years old because of problems they have in understanding the notion of rating fear on a 5-point scale. In a revision and restandardization of the scale, Ollendick (1983a) found that when a 3-point scale was used younger children were able to rate their fear reliably and validly. These examples show us that assessment methods should be designed with the cognitive and verbal skills of children in mind.

In the behavioural assessment of childhood fears and phobias a fundamental question is whether the fear behaviour warrants clinical attention. As noted by Mash and Terdal (1981), behavioural assessment has concentrated upon intra-individual comparisons as seen in evaluations of therapeutic intervention. In recent years, attention has turned to normative comparisons since they provide information about the child's behaviour relative to the behaviour of other children in an appropriate reference group (e.g. age, sex and culture) (Ollendick & Hersen, 1984). In relation to childhood fears, research studies have described 'normal' age trends that can assist in problem identification. As we noted in Chapter 1, specific fears occur with regularity during the course of normal development. From a normative standpoint, a 4-year old child who evinces a fear of the dark is not exhibiting deviant behaviour. On the other hand, a 10-year old child who is afraid of the dark is outside the developmental norms. When the fear appears to be part of normal child development and to have a good prognosis, the focus should be on the parents' perception. A discussion about the common fears of children and the age-related decline in fears is usually reassuring to parents. In addition, practical information can be given about the prevention of excessive fears and the role of parents (see Chapter 7).

In view of the methodological problems associated with the research on children's fears, however, we should be cautious in the clinical application of normative data (see Chapter 1). Certainly, there is a need to update norms and establish appropriate referenced norms for different cultures and countries, as well as continuing to research the reliability and validity of fear assessment methods (Harris & Ferrari, 1983; Ollendick, Huntzinger & King, 1987). Even with a stronger data base on what children normally fear, it will be appreciated that there are other clinical issues in problem identification. The regular occurrence of fears, and their consistency with the developmental pattern, does not necessarily imply that such fears are transitory or not problematic to the child (Graziano, DeGiovanni & Garcia, 1979). An important practical question concerns the short- and long-term consequences for the child should treatment be withheld (Barrios et al., 1981). Because of the possible health risks, this is a critical issue in the assessment of children with fears of dentists and doctors that appear to be age-appropriate. In behavioural assessment we must therefore obtain detailed information on the intensity, persistence and maladaptiveness of the individual child's fear. After all, these have long been recognized as useful criteria in differentiating clinical fears (or phobias) from normal fears (Barrios *et al.*, 1981; Graziano, DeGiovanni & Garcia, 1979; Morris & Kratochwill, 1983).

Childhood phobias need to be differentiated from other emotional and behavioural disorders. Following the DSM-III-R, children with 'overanxious disorder' engage in excessive worrying and fearful behaviour that is not focused on a specific object or situation. Complaints about 'feeling nervous' are common, along with worries about future events such as examinations and peer-group activities. Although frequently treated as a unitary problem, 'examination anxiety' can be part of the clinical picture seen in overanxious disorder. Occasionally, non-compliance and temper tantrums can be mistaken for a fear problem. A child who is non-compliant as regards bedtime routines (sleeps with his or her parents, for example) might be thought by the clinician to have an excessive fear of the dark especially when the rationale of the family is that of fear rather than disobedience. In addition to more consistent verbal complaints of fear, the child who is really afraid of darkness is likely to display fear in various darkness situations. The non-compliant child would likely be diagnosed as having an 'oppositional defiant disorder' within the DSM-III-R classification. Obviously we should be aware of the true clinical picture before setting treatment goals and selecting intervention strategies.

FUNDAMENTAL QUESTIONS FOR TREATMENT DESIGN

Children with excessive fears are frequently diagnosed as having separation anxiety disorder, simple phobia, school phobia, and so forth. Notwithstanding the problems inherent in diagnostic systems like the DSM-III-R, we believe that a diagnosis can be useful in signalling broad concerns and generalizations about the problem. In fact, a diagnosis can provide a starting point for the behavioural assessment of particular responses and specific controlling variables. In obtaining such idiographic data on a child's phobia, there are a number of questions which must be addressed in behavioural assessment (Barrios *et al.*, 1981; Kennedy, 1983; Miller, 1983). Foremost of these issues is the specification of the phobia in terms of multi-target behaviours encompassing cognitive, physiological and overt behavioural responses. The standard functional analysis is mandatory in order to determine the antecedents and consequences of the phobia. In contrast to previous years, cognitions are now recognized in the selection of target behaviours and in the mediation of antecedents and consequences. The available resources and practical constraints should also be anticipated by the clinician. As will become evident, the selection of behavioural procedures depends upon the extent to which we are able satisfactorily to address these issues in behavioural assessment.

Target behaviours

A fundamental step in the behavioural assessment of a child's phobia is the specification of the fear problem in terms of target behaviours. Here the clinician must ascertain the nature of the disruptive and/or distressing responses which result from actual or anticipated exposure to the fear-evoking stimuli. As noted above, the disruptive behaviours may be within the overt behavioural, physiological and cognitive spheres. Knowing the response systems in which disturbance occurs provides the clinician with a tentative indication as to the selection of behavioural procedures (Barrios *et al.*, 1981, Borkovec *et al.*, 1977; Hugdahl, 1981).

The most common *overt behavioural* response of phobic children is avoidance of what is feared or escape if the fear-evoking stimuli are encountered unexpectedly. When escape or avoidance is not possible the child may display inappropriate behaviour for the situation. A child with a phobia of physical examinations, for example, may become uncooperative and aggressive in the doctor's office. Problematic overt behaviours are customarily treated by behavioural techniques such as participant modelling and operant procedures that are designed to enhance approach and adaptive behaviours (Borkovec *et al.*, 1977).

The *physiological* responses of phobic children to fear-evoking stimuli (actual or imagined) are varied but typically include increases in heart rate, changes in respiration, dryness of the mouth and diffuse muscle tension. In order to overcome extreme physiological reactions, progressive relaxation, systematic desensitization or emotive imagery might be employed (Barrios *et al.*, 1981; Borkovec *et al.*, 1977). These procedures entail the introduction of emotional states incompatible with the state of physiological arousal that occurs in the phobic reaction and teach the child a competing emotional response.

The *cognitive* responses of phobic children include maladaptive thoughts and images (Barrios *et al.*, 1981). Negative expectations are frequent in the thinking of such children (e.g., 'This has been bad for me before... it will be bad again'). Phobic children may exaggerate or catastrophize about the seriousness of the situation (e.g., 'This is terrible... I will get hurt'). Also, phobic children often perceive themselves as being helpless in the situation (e.g., 'I won't know what to do ... someone must help me'). Evidence of such cognitive–verbal disturbance would suggest the possible implementation of cognitive procedures like rational–emotive therapy (Ellis, 1970), self-instructional training (Meichenbaum, 1977) or some other cognitive training procedure (e.g. Graziano & Mooney, 1980; Kanfer, Karoly & Newman, 1975).

In the behavioural assessment the clinician needs to be aware of individual differences among children in relation to the pattern of subjective, physiological and overt behavioural responses (Borkovec *et al.*, 1977). A child who is anxious about a particular situation may display strong reactions in only one or two response systems. For example, a child may report fear about dentistry and show intense physiological activity in the dentist's chair, but not display escape or avoidance behaviour. An adolescent may demonstrate fear of darkness on physiological and behavioural criteria but not report being afraid. On the other hand, there are children with phobias who evince disruptive changes in all three response systems. A child with school phobia may report feeling terrified about school, demonstrate marked physiological changes each morning before school, and refuse to attend school voluntarily. As we have seen, the manifestation of the phobia has an important impact on the choice of treatment methods. The extent to which all three response systems are involved will influence the selection of multiple behavioural procedures in treatment. An issue of clinical significance is the fact that changes in any one of the three response systems throughout treatment do not necessarily correlate with changes in the other response systems (Barlow & Mavissakalian, 1981; Hodgson & Rachman, 1974). We return to this issue in the final chapter.

Antecedents

An important step in the behavioural assessment of a child's phobia is the identification of the antecedent stimuli that elicit the targeted response components. The most obvious antecedents are those of an external nature (e.g. darkness, animals, dental procedures) which are agreed upon by the child and care providers to be of functional significance. In addition, considerable discomfort can be produced in the child by cognitive representations (thoughts and images) of the fear-evoking stimuli. The potency of these antecedents can be exacerbated through a process of self-arousal in which the child actively imagines and thinks about the fear-evoking situation as in anticipatory anxiety. Of course, the identification of antecedent conditions may not tell exactly what it is about the situation or event that produces fear. From the viewpoint of individualized behavioural treatment, the clinician should attempt to identify the dimensions or variables which control the child's cognitive–verbal, physiological, and overt behavioural reactions. Foremost of these are temporal and/or spatial considerations, the number and type of people present, what is expected of the child, and the nature of the environment in which exposure occurs. A child who evinces an excessive fear of darkness, for example, may indicate that intensity of darkness is the crucial factor. Invariably other considerations come into play, such as whether the child is alone and the nature of the environment.

Obtaining detailed information about the controlling stimulus conditions can be problematic in working with children. In addition to the assessment strategies described in this chapter, we have used several techniques to obtain such information. Showing slides or pictures of fear-related stimuli interspersed among those of a non-threatening nature is helpful in eliciting the child's perception of the critical stimulus dimension(s). Walking with the child in the proximity of the feared situation or object can elicit physiological reactions and useful comments about what is feared (Yule, 1979). Another ploy is to have the child visualize and describe a typical day that includes one or more encounters with the frightening event or situation (Smith & Sharpe, 1970). The clinician notes the child's verbal and non-verbal behaviour at critical stages in order to gauge the child's likely reactions. Nevertheless, it must be acknowledged that there are times when the clinician has to formulate hypotheses about the antecedent conditions partly on the basis of clinical experience as well as on information obtained from the child and care providers.

For a small but consistent number of phobic children who appear at clinics the potency of the fear-evoking stimuli may be attributed to severe trauma. In most cases the child has developed a fear reaction that is inappropriate in terms of any real danger or threat. A child that has been mauled by a dog, for example, may become panic-stricken at the sight of all dogs regardless of whether or not there is any risk of physical harm. In the case of a child's phobia that is a function of direct (trauma) conditioning, the clinician might select systematic desensitization or some deconditioning procedure given the research foundations of these procedures (Wolpe, 1958). However, in our eagerness to apply deconditioning procedures we should not overlook the possibility of the presenting fear complaint having a realistic basis. Here the clinician should heed Kennedy's (1983) admonition about 'correct-sign' behaviour in which appropriate discriminations are evinced by the child. In the behavioural assessment of a boy with a trauma-induced dog phobia, Kennedy found that the dog responsible for a vicious attack on the boy was owned by a neighbour. Further, the neighbour had kept the dog since the attack and because of inadequate security it was a constant threat to the child. Throughout the high-risk period the child's behaviour with other dogs was appropriate. In this case intervention took the form of a law suit to remove the dog, which rendered treatment unnecessary. Thus the possible correctness of the fear should be examined before assuming that the treatment of a phobia is in order.

A factor that has not been sufficiently emphasized concerns the child's skill deficits (Barrios et al., 1981). A requisite to coping with many of the feared stimuli that elicit phobic reactions is a certain level of behavioural competency. Frequently, phobic children seem to lack important behavioural skills. For example, a child's phobia of water can be confounded by an inability to swim. Animal-phobic children often display poor verbal command and inadequate handling skills when interacting with animals. Because of the persistent avoidance of the phobic stimuli, the child never acquires or maintains the skills for coping with the feared situation that are taken for granted in non-phobic children. Over a period of years, a vicious cycle may occur in which physiological arousal and skill deficits interact to the detriment of the child. Participant modelling and reinforcement are recommended for the development of behavioural competencies in phobic children.

Clinically, it is important to consider other relevant antecedents that may be more difficult to identify in the temporal sequence of events associated with the child's phobia (sometimes referred to as 'setting events'). Here the possibility of significant others (parent, siblings, friends) modelling fearful behaviour needs to be assessed (Klesges, Malott & Ugland, 1984; Windheuser, 1977). This process can be very subtle, thus making an assessment decision very difficult. When the parent (or whoever) confirms that they have fear problems, the starting point of therapy can be with that person. As general advice to parents and other care providers, however, the necessity for good coping models in the child's social environment needs to be pointed out.

Another possible antecedent somewhat removed temporally from the phobia involves the amount of general stress in the child's life (see Chapter 2). Children who are undergoing high levels of stress (e.g. peer relationship difficulties, academic problems at school, a dying parent or sibling) may be more prone to develop phobias because of their heightened level of physiological arousal. An obvious problem is the question of what circumstances are to be considered stressful. This will be a clinical judgement on the part of the clinician, based on observations of the child and the general circumstances of the case. For those individuals in which the model seems to apply, behavioural assessment and intervention need to focus upon the stressor(s) in addition to the more specific antecedents. The nature of intervention will depend upon the stressor(s) but quite conceivably address educational, behavioural, family or economic problems.

Consequences

Given that the problem behaviour of children can be reinforced inadvertently by care providers, behavioural assessment should address the consequent events within the social network. When present on those occasions in which the child is exposed to the fear-evoking stimuli, the care provider's reaction to the cognitive, physiological and overt behavioural aspects of the phobia can be of functional significance. Care providers usually intervene in a protective and comforting manner in which there are elements of both negative and positive reinforcement. Depending upon the circumstances, the care provider may remove the child from the fear-evoking situation or neutralize the situation, thus terminating the aversive experience (negative reinforcement). For example, parents of animal-phobic children may provide some form of 'physical protection' from the animal, take the child away from the feared animal or have the animal removed. In addition, efforts to comfort the child both at the time and after the exposure may serve to strengthen the cognitive, physiological and overt behavioural components of the phobia (positive reinforcement).

Similarly, the clinican needs to appraise the reaction of care providers to the cognitive, physiological and overt behavioural changes displayed by children in anticipation of exposure to the feared stimuli. Parents and other care providers frequently attend to verbal complaints and physiological indicators of distress and finally allow the child to avoid the feared situation. In this way the child learns the functional value of the marked or subtle changes in one or more of the response systems on those occasions in which exposure is anticipated. This process is invariably seen in school phobia in which confrontation with the feared situation is highly predictable to the child.

Of course, care providers may be proactive in the facilitation of avoidance behaviour. For example, many parents of children who are afraid of darkness habitually ensure that all the necessary lights are switched on in their house at night to ensure peace and quiet for the family. Parents of dog-phobic children tend to check out localities and plan family outings in order to minimize the chances of contact with dogs. Certainly, the manner in which parents and other care providers accommodate their lifestyle to the child's phobia must be addressed. Occasionally, the reinforcement that is contingent upon the child's phobia can be fulfilling a need of the care provider (e.g. a lonely single parent who sleeps with his or her child on the grounds that the latter is afraid of the dark). Hence, the clinician needs to be attuned to the reciprocity of reinforcement within the family system. Contingency management would be a logical component of therapeutic programmes for children's phobias in which reinforcement plays a significant role.

However, the identification of consequent events can be a difficult task for the clinician. In the assessment of direct contingencies there are several issues. The subtle nature of social reinforcement is a concern; parents say they do not make a fuss about the child's phobia, but for the child a reassuring comment, a brief hug or even just eye contact can be very encouraging. In relation to the intermittent nature of the reinforcement, parents say 'never' when they mean 'hardly ever', with the latter having a significant impact on the persistence of the child's phobic reaction. Another issue concerns the various sources of reinforcement. In addition to parents, the child has interactions with many other people that are frequently overlooked in terms of their role in maintaining the phobia. As noted by Kennedy (1983), parents and the child are poor informants regarding indirect contingencies. For example, during the night a child runs to his parents expressing fear about 'something' at the window, which serves to terminate an argument between the parents that is upsetting to him. The parents comfort the child and tuck him into bed, but the crucial contingency is the cessation of the argument rather than parental comfort. Kennedy also points out that there are times when the contingency is purely superstitious. A child has a fear of dying, for example, and runs in terror to the parents' bed for help. The mother wakes up, speaks to the child and the child does not die. The child's fear is unfounded and the mother's behaviour is really ineffective, but in the child's eyes the phobic reaction produces behaviour that is effective. Hence the clinician needs to be very thorough in the assessment of consequences, and alert to the various ways in which a child's phobia can be inadvertently reinforced by care providers.

Resources

The behavioural assessment of children's phobias should address the resources available to children and their families. Child variables such as age, health, compliance, intelligence, verbal skills, and imaginal ability, are all important in the choice of therapeutic technique. For example, systematic desensitization in imagination requires children and adolescents with good concentration and imaginal skills. Further, in many phobic reduction programmes for children, the care provider may be involved in the implementation of the programme under the direction of the therapist. Consequently, the suitability of the 'mediator' needs to be carefully assessed. The mediator's availability and motivation, understanding and acceptance of the programme, and competence to execute prescribed tasks, should be considered. In addition, setting variables may be important in terms of the physical structure of the treatment location, the availability of peers to assit in therapy (e.g. modelling), and access to appropriate fear-evoking stimuli for exposure treatments. The importance of resources and practical problems cannot be overemphasized in effective behavioural intervention.

SPECIFIC ASSESSMENT STRATEGIES

Consistent with current thinking about child behavioural assessment (Mash & Terdal, 1981; Ollendick & Hersen, 1984), we advise a multi-method approach to the behavioural assessment of childhood fears and phobias. Nowadays, child behavioural assessment involves the use of behavioural interviews, checklists and rating forms, traditional standardized instruments, self-reports, behavioural observations, self-monitoring, physiological instruments, and so forth. Collectively, these varied sources of information help us obtain a 'complete picture of the child', his or her behaviour, and the treatment context (Ollendick & Hersen, 1984). Of course, it is not always necessary or possible to use all of these assessment strategies. The specific assessment methods used depend upon the nature of the referral problem and the time and resources available to the clinician (Ollendick & Cerny, 1981). As noted by Evans (1982): 'Taking careful aim is still more important than the bore of the barrel or gauge of the shot' (p. 124). Nevertheless, we recommend that as many procedures as possible be used to develop an effective programme. Because of their specific relevance to the behavioural assessment of childhood fears and phobias, we shall address the behavioural interview, self-reports, behavioural observations, self-monitoring, and physiological recordings.

Behavioural interviews

The interview is an integral part of behavioural assessment and the chief means by which clinical information is gathered. In order to facilitate the ease and thoroughness of the initial interview, the use of an interview schedule or checklist of issues is recommended. Murphy, Hudson, King and Remenyi (1985) have developed one such interview schedule that can be used in the initial stages of behavioural assessment in relation to childhood problems, and this is summarized in checklist form in Table 3.1. It can be conveniently located on a

Table 3.1 Interview schedule for children's problems

Date ——————————— Client ———————————
Interviewer——————————— Observer———————————
Time started ——————————— Time finished ———————————

(1) The establishment
  (a) Introduction
  (b) Small talk
  (c) Seating

(2) General
  (a) Purpose of interview
  (b) Permission of note-taking
  (c) Client perception of problem
  (d) Referral agency

(3) Background information
  (a) Biographic information
    (i) Name
    (ii) Age
    (iii) Address
    (iv) Telephone
  (b) Family background
    (i) both parents present
    (ii) employment of parents
    (iii) number and ages of siblings
    (iv) unusual family organization
    (v) child's relation with family members.
  (c) Educational background
    (i) number and type of schools attended
    (ii) school progress
    (iii) relationship with teachers
    (iv) current teacher's name
    (v) relationship with peers
  (d) Medical background
    (i) developmental milestones and behaviour patterns:
      feeding
      sleeping
      eating
      gross motor
      toileting
      language
    (ii) childhood illnesses
    (iii) medication

(4) Problem-specific information
  (a) Precise statement of problem
  (b) Extent of problem
  (c) Antecedents and consequences
  (d) Previous attempts to handle problem

(5) Clarification of expectations
  (a) Agreement of goal
  (b) Statement of suitability of agency
  (c) No magic wand
  (d) Involvement of consultee

(6) Homework
  (a) Baseline
  (b) Identification of A's and C's

(7) Scheduling next appointment

(8) Termination of interview

SOURCE: Murphy, Hudson, King and Remenyi (1985). Reproduced by permission of the Australian Behaviour Modification Association.

Table 3.2 Content of each stage in the behavioural interview

---

(1) *Establishment*
  (a) Introduce yourself to consultee (name and profession; how you like to be addressed; introduce observer or colleague—name and role).
  (b) Engage in 'small talk' to put consultee at ease.
  (c) Direct client to appropriate chair if interview is in office (have chairs and furniture prearranged to facilitate communication).

Remember that this period is critical to the development of a good client–therapist relationship. Such a relationship is essential for therapeutic success.

(2) *General*
  (a) Purpose(s) of interview
  (b) Permission on notetaking, etc.
  (c) Client's perception of problem
  (d) Referral agency

The client should be given a general statement on the purpose of the interview. This is important because some clients expect an immediate answer to their problem. Over the course of the interview it may be necessary to remind the client that management advice is not possible at this stage.

Permission should be obtained from the client on note-taking—usually this is not a problem in terms of client permission. Should audio- or video-recording be thought to be an advantage, seek permission prior to recording.

At this stage it is helpful to ask the consultee about the nature of the problem. This is simply to prompt consultees to give their perception of why they have come to see you. The description given may not be satisfactory to you or the client at this stage, but continued exploration about the nature of the problem would follow later in the interview. The idea of asking the question here is partially to set the stage for the next step, gathering general background information. Terminate this step by saying that you will come back to talking about the problem later, but first you want to obtain some other information about the child.

Obtain or check details on referring agency (professional's name, agency, and phone number). Remember that good liaison with other agencies in the community is essential, and dual management can be wasteful, confusing or deleterious.

(3) *Background information*
  (a) Biographic information of child:
     (i) name
     (ii) age (including date of birth)
     (iii) address
     (iv) telephone number

  (b) Family background

Here the interviewer collects information about:

     (i) whether in fact the mother and father (or others filling these roles) are present in the household
     (ii) what employment, if any, parents (or other careproviders) have
     (iii) number of and ages of siblings in the family
     (iv) any unusual family organizational pattern, like an aunt or cousin living with the family
     (v) quality of relationship between target child and other family or household members

(contd.)

Table 3.2 (*contd.*)

(c) Educational background

Here careful detail of educational background is recorded, including:
- (i) number and type of schools attended
- (ii) general progress while at school, including any grades repeated
- (iii) any history of conflict with teachers
- (iv) current teacher's name
- (v) relations with peers

(d) Medical background

The interviewer should list any information regarding the child's medical background, particularly anything that is slightly out of the ordinary. Remember to question regarding:
- (i) general development milestones and behaviour patterns
- (ii) childhood illnesses
- (iii) any medication child is currently on

If the behavioural interviewer is unsure about 'normal' development rates of infants and children in particular areas, standardized scales such as those of Bayley (1969) should be used.

The above areas need to be explored because (a) most clients receiving clinical service expect such areas to be addressed, and (b) the information helps the clinician appreciate the context of the problem, assists the clinician's choice of target behaviours, guides selection of assessment devices to be used and identifies possible barriers to particular treatment programmes.

(4) *Problem-specific information*
(a) What precisely is the problem?

Here the interviewer seeks to have the consultee state precisely what the nature of the problem is. Some clients may need extra time to articulate the problem.

(b) What is the extent of the problem?

Here the interviewer seeks to obtain some estimate from the consultee about the frequency or the duration of the previously described behaviour(s). At this point self-report data is relied upon; at a later stage more objective methods of assessment can be introduced.

(c) What appear to be the antecedents and consequences of the problem?

Here the interviewer seeks to draw from the consultee a rough idea of what s/he perceives to be the antecedents and consequences associated with the particular behaviour(s).
   Choice of language on the part of the clinician is very important. Phrases like 'what happens before', 'events that trigger' (antecedents) and 'what happens during and after' (consequences) are better for most clients.

(d) Clients should be assisted to state previous attempts to handle the problem and advice received from other agencies, previously or currently involved.

(5) *Clarification of expectations*
This is where the interviewer has to do four things:
(a) come to agreement with the consultee regarding the goal of treatment
(b) state whether or not this agency is suitable for helping to achieve that goal

Table 3.2 (*contd.*)

(c) ensure that the consultee is aware that the therapist does not have a magic wand to wave over the problem child and be able to immediately convert him/her from being a problem to no problem at all; and

(d) impress upon the consultee the need for him/her to be actively involved in the intervention programme, and if they decide to proceed that this will necessarily require active participation by the consultee.

(6) *Setting of homework*
The interviewer may need to set very precise homework for the consultee to carry out during the subsequent period of time. Usually one week elapses between first and second interview. The specific instructions would usually require the collection of baseline data and the identification of the antecedents and consequences associated with the target behaviour. Appropriate antecedent stimulus control of the consultee's behaviour is usually best achieved through the use of structured data-collection sheets that the consultee has to fill in during the week and return at the next interview. It is important at the conclusion of the interview to make sure that the consultee is able to repeat precisely what is expected of him by the interviewer. (In many cases this homework setting can take up to one hour, so a separate interview for this purpose may be necessary.)

(7) *Scheduling of next appointment*

(8) *Termination of interview*
Remember the importance of a good client–therapist relationship.

SOURCE: Murphy, Hudson, King and Remenyi (1985). Reproduced by permission of the Australian Behaviour Modification Association.

desk or clipboard during the initial interview(s). More detailed information on each area of the checklist is given in Table 3.2. As would be appreciated from an examination of these tables, many areas need to be addressed.

From the interview first-hand observations can be obtained from various family members about the problematic fear and the controlling antecedent and consequent stimuli. The interview also provides an opportunity to assess resources within the family that may be employed in treatment programming. Hence the first interview is invaluable in the attempt to obtain as complete a picture of the child and family as possible (Ollendick & Cerny, 1981).

Several important issues should be raised about the interview schedule. A fundamental point is the reliance upon the child's care providers (e.g. parents and teachers) for most of the information. There are several reasons for this. First, the referral is typically made by the child's care providers on the basis of their experience with the child. Consequently, their perception of the problem must be investigated. Second, the expressive language problems of children force the therapist to rely on the care providers for a histroy. Expressive language problems are certainly an obstacle for young children. Older children and adolescents can be involved more directly in the behavioural interview. Third, it is likely that the careproviders will have an important role in the implementation of the phobia-reduction programme; thus it is prudent to involve them in the initial interviews to ensure understanding and motivation. But it must be acknowledged that children are playing a more central role in the behavioural interview nowadays. Ollendick and his colleagues (Ollendick, 1983a; Ollendick & Cerny, 1981; Ollendick & Francis, in press) routinely interview the child (regardless of age) prior to requesting that rating forms be completed by parents and teachers or prior to observation of the child in the home or school setting. This is done for ethical reasons and to obtain the explicit cooperation of the child.

Another important issue concerns the manner in which the interview schedule is employed. A tendency of inexperienced therapists is to follow the schedule in a very rigid and insensitive manner. Being logical and thorough are admirable clinical qualities, but they must be combined with essential human qualities like warmth and a sense of humour. Contrary to the myth of the 'behaviour therapist' being cold and mechanistic, the clinician needs to relate to the child and careproviders in a warm and genuine manner. This is certainly necessary if the therapist is to gain all the necessary information about the problem, and secure the confidence of the child and careproviders about treatment recommendations. The therapist can establish rapport with the young child in numerous ways (e.g. chatting, use of edibles, playing games and lending toys). Individual differences in response to 'warmth and genuineness' must be recognized as some children and care providers respond better to a more formal clinician (Lazarus, 1971). Another concern about the use of the interview schedule is the way in which questions are phrased. For example, many of the interviewer enquiries about issues like 'developmental milestones' can be made in a conversational manner. It is recommended that behavioural and psychological jargon in general be kept to a minimum during the interview, as such language can be off-putting to some clients (Woolfolk, Woolfolk & Wilson, 1977).

Of course, the reliability and validity of report information can be called into question. For example, how reliable and valid is the parental report about John's school phobia? Was he *really* attending school on a voluntary basis for 'several' months and then evidenced a relapse upon the birth of a sibling? Does John *never* follow directions? Or does he follow directions at certain times but not others? Although we should be cautious abouts accepting interview data as reliable and valid sources of information, it would be impractical and unwise to 'throw out' the interview. It is expected that the recency of the behaviour in question and the specificity of information sought through the interview have a significant bearing on the reliability and validity of information gleaned from the interview. As noted by Ollendick and Cerny (1981): 'the interview is an important and necessary first step in the assessment process. When combined with other procedures like rating scales, inventories, and naturalistic observation, it serves as an important source of information' (p. 35).

Self-reports

Traditionally, the use of self-reports have been played down in behavioural assessment because of their questionable validity. In recent years, however, it appears that self-report measures have won acceptability in behavioural assessment. To a certain extent this is due to the current emphasis upon consumer satisfaction. Accordingly, the client's own perspective of the problem, treatment and outcome is crucial in evaluation. Another factor responsible for the growing acceptability of this form of assessment concerns the advent of cognitive-behaviour modification with the explicit focus upon cognitive processes underlying behavioural problems (Barrios *et al.*, 1981; Morris & Kratochwill, 1983). Naturally, an assessment of cognitive processes is required before such intervention is possible. Although information about all response systems can be collected by means of self-report, these instruments are used primarily to assess the cognitive–verbal response system.

In research studies on adult phobias, the 'fear thermometer' (Walk, 1956) has been a very popular assessment device. In essence, the fear thermometer entails a rating by the subject on his or her fear level, usually just after exposure to the fear/phobia stimulus as in avoidance tests. Some interesting variations of the fear thermometer for children have been reported. In her research study on children with fear of darkness, Kelley (1976) developed an elaborate version of the fear thermometer. As Kelley explains: 'Subjective fear was measured by means of a fear thermometer (FT) consisting of a vertically slotted board and inserted lever which could be moved by S to denote one of five levels of fear differentiated by color' (p. 79). A similar procedure was adopted by Sheslow, Bondy and Nelson (1982) in their assessment of children with fear of darkness. Each child was required to give a fear rating subsequent to an avoidance test. The children were told that 'this toy can tell me how much you like some things and how much you are afraid of some things by moving the arrow' (p. 36). Several trials were given with items unrelated to the fear stimulus (hamburgers, spinach, ice-cream, lions and sharks) to assure an understanding of the rating system. In a study involving retarded children with a fear of strange adults, Matson (1981) employed another variation of the fear thermometer. After a prearranged meeting with an adult stranger, each child was required to indicate the degree of fear experienced in the encounter. The numbers 1 to 7 were displayed on a wall, above which were yellow bar graphs of increasing size. In the experiment, the mothers of the children implemented this part of the assessment. The mother pointed to the numerals and bar graphs, and asked her child to point out the one that represented the amount of fear experienced when asked to speak to the stranger.

Another interesting self-report instrument developed especially for children is the Snake Attitude Measure (Kornhaber & Schroeder, (1975). This was designed to measure the attitudes of snake-avoidant children towards the fear stimulus, without having to rely on verbal or written questions. Kornhaber and Schroeder state:

> It consists of 10 sets of pictures, each set containing pictures of three different animals. Nine of the sets contained one picture of a snake while the 10th set had two snake pictures. The remaining pictures in each set were of various reptiles (i.e. lizard, alligator), amphibians (i.e., frog), mammals (i.e., beaver, panther), and insects

(i.e., water bug, beetle). In selecting the pictures an attempt was made to vary the popularity, esthetic beauty, and threat potential of the pictures. The SAM also includes six buffer picture sets in which no snakes appear.

In each second-grade and third-grade class, the experimenter explained the test procedure to the entire class. The SAM was then administered individually. For each picture set, children were asked 'which animal do you like' and 'which animal don't you like'. A subject's score on the SAM was determined by the number of snake pictures liked minus the number of snake pictures disliked. A positive score on the SAM therefore indicated a tendency to prefer snake pictures, whereas a negative score indicated a dislike of snake pictures. The range of possible scores is + 10 to − 10. (p. 602)

Obviously the same procedure could be applied to the assessment of other childhood fears and phobias.

The major self-report instruments used in the assessment of children's fears and phobias include the Children's Manifest Anxiety Scale (Castaneda *et al.*, 1956), the State–Trait Anxiety Inventory for Children (Spielberger, 1973), the Louisville Fear Survey For Children (Miller *et al.*, 1972b), the Fear Survey Schedule for Children (Scherer & Nakamura, 1968) and the Children's Fear Survey Schedule (Ryall & Dietiker, 1979). Recently both the Children's Manifest Anxiety Scale (Reynolds & Richmond, 1978, 1979) and the Fear Survey Schedule for Children (Ollendick, 1983b; Ollendick *et al.*, 1985a) have been revised. The fear survey schedules are frequently used by clinicians as ipsative instruments to identify specific fear sensitivities in individual children, as well as a means of assessing generalization effects following treatment. Other less frequently used self-report instruments have also been employed in studies on children's fears and phobias. These include Amen's Projective Test (Vernon, 1973), the General Anxiety Scale for Children (Sarason, Davidson, Lighthall, Waite & Ruebush, 1960), the Hospital Fears Rating Scale (Melamed & Siegel, 1975), Human Figure Drawing (Melamed & Siegel, 1975), Memory for Objects (Radaker, 1961), and the Personal Report of Confidence as a Speaker (Paul, 1966).

The self-report instruments used in the assessment of children's fears and phobias have been nicely summarized by Barrios *et al.* (1981). An updated version of their summary is presented in Table 3.3. The self-report instruments are analysed in terms of the targeted fear, channel of anxiety/fear, reliability/validity, with some general comments. Certainly, an extensive range of self-report instruments are available for general screening, individual assessment and for treatment measures.

The major issue associated with self-report instruments concerns their questionable reliability and validity. However, it would be unfair to dismiss all self-report instruments in the same breath since they vary with respect to their research foundations and subsequent reliability and validity. Fear thermometers are the most vulnerable. Given their simplicity and minimum reliance on language skills, it is understandable that fear thermometers have been tried with children (Barrios *et al.*, 1981; Morris and Kratochwill, 1983). The value of the information, however, is questionable. Miller *et al.* (1974) have been disappointed in their use of the fear thermometer. They state: 'We used a fear

Table 3.3 Self-report instruments

Title	Reference	Fear	Channel	Reliability/validity	Comments
Amen's Projective Test	Vernon (1973)	Hospitalization	Cognitive	No data on reability, but some data on validity. Scores correlated with nurses' ratings of children's general level of fear and nervousness during hospitalization.	Instrument lacks specificity. The faces format has been found to be insensitive and unstable in assessing children's fears.
Children's Fear Survey Schedule	Ryall & Dietiker (1979)	General	Motor	Good test–retest reliability over 1 week. Some data on clinical and non-clinical children which supports validity. Overall, insufficient data on reliability and validity.	Administration of scale incorporates a fear word choice in recognition of the child's limited language ability.
Children's Manifest Anxiety Scale	Castaneda *et al.* (1956)	General	Cognitive	Good test–retest reliability for up to 1 month. Scores relate to learning task errors and to behaviour problems. No relationship with teachers' ratings and IQ measures.	Normative data available for a variety of child groups. Items lack situational specificity. Could be used as a rough screening device for generalized treatment effect and cross-situational cognitive strategies.

(*contd.*)

Table 3.3 (*Contd.*)

Title	Reference	Fear	Channel	Reliability/ validity	Comments
Children's Manifest Anxiety Scale—Revised	Reynolds & Richmond (1978)	General	Cognitive	Internal consistency adequate. Temporal stability and validity data lacking.	Revised scale lessens administration time, increases clarity of items, and lowers the reading level. Suitable for primary-grade children. Limitations and potential utility same as for Children's Manifest Anxiety Scale.
Fear Survey Schedule for Children	Scherer & Nakamura (1968)	General	Motor	Good internal consistency and temporal stability. Correlates with Children's Manifest Anxiety Scale and physiological measures.	Utility as a screening measure and for assessing generalization effects. By combining items and expanding certain fear categories, instrument can be used to assess specific fear.
Fear Survey Schedule for Children—Revised	Ollendick (1983b) Ollendick et al. (1985a, b) Ollendick et al. (1987)	General	Motor	Good internal consistency, high test-retest reliability over a 1 week interval, moderately reliable and stable over a 3 month interval. Correlates with psychometric instruments, including Trait scale of the Stait–Trait Anxiety Inventory for Children. Discriminates between normal and clinical	Revised scale makes for easier administration with children. Normative data available for a variety of child groups (USA and Australia). Clinical utility as a screening device and ipsative inventory.

Fear Thermometer	Kelley (1976)	Darkness	Motor	No data on temporal stability. Low negative relationship with BAT	Simple to administer; may need to be increased beyond five scoring categories in order to achieve adequate sensitivity for detection of change.
Fear Thermometer	Melamed et al. (1978)	Dental treatment	Motor	High temporal stability and significant correlations with Fear Survey Schedule for Children and observational ratings.	Administration simple; interpretation of scores straightforward. Research on its utility with other target behaviours needed.
General Anxiety Scale for Children	Sarason et al. (1960)	General	Cognitive	No reliability data available. Positive correlations with Test Anxiety Scale for Children. Low negative correlations with IQ and achievement measures.	Items lack detail and specificity. Potentially useful as a screening procedure and for assessing cross-situational cognitive style.
Global Self-Ratings	Glennon & Weisz (1978)	Separation	Motor	No adequate reliability and validity data. No relationship with other self-report, observational, and performance measures.	Not recommended.
Hospital Fears Rating Scale	Melamed & Siegel (1975)	Hospitalizations & surgery	Motor	No within-group changes across measurement periods. Not related to physiological measures and behavioural observation scores.	Not recommended at this time.

(contd.)

Table 3.3 (*Contd.*)

Title	Reference	Fear	Channel	Reliability/ validity	Comments
Human Figure Drawing	Melamed & Siegel (1975)	Surgery	Cognitive	Inter-rater agreements excellent. No relationship with measures of motor and physiological channels and other estimates of the cognitive channel. Not sensitive to treatment.	Not recommended.
Louisville Fear Survey Schedule	Miller *et al.* (1972b)	General	Motor	Internal consistency high. Data lacking on temporal stability and validity. Little congruence between child's ratings and parents' observations of level of fear.	Potentially useful for screening and assessment of generalization effects. Possibly useful for assessment of specific fears by combining related items and describing items in greater detail.
Memory for Objects	Radaker (1961)	None (imagery)	Cognitive	Test–retest reliability adequate. Scores related to Memory for Word Forms and to Memory for Designs.	Employed exclusively with retarded children.
Personal Report of Confidence as a Speaker	Paul (1966); Cradock *et al.* (1978); Johnson *et al.* (1971)	Public speaking	Motor	Acceptable reliability and relationship to other measures.	Employed primarily with adults. Norms not available. Easy to administer and interpret. Provides detailed information on fear of public speaking.

Measure	Reference	Stimuli	Mode	Reliability/Validity	Comments
Snake Attitude Measure	Kornhaber & Schroeder (1975)	Snakes	Motor	No data on temporal stability, but children in a no-treatment control condition exhibited small mean change scores for an unknown time interval. Scores correlate highly with BAT.	Administration and scoring of responses relatively simple. Employed only with second- and third-grade girls. Norms not available. More data needed on sensitivity.
State–Trait Anxiety Inventory for Children	Spielberger (1973)	General	Cognitive	Good reliability. Negative correlations with verbal IQ, aptitude, and achievement; positive correlations with school grades and Children's Manifest Anxiety Scale. Scores change as a function of stress and other anxiety producing stimuli.	Possibly useful as preliminary screening device or for assessment of generalization effect and cross-situational cognitive styles.
Test Anxiety Scale for Children	Sarason et al. (1960)	Test	Cognitive	Good reliability. Some data on construct validity.	Not widely employed by behaviour therapists because of lack of specificity. Slight modifications may make the scale useful.
Visual Imagery Index	Radaker (1961)	None (imagery)	Cognitive	Good test–retest reliability over 2 week period. No data on relationship with other instruments.	Used exclusively with mentally retarded children.

SOURCE: Adapted from Barrios et al. (1981). Original © 1981 The Guilford Press.

thermometer with children, but did not analyze the data, since our clinical observer thought that many of the estimates were random guesses by children' (p. 99). Although reliability and validity are still of concern, the fear survey schedules and anxiety scales are much stronger than the fear thermometer on these criteria. The Fear Survey Schedule for Children appears to be quite promising as a self-report instrument in the light of recent research findings on reliability and validity (Bondy et al., 1985; Ollendick, 1983b); Ollendick et al., 1985a). Further, the State–Trait Anxiety Inventory for Children and the Children's Manifest Anxiety Scale (Revised) have good reliability and moderate validity (review by Finch & Rogers, 1984).

It will be recalled that one of the factors responsible for the acceptance of self-report measures is the emergence of cognitive-behaviour modification. With the belief that cognitive processes underly negative emotional states, it becomes important to quantify these processes in behavioural assessment and research. As can be seen from Table 3.3 a number of the self-report instruments used in the assessment of children's fears/phobias are directed at the cognitive 'channel'. The fear survey schedules, however, are given a motor classification. In any case, self-report instruments alone do not provide detailed information on the child's cognitions. Barrios et al. (1981) maintain that alternative methods of assessing the cognitive component of children's fears and phobias are needed. Having the child 'think out aloud' during performance tests such as the Behavioural Avoidance Test, and viewing videotapes of performance with recall of the cognitions present at the time, have been suggested (Meichenbaum, 1976; Smith & Sharpe, 1970). In view of the problems associated with the fear thermometer and fear survey schedules, the latter suggestions are likely to be problematic in terms of reliability and validity.

Physiological assessment

The physiological assessment of phobias is important since physiological arousal is a significant component of most phobic reactions. Scientific instrumentation permits the recording of many physiological responses (heart rate, blood pressure, muscle tension, GSR and so forth) in the assessment of the individual's reactivity to phobic stimuli. Heart rate and electrodermal activity are the most frequently used physiological indices, especially for children. Physiological assessment, however, can present a variety of problems, including access to equipment, selection of electrodes, recording, and controlling movement artifacts. Furthermore, it is doubtful that one physiological measure of arousal is sufficient. The existence of individual differences in autonomic response patterns ('autonomic response specificity') is well established (Lacey, Bateman & Van Lehn, 1953; Lacey & Lacey, 1958). Therefore, the ideal physiological assessment of phobias entails multiple-response measures.

Despite these problems, a rich literature has grown on the physiological assessment of anxiety and phobias in adults. Children's fears and phobias, however, have received less attention from researchers interested in physiological recordings. Presumably, the major obstacle to the physiological assessment of phobic children concerns their inability to remain stationary throughout the recording period (Barrios *et al.*, 1981). Nevertheless, physiological measures have been taken in several research studies on children's fears and phobias.

Possibly the first recording of a child's physiological response to a fear stimulus was that reported by Jones (1924a) in the laboratory study of 'Peter', who feared rabbits:

> Early in the experiment an attempt was made to get some measure of the visceral changes accompanying Peter's fear reactions. On one occasion Dr. S. determined Peter's blood pressure outside the laboratory and again later, in the laboratory while he was in a state of much anxiety caused by the rabbit's being held close to him by the experimenter. The diastolic blood pressure changed from 65 to 80 on this occasion. (p. 314)

Physiological measures of children's fears and phobias have continued in more recent years. Shapiro (1975) monitored anticipatory heart rate and finger sweat activity in a study of the behaviour of kibbutz and urban children receiving an injection. In the 'tripartite' assessment of an 11-year-old multi-phobic boy, Van Hasselt *et al.* (1979) assessed the child's responses in the motoric, cognitive and physiological response systems. In this case, heart rate and finger pulse volume were taken as measures of physiological arousal. A significant development has been the use of the Palmar Sweat Index by Melamed and her colleagues (Melamed & Siegel, 1975; Melamed, Weinstein, Hawes & Katin-Borland, 1975; Melamed, Yurcheson, Fleece, Hutcherson & Hawes, 1978) in their work on the preparation of children for dental treatment and hospitalization. The Palmer Sweat Index is a quantification of sweat gland activity of the hand obtained by a plastic impression method. Since the sweat glands of the hand are primarily affected by emotional factors, the number of active sweet glands provides a reliable measure of transitory physiological arousal; and because of the ease of administration and reliability of scoring the index is a useful physiological measure in individual assessment as well as in large-scale research investigations.

We believe that future years will see more research on the physiological assessment of children's phobias.

Behavioural observations

It is maintained that the direct observation of behaviour, which is emphasized in the behavioural approach to assessment, is the most 'meaningful' method of assessment. Thus it is not surprising that behavioural observation has been given preference in the behavioural assessment of children's phobias. Behavioural observation of children's phobias can involve observation in structured laboratory situations or in natural settings.

Observations in structured situations

Therapists and researchers often observe children in structured or analogue situations in the clinic or laboratory when direct observations in the natural setting are impractical or impossible. In the behavioural assessment of children's phobias, this appears to have been the preferred means of taking behavioural measures. The common analogue test of phobic behaviour is referred to as the 'Behavioural Avoidance Test' (BAT) and was first reported by Lang and Lazovik (1963). Although the BAT is invariably associated with the assessment of animal phobias, it has also been used in the assessment of, for example, darkness and water phobias (Kelley, 1976; Lewis, 1974).

The BAT entails a series of graduated performance tasks related to the phobic stimulus. The notion of a graduated series of stimulus-related tasks is quite sound as it provides a more sensitive measure of the child's approach behaviour and skill than a non-graduated 'all or nothing' avoidance test (McGlynn & Williams, 1970). A distinction has been drawn between active and passive types of BATs (Murphy & Bootzin, 1973). In the active BAT the child is required to approach the phobic stimulus, while in the passive type the child is stationary and the phobic stimulus is brought to the child by the experimenter. Although active and passive BAT performance correlate highly in children (Murphy & Bootzin), the active BAT has been preferred in behavioural assessment.

In view of the importance of the BAT in the assessment of children's phobias, a sampling of its use will now be given across a range of phobic problems. Prior to the BAT, the child should be informed that there is no danger associated with the fear stimulus, particularly in the case of animals. Ritter's (1968) assessment of snake avoidance entailed a 29-item performance test requiring increasingly more direct interactions with a harmless 4-foot snake:

> Initial tasks of the avoidance test required the S to move from a point 15 ft away from the caged snake to a point 1 ft away (items 1 through 4). Tasks 5 through 12 involved the following: standing directly in front of the cage, looking down at the snake, touching the cage with gloved and bare hands, and inserting gloved then bare hand into the cage up to the wrist. Task 13 and 14 required the S to briefly touch the snake with one gloved and bare hand respectively. Items 15 through 20 required the S to lift the snake within the cage with one bare or gloved hand for periods ranging from 5 to 30 sec. Ss were subsequently requested to lift the snake out of the cage with two gloved or two bare hands until told to put him back within 5–30 sec (tasks 21 through 26). Task 27 involved taking the snake out of the cage with bare hands, placing it on the floor, lifting it after a few seconds then holding it until told to put it back in 30 sec. Task 28 required holding the snake approximately 5 in. from the face for 30 sec. Finally the S was asked to sit in a chair with his arms at his sides while the snake was in his lap for 30 sec (terminal behavior, item 29) (pp. 2–3).

Similarly, Bandura *et al.* (1967) had their dog-fearful children undertake a graded sequence of 14 performance tasks with a cocker spaniel:

> The strength of avoidance responses was measured by means of a graded sequence of 14 performance tasks in which the children were required to engage in increasingly intimate interactions with a dog. A female experimenter brought the children

individually to the test room, which contained a brown cocker spaniel confined in a modified play pen. In the initial tasks the children were asked, in the following order, to walk up to the playpen and look down at the dog, to touch her fur, and to pet her. Following the assessment of avoidance responses to the dog in the protective enclosure, the children were instructed to open a hinged door on the side of the playpen, to walk the dog on a leash to a throw rug, to remove the leash, and to turn the dog over and scratch her stomach. Although a number of the subjects were unable to perform all of the latter tasks, they were nevertheless administered the remaining test items to avoid any assumption of a perfectly ordered scale for all cases. In subsequent items the children were asked to remain alone in the room with the animal and to feed her dog biscuits. The final and most difficult set of tasks required the children to climb into the playpen with the dog, to pet her, to scratch her stomach, and to remain alone in the room with the dog under the exceedingly confining and fear-provoking conditions. (p. 17–18)

In this particular study, Bandura *et al.* adopted the following scoring system:

The strength of the children's avoidant tendencies was reflected not only in the items completed, but also in the degree of vacillation, reluctance, and fearfulness that preceded and accompanied each approach response. Consequently, children were credited 2 points if they executed a given task either spontaneously or willingly, and 1 point when they carried out the task minimally after considerable hesitancy and reluctance. Thus, for example, children who promptly stroked the dog's fur repeatedly when requested to do so received 2 points, whereas subjects who held back but then touched the dog's fur briefly obtained 1 point. In the item requiring the children to remain alone in the room with the dog, they received 2 points if they approached the animal and played with her, and 1 point if they were willing to remain in the room but avoided any contact with the dog. Similarly, in the feeding situation children were credited 2 points if they fed the dog by hand, but a single point if they tossed the biscuits on the floor and thereby avoided close contact with the animal. The maximum approach score that a subject could attain was 28 points. (p. 18)

In assessing children afraid of the dark by means of a BAT, Kelley (1976) manipulated light intensity and duration of exposure:

The behavioural avoidance test (BAT) took place in a room which was totally dark without artificial light. A fluorescent light was suspended from the ceiling and calibrated so that light intensity in the room could be reduced from full brightness to complete darkness in five steps: (a) 10.8, (b) 3.3, (c) 0.07, (d) 0.003 and (e) 0.0 foot candles. The S was seated beneath the light near a response box with illuminated key, depression of which resulted in a 10-db tone and automatic restoration of full light intensity. ... Light intensity was reduced in the five steps previously described with light duration at 15, 45, 45, 45, and 60 sec during successive steps. The child was seated in the fully lighted experimental room and instructed:

This is a test to see how long you can stay in a dark room. The light will get darker ... If you feel afraid, push the button and the light will come back on. If you don't feel afraid, do not push the button.

Each BAT trial was terminated when S pushed the button, thus turning the light back to full intensity, or when S endured the full 210 sec of progressive darkness. (p. 79)

Despite the fact that the BAT is often employed in phobia-reduction studies with children, there are several problems associated with its use. These include issues related to its standardization, reliability and validity. A related issue concerns the reactive effects of this method of assessment with children. With respect to standardization, there is surprising variation between BATs on the number of steps or tasks involved, the amount of information given to subjects about the characteristics of the fear stimulus, the actual 'threat' posed by the stimulus, and instructions about terminating the approach performance (Barrios et al., 1981; Morris & Kratochwill, 1983). Obviously, this lack of standardization makes comparison across studies difficult, if not impossible.

Although the BAT has excellent inter-observer reliability, the test–retest reliability of the BAT has been assumed rather than demonstrated. In a study of the test–retest reliability of the BAT with 14 animal-phobic children, the present authors obtained a high correlation (0.97) between the two administrations (seven days apart). Nevertheless, further research should be undertaken on the test–retest reliability of the BAT, especially for longer periods of time.

The possibility of 'demand characteristic' is an obvious threat to the validity of the BAT, especially when the BAT is being used to assess treatment effectiveness. As the clinician or researcher is eager to demonstrate a treatment effect, it is quite feasible that the amount of pressure or demand placed upon the child may change (increase) from the pre-treatment to the post-treatment avoidance test. As Lick and Unger (1977) explain:

> ...the major concern thus far has been that differences in demand for fearful verus fearless performance between pre- and posttreatment assessment may affect subjects' responses on behavioral tests. If this occurred, laboratory assessment could overestimate the amount of 'real' therapeutic change subjects experienced, since pretreatment demand characteristics are presumed to 'pull' for high levels of fear, while those associated with posttreatment assessment 'pull' for less fearful performance. (p. 292)

The potency of a high-demand BAT with fearful children has been demonstrated by Kelley (1976). After negative findings were obtained on low-demand pre- and post-treatment BATs, Kelley tried out a high-demand BAT that succeeded in producing a significant change in the children's behaviour (endurance of darkness). However, it must not be concluded that therapeutic gains reported by researchers using the BAT are to be explained only in terms of demand characteristics. At the moment it is a 'plausible rival hypothesis', which has yet to be validated. In fact, very little is known about the effects of obtrusive assessment on children's responses to phobic stimuli.

The extent to which BAT scores reflect 'real-life' functioning is a serious issue. Avoidance tests are restricted to fairly safe exercises with the clinician and perhaps care provider in close proximity to the child. This, of course, constitutes a situation quite different from the exposures which occur in the natural setting. For example, in an avoidance test the dog-phobic child is required to approach a dog that is secured in some way. But in the community the dog may be unrestrained and approach the child, thus involving a different set of antecedent conditions. Beyond impressionistic data, little systematic attention has been paid to the cross-validation of the BAT. Lick and Unger (1977) suggest that several different approaches can be taken in the cross-validation of the BAT, including (a) unobtrusive observation, (b) obtrusive observation, (c) use of informants, and (d) self-reports. These approaches are yet to be explored systematically.

The possible reactive effects of the BAT have been discussed by Rowland and Canavan (1983). Because of the unreinforced presentation of the phobic stimuli (extinction), it can be argued that the BAT may be therapeutic. On the other hand, it can be argued that in view of the 'incubation' phenomenon, the BAT may exacerbate the phobia since it involves short exposures—a condition which favours incubation (Eysenck, 1979). In the experience of the present authors, the BAT *per se* has a therapeutic effect for a minority of phobic children, especially if repeated several times. Whether this is predictable outcome for mildly phobic children is an issue for further research.

Observations in the natural setting

Observing the child in the natural setting has obvious appeal in terms of validity. However, the behavioural practitioner needs to be cautioned on several issues. Foremost, the target behaviour needs to be well-defined for the observer, otherwise ambiguity and unreliability will occur. A measurement strategy must be determined bearing in mind numerous options (frequency recording, duration recording, interval recording, and permanent products). A recording system needs to be developed that is clear and easy to follow for the observer (a basic point that is often overlooked). The observer may need preliminary training, especially when elaborate recording systems are involved. In any case, it is prudent to keep regular contact with the observer in case of any misunderstandings. In view of the possibility of human error, it is advisable to determine the reliability of the observations. An inter-observer reliability check can be made with the assistance of another observer (usually about one-third of the observation periods are checked). A percentage agreement of 80% (or a correlation of 0.80) or above is regarded as an acceptable level of reliability. For more information on the salient points of recording in the natural setting and the various way of calculating reliability, the reader should consult other sources (Gelfand & Hartmann, 1984; Ollendick & Hersen, 1984).

Many case reports and experimental studies on children's fears and phobias have employed observations in the natural setting. For example, Neisworth, Madle and Goeke (1975) recorded the duration of anxious behaviours (crying, screaming and sobbing without being injured) displayed by a pre-school child. In a programme for an institutionalized 15-year-old boy with a toileting phobia, Luiselli (1977) had attendant staff record each instance of observed pants wetting. Hence an indirect measure of the boy's toilet phobia was employed. In the assessment of school phobia, data are usually collected on school attendance, such as the number of hours at school per day or days at school per week (Vaal, 1973). In work with children suffering from night-time fears, researchers have had parents record the frequency of night-time disturbances (Graziano, Mooney,

Table 3.4 Behaviour observation rating scales

Reference	Fear	Reliability/validity	Comments
Glennon & Weisz (1978)	Separation	Inter-rater reliability is high. Scores relate to teacher and parent reports.	Items selected on basis of a literature search of behavioural indications of anxiety in children, recommendations by child clinical psychologists, and pilot testing indicating potential for accurate and reliable observation. System's usefulness may be limited by large number of response categories (30) and extensive training procedures required of observers. Response categories include physical complaint, cry, whisper, nail biting, lip licking, chewing or sucking objects, and touching genitals.
Melamed & Siegel (1975)	Surgery	Average inter-rater reliability is excellent. Relationships with other measures not reported.	29 categories of verbal and skeletal–motor behaviour thought to represent behavioural manifestations of anxiety in children. Categories include crying, trembling hands, stutters, and talks about going home. Complexity of the scale and the necessity of possibly extensive observer training may make it impractical for clinical use.
Melamed et al. (1978); Melamed, Weinstein, Hawes & Katin-Borland (1975); Melamed, Hawes, Heiby & Glick (1975)	Dental treatment	Excellent inter-rater reliability. Substantial correlations between scores and dentists' ratings and children's self-report.	27 response categories (e.g. crying, refusal to open mouth, white knuckles, rigid posture, verbal complaints, kicking, leaves or stands up in chair, eyes closed, choking, cries at injection, clings to parent and faints) that lead to disruption of the dental treatment procedure. Categories weighted by a factor that indicates the degree of a disruption as

Neisworth *et al.* (1975)	Separation	Inter-rater agreement quite high. Scores obtained in experimental setting related to mother's reports of similar behaviour exhibited in different settings.	Duration recording of crying, screaming, and sobbing. Small number of response categories makes system feasible for clinical practice. Idiosyncratic responding on part of child may render system inappropriate for assessment.
O'Connor (1969)	Social interaction	Inter-observer reliability is extremely high.	Five response categories include physical proximity, verbal interaction, looking at, and interacting with. May be used in naturalistic or laboratory settings. Certain categories emphasize the reciprocal quality of social interaction, which may make scoring difficult for non-professionals or minimally trained observers.
Paul (1966)	Public speaking	Excellent inter-rater reliabilities. Scores correlate significantly with self-report and physiological measures.	20 response categories, such as speech blocking, pacing, swaying, foot shuffling, hand tremors, perspiration, and quivering voice. Training of observers usually involves practice with both live and videotaped speech presentation; thus may not be feasible for typical clinical use. Only one investigation (Cradock, *et al.*, 1978) has employed the rating system for assessment of speech-anxious children.
Ross *et al.* (1971)	Social interaction	High inter-rater agreement.	11 response categories denoting social interaction and avoidance behaviour (e.g. physical contact, verbal interaction, nonverbal motor interaction). Interval recording procedure may present problems for the non-professional, but should be relatively straightforward for professionals and experienced therapists.

(contd.)

Table 3.4 (*Contd.*)

Reference	Fear	Reliability/validity	Comments
Sarason *et al.* (1960)	Test	No reliability estimates reported. Significant correlations found between scores and children's self-report. Fairly high negative correlations found between scores and achievement.	Using five-point Likert scale, teacher rates the child on 17 items (e.g. voice trembling when asked to recite, physical complaints on test days, upset when corrected). Infrequently employed by behaviour therapists, the instrument generally lacks precision and situational specificity. May have some utility as relatively quick and simple screening measure.
Vernon (1973)	Anesthesia induction	Inter-rater agreement adequate. Significant relationships between scores and physiological measures and doctors' ratings.	Ratings of the global mood of the child according to a seven-interval scale at various time periods. Scale intervals are anchored with ambiguous behaviour descriptions. Simplicity of system makes it attractive, but amount of information generated is limited.
Vernon *et al.* (1966)	General	Some evidence of test–retest reliability and validity. Scores related to data obtained from interviews.	27 items describing a specific behaviour, such as refusal to leave home, enter the dark, or leave presence of parents. Parents compare children's behaviour at various times.

SOURCE: Adapted from Barrios *et al.* (1981). Original © 1981 The Guilford Press.

Huber & Ignasiak 1979; Jackson & King, 1981). In addition to the use of the BAT in the assessment of a dog-phobic child, Chudy *et al.* (1983) had the mother collect data on the number of times the child left the house alone and the number of times the child interacted with peers. Because the dog phobia had made the child a 'prisoner in his home', this was very pertinent data. As would be apparent, observations of the child in the natural setting can be used to supplement data derived from the BAT.

A number of observational rating scales have been developed for use with children in various settings. They are particularly useful when many response categories (e.g. stuttering, hand tremors, crying, screaming, biting) are pertinent to an assessment of the child's behaviour. In relation to the assessment of

Table 3.5 Behavior Profile Rating Scale

	Successive 3-minute observation periods									
SEPARATION FROM MOTHER	1	2	3	4	5	6	7	8	9	10
(3) Cries										
(4) Clings to mother										
(4) Refuses to leave mother										
(5) Bodily carried in										
OFFICE BEHAVIOUR										
(1) Inappropriate mouth closing										
(1) Choking										
(2) Won't sit back										
(2) Attempts to dislodge instruments										
(2) Verbal complaints										
(2) Over-reaction to pain										
(2) White knuckles										
(2) Negativism										
(2) Eyes closed										
(3) Cries at injection										
(3) Verbal message to terminate										
(3) Refuses to open mouth										
(3) Rigid posture										
(3) Crying										
(3) Dentist uses loud voice										
(4) Restraints used										
(4) Kicks										
(4) Stands up										
(4) Rolls over										
(5) Dislodges instruments										
(5) Refuses to sit in chair										
(5) Faints										
(5) Leaves chair										

SOURCE: Melamed, Weinstein, Hawes & Katin-Borland (1975). Copyright by the American Dental Association. Reprinted by permission.

children's fear/phobic behaviour, observational rating scales have proved to be very useful in health-care settings and schools. Observational rating scales should be completed by trained observers in order to enhance the reliability of the recordings. A summary of the major observational rating scales is presented in Table 3.4.

A particularly well-researched observational rating scale is the Behavior Profile Rating Scale (Melamed, Hawes, Heiby & Glick, 1975; Melamed, Weinstein, Hawes & Katin-Borland, 1975; Melamed *et al.*, 1978). Reproduced in Table 3.5, this scale is very useful in the assessment of dental fearful children. As can be seen from the 27 categories of behaviours, the scale provides a measure of disruptive behaviour during dental treatment. The scale can be used by a dentist (or assistant) over successive 3-minute observation periods. Each response category has a weighting factor (given in parentheses) based on dentists' ratings of the degree of disruptiveness involved. A total score is obtained by multiplying the frequency at which the behaviour in each category occurred by its weighted factor and then adding the category scores. This score is divided by the number of 3-minute observation periods to give the average frequency of disruptive behaviours per 3-minute interval. An investigation of the inter-rater reliability of the scale yielded a Spearman rank correlation coefficient of 0.97. Dentist ratings of cooperation and anxiety correlate with the scale, and it has also been successful in differentiating treated from untreated children (Melamed, 1979).

A more recent example of an observation behaviour rating scale is the Procedure Behavior Rating Scale developed by Katz, Kellerman and Siegel (1980). The scale was developed in order to measure anxiety/distress in children with cancer undergoing bone-marrow aspirations. An important feature of the scale concerns the use of operational definitions for each of the 25 items (see Table 3.6). Katz *et al.* reports the use of the scale with 115 children undergoing bone-marrow aspirations. In their study, the bone-marrow procedure was divided into four phases:

	ON	OFF
Phase 1:	Child is called from waiting room	Child reaches door of treatment room
Phase 2:	Child enters treatment room	Clothes are removed
Phase 3:	Site is cleansed local anesthetic is administered, procedure carried out	Needle is withdrawn
Phase 4:	Dressing is placed	Child leaves room

Five observers recorded the behaviour of the children using the Procedure Behavior Rating Scale. In addition to behavioral observations, the nurse performing the bone-marrow aspiration was asked to rate the child's anxiety using a 5-point Likert scale. Nurses' ratings were conducted independently of behavioural observations, immediately after the child left the treatment room. An inter-rater reliability check on the scale yielded the following Pearson correlations: phase 1, $r = 0.94$; phase 2, $r = 0.88$; phase 3, $r = 0.91$; phase 4, $r = 0.92$. Thus, high inter-rater reliability was obtained. There was also a

Table 3.6. Procedure Behavior Rating Scale

Item	Operational definition
Cry	Tears in eyes or running down face
Cling	Physically holds on to parent, significant other or nurse
Fear verbal	Says 'I'm scared', 'I'm afraid', etc.
Pain verbal	Says 'Ow', 'Ouch', 'It hurts', 'You're hurting me', etc.
Groan*	Non-verbal, vocal expression of pain or discomfort
Scream	No tears, raises voice, verbal or non-verbal
Laugh*	Smiling with a chuckling sound
Stall	Verbal expression of delay ('Wait a minute', 'I am not ready yet', etc.) or behavioral delay (ignores nurse's instructions)
Stoic silence*	Child does not respond to questions or remarks of others, may appear 'trancelike'
Carry	Has to be physically carried into or out of room or placed on table, not because of physical inability to do so on his or her own
Flail	Random gross movements of arms or legs, without intention to make aggressive contact
Nausea verbal*	Says 'I'm sick', 'I feel nauseous', 'My stomach feels like I'm going to throw up'
Vomit*	Includes retching, dry heaves
Urinate/defecate*	Soils or wets self
Kick*	Intentional movement of leg(s) to make aggresive physical contact
Hit*	Intentional movement of arm(s) or hand(s) to make aggresive physical contact
Bite*	Intentional closing of jaw to make aggressive physical contact
Verbal hostility*	Says 'I hate you', 'You're mean', etc.
Refusal position	Does not follow instructions with regard to body placement on treatment table
Restrain	Has to be held down because of lack of cooperativeness
Curse*	Verbally utters profanity
Muscular ridigity	Any of following behaviors: clenched fists, white knuckles, gritted teeth, clenched jaw, wrinkled brow, eyes clenched shut, contracted limbs, body stiffness
Questions*	Non-delay, information-seeking verbal behavior ('what are you doing now?', 'Is it over yet?', etc.)
Emotional support	Verbal or non-verbal solicitation of hugs, physical comfort, or expression of empathy from parent, significant other or nurse
Request termination	Verbally asks/pleads that procedure be stopped

*These items were subsequently eliminated.
SOURCE: Katz, Kellerman and Siegel (1980). Copyright (1980) by the American Psychological Association. Adapted by permission of the publisher.

significant correlation between the Procedure Behavior Rating Scale scores and the nurses' ratings of anxiety.

The reactive effects of behaviour observation rating scales are of concern in the behavioural assessment of children's phobias (Morris & Katochwill, 1983).

In those instances of obtrusive data gathering, the child's behaviour may change, making the data fairly questionable in terms of its validity. A number of strategies can be used to reduce or minimize reactivity. According to Haynes and Horn (1982):

(1) participant observers can be used;
(2) alternative measures can be used to supplement the regular measures;
(3) covert observation can be implemented;
(4) procedures can be implemented to reduce or minimize the obtrusiveness of observation;
(5) various technologies can be used (e.g. telemetry, video-cameras, tape recorders);
(6) the therapist can minimize subject-observation and other discriminative properties of the observation;
(7) the therapist can train and instruct observers to act naturally;
(8) during data collection, the therapist can (should) allow sufficient time for dissipation of reactive slope and variability in observations;
(9) the therapist can use a number of observers and observation procedures to help cancel out differential effects.

Provided attention is given to psychometric characteristics and the problem of reactive effects, observational rating scales should continue to provide useful information in the behavioural assessment of children. Their use, of course, need not be restricted to phobic children; they can also be employed in the assessment of normal children being prepared for hospitalization and surgery and in other medically related situations.

Self-monitoring

The procedure known as self-monitoring requires children to first self-observe and then systematically self-record the occurrences of behaviour (Haynes, 1978). Self-monitoring is a potentially useful method of gathering baseline data on the frequency of the target behaviour, as well as antecedent and consequent events. In certain instances, self-monitoring can be used to gather data on children's cognitions about the problem. A number of methods have been developed to facilitate self-monitoring, including the behavioral diary and counting devices such as wrist counters. When self-monitoring procedures are applied to children it is imperative that the behaviours be well-defined and that the recording procedures be uncomplicated (Shapiro, 1984). As noted earlier, the age of the child is an important factor in deciding on the use of self-monitoring, with young children not having the necessary abilities for self-recording.

When self-monitoring is selected as an assessment strategy, attention should be given to several issues. A primary concern is the accuracy of self-monitoring. Accuracy can be enhanced with some preliminary training, which might include explanation and examples. Telephone contact between sessions provides a good

SELF-MONITORING DIARY

Client's name: __Jill Tucker__

Target behaviour: __Excessive fear of dogs__

Time and date	Location	Persons present	Preceding event	Target behaviour	Subsequent thoughts	Consequent actions and events
6.00pm Monday March 15	Outside Supermarket	Mum	Dog jumped out of a van in front of me	Panic. Fast breathing stays on spot	Embarrassed I thought it was stupid to behave like that. Hope I dont run into a dog at the supermarket again	Mum got me away from the dog. We sat outside supermarket until I felt better.
8.15am Thursday March 18	Walking to School down Pitt Street	Alone	Large dog sitting on footpath. Saw me & barked	Stopped – felt sick	The dog might get up and come at me. I didn't want friends to see what was happening	Walked along another street to school.

Fig. 3.1 Example of a self-monitoring diary of a child with a phobia of dogs.

opportunity to remind or praise children for their efforts. Although the purpose of self-monitoring may be assessment, a change in behaviour is by no means infrequent prior to treatment. We have observed such reactive effects for various childhood fears (especially night-time fears) within 2–3 weeks of recording. While the factors that account for reactivity are unclear, some form of behavioural self-management is presumably being instigated by children. This is likely to entail exposure to the fear-eliciting stimuli on the part of the child.

Self-monitoring has been applied relatively infrequently to childhood fears and phobias. Figure 3.1 shows the self-recording of a 14-year-old girl who exhibited an excessive fear of dogs. Conducted for several weeks prior to intervention, self-monitoring in this case provided information on the frequency of encounters with the feared stimulus. As can be seen, significant clinical information was also obtained on antecedent and consequent events, as well as the subject's immediate thoughts about contact with dogs. Self-monitoring also played a central role in a self-control programme for children's night-time fears developed by Graziano and colleagues (Graziano, Mooney, Huber & Ignasiak, 1979; Graziano & Mooney, 1980). The 6–13 year old children were given a booklet which contained both written instructions for the daily practice of self-control exercises and space to record the number of tokens earned each night. Hence the children were able to record their progress through self-monitoring. In conclusion, self-monitoring deserves more frequent use in the behavioural assessment of childhood fears and phobias.

SUMMARY

As noted by Ollendick and Hersen, child behavioural assessment is defined as an exploratory, hypothesis-testing process in which a range of specific procedures is used in order to understand a given child, group or social ecology and to formulate and evaluate specific intervention strategies. Furthermore, child behavioural assessment is empirically based, developmentally sensitive, and multi-method in its approach. The clinical usefulness of normative data on childhood fears has been highlighted, although further research is required on the reliability and validity of our current database. Problem identification necessitates an understanding of the intensity, persistence and maladaptiveness of the child's fear.

The design of individualized treatment programmes depends upon a number of considerations. Following a behavioural approach to assessment, 'specification' of the presenting problem is mandatory. The target behaviours encompass overt behaviour, physiological states and cognitions. Although the aetiology of the child's phobia is usually explored, an understanding of the current situation is more helpful. A functional analysis gives us vital information on the controlling antecedents (specific stimulus events plus more general setting events) and consequences (e.g. reactions of care providers). In addition, many practical considerations have to be entertained at this stage (e.g. the suitability of a care provider to act as a behaviour-change agent).

Consistent with the notion of multi-method child behavioural assessment, a variety of assessment strategies can be used with phobic children. Nowadays, behavioural interviews, checklists and rating forms, traditional standardized instruments, self-reports, behavioural observations, self-monitoring, and physiological instruments, are all used in child behavioural assessment. Particular attention has been given here to the behavioural avoidance test (BAT) in the assessment of children's phobias. Despite its continued use, the reliability and validity of the BAT with children has not been thoroughly investigated. Of course, behavioural observation methods are not necessarily 'better' than self-report or physiological ones; all of these methods provide potentially important information in our pursuit to obtain as 'complete' a picture as possible of phobic children and the treatment context.

Section 2

Treatment Principles and Procedures

CHAPTER 4

Systematic desensitization, emotive imagery, flooding and implosion

INTRODUCTION

A number of behavioural procedures can be used in the treatment of children's phobias. These include systematic desensitization, emotive imagery, flooding, implosion, modelling, and contingency management. More recently, cognitive procedures have been employed with increasing frequency. As will become evident, phobia-reduction methods have been derived from several different conditioning paradigms (i.e. classical conditioning, operant conditioning and vicarious conditioning). However, the overall rationale for the behavioural treatment of children's phobias is *exposure*. Behavioural programmes are fundamentally exposure-based in the arrangement of therapeutic tasks and advice to parents. Accordingly, the various behavioural procedures can be regarded as different pathways—imaginal or real-life, low or high intensity, passive or active—by which the child is required to face the feared stimulus.

The notion of exposure is by no means new to behaviour therapy. In fact the wisdom of exposure appears to have been recognized by Freud (1919/1959) who offered the following advice: 'One can hardly ever master a phobia if one waits till the patient lets the analysis influence him to give it up. ... One succeeds only when one can induce them ... to go about alone and to struggle with their anxiety while they make the attempt' (pp. 399–400). In recent years Marks (1975) recognized exposure as the underlying mechanism in the use of behavioural procedures: 'an important mechanism shared by all of these methods is exposure of the frightened subject to a frightening situation until he acclimatizes' (p. 67). Of course, we are not trying to completely eradicate fear using exposure-based procedures, so much as to help the child learn to *discriminate* between threatening and non-threatening stimuli. A dog phobic child, for example, should retain a 'healthy respect' for savage or unknown dogs. Discrimination learning of this kind is either implicit or explicit in successful phobia-reduction programmes for children.

91

The behavioural methods to be examined in this chapter—systematic desensitization, emotive imagery, flooding and implosion—are derived mainly from the classical conditioning paradigm; the remaining phobia-reduction procedures (modelling, contingency management, and cognitive therapies) are reviewed in Chapter 5. Interestingly, most of the phobia-reduction techniques used today appear to have been suggested several decades ago. Thus, a section of the present chapter will deal with these historical developments. Each therapeutic strategy is described in terms of its rationale and procedures and clinical-research applications. A brief comment is given on the status of the technique in clinical practice. In the discussion of behavioural methods in this chapter, the focus is on the specific phobias of children. The application of behavioural methods to school phobia is addressed in Chapter 6.

HISTORICAL LANDMARKS

Most contemporary phobia-reduction techniques for children were anticipated by clinicians and researchers in the 1920s and 30s. For example in a series of uncontrolled case studies, Jones (1924b) tried seven different methods of removing fear, including:

(1) elimination through disuse (child is carefully shielded from the fear stimulus);
(2) verbal appeal (talking about the fear object and connecting it verbally with pleasant experiences);
(3) negative adaptation (repeated fear stimulus presentations);
(4) repression (peer ridicule and scolding);
(5) distraction (use of substitute activity in presence of feared object);
(6) direct conditioning (specific attempts to associate the fear-object with a definite stimulus, capable of arousing a positive and pleasant reaction;
(7) social imitation (child watches peers handle feared object).

The most reliable methods for removing fear responses were purported to be direct conditioning and social imitation.

In her now classic case study, Jones (1924a) successfully deconditioned Peter, a 2-year and 10-month old boy, with a fear of animals. In pretreatment assessment, Peter was found to have several fears: 'He was afraid of a white rat, and this fear extended to a rabbit, a fur coat, a feather, cotton wool, etc., but not to wooden blocks and similar toys' (p. 309). In this study, Jones addressed two primary issues: deconditioning a fear response to an animal, and determining whether deconditioning to one fear stimulus would generalize to other fear stimuli. In relation to the first issue, it was decided to use the rabbit for deconditioning as Peter showed even more marked fear responses to the rabbit than to the rat. Initially, Peter was gradually introduced to new situations in a series of toleration steps requiring closer contact with the rabbit until he was finally able to let the rabbit nibble from his fingers. This graduated exposure to the rabbit appeared to sucessfully inhibit his fear. Shortly after the 'toleration series', however, Peter developed scarlet fever unexpectedly and was taken to the hospital. On his return two months later, Peter's early fear of the rabbit appeared to resurface. This time the method of 'direct conditioning' was attempted. According to Jones:

> Peter was seated in a high chair and given food which he liked. The experimenter brought the rabbit in a wire cage as close as she could without arousing a response that would interfere with the eating. Through the presence of the pleasant stimulus (food) whenever the rabbit was shown, the fear was eliminated gradually in favour of a positive response. Occasionally also other children were brought in to help with the 'unconditioning'. (pp. 312–13)

Thus, Jones was successful in overcoming Peter's fear of the rabbit. The clever use of graduated exposure and 'pleasant stimulus' anticipate Wolpe's (1958) research on systematic desensitization involving an anxiety inhibitor. Although the fact is not usually highlighted by most writers, Jones also made deliberate use of other children to act as fearless models. The notes for one particular session read:

> Lawrence and Peter sitting near together in their high chairs eating candy. Rabbit in cage put down 12 feet away. Peter began to cry. Lawrence said, 'Oh, rabbit'. Clambered down, ran over and looked in the cage at him. Peter followed close and watched. (p. 313)

In another session, a child model of non-fearful behaviour produced-dramatic change:

> Peter with candy in high chair. Experimenter brought rabbit and sat down in front of the tray with it. Peter cried out, 'I don't want him', and withdrew. Rabbit was given to another child sitting near to hold. His holding the rabbit served as a powerful suggestion; Peter wanted the rabbit on his lap, and held it for an instant. (p. 313)

Regarding the question of generalization, it was observed that Peter's fear of cotton, a fur coat and feathers also disappeared. Peter's reaction to rats also greatly improved, and the introduction of a strange animal (mouse) was greeted with interest.

On the basis of Jones' work, Holmes (1936) attempted to demonstrate more carefully the effectiveness of a combination of procedures; i.e. 'verbal urging and reassurance by the experimenter, gradual familiarization with the fear situation, and play with various games at the end of each exposure' (p. 10). Holmes emphasized that this method 'could easily be applied by anyone dealing with young children in the home and nursery school' (p. 10).

Twenty nursery school children participated in the experiment. The children were exposed to two experimental fear situations, which were a high board and a dark room. Of these children, only two showed definite fear of the high board. However, 14 children showed fear of the dark. Holmes was successful in reducing the fear of one of the two children afraid of the high board and 13 of the 14 children afraid of the dark room. Holmes also used elements of counter-conditioning (she ensured that the children trusted her prior to treatment) and participant modelling (she accompanied the children into the dark room).

Therefore, it is difficult to determine which aspects of the treatment were effective (Ollendick, 1979b). Nevertheless, the study anticipates the contemporary use of shaping and reinforced practice with phobic children (Leitenberg & Callahan, 1973; Obler & Terwilliger, 1970).

Early researchers were also interested in the question of how parents handle their children's fears in the natural setting. In interviewing the parents of 47 children (aged 16 to 84 months), Jersild and Holmes (1935b) made a number of interesting observations of the methods used by parents to overcome their children's fears. The fears which parents tried to overcome were classified under two headings: 'Fears elicited apparently by concrete, tangible events such as a certain object, person, noise, animal, etc., are distinguished from fears apparently influenced by imaginary elements, such as fear of dangers lurking in the dark or fear of bogeys' (p. 80). The major methods of overcoming children's fears included:

(1) verbal explanation and reassurance;
(2) verbal explanations and reassurance, combined with a demonstration (by the adult) of the nature of the thing that is feared;
(3) example of fearlessness in others;
(4) positive but 'passive' conditioning in the form of attempts to associate the feared stimulus with a pleasant, familiar, unfeared stimulus or reward;
(5) attempts to compel the child to make contacts with or to participate in the feared situation, by means of physical force or ridicule and invidious comparisons with other children;
(6) giving the child an opportunity for growing familiar with the feared event in the daily routine;
(7) graded presentation of the fear stimulus, introducing the child to it by degrees;
(8) definite attempts to promote skill in dealing with the feared stimulus;
(9) ignoring the child's fear;
(10) removing the cause of fear.

The most ineffective techniques included ignoring the child's fears, coercing the child into contact with the feared situation, and removing the cause of fear. On the other hand, the most helpful techniques entailed prompting the child to acquire specific skills, gradual contact and participation with the fear situation, and allowing the child 'to become acquainted with the feared stimulus on his own accord, by making it readily accessible to him in his normal environment' (p. 103). Clearly, these early attempts set the stage for the development and refinement of most behavioural procedures used currently.

SYSTEMATIC DESENSITIZATION

Rationale and procedures

For many years, systematic desensitization was the technique of choice in the treatment of phobias. In terms of its theoretical basis, systematic desensitization is derived from the classical conditioning paradigm. As stated in Chapter 2, the traditional behavioural account of phobias is in terms of classical aversive conditioning and negatively reinforcing avoidance responses. Systematic desensitization was developed by Wolpe (1958) as a result of research with laboratory cats. Wolpe found that classically conditioned anxiety could be inhibited by the eating response with a graduated approach to the fear stimulus. Following the physiologist Sherrington (1906), Wolpe evoked the principle of reciprocal inhibition. According to Wolpe:

> If a response antagonistic to anxiety can be made to occur in the presence of anxiety-evoking stimuli so that it is accompanied by a complete or partial suppression of the anxiety responses, the bond between these stimuli and the anxiety responses will be weakened. (p. 71)

Working from the principle of reciprocal inhibition, anxiety was said to be overcome by superimposing a response that was incompatible with anxiety. In clinical practice, relaxation is the anxiety inhibitor most often employed.

Systematic desensitization entails three steps: relaxation training, development of the anxiety hierarchy, and systematic desensitization proper (Wolpe, 1958). Each of these steps will be described, with special reference to phobic children.

Relaxation training

Relaxation usually involves training in abbreviated progressive muscle relaxation (Bernstein & Borkovec, 1973; King, 1980). Here the client works on the major muscle groups of the body, engaging in systematic tension-release exercises. The following muscle groups are usually tackled: dominant hand and forearm; dominant biceps; non-dominant hand and forearm; non-dominant biceps; forehead; upper cheeks and nose; lower cheeks and joins; neck and throat; chest; shoulders and upper back; abdominal or stomach region; dominant thigh; dominant calf; dominant foot; non-dominant thigh; non-dominant calf; non-dominant foot. In tensing and relaxing these muscle groups the individual learns to recognize tension, and induce a more relaxed state. The person is instructed to practise the relaxation exercises outside the training sessions (maybe once or twice a day for about 15 minutes). Sometimes the therapist has the client vocalize or subvocalize a word like 'relax' or 'calm' as the individual breathes out and lets go the tension (known as 'cue-contolled' relaxation training). In this way the word 'relax' can be used by the client to combat feelings of tension or anxiety in imaginal desensitization and/or aversive real-life situations. When teaching relaxation to clients it is important that its real-life application(s) be stressed. Most relaxation training scripts incorporating abbreviated progressive relaxation and cue-controlled relaxation have been written for adults (Bernstein & Borkovec, 1973; Rimm & Masters, 1974). Usually, adolescents are able to profit sufficiently from adult scripts. However, children often find the instructions difficult to comprehend or are bored by the lengthy tension-release routine.

In recent years, relaxation training formats for children have been developed.

Table 4.1. Pre-test: readiness procedures

The following pre-test should be administered to the child. Give three trails for each response.

Name of child ————————————————— CODE: √ = Correct
Date ——————————————————————— X = Incorrect
Teacher/parent ————————————————— NR = No response

BASIC SKILLS	Trial 1	Trial 2	Trial 3
(1) Ask the child to sit quietly in a chair for 5 seconds, feet still, back straight, head up, without moving or vocalizing. Repeat 2 more times.			
(2) Say 'Look at me', and ask the child to maintain eye contact for 3 seconds. Child must respond within 5 seconds. Repeat 2 more times.			

IMITATIVE SKILLS

(3) Say 'Do this', and raise your hand above your head. Child should imitate this response correctly within 5 seconds. Repeat 2 more times.			
(4) Say 'Do this', and you tap the table. Child should be able to imitate this response correctly by tapping the table. Repeat 2 more times.			
(5) Say 'Do this', and you tap your chest. Child should be able to imitate correctly by tapping his chest. Repeat 2 more times.			

FOLLOWING SIMPLE INSTRUCTIONS

(6) Say 'Stand up'. Child should stand up in front of his chair within 5 seconds. Repeat this instruction 2 more times.			
(7) Say 'Sit down'. Child should sit down in his chair within 5 seconds. Repeat this instruction 2 more times.			
(8) Stand 6 feet from the child and say 'Come here'. Child should stand up and walk toward you without inappropriate movements or vocalizations. Repeat 2 more times.			

SOURCE: Cautela and Groden (1978). © 1978 the authors. Reproduced by permission of Researc Press, Champaign, Illinois.

Table 4.2 Relaxation training script for children with imagery

---

Hands and arms

Pretend you have a whole lemon in your left hand. Now squeeze it hard. Try to squeeze all the juice out. Feel the tightness in your hand and arm as you squeeze. Now drop the lemon. Notice how your muscles feel when they are relaxed. Take another lemon and squeeze it. Try to squeeze this one harder than you did the first one. That's right. Really hard. Now drop your lemon and relax. See how much better your hand and arm feel when they are relaxed. Once again, take a lemon in your left hand and squeeze all the juice out. Don't leave a single drop. Squeeze hard. Good. Now relax and let the lemon fall from your hand. (Repeat the process for the hand and arm.)

Arms and shoulders

Pretend you are a furry, lazy cat. You want to stretch. Stretch your arms out in front of you. Raise them up high over your head. Way back. Feel the pull in your shoulders. Stretch higher. Now just let your arms drop back to your side. Okay, kitten, stretch again. Stretch your arms out in front of you. Raise them over your head. Pull them back, way back. Pull hard. Now let them drop quickly. Good. Notice how your shoulders feel more relaxed. This time let's have a great big stretch. Try to touch the ceiling. Stretch your arms way out in front of you. Raise them way up high over your head. Push them way, way back. Notice the tension and pull in your arms and shoulders. Hold tight, now. Great. Let them drop very quickly and feel how good it is to be relaxed. It feels good and warm and lazy.

Shoulders and neck

Now pretend you are a turtle. You're sitting out on a rock by a nice, peaceful pond, just relaxing in the warm sun. It feels nice and warm and safe here. Oh-oh! You sense danger. Pull your head into your house. Try to pull your shoulders up to your ears and push your head down into your shoulders. Hold in tight. It isn't easy to be a turtle in a shell. The danger is past now. You can come out into the warm sunshine, and, once again, you can relax and feel the warm sunshine. Watch out now! More danger. Hurry, pull your head back into your house and hold it tight. You have to be closed in tight to protect yourself. Okay, you can relax now. Bring your head out and let your shoulders relax. Notice how much better it feels to be relaxed than to be all tight. One more time, now. Danger! Pull your head in. Push your shoulders way up to your ears and hold tight. Don't let even a tiny piece of your head show outside your shell. Hold it. Feel the tenseness in your neck and shoulders. Okay. You can come out now. It's safe again. Relax and feel comfortable in your safety. There's no more danger. Nothing to worry about. Nothing to be afraid of. You feel good.

Jaw

You have a giant jawbreaker bubble-gum in your mouth. It's very hard to chew. Bite down on it. Hard! Let your neck muscles help you. Now relax. Just let your jaw hang loose. Notice how good it feels just to let your jaw drop. Okay, let's tackle that jawbreaker again now. Bite down. Hard! Try to squeeze it out between your teeth. That's good. You're really tearing that gum up. Now relax again. Just let your jaw drop off your face. It feels so good just to let go and not have to fight that bubble gum. Okay, one more time. We're really going to tear it up this time. Bite down. Hard as you can. Harder. Oh, you're really working hard. Good. Now relax. Try to relax your whole body. You've beaten the bubble gum. Let yourself go as loose as you can.

(contd.)

Table 4.2 (*contd.*)

Face and nose

Here comes a pesky old fly. He has landed on your nose. Try to get him off without using your hands. That's right, wrinkle up your nose. Make as many wrinkles in your nose as you can. Scrunch your nose up real hard. Good. You've chased him away. Now you can relax your nose. Oops, here he comes back again. Shoo him off. Wrinkle it up hard. Hold it just as tight as you can. Okay, he flew away. You can relax your face. Notice that when you scrunch up your nose that your cheeks and your mouth and your forehead and your eyes all help you, and, they get tight, too. So when you relax your nose, your whole face relaxes too, and that feels good. Oh-oh. This time that old fly has come back, but this time he's on your forehead. Make lots of wrinkles. Try to catch him between all those wrinkles. Hold it tight, now. Okay, you can let go. He's gone for good. Now you can just relax. Let your face go smooth, no wrinkles anywhere. Your face feels nice and smooth and relaxed.

Stomach

Hey! Here comes a cute baby elephant. But he's not watching where he's going. He doesn't see you lying there in the grass, and he's about to step on your stomach. Don't move. You don't have time to get out of the way. Just get ready for him. Make your stomach very hard. Tighten up your stomach muscles real tight. Hold it. It looks like he is going the other way. You can relax now. Let your stomach go soft. Let it be as relaxed as you can. That feels so much better. Oops, he's coming this way again. Get ready. Tighten up your stomach. Real hard. If he steps on you when your stomach is hard, it won't hurt. Make your stomach into a rock. Okay, he's moving away again. You can relax now. Kind of settle down, get comfortable, and relax. Notice the difference between a tight stomach and a relaxed one. That's how we want it to feel—nice and loose and relaxed. You won't believe this, but this time he's really coming your way and no turning around. He's headed straight for you. Tighten up. Tighten hard. Here he comes. This is really it. You've got to hold on tight. He's stepping on you. He's stepped over you. Now he's gone for good. You can relax completely. You're safe. Everything is okay, and you can feel nice and relaxed.

This time imagine that you want to squeeze through a narrow fence and the boards have splinters on them. You'll have to make yourself very skinny if you're going to make it through. Suck your stomach in. Try to squeeze it up against your backbone. Try to be as skinny as you can. You've got to get through. Now relax. You don't have to be skinny now. Just relax and feel you stomach being warm and loose. Okay, let's try to get through that fence now. Squeeze up your stomach. Make it touch your backbone. Get it real small and tight. Get as skinny as you can. Hold tight now. You've got to squeeze through. You got through that skinny little fence and no splinters. You can relax now. Settle back and let your stomach come back out where it belongs. You can feel really good now. You've done fine.

Legs and feet

Now pretend that you are standing barefoot in a big, fat, mud puddle. Squish your toes down deep into the mud. Try to get your feet down to the bottom of the mud puddle. You'll probably need your legs to help you push. Push down, spread your toes apart, and feel the mud squish up between your toes. Now step out of the mud puddle. Relax your feet. Let your toes go loose and feel how nice that is. It feels good to be relaxed. Back into the mud puddle. Squish your toes down. Let your leg muscles help you push your feet down. Push your feet. Hard. Try to squeeze that mud puddle dry. Okay. Come back out now. Relax your feet, relax your legs, relax your toes. It feels so good to be relaxed. No tenseness anywhere. You feel kind of warm and tingly.

SOURCE: Koeppen (1974). Reproduced by permission.

Table 4.3 Relaxation training script for children without imagery.

Hands and arms

Make a fist with your left hand. Squeeze it hard. Feel the tightness in your hand and arm as you squeeze. Now let your hand go and relax. See how much better your hand and arm feel when they are relaxed. Once again, make a fist with your left hand and squeeze hard. Good. Now relax and let your hand go. (Repeat the process for the right hand and arm.)

Arms and shoulders

Stretch your arms out in front of you. Raise them high up over your head. Way back. Feel the pull in your shoulders. Stretch higher. Now just let your arms drop back to your side. Okay, let's stretch again. Stretch your arms out in front of you. Raise them over your head. Pull them back, way back. Pull hard. Now let them drop quickly. Good. Notice how your shoulders feel more relaxed. This time let's have a great big stretch. Try to touch the ceiling. Stretch your arms way out in front of you. Raise them way up high over your head. Push them way, way back. Notice the tension and pull in your arms and shoulders. Hold tight, now. Great. Let them drop very quickly and feel how good it is to be relaxed. It feels good and warm and lazy.

Shoulder and neck

Try to pull your shoulders up to your ears and push your head down into your shoulders. Hold in tight. Okay, now relax and feel the warmth. Again, pull your shoulders up to your ears and push your head down into your shoulders. Do it tightly. Okay, you can relax now. Bring your head out and let your shoulders relax. Notice how much better it feels to be relaxed than to be all tight. One more time now. Push your head down and your shoulders way up to your ears. Hold it. Feel the tenseness in your neck and shoulders. Okay. You can relax now and feel comfortable. You feel good.

Jaw

Put your teeth together real hard. Let your neck muscles help you. Now relax. Just let your jaw hang loose. Notice how good it feels just to let your jaw drop. Okay, bite down again hard. That's good. Now relax again. Just let your jaw drop. It feels so good just to let go. Okay, one more time. Bite down. Hard as you can. Harder. Oh, you're really working hard. Good. Now relax. Try to relax your whole body. Let yourself go as loose as you can.

Face and nose

Wrinkle up your nose. Make as many wrinkles in your nose as you can. Scrunch your nose up real hard. Good. Now you can relax your nose. Now wrinkle up your nose again. Wrinkle it up hard. Hold it just as tight as you can. Okay. You can relax your face. Notice that when you scrunch up your nose that your cheeks and your mouth and your forehead all help you and they get tight, too. So when you relax your nose, your whole face relaxes too, and that feels good. Now make lots of wrinkles on your forehead. Hold it tight, now. Okay, you can let go. Now you can just relax. Let your face go smooth. No wrinkles anywhere. Your face feels nice and smooth and relaxed.

Stomach

Now tighten up your stomach muscles real tight. Make your stomach real hard. Don't move. Hold it. You can relax now. Let your stomach go soft. Let it be as relaxed as you can. That feels so much better. Okay, again. Tighten your stomach real hard. Good. You can relax now. Kind of settle down, get comfortable, and relax. Notice the difference between a tight stomach and a relaxed one. That's how we want it to feel. Nice and

(contd.)

Table 4.3 (*contd.*)

---

loose and relaxed. Okay. Once more. Tighten up. Tighten hard. Good. Now you can relax completely. You can feel nice and relaxed.

This time, try to pull your stomach in. Try to squeeze it against your backbone. Try to be as skinny as you can. Now relax. You don't have to be skinny now. Just relax and feel your stomach being warm and loose. Okay, squeeze in your stomach again. Make it touch your backbone. Get it real small and tight. Get as skinny as you can. Hold tight now. Your can relax now. Settle back and let your stomach come back out where it belongs. You can really feel good now. You've done fine.

Legs and feet

Push your toes down on the floor really hard. You'll probably need your legs to help you push. Push down, spread your toes apart. Now relax your feet. Let your toes go loose and feel how nice that is. It feels good to be relaxed. Okay. Now push your toes down. Let your leg muscles help you push your feet down. Push your feet. Hard. Okay. Relax your feet, relax your legs, relax your toes. It feels so good to be relaxed. No tenseness anywhere. You feel kind of warm and tingly.

Conclusion

Stay as relaxed as you can. Let your whole body go limp and feel all your muscles relaxed. In a few minutes I will ask you to open your eyes and that will be the end of the session. Today is a good day, and you are ready to go back to class feeling very relaxed. You've worked hard in here and it feels good to work hard. Shake your arms. Now shake your legs. Move your head around. Slowly open your eyes. Very good. You've done a good job. You're going to be a super relaxer.

SOURCE: Ollendick and Cerny (1981). Reproduced by permission of Plenum Publishing Corp.

Cautela and Groden (1978) have written a manual on relaxation training for use with children. An important feature of their manual is the relaxation readiness pretest (see Table 4.1) which is designed to assess the child's suitability (compliance with basic instructions) for training in relaxation. Another interesting development was proposed by Koeppen (1974). She has incorporated fantasy into the muscle-tension release exercises in order to elicit and maintain the child's interest. In relation to the muscles of the arms and shoulders, for example, the following instructions are given: 'Pretend you are a furry, lazy cat. You want to stretch. Stretch your arms out in front of you ...' (Koeppen, 1974, p. 17). The full script is presented in Table 4.2. Koeppen suggests that 15-minute training sessions be adopted with no more than three muscle groups being introduced per session. Two or three sessions per week are recommended for the rapid learning of the relaxation skills. On the grounds that some children become overly involved in the fantasy, Ollendick and his colleagues (Ollendick & Cerny, 1981) have developed a relaxation script without reference to fantasy creatures (see Table 4.3). Ollendick *et al.* also suggest 15 to 20-minute training sessions, and that no more than three muscle groups be introduced in any one training session. The level of relaxation attained by the child is inferred by the therapist from observations of the child during the training sessions and the child's subjective report. Physiological measures (e.g. heart rate) may be possible

Table 4.4 Anxiety hierarchies

FEAR OF INJECTIONS

(1) Hearing about another child receiving an injection from doctor
(2) Parents saying that it is necessary to visit doctor
(3) Travelling in car with parents to doctor
(4) Being greeted by the receptionist
(5) Sitting in waiting room with parents
(6) Entering the doctor's office
(7) Being told by doctor that an injection is necessary
(8) Listening to conversation between doctor and nurse about injection
(9) Seeing various medical instruments and syringe on table
(10) Being prepared for an injection (arm rubbed with swab)
(11) Doctor picking up syringe
(12) Doctor holding arm and asking you to look away
(13) Feeling needle prick skin
(14) Feeling needle start to enter skin
(15) Feeling increased pressure as doctor gives injection

FEAR OF DENTIST

(1) Being told by parents that it is time for a dental check-up
(2) Sitting in waiting room outside the dentist's office
(3) Nurse asking you to come into dentist's office
(4) Sitting in dentist's chair waiting for instructions
(5) Hearing conversation between dentist and nurse
(6) Dentist asking you to 'open your mouth wide'
(7) Dentist looking into mouth
(8) Dentist using probe on side of tooth
(9) Receiving an injection in gums
(10) Listening to sound of drill
(11) Feeling drill go into tooth
(12) Being told by dentist that a tooth has to be removed
(13) Feeling the pressure of the tooth being pulled
(14) Observing a little blood in saliva
(15) Hearing the crunching sound of the tooth being pulled

FEAR OF DARKNESS

(1) Watching television in darkness
(2) Watching movie at cinema
(3) Observe darkening sky after sunset
(4) Travelling in car at night with parents
(5) Walking from car to house at night
(6) Going to another part of house in semi-darkness
(7) Room light briefly switched off
(8) House lights going out for a long interval because of interruption to electricity supply
(9) Going outside at night to find or check something (assistance of flashlight)
(10) Sitting in car (alone) waiting for parents
(11) Parent switching off bedroom light before you fall asleep
(12) Waking up through the night with bedroom in darkness
(13) Walking to neighbour's house at night on errand for parents
(14) Staying overnight at friend's house
(15) Sleeping in a tent for the night

(contd.)

Table 4.4 (*contd.*)

FEAR OF DOGS

(1) Seeing a television advertisement that involves a dog
(2) Hearing dog bark in neighhbourhood (distant)
(3) Hearing dog bark in neighhbourhood (close)
(4) Looking at puppies at market or pet shop
(5) Touching puppies at market or pet shop
(6) Holding a puppy at market or pet shop
(7) Looking out window of house—see dog in street
(8) Visiting relatives or friends—see dog in back yard
(9) Visiting relatives or friends—see dog asleep in the house
(10) Patting a dog secured to kennel
(11) Walking a dog on a leash
(12) Playing with a dog off the leash
(13) Dog licks your face during play
(14) Walking along footpath—encounter unknown dog
(15) Walking along footpath—encounter unknown dog (barks)

FEAR OF TESTS

(1) Teacher announces that there will be a major test in two weeks
(2) Studying at home a week before the test
(3) Parents ask about the test
(4) Studying 3 nights before the test
(5) Studying 2 night before the test
(6) Studying the night before the test
(7) Thinking about the test as you walk to school
(8) Studying during break just before the test
(9) Hearing other children talk about the test
(10) Sitting in class waiting for test papers to be distributed
(11) Listening to the instructions given by teacher
(12) Hearing the teacher speak to a student about his misconduct
(13) Notice other students at work as you study the questions
(14) Hearing the teacher say you have 15 minutes left to finish the test—notice that a number of students have finished
(15) Hearing the teacher say you have 5 minutes left—must decide on how to spend remaining time.

FEAR OF READING

(1) Parents asking about progress on reading at school
(2) Reading in bed before going to sleep
(3) Looking at books in library at school
(4) Lesson before 'reading class' at school
(5) Teacher explains nature of reading exercise
(6) Teacher calls out name of someone else to read
(7) Listening to another child read to class
(8) Teacher asking child to pronounce certain words
(9) Teacher asking child questions about text
(10) Hearing own name being called out to read by teacher
(11) Starting to read aloud to class
(12) Encountering a word that is difficult to pronounce when reading aloud to class
(13) Thinking that you have another half-page of reading
(14) Teacher asking you to pronounce certain words
(15) Teacher asking you questions about text

depending upon the circumstances. Of course, the introduction of equipment and electrodes would have to be done carefully so as not to frighten the child. Giggling and laughter, persistent shuffling and fidgetting, excessive eyelid movements, and facial tension and grimacing all indicate that the child is experiencing difficulties with the procedure. If these obstacles cannot be overcome, other forms of anxiety inhibitors (e.g. interpersonal relationships, games, edibles) should be considered. Young children are better suited for the latter variety of anxiety inhibitors. The choice of anxiety inhibitor can be determined by the therapist in consultation with the care provider(s).

Development of the anxiety hierarchy

The anxiety hierarchy consists of a series of anxiety-provoking items related to the phobic stimulus, ranging from least anxiety-provoking to most anxiety-provoking. The construction of the anxiety hierarchy can be facilitated by giving clients index cards upon which they can briefly describe different situations that elicit distress. Clients are often required to rate their reaction to each of these situations on a 0 to 100 scale (0—comfortable and relaxed; 100—extremely tense and anxious). This allows for the proper sequencing of the items in the anxiety hierarchy. Anxiety hierarchies consist of about 15 to 25 items (see Table 4.4 for examples). It is important to identify the critical antecedents of the phobic reaction, and ensure that the appropriate stimulus dimensions run through the anxiety hierarchy. Older children and adolescents are usually capable of participating in the construction of the anxiety hierarchy. For young children, however, the therapist tends to rely upon the care provider for information about antecedent stimuli, choice of items, and the appropriate sequencing of items in the anxiety hierarchy.

The child's ability to imagine the anxiety-provoking scenes may have to be addressed by the therapist at this stage. Unfortunately for the therapist, there is a dearth of literature on the assessment of children's imagery, especially in relation to systematic desensitization and other imagery-based behavioural techniques. Several interesting suggestions have been made by Morris and Kratochwill (1983). For example an informal imagery test might be conducted in which the child is shown a certain picture for 20 seconds by the therapist, after which he or she has to recall the objects and their location on a separate piece of paper. Morris and Kratochwill also suggest that children could be presented with incongruous pictorial descriptions (e.g. fish smoking a cigar) with the task of imagining the descriptions as quickly as possible. The speed at which he or she imagines the description (indicated by raising a hand) might provide useful information about the child's imagery level. Finally, the Bett's (1909/1969) Vividness of Mental Imagery Scale is presented as a more formal method of measuring imagery ability. Here the individual is asked to rate the vividness of certain images along specified dimensions. At the moment it appears that therapists are guided by their clinical judgement about the child, and his or her reaction to instructions regarding the visualization of anxiety-provoking scenes for desensitization (which, after all, is the acid test).

Systematic desensitization proper

At this stage, the client is given several minutes to reach a state of deep relaxation. The client is then asked to imagine being in the least anxiety-provoking scene of the hierarchy. The therapist describes the situation, asks the client to imagine being in the scene, and then stop imagining the scene after about 10 to 15 seconds. The client is instructed to raise the forefinger if excessive anxiety is experience during the imagery. Should this be the case, the scene is usually re-presented in a milder form or briefer exposure. When the scene concerned no longer evokes anxiety, the next scene on the anxiety hierarchy is tackled. The procedure is followed until the most anxiety-provoking item can be imagined as the client relaxes. The number of sessions to complete systematic desensitization proper varies considerably depending upon how may items there are in the hierarchy and what problems are encountered. Older children and adolescents are able to participate in this procedure. When there are problems in imagining the anxiety-provoking scenes, as with young children, real-life sytematic desensitization may be pursued. Depending on the fear problem, we incorporate representational stimuli (e.g. slides, pictures, toys, sound recordings) in the initial stages of real-life desensitization. Typically, parents are supplied with such materials for use at home with their child. In accordance with the principle of reciprocal inhibition, an anxiety inhibitor of some kind is still employed to counter any tension or distress experience at each exposure. Invariably, we rely on the warm and trusting relationship the child has with the parents, as well as encouraging parents to make the exposures 'fun activities' whenever possible. The implementation of real-life desensitization calls for some advanced planning and antecedent stimulus control on the part of the therapist. In the treatment of animal-phobic children, for example, it is important that the animal does not get out of control. A dog that growls savagely or leaps at the child may serve to reinforce the child's phobia, and make further efforts at desensitization difficult. The rate of progress through the anxiety hierarchy in real-life desensitization (consider number of exposures per item, duration of exposures) depends upon the child's verbal, physiological and behavioural reactions to the exposures. We proceed fairly cautiously not wishing to risk the benefits of desensitization. Extra steps can be added to help the child who finds a particular exposure to be move threatening than anticipated. Finally, a clinical judgement has to be made about the extent of desensitization and whether it is necessary to proceed beyond what is normally encountered in the interests of overlearning.

The use of real-life or *in vivo* exposures in systematic desensitization has been given high priority in recent years. Even for older children and adolescents, it appears that real-life exposures are more potent than imaginal exposures (Ultee, Griffioen & Schellekens, 1982). This conclusion is consistent with that found in the treatment of anxiety and phobias in adults, where real-life exposures are more effective than imaginal exposures (Emmelkamp, 1982).

There are many reasons for the superiority of real-life exposures over imaginal exposures. As previously observed, some children have difficulty in imagining the anxiety-provoking items during systematic desensitization. Other children can imagine the items, but do not experience any physiological reaction. Furthermore, many children point out that they can handle the feared object/situation in their imagination but have no confidence in their ability to cope with real-life confrontations. Thus, preference should be given to the inclusion of real-life exposures in the systematic desensitization treatment of children's phobias.

However, there are phobias in which real-life exposures cannot be arranged and which remain suited for imaginal desensitization. As Ollendick and Cerny (1981) state:

> Although *in vivo* presentation of the anxiety-arousing stimuli is effective, not all fears and anxiety are amenable to *in vivo* procedures. For instance, it is cumbersome, if not impossible, to treat *in vivo* such common but ephemeral fears as fear of rejection, fear of punishment, fear of bodily injury, and fear of death. (p. 73)

Although it cannot be disputed that imaginal systematic desensitization has a vital role to play in the management of such fears and phobias, the behavioural practitioner should strive to employ real-life exposures whenever this is feasible.

Clinical and research applications

Many uncontrolled case studies involving systematic desensitization and its variants have been reported. A brief review of these cases illustrates the special consideration often needed when using systematic desensitization with children. Tasto (1969) relied upon systematic desensitization in imagination and muscle relaxation as the anxiety inhibitor in the treatment of a 4-year-old child's phobia of sudden loud noises. Interestingly, the child moved through the anxiety hierarchy in his imagination without signalling anxiety. However, when subsequently tested *in vivo*, his fear had not diminished. Thereafter, *in vivo* desensitization was embarked upon with good results. In the treatment of an 11-year-old girl with dog phobia, Kissel (1972) also attempted traditional systematic desensitization. After the first session, however the therapist's interpersonal relationship with the child was used as the anxiety inhibitor instead of muscle relaxation. Much of the desensitization involved the girl tape recording a story of her own creation about dogs, and then listening to the story while creating images in her mind. Danquah (1974) treated an $8\frac{1}{2}$-year-old boy with a frog phobia using systematic desensitization. The anxiety inhibitor was relaxation (induced by mild hypnosis). Pictures of frogs, toy frogs and specimens of frogs were systematically presented to the child. A galvanometer was used to gauge the child's autonomic response to the phobic stimuli. Croghan and Musante (1975) successfully treated a 7-year-old boy with a phobia for high buildings. Game-playing in the presence of the phobic object was used as the counter-conditioning agent. Freeman, Roy and Hemmick (1976) extinguished the phobic response of a 7-year-old mentally retarded boy to physical examinations conducted by male doctors. A hierarchy of requirements for the physical examination was established, and the comfortable relationship the boy had with a nurse on the ward was used as the anxiety inhibitor.

Wish, Hasazi and Jurgela (1973) used an 'automated direct conditioning' technique to treat an 11-year-old child with an excessive fear of loud noises. Treatment was self-administered by the child in his home. Following relaxation in a darkened room, he listened to increasingly longer portions of a tape recording in which feared sounds were superimposed upon selections of his favourite music. Participation in the session was reinforced by the child's parents. In the reciprocal inhibition of a 1-year-old infant with a phobic reaction to water, Bentler (1962) made use of toys and body-contact with the mother as anxiety inhibitors. Jackson and King (1982) employed laughter as an anxiety inhibitor in the *in vivo* desensitization of an autistic child's phobia of noises associated with toilet flushing. As the child loved being tickled to the point of laughter, this activity was introduced during the toileting and flushing procedure (with no adverse effect upon urination or defecation).

Thus, a range of anxiety inhibitors have been tried with children, including muscular relaxation, hypnosis, edibles, games, interpersonal relationships, and laughter. Successful graduated-exposure programmes have been developed for phobic children in which anxiety inhibitors were omitted, although it may be argued that the child's relationship with the therapeutic agent served as the anxiety inhibitor (Stableford, 1979; Wilson & Jackson, 1980).

In a somewhat controversial study, Obler and Terwilliger (1970) examined the effectiveness of a 'modified version of Wolpe's systematic desensitization' with neurologically impaired children suffering from phobic symptoms. Two hypotheses were tested: (a) 'a non-verbal therapeutic technique not requiring motivation will produce successful symptom reduction of these children'; and (b) 'awareness of therapeutic procedure is not necessary for successful results' (p. 314). Neurologically impaired children with either fears of buses or dogs were selected for the study. Fifteen children were assigned to the treatment group, while another 15 served as controls and were matched with the treatment group on age, sex, intelligence and phobia. Treatment consisted of a 5-hour session per week for 10 weeks, and was described as follows:

> Prior to exposure to the real phobic stimulus, Ss were asked to look at pictures or models of the fear-inducing stimulus (bus or dog). This eliminated the need for S to imagine the stimulus. Cooke (1966) showed that actual exposure to the fear-inducing stimulus was more effective than merely imagining the stimulus. When S's behavior indicated a tolerance of the picture or model, he was then exposed to the actual fear-producing stimulus (bus or dog). The therapist continuously rewarded S through encouragement for moving closer and closer to the object. Eventually, Ss were able to move up the scale to more anxiety-producing stimulus (e.g., touching the bus or dog). At this point, S was given the option of exposure to the stimulus without the presence of the therapist. A new reward was offered at this time which included toys, books, pets, and candy chosen by S at an earlier session with the therapist.
>
> These rewards were dispensed immediately at the time of successful completion of the defined task (e.g., talking to the bus driver, putting a token in the box, staying in the room with a dog). If an S overcame the phobia prior to completion of the

tenth session, he continued to be reinforced by the therapist for his success. Successful handling of the fear-inducing stimulus was considered to be its generalization to S's daily life without the presence of the therapist. This was measured by a parent report scale administered to all E and C group members prior to and at the completion of the treatment period. (p. 316)

Whether subjects were aware or unaware of treatment was assumed to be related to the children's IQ score obtained on the Wechsler Intelligence Scale for Children (Wechsler, 1949). An arbitrary cut-off point (a score of 75) was established as the critical value. Those subjects with IQ scores below 75 were assumed to be minimally aware of treatment procedures, while those above 75 were considered more likely to be aware. The basic measure for treatment effectiveness was a parent rating before and after treatment. The scale consisted of 10 questions concerning the child's functioning; one of the questions tapped the critical phobic behaviour on a 0–2 rating. As measured by parent ratings, the treated subjects were significantly affected by the 'modified systematic desensitization method'. Control group subjects, on the other hand, showed no significant change in reduction of their phobic symptoms. The children's intellectual ability, presumably indicating awareness of being treated, did not affect the outcome.

In a critique of Obler and Terwilliger's (1970) study, Begelman and Hersen (1971) make a number of critical points about the conclusions drawn by Obler and Terwilliger. A major criticism is the conceptualization of their treatment as systematic desensitization, in that therapeutic intervention is seen to be more akin to shaping. According to the researchers themselves, 'The therapist continuously rewarded S through encouragement for moving closer and closer to the object' (p. 316). Tangible rewards (toys, books, pets and candy) were also employed. Begelman and Hersen are also critical of the unsystematic administration of primary and secondary reinforcers, lack of clarity concerning the therapist's role, absence of behaviourally based pre-treatment and post-treatment measures, arbitrary assessment of awareness and unawareness of treatment, and the use of subjective and retrospective parent ratings.

In a subsequent article, Terwilliger and Obler (1971) addressed these criticisms. According to them: 'The aim was not to do in vivo desensitization per se, but to do therapy on brain-injured patients. That consideration rather than methodological concerns determined the use of 'in vivo' tactics' (p. 15). Terwilliger and Obler quite correctly point out the need for modified desensitization procedures when working with low-functioning and hyperactive individuals. In addition, it is maintained that all desensitization is carried out within a social interaction in which shaping and modelling are inevitable. To conclude, it can be stated that the study is an interesting adaptation of systematic desensitization for a special population. However, the findings cannot be interpreted as hard evidence for the efficacy of systematic desensitization as it is usually conceptualized.

A more carefully controlled study was conducted by Kelley (1976) on the therapeutic efficacy of 'play desensitization' and the contribution of reinforcement as an adjunct to the basic treatment procedure. In contrast to the aforementioned studies on shaping, Kelley made an attempt to control for demand characteristics with the inclusion of a placebo condition and a condition entailing the non-contingent administration of reinforcers. The children in the experiment were afraid of darkness. The target behaviour was assessed by behavioural (BAT) and subjective (fear thermometer) measures. On the basis of the pre-test BAT scores, children 4 to 5 years old were randomly assigned to one of five treatment conditions: (1) no-treatment control, (2) play placebo, (3) play desensitization, (4) play desensitization with non-contingent M & Ms, and (5) play desensitization with contingent M & Ms. Subjects in the treatment groups received three half-hour therapy sessions distributed over a 3-week period. In the three desensitization groups, a standard 15-item hierarchy paralleled in play with a doll the procedure and dialogue actually conducted during the BAT. Each item on the hierarchy was presented until a criterion of two presentations without signalled fear was met. Subjects in the placebo group engaged in sessions where play consisted of 15 items involving daily activities at pre-school but with no reference to darkness or the BAT situation. The M & Ms were dispensed on a non-contingent or contingent basis as the children progressed up the hierarchy during play desensitization depending upon group condition. After treatment, the children were given two BAT trials. On the second of the BAT trials, 'high-demand' instructions were deliberately given to the children: 'Now try it again, but this time try as hard as you can not to push the button' (p. 80). The two primary outcome measures—behavioural avoidance of the dark and subjective report of fear while in the dark—were expressed as change scores from pre-test to post-test under low-demand and high-demand post-test conditions. None of the treatment conditions resulted in significant decreases in fear of darkness on either behavioural or self-report measures. However, instructions alone had a significant effect on outcome. Increased endurance of the dark could be produced for most subjects by verbal instructions to remain longer in the dark room.

Kelley's (1976) experiment is important in a number of ways. It was an attempt to assess the specific contribution of a range of therapeutic procedures that are often placed together (Obler & Terwilliger, 1970). The sobering aspect of Kelley's experiment is the negative outcome for each of these component parts. Possible explanations of the negative findings include:

(1) The small number of treatment sessions was spread over three weeks.
(2) The children may have been distracted by the doll from the real task, i.e. their own desensitization.
(3) The M & Ms may have been of little reinforcing value to the children.
(4) The fear expressed by these 'normal' children was possibly non-phobic.

A great deal of research has been carried out on systematic desensitization in educational settings. On the assumption that poor test results and reading difficulties can be due to high levels of tension or anxiety, systematic desensitization is seen to be an appropriate method of intervention. Deffenbacher and

Kemper (1974b) report the use of systematic desensitization with 28 test-anxious junior high school students. Systematic desensitization was administered in small groups of 2 to 5 students. The students worked through a standard anxiety hierarchy, with the slowest student determining the pace of the group. Eight sessions were devoted to this form of counselling. Students underwent a significant improvement in their grade point average. However, a control group was not included in the study. In a controlled investigation, Deffenbacher and Kemper (1974a) evaluated the effectiveness of systematic desensitization as treatment for test-anxious sixth graders. Students were randomly assigned to desensitization counselling ($n = 11$) or a non-counselled control group ($n = 10$). Desensitization was performed in two small groups. Compared with students in the non-counselled control group, those who underwent systematic desensitization experienced significant improvements in their grade point averages. In addition, 4 of the 5 failing students who received systematic desensitization achieved a C average or better by the end of counselling, while none of the failing students improved to this level in the non-counselled control group.

The comparative effectiveness of relaxation *per se* and systematic desensitization is an important practical issue for behavioural practitioners. Traditionally, relaxation *per se* has been thought to be of limited or no value in the treatment of children's phobias. A small amount of evidence suggests that relaxation may have been underestimated in overcoming children's phobias. As a case illustration, Walker and Werstlein (1980) sucessfully employed abbreviated progressive relaxation (aided by cassette tapes and homework practice) in the treatment of a 4-year-old encopretic boy with a toilet phobia. In an experiment on the reduction of examination anxiety and 'stage fright', Kondas (1967) compared the effects of group desensitization, autogenic relaxation training, and the imagination of items on the anxiety hierarchy. The subjects consisted of 23 children (aged 11 to 15 years) and 13 psychology students. Interviews, an adapted fear survey schedule, and a test of palmer perspiration were used in the assessment of treatment effects. Systematic desensitization was effective in reducing 'stage fright' on these measures. Autogenic relaxation training produced encouraging results for the children but not the psychology students. Apparently the children had an advantage over the psychology students in that relaxation had been carried out at the beginning of a lesson just before an examination. The imagination of fear-inducing examination scenes alone was not successful in overcoming examination anxiety. A 5-month follow-up of a limited sample suggested that the effects of systematic desensitization were fairly stable, whereas the effects of autogenic relaxation training were more transient.

Laxer, Quarter, Kooman and Walker (1969) assigned high test-anxious secondary school students to either systematic desensitization or relaxation training conditions. Small groups of 2 to 4 students met with their counsellor for 20 minutes daily over a 6-week period. Three anxiety measures as well as academic and non-academic grades were used to evaluate the success of the interventions. In comparison with a no-treatment control group, both experimental conditions produced a significant reduction in anxiety. However, generalization to academic work was very slight and only evident for students in the 13th grade (the highest grade in the study). Relaxation *per se* seemed more effective in reducing manifest anxiety, and equally effective in lowering debilitating test anxiety. According to these researchers:

> One possible explanation for these results is that Ss in a relaxed state might inadvertently imagine anxiety-provoking stimuli and form new associations between these stimuli and relaxation. For Ss in the relaxation *per se* condition the new associations might have been more general than those for Ss who were systematically desensitized. (p. 451)

Another possible explanation is that the students worked at applying relaxation in real-life situations including school activities. The findings of the Kondas (1967) and Laxer *et al.* (1969) studies suggest that relaxation (autogenic training and abbreviated progressive relaxation training) may be as effective as systematic desensitization for the less-severe anxieties of older children and adolescents.

As already intimated, the comparative effectiveness of real-life and imaginal exposures in systematic desensitization is an important practical question. Mainly on the basis of adult studies, it is generally conceded that real-life exposures are more effective than imaginal exposures in systematic desensitization (Marks, 1975; Sherman, 1973). Whether imaginal exposure helps facilitate subsequent real-life exposures in systematic desensitization is another important practical issue. In fact, imaginal exposures might be viewed as an opportunity to rehearse coping with real-life exposures (Goldfried, 1971). A study conducted by Ultee, *et al.* (1982) examined these issues in relation to children. Twenty-four children aged 5 to 10 years participated in the experiment. The children had a fear of water as judged by parents and two swimming teachers. Three groups were formed, namely, an *in vitro* treatment group ($n = 7$), an *in vivo* treatment group ($n = 8$), and a control group ($n = 9$). Children were matched for age with a random distribution over the treatment conditions.

Subjects in the *in vitro* treatment group received four sessions of gradual imaginal exposure to the fear-evoking stimuli followed by four sessions of real-life exposure to the feared stimuli. Subjects in the *in vivo* treatment group were given eight sessions of gradual real-life exposure. In both treatment conditions, exposure to the feared stimuli was guided by reference to items from a standard hierarchy. When children reported anxiety during *in vitro* exposure, the therapist immediately induced an antagonistic response by the instruction to imagine a pleasant situation (Lazarus & Abramowitz, 1962). If during *in vivo* exposure an item elicited anxiety, the child was told to leave the situation and to relax by imagining something pleasant. The control group took part only in the tests, which were administered at the commencement of treatment, after four sessions, and at the end of the course of treatments. A pre-coded behaviour observation record was used to evaluate the avoidance behaviour of the children in two different feared 'swimming pool situations'. In addition, swimming teachers recorded anxiety in each situation using two records. Teacher record I was used to gauge the performance of children in the water. Teacher record

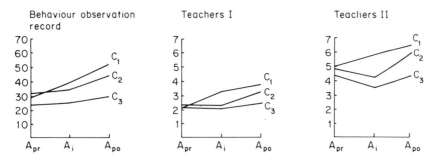

Fig. 4.1 Average scores per instrument for the *in vivo* condition (C$_1$), the *in vitro* condition (C$_2$) and the control condition (C$_3$) on preliminary test (A$_{pr}$), intermediate test (A$_i$) and post-test (A$_{po}$). Reproduced from Ultee, Griffioen and Schellekens (1982) by permission of Pergamon Press.

II was used to predict the development of anxiety given the behaviour of the children in the water.

As is evident in Fig. 4.1, the *in vivo* desensitization group showed greater gains than the *in vitro* desensitization group and control group. After the initial eight sessions, the differences between the *in vitro* group and control group were not statistically significant. It will be noted that there was a marked improvement in the performance of the *in vitro* desensitization group over the last four sessions. These sessions were devoted to *in vivo* desensitization, thus suggesting the superiority of real-life exposures. Ultee *et al.* state:

> The findings suggest that in desensitization treatment of anxiety in children, real-life exposure to the feared stimuli is superior to exposure in imagination, and that prefacing *in vivo* desensitization with *in vitro* desensitization is not better than a complete *in vivo* desensitization treatment; the tendency, if anything, is in the other direction. (p. 66)

Another interesting question is the comparative effectiveness of systematic desensitization and psychotherapy in overcoming children's phobias. Miller *et al.* (1972a) report a comparative study on systematic desensitization and psychotherapy as treatments for phobic children. Efforts were made to obtain subjects aged 6 to 15 years who represented the domain of clinical level childhood monophobias and multiphobias from all socio-economic classes of the community. The target phobias comprised mainly fear of school (69%) and fear of storms, the dark and domestic animals. Sixty-seven phobic children were randomly assigned to one of three conditions: systematic desensitization (called 'reciprocal inhibition therapy'), psychotherapy, and waiting-list control. Children in the two treatment conditions received three 1-hour therapy weekly sessions over a period of 8 weeks. In the systematic desensitization condition, children were taught muscular relaxation and underwent imaginal desensitization. After all items of a fear hierarchy could be imagined comfortably, an *in vivo* test was arranged. No problems were reported by the researchers in relation to the young children coping with muscular relaxation, the construction of the anxiety hierarchy, and the imaginal desensitization procedure. Additional behavioural methods were employed depending upon the family situation:

> Where parent–child interaction patterns appeared to reinforce fear behaviour, behaviour therapy principles were employed to restructure contingency schedules, for example, eliminating television during school hours for a school phobic who stayed home. Assertive training was used for inhibited children. (p. 271)

Thus the therapists who conducted this treatment were by no means restricted to pure systematic desensitization. Psychotherapy entailed mainly play therapy which 'concentrated on the child's "inner experiences", his hopes and his fears, particularly his aggressive and sexual fears and dependent needs' (p. 271). The children were encouraged to vent their anger and disappointment. When secondary gains at home became apparent, the therapist involved the parents and attempted to remove various gratifications (e.g. television watching on school days). Therapy was evaluated on the basis of 'severity scores' obtained at pre-treatment, post-treatment and 14th-week follow-up. The severity scores were derived from ratings provided by the child's parents (usually the mother) and by an independent clinician (the 'primary evaluator'). Ratings reflected the intensity of the target phobia and its extensity (i.e. the degree to which the fear

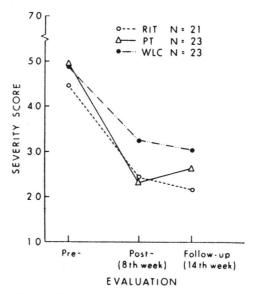

Fig. 4.2 Mean primary evaluator severity score for reciprocal inhibition, psychotherapy and waiting-list control subjects at pre-treatment, post-treatment and follow-up. Reproduced from Miller, Barrett, Hampe and Noble (1972a). Copyright (1972) by the American psychological Association.

affected the child's life sphere). In addition, parents completed the Louisville Behaviour Check List and the Louisville Fear Survey for Children.

Parents of the children in the two treatment groups reported a greater reduction in fear in their children than did parents in the waiting-list group. On parent ratings, however, there was no difference between the effectiveness of the two treatment groups. Moreover, the clinician evaluations failed to confirm any differences between the three groups at post-treatment or follow-up (see Fig. 4.2). In a *post hoc* analysis of the data, Miller *et al.* found a relationship between the child's age and treatment outcome. The young children in both treatment conditions improved significantly more than the waiting-list control children, whereas differences were less apparent for the older children. Taking the combined statistics for the three groups, 31 of the 38 young children (6 to 10 years) were successfully treated, compared with 13 of the 29 older children (11 to 15 years). Hampe *et al.* (1973) conducted a 1- and 2-year follow-up evaluation of 62 of the 69 children who had participated in the original study. Many of the children on the waiting list as well as those who had been unresponsive to the initial treatment received some form of therapeutic assistance. At the follow-up evaluation, 80% were either symptom-free or significantly improved, and only 7% still had a severe phobia.

Discussion

Systematic desensitization has gained much acceptance as a phobia-reduction technique for children. From the viewpoint of clinical practice, a positive feature of systematic desensitization concerns the very clear procedural guidelines set down for the therapist. An intriguing question is the underlying mechanism of systematic desensitization. Wolpe (1958) argues that reciprocal inhibition accounts for the success of systematic desensitization. Contrary to Wolpe's principle of reciprocal inhibition, however, researchers have found that the presence or absence of relaxation has little effect on treatment outcome (e.g. Cooke, 1968; Freeling & Shemberg, 1970; Waters, McDonald & Koresko, 1972). Moreover, in relation to Wolpe's procedural guidelines, many variations of the recommended procedure have been tried and found to be successful. For example, standardized or group anxiety hierarchies have been used with good results (e.g. Cotler, 1970; McGlynn, 1971). Furthermore, progress through the anxiety hierarchy has been made with subjects proceeding in descending or random order of aversive items (Krapfl & Nawas, 1970). Flooding, of course, may be interpreted as the ultimate violation of Wolpe's theoretical position. An alternative explanation of systematic desensitization is that of extinction. Here, repeated non-reinforced exposure to the phobic stimulus is seen to be the crucial element (Wilson and O'Leary, 1980).

In an early article on this issue, Lomont (1965) argues that the therapist's instructions to the client to confront the anxiety-provoking stimulus prevents normal avoidance, and that the repeated exposure eventually results in the extinction of the response. Even when the client signals anxiety, there is a brief delay before the therapist terminates the exposure, thus contributing to the extinction of the response. On the basis of a review of the relevant animal literature, Wilson and Davidson (1971) conclude that extinction is the most likely mechanism. However, it is pointed out that relaxation (or other incompatible responses) appears to facilitate extinction, encouraging exposure to the conditioned stimulus by reducing the unpleasant responses it evokes.

An obvious question concerns the implications of this issue for the clinician interested in the utilization of systematic desensitization with phobic children. Although not essential ingredients from a research viewpoint, relaxation and graduated stimulus presentations are considered useful in facilitating non-reinforced real-life exposure. These aspects of desensitization seem to make the exposures more tolerable or acceptable. To this extent systematic desensitization is well-suited for those phobic reactions involving a high level of physiological reactivity and extreme avoidance. It is also a useful procedure for phobic children with medical conditions (e.g. heart problems and asthma) which the therapist would prefer not to risk exacerbating through more-confronting behavioural techniques. However, it is not the treatment of choice for those phobias due primarily to a lack of skills, inadvertent reinforcement from significant others, or other maintenance factors.

EMOTIVE IMAGERY

Rationale and procedures

Emotive imagery is a procedural variation of systematic desensitization and was developed by Lazarus and Abramovitz (1962), in response to the problems that children experience in traditional systematic desensitization. Some children have difficulty with relaxation training and the evocation and control of images during systematic desensitization proper. In their now classic paper, Lazarus and Abramovitz use the term 'emotive imagery' in reference to 'those classes of imagery which are assumed to arouse feelings of self-assertion, pride, affection, mirth, and similiar anxiety-inhibiting responses' (p. 191). The basic idea is to incorporate these images into an engaging story, with a strong positive affect being established in the child. As in systematic desensitization, anxiety-provoking items are introduced in a gradual manner by the therapist. The positive emotional feelings are expected to counteract any anxiety elicited by these stimuli. It will be appreciated that the rationale is the same as that of systematic desensitization (i.e. reciprocal inhibition).

The procedure involved in emotive imagery is outlined by Lazarus and Abramovitz (1962) as follows:

(a) As in the usual method of systematic desensitization, the range, intensity, and circumstances of the patient's fears are ascertained, and a graduated hierarchy is drawn up, from the most feared to the least feared situation.

(b) By sympathetic conversation and enquiry, the clinician establishes the nature of the child's hero-images—usually derived from radio, cinema, fiction, or his own imagination—and the wish-fulfilments and identifications which accompany them.

(c) The child is then asked to close his eyes and told to imagine a sequence of events which is close enough to his everyday life to be credible, but within which is woven a story concerning his favourite hero or *alter ego*.

(d) If this is done with reasonable skill and empathy, it is possible to arouse to the necessary pitch the child's affective reactions. (In some cases this may be recognized by small changes in facial expression, breathing, muscle tension, etc.).

(e) When the clinician judges that these emotions have been maximally aroused, he introduces, as a natural part of the narrative, the lowest item in the hierarchy. Immediately afterwards he says: 'if you feel afraid (or unhappy, or uncomfortable just raise your finger.' If anxiety is indicated, the phobic stimulus is 'withdrawn' from the narrative and the child's anxiety-inhibiting emotions are again aroused. The procedure is then repeated as in ordinary systematic desensitization, until the highest item in the hierarchy is tolerated without distress. (pp. 191–2)

In addition to the above guidelines on emotive imagery, Rosenstiel and Scott (1977) provide four procedural recommendations on the use of imagery techniques with children. The following suggestions have been adapted from Rosenstiel and Scott:

(1) Imagery scenes should be tailored to the age of the child. There is some evidence that between 6 and 8 years children can begin to utilize complex images to alter their behaviour. Although 4-year-olds can use simple images when directed by others, no lower age limit has been established. Leaving aside the arbitrariness of the cut-off age, some attempt should be made to adjust the complexity of the imagery according to the age of the child.

(2) Treatment should incorporate children's existing fantasies and cognitions. Children have an active and psychologically important fantasy life, incorporating imaginary playmates, superheroes, and so on. Tapping children's naturally occurring imagery as the basis for therapeutic techniques may be advantageous in a number of ways. The use of pre-existing cognitive activities may decrease the complexity and increase the familiarity of the scenes, as well as heighten the child's overall interest. This in turn might increase the child's involvement in the scenes. Including elements of children's natural fantasies into treatment may also improve children's ability to continue to practise the tasks.

(3) Non-verbal cues supply important information about the treatment process. Given that children have difficulty in describing emotional arousal during the imagery based treatments, the therapist should be alert to the non-verbal cues as a means of gauging the child's progress. Non-verbal cues include flushing of the skin, alterations in breathing patterns, changes in facial expression, increased body movements and muscular tension, and crying.

(4) Children's reports of their images should be utilized in treatment. Having children describe their images seems to help them obtain more accurate and detailed images. This is important given the imaginal problems that many children report.

Clinical and research applications

The following case illustration of emotive imagery is adapted from Lazarus and Abramovitz (1962, p. 192):

> The client, a 14-year-old-boy, suffered from an intense fear of dogs which had lasted for $2\frac{1}{2}$-3 years. He would take two buses on a roundabout route to school rather than risk exposure to dogs on a direct 300-yard walk. He was rather a dull (IQ = 93), sluggish person, very large for his age, trying to be cooperative, but sadly unresponsive—especially to attempts at training in relaxation. Training in relaxation was eventually abandoned, and an attempt was made to establish the nature of his aspirations and goals. By dint of much questioning and after following many false trails because of his inarticulateness, a topic was eventually tracked down that was absorbing enough to form the subject of his fantasies, namely, racing motor-cars. He had a burning ambition to own a certain Alfa Romeo sports car and race it at the Indianopolis 500. Emotive imagery was induced as follows: 'Close your eyes. I want you to imagine, clearly and vividly, that your wish has come true. The Alfa Romeo is now in your possession. It is your car. It is standing in the street outside your house. You are looking at it now. Notice the beautiful sleek lines. You decide to go for a drive with some friends of yours. You sit down at the wheel, and you feel a thrill of pride as you realize that you own this magnificent machine. You start up and listen to the wonderful roar of the exhaust. You let the clutch in and the car streaks off. You are out in a clear open road now; the car is performing like a pedigree; the speedometer is climbing into the nineties; you have a wonderful feeling of being in perfect control; you look at trees whizzing by and you see a little dog standing next to one of them—if you feel any anxiety, just raise your finger. ...'
> An item fairly high up on the hierarchy was: 'You stop at a cafe in a little town, and dozens of people crowd around to look enviously at this magnificent car and its lucky owner; you swell with pride; and at this moments a large boxer comes up and sniffs at your heels. If you feel any anxiety. ...'
>
> After three sessions with this method, the client reported a marked improvement in his reaction to dogs. He was given a few field assignments during the next two sessions, after which therapy was terminated. Twelve months later, reports received from both the patient and his relatives indicated that there was no longer any trace of his former phobia.

Lazarus and Abramovitz (1962) applied emotive imagery to 9 phobic children aged between 7 and 14 years in this study. Seven children recovered in a mean of only 3.3 sessions The method failed with one child who refused to cooperate and who later revealed widespread areas of disturbance, which required broader therapeutic handling. The other failure was a phobic child with a history of encephalitis. He was unable to concentrate on the imagery and could not enter into the spirit of the 'game'. Since the early work of Lazarus and Abramowitz, several more case studies using emotive imagery have been reported by Lazarus and his colleagues (Lazarus, 1971; Lazarus, Davison & Polefka, 1965).

Jackson and King (1981) employed emotive imagery in the treatment of a $5\frac{1}{2}$-year-old boy with a phobia of darkness. He was also afraid of noises and shadows associated with the night, which caused many sleepness nights for the child and family. The phobia seemed to have been caused by a frightening incident involving a prowler breaking into the house. The boy's mother was asked to keep a record of her son's behaviour at night following a particular coding system, so that treatment could be evaluated. Systematic desensitization was attempted, using a 19-item anxiety hierarchy, but this appeared too difficult for the boy to manage. As the parents lacked confidence in their ability to act as therapeutic agents in an *in vivo* desensitization programme, emotive imagery was decided on. The anxiety hierarchy constructed for the purpose of systematic desensitization was adopted for emotive imagery. The boy was also given a flashlight to enhance treatment effects and develop positive coping skills. In view of the boy's great interest in Batman, he was asked to imagine that he had joined forces with Batman as a special agent. The following transcript illustrates the build-up of the imagery and the introduction of anxiety-provoking items. Following Rosenstiel and Scott's recommendations, the child's active involvement in the treatment (shown here in italic) is also evident:

> Close your eyes—now I want you to imagine that you are sitting in the lounge room watching TV with your family. You're dressed for bed and the last program before bedtime has finished. Your mother tells you it's time for bed but just then Batman who you really wish you knew, appears out of nowhere and sits down next to you. Think about it as best you can. Can you see Batman in your head?
>
> *Yes.*
>
> Can you tell me what Batman's wearing?
> What color are his clothes?
>
> *He's got black and red clothes and big shoes and a gun.*
>
> Oh, you can see him with a gun?
>
> *Yeah he needs it for the Joker.*
>
> That's terrific M. Now I want you to imagine that Batman tells you he needs you on his mission to catch robbers and other bad people and he's appointed you as his special agent. However, he needs you to get your sleep in your bedroom and he will call on you when he needs you. You're lucky to have been chosen to help him.
>
> *Yes.*
>
> Now your mother puts you in your bed and leaves both the lights on and leaves the three blinds up. Batman is also there looking as strong as he always does. Think about it as clearly as you can. Can you see it?
>
> *Yes, I can see mummy and Batman in my room and all the lights are on.*
>
> Well if you're scared raise your finger
> (p. 327)

Altogether there were four sessions of emotive imagery. At the completion of treatment the boy was free of his phobia and slept soundly through the night. An 18-month follow-up revealed that treatment gains had been maintained. Because of the use of the flashlight, however, the positive treatment outcome cannot be attributed solely to emotive imagery.

Chudy, *et al.* (1983) applied emotive imagery in the treatment of a 7-year-old boy with a dog phobia. The subject's phobia was induced by a traumatic incident with a German Shepherd dog. Interestingly, the parents attempted to deal with the problem by buying their son a puppy. However, the puppy unintentionally scratched the child, thus making him more fearful. The child became reluctant to leave the house or yard to play with his peers. As judged by the boy's performance in a BAT, his reaction was too severe for *in vivo* desensitization. A graduated hierarchy of 10 scenes involving dogs was developed at home jointly by the father and his son. Initially, muscle relaxation was attempted for use as a competing response but proved too difficult for the subject (moving and fidgeting). Emotive imagery was then chosen using a fantasy called 'Super Johnny' (after the subject's name). Super Johnny was an omnipotent fearless individual from outer-space who had an arsenal of self-defence devices. However, the subject became bored in the two sessions which attempted to interweave Super Johnny into the imaginal scenes.

At this point an interesting strategy was pursued. When he felt only excessive fear in imagining the scenes, he was permitted to play out how Super Johnny would handle the situation (real dogs not involved). The transformation to Super Johnny was fairly elaborate, and involved the subject putting on a cape and drinking a 'power-inducing potion'. Following the transformation and play, the subject tackled the imaginal scene as Super Johnny with his imaginal weapons. The subject was then instructed to imagine the same scene again as himself but employing the adaptive behaviours modelled by Super Johnny. The subject successfully completed the hierarchy in eight sessions. This modified form of desensitization and emotive imagery was very successful in overcoming the child's dog phobia as measured by the number of times the child left the house unaccompanied and the frequency of social contacts with peers. A 15-month follow-up over a 3-day period indicated that he could still make unaccompanied excursions. According to the parents, he was still cautious of dogs, but no longer phobic of them.

Discussion

Despite the fact that emotive imagery with phobic children was reported in the early 1960s (Lazarus & Abramovitz, 1962), it has not been subject to intensive research investigation. Moreover, Sherman (1973) has raised an interesting point with respect to emotive imagery. He states:

> Emotive imagery can deeply involve children in stories since play activities and fantasies are very real to youngsters. However, there is a puzzling aspect of the mechanisms presumed to underlie the emotive imagery method: why is it that the youngster, when he encounters the feared situation in reality, does not discriminate between the unrealistic fantasies in which he is alone without his Alfa Romeo or the help of his best friend, Superman?
>
> Has he learned to imagine that these supports are with him when he encounters the feared objects in real life? If so, this would seem to create more problems than it resolves. Instead, it seems the child is expected to discriminate between the imagined and the real events with respect to the fantasied supports, but not with

respect to the phobic features (Sherman, 1971). This aspect of the child's cognitive experience in emotive imagery therapy would appear to be quite complex and worthy of further study. (pp. 71–2)

These problems not with standing, the results of the few case studies involving the use of emotive imagery in the treatment of phobic children are quite encouraging. It also appears that emotive imagery is very acceptable to children and their families, and is fairly economical in terms of the amount of time involved. It is to be hoped that well-controlled research will be undertaken to establish its efficacy.

FLOODING AND IMPLOSIVE THERAPY

Rationale and procedures

Systematic desensitization and emotive imagery are phobia-reduction techniques that entail a graduated approach and an anxiety inhibitor (e.g. muscular relaxation, strong positive affect). The exposures to anxiety-provoking items are fairly brief and not too frightening. Consequently, the child undergoing treatment experiences little distress in overcoming the phobia. An alternative approach to phobia reduction is to expose the child to the most threatening aspects of the phobic situation. Flooding and implosive therapy are treatment procedures of this nature.

Flooding involves exposing the child to full-intensity phobic stimuli for prolonged durations. According to Marshall, Gauthier and Gordon (1979):

> Flooding is a generic term for procedures that have as their goal the extinction of classes of maladaptive responses to aversive stimuli by exposure to high-intensity subsets of these aversive stimuli for prolonged periods in the absence of actual physically injurious consequences. (p. 215)

The rationale of flooding was orginally based on two-factor learning theory and extinction. Accordingly, a conditioned fear response can be extinguished by repeatedly presenting the stimuli that elicit that response, in the absence of traumatic or aversive events. However, there are other explanations of flooding. Physiological habituation may be an important process. According to Lader and Mathews (1968), habituation is facilitated under conditions of low arousal. Flooding may exhaust the capacity for arousal so that a minimal anxiety state is finally induced. Similarly, Rachman (1969) notes that it is as if the subject is brought to a point of rapid habituation by first exhausting his capacity for emotional arousal.

Flooding has several important features (i.e. stimulus aspects, exposure duration and response aspects) (Marshall *et al.*, 1979). Stimuli can be presented in three modes: imaginal, representational (e.g. pictures, toys), and real-life. Real-life exposures seem to have been preferred with children. With respect to exposure duration, it is recommended that clinicians make length of exposure a function of the subject's responses. Rather than exposures being limited to a set time (e.g. 20 minutes), exposures should continue until the child's phobic reaction has dissipated. Should the development of coping skills be considered an important part of treatment, the duration of exposure can be extended in order that the child works on the development of the appropriate coping skills. In relation to response aspects, the allowed responses during treatment need to be clarified. The child's initial reaction is usually one of extreme distress. However, the child is prevented from avoiding the aversive stimuli by either physical or instructional means (response prevention). Although response prevention seems to be the preferred way of operating, a possible alternative is 'response freedom'. Here the child is allowed to avoid, but such behaviour does not terminate the phobic stimuli. A dog-phobic child might during flooding, for example, avoid a certain dog but immediately be encountered by another dog. Although the child's avoidance behaviour is blocked, the child's behavioural repertoire may range from extreme passivity to active coping. Hence the role of the therapist or mediator is in need of clarification. There are, of course, varying degrees of involvement in terms of encouragement, suggestions about coping and verbal praise for performance accomplishments.

Implosive therapy was developed by Stampfl and his associates (Stampfl & Levis, 1967, 1968). In this procedure the clinician asks the child to imagine being in the phobic situation, and suffering the worst possible consequences of the experience. As with flooding, the intent is to eliminate avoidance behaviour by the process of extinction. According to Stampfl and Levis (1967):

> The fundamental hypothesis is that a sufficient condition for the extinction of anxiety is to re-present, reinstate, or symbolically reproduce the stimuli (cues) to which the anxiety response has been conditioned, in the absence of primary reinforcement. (pp. 498–9)

Following assessment of the child, hypotheses are generated by the therapist concerning the important 'cues' (stimuli) of the child's phobia. A hierarchy of scenes is constructed by the therapist on the basis of these hypothesized cues. This is referred to as the 'avoidance series cue hierarchy'. Many of the cues are situational or environmental ('symptom-contingent cues'). In the case of a child with a darkness phobia, such cues may include the intensity of darkness and hearing a noise in the dark. Other cues represent internal representations of the phobia ('hypothesized-sequential cues'). For the child with a darkness phobia, this may entail what the child fears might happen (stranger entering room) and the resulting consequences (being harmed). These cues are thought to be related to a number of dynamic themes (i.e. aggression and hostility, oral and anal activity, sexual activity, punishment, rejection, bodily injury, loss of impulse control and guilt). Although implosive therapy involves a hierarchical order in terms of symptom-contingent cues followed by the hypothesized-sequential cues, this should not be confused with the anxiety hierarchy constructed for systematic desensitization. The avoidance serial cue hierarchy consists only of scenes that produce maximum anxiety.

Numerous attempts have been made to differentiate flooding and implosive therapy. Morganstern (1973) notes that flooding is a procedure in which 'intense stimuli are simply presented for an extended period of time', while implosive procedures 'expose patients to unrealistic, but horrifying and vivid scenes related to the phobic stimuli' (p. 320). For Levis (1974) the inclusion of cues related to the dynamic aspects of the problem is crucial. Psychodynamic areas are addressed depending upon the case. Bandura (1969) concluded that the 'adverse consequences' in implosive imagery constitute its distinguishing characteristic. Despite the difference(s) between flooding and implosive therapy, both techniques have in common the principle of confronting the child with high-intensity stimulation (Marshall *et al.*, 1979).

Clinical and research applications

The use of flooding and implosive therapy with phobic children is not well-researched. The reason for this is probably due to the fact that most parents are unwilling to allow their children to undergo such an anxiety-provoking procedure. For whatever reason, only a few case reports of flooding and implosive therapy with phobic children appear in the literature. Yule, Sacks and Hersov (1974) used flooding with an 11-year-old boy (Bill) afraid of sudden, loud noises (balloons bursting, cap-guns being fired, motor cycles and pneumatic drills). Systematic desensitization *in vivo* was pursued, but was only partially successful. At a 9-month follow-up, Bill was still afraid of balloons. Thus, 2 sessions of *in vivo* flooding was employed:

> The therapist explained that the treatment would be unpleasant for a short time, but despite this Bill wanted to try it. After settling him in a very small room, the door was opened and about 50 fully inflated balloons were taken in. He was obviously scared by this. He cowered into his chair, started to sweat and shake, and put his fingers into his ears. He refused to burst any balloons himself, so the therapist burst half a dozen. In the confined space, the noise was unpleasant. Bill started to cry, but the therapist continued bursting balloons until he (Bill) no longer flinched.
>
> After much persuasion, Bill used his feet to push balloons against a nail held by the therapist. In rapid succession, 20 were burst in this fashion, and Bill no longer flinched. Next, following further verbal pressure, he agreed to burst one by hand, whilst keeping the other hand covering one ear. Immediately, about 30 more were presented in quick succession. Lastly, he was persuaded to burst about six while both ears were uncovered.
>
> At this stage, the first session was terminated. In one and a half hours approximately 220 balloons had been burst. The patient was a little shaken by the experience, but agreed to return the next afternoon for a second session.
>
> The second session was started by surrounding Bill with 100 to 150 balloons, and telling him to burst them. Initially he was still anxious, but energetic verbal persuasion coupled with actual prompting (i.e. moving his hand to the balloon, and gradually withdrawing adult pressure) soon had him bursting the balloons with occasional signs that he was actually enjoying the experience.
>
> This session lasted 45 min, and by the end of it he was bursting balloons next to his uncovered ears, bursting them with his bare hands, and stamping on them

in a determined fashion. During this second session, 320 balloons were dispatched. The total cost of balloons for the two sessions was £4.50. (p. 210)

Twenty-five months after the flooding sessions, Bill was found to be immune to the noises that previously had disturbed him. Given the failure of systematic desensitization, the use of flooding was felt to be justified in this case.

Sreenivasan, Manocha and Jain (1979) were also successful in the use of flooding with an 11-year-old dog-phobic girl (Colleen) for whom systematic desensitization had been only partially successful. Colleen's reaction and progress during the six flooding sessions was described as follows:

> For the first session, Colleen was apprehensive for several hours before. On arrival in the treatment room she was anxiously scanning the area for the dog. When the dog was led in she froze, visibly paled and her pupils were dilated. Staff talked reassuringly to Colleen, but when the dog was freed she jumped on a chair. She cried and pleaded that the dog should be placed on its leash. Gradually she relaxed slightly but stayed on the chair, becoming anxious and entreating if the dog moved towards the chair. Two of the staff played table tennis and tried unsuccessfully to persuade Colleen to join them. In the second session she was equally anxious but would get down from the chair or table she stood on for a few seconds but was never at ease. Prior to the third session Colleen appeared excited, although she expressed fear and dislike of the sessions. She managed to take part in the table tennis game for brief periods, sitting on the table if the dog ambled towards the table. In the fourth session she could pat the dog if it was not facing her. In the sixth session she tolerated the dog in her lap, and then took the dog for a walk holding the leash to the amazement of her parents who happened to arrive. After this, she was able to take the family pet for a walk and then to go for a drive with the puppy in the car. She spent a weekend at home without the puppy having to be isolated and was discharged from the inpatient unit at the end of May, 1977, 7 weeks after admission. (pp. 257–8)

Sellick and Peck (1981) report the use of flooding with a 2-year-old boy, diagnosed as having cerebral palsy following a history of severe fetal distress. The boy displayed an intense fear of situations where direct physical support was not provided, such as being placed on the floor, in the bath, or sitting in a high chair. As part of behavioural assessment, the mother exposed the child to a range of situations associated with the phobia and recorded his reactions. This facilitated the construction of a hierarchy (see Table 4.5), as well as desensitizing the mother to the proposed flooding programme. Items 2 and 3 on the hierarchy were selected as the target situations, and the mother was issued with the following instructions:

(1) Place the child in situation 2 or 3 and leave him alone.
(2) When he stops crying, go in and sit with him.
(3) If he cries when you return to the room or before the 10 seconds, then leave the room and repeat the procedure.

The mother was instructed to give her child two treatment sessions per day, alternating between situations 2 and 3. Because of an unexpected illness there was a 10-week delay in the programme after flooding before situations 2 and 3 had been completed. In the second phase of treatment, item 1 on the

Table 4.5 Hierarchy of phobic situations

Situations	Mean fear intensity as rated by mother (1–5 rating scale)
(1) Sitting in bath with support	3.3
(2) Sitting on floor alone with support	3.0
(3) Lying on floor alone	3.0
(4) Lying on floor with mother present	3.0
(5) Sitting on floor with support and mother present	2.3
(6) Lying in bath with support	2.3
(7) Sitting on floor between mother's legs	1.6
(8) Sitting in high-chair	1.0
(9) Sitting on top of mother's bed	0.6
(10) Lying on top of mother's bed	0.3
(11) Sitting on mother's lap on floor	0.3

hierarchy was selected as the target situation. Instructions similar to those previously issued were given to the mother. Because a bathing situation was involved, however, she did not have to leave the room.

The flooding procedure was successful in overcoming the child's phobia. Interestingly, situations 9, 10 and 11 on the hierarchy extinguished during baseline. The child's reaction to the early part of treatment dealing with situations 2 and 3 was extremely severe. As can be seen from Fig. 4.3, the initial phobic responses lasted 40–50 minutes. Early reactions included crying, fear responses and falling asleep exhausted. By the seventh day the child settled spontaneously in both situations, played happily on his own and moved freely around the floor. In relation to phobic situation 1, it took the child 10 minutes to settle down on the first day of treatment. (see Fig. 4.4). However, after 3 days

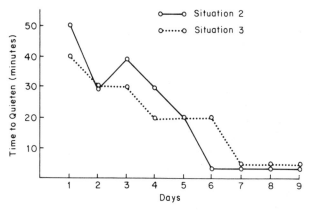

Fig. 4.3 Duration of fear response in phobic situations 2 and 3. Reproduced from Sellick and Peck (1981) by permission of the American Congress of Rehabilitation Medicine.

124

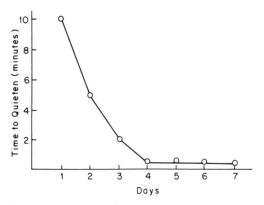

Fig. 4.4 Duration of fear response in phobic situation 1. Reproduced from Sellick and Peck (1981) by permission of the American Congress of Rehabilitation Medicine.

of treatment, there were no signs of distress, with the child playing in the bath for up to 60 minutes. Follow-up meetings with the mother at two, three and six months indicated that the treatment gains had been maintained.

An illustration of the way in which implosive therapy might be used in the treatment of children's phobias is provided by Ollendick and Gruen (1972). The case involved an 8-year-old boy (Tommy) with a severe body-injury phobia of some 3 year's duration. The phobia was expressed in the behavioral symptoms of sleepless nights, hives and asthmatic bronchitis. Tommy was seen for only two sessions of implosive therapy separated by 1 week. During each session he was asked to imagine as vividly as possible scenes involving the hypothesized anxiety-arousing cues. The following scenes were typical of those presented during the two sessions:

(1) You are alone walking through a forest going to a lake to fish and you hear weird noises and see strange things.
(2) The wind begins blowing very hard and you trip and hit your head on a rock.
(3) When you get up, blood trickles down your forehead into your eyes, nose, and mouth.
(4) You feel dizzy and lost. You cry and no one is there to help you. You feel all alone and the blood continues to trickle.
(5) You fall down again and when you open your eyes you see brown, hairy rats all around you. There are hundreds of them and they are coming after you ... to eat you.
(6) They begin nibbling at your feet, biting your toes, and pulling them off. They are scratching and showing their teeth. It is getting very dark now and it is raining.
(7) Now they are over your whole body, running across it, and biting you all over. Blood runs from all parts of your body and you hear the thunder and there is lightning.
(8) They pierce your neck. You wish someone would come, even an ambulance, but it doesn't. You scream and a big, hairy rat jumps in your mouth. You feel him biting your tongue and scratching you.

(9) Finally, the rats that feed on your blood grow and become man-size. They tear off your arms and just keep attacking you. They tear out your eyes and you can't get away from them. (p. 391)

Tommy was required to imagine each scene until a visible reduction in anxiety had occurred. At the conclusion of both sessions, Tommy was reassured that he was all right and given some brief relaxation training. Following two sessions of implosive therapy, the number of sleepless nights diminished from five to seven per week to two per week. In addition, there was no recurrence of hives or asthmatic bronchitis during treatment nor at the 6-month follow-up.

Discussion

In general, authorities have been fairly critical of the use of flooding and implosive therapy with children. Graziano (1975) points out that ethical and humanitarian issues are involved in the deliberate and repeated frightening of children, and emphasizes that the child does not have the option of disengaging therapy that an adult has in flooding and implosive therapy. Gelfand (1978) maintains that the treatment setting may become so aversive that the child may refuse to engage or cooperate in subsequent treatment sessions. Marshall, Gauthier, Christie, Currie and Gordon (1977) warn that a person's fear may possibly be *strengthened* by imaginal exposures to extremely frightening and horrifying situations. This would seem to be of real concern in working with children. Morris and Kratochwill (1983) urge that flooding and implosive therapy be used with caution. They emphasize the need for a sound client–therapist relationship so that the anxiety-provoking experience will be associated with the phobic stimulus and not with the therapist. As noted by Morris and Kratochwill: 'The therapist must also be capable of dealing with a child who might have a very negative experience to the anxiety-provoking scenes that are presented' (p. 167). Given the aversive nature of flooding and implosive therapy, combined with the fact that most parents object to their children receiving such treatment, these particular phobia-reduction techniques should be given low priority in clinical practice.

SUMMARY

In this chapter we have commenced our discussion of behavioural methods used in the treatment of children's phobias. Several techniques have been examined; based upon classical conditioning principles, their aim is to overcome conditioned fear responses through counter-conditioning and extinction.

In pioneering work carried out in the 1920s and 30s, an historical landmark was M. C. Jones' treatment of a small boy's fear of a white rabbit using a graduated approach to the feared stimulus (food) whenever the rabbit was shown.

Systematic desensitization has been the traditional method of treating phobias, and consists of three steps: (1) relaxation training (noting scripts for children),

(2) development of the anxiety hierarchy, and (3) systematic desensitization proper (the client relaxes and imagines the aversive scenes introduced in a graduated manner). The need for anxiety inhibitors other than relaxation has been emphasized, especially for young children, along with preference for real-life exposures. Although there is disagreement about the mechanism (Wolpe thought it was reciprocal inhibition), systematic desensitization remains a particularly useful technique in the treatment of children's phobias. Emotive imagery is a variant of systematic desensitization. Basically, positive emotional feelings are induced by a story concerning a favourite hero; when the clinician is satisfied that a positive affect has been established the phobic stimulus is gradually interwoven. Several case illustrations of emotive imagery have been presented here, but as yet a solid research foundation is lacking.

Flooding and implosive therapy require the child to confront the phobic stimulus at its maximum or near-maximum strength. The flooding procedure can be analysed in terms of stimulus aspects, exposure duration and response aspects. Usually, flooding is carried out in vivo with the child being prevented from avoiding the feared situation. Implosive therapy requires the child to imagine being in the phobic situation into which symptom-contingent cues are introduced by the therapist. Horrifying and vivid scenes with dynamic themes (e.g. aggression and hostility, oral and anal activity) frequently characterize implosion. Numerous authorities have been critical of the use of flooding and implosive therapy with children; concerns about these procedures centre on the aversive nature of the intervention and possible implications for the child. In addition, they are in need of considerable research before their routine use can be endorsed (Ollendick, 1986).

CHAPTER 5

Contingency management, modelling, cognitive procedures and self-control

INTRODUCTION

The previous chapter examined the role of systematic desensitization, emotive imagery, flooding and implosion in overcoming children's phobias. The use of these procedures is predicated upon the assumption that a high level of physiological arousal is the crucial feature of the child's phobic reaction and that the child's phobia was directly conditioned. The aim of the present chapter is to review contingency management, modelling, cognitive procedures and self-control. As will become evident, these procedures are based on different theoretical under-pinnings and do not necessarily hypothesize directly conditioned fears. Each technique will be described in terms of its rationale and procedure, and clinical and research applications, with a brief comment on the status of the technique in clinical practice. Consistent with the previous chapter, these therapeutic procedures will be discussed in relation to the specific maladaptive fears or phobias of childhood.

CONTINGENCY MANAGEMENT

Rationale and procedures

Contingency management, involves a number of treatment procedures derived from the principles of operant conditioning. From an operant perspective, an individual operates on the environment (hence 'operant'), emitting an action to which the environment reacts. The environment's reaction to the individual's response is crucial in terms of whether the response is likely to be repeated under similar circumstances. Thus, consequences of behaviour are basic in contingency management procedures.

Because of the emphasis on overt behaviour and its relationship with the environment, operant researchers and clinicians have little time for the notions of 'anxiety' and 'phobic reactions'. It is believed that these terms refer to constructs that cloud the basic issue of changing overt, avoidant behaviours. As Morris and Kratochwill (1983) have illustrated, one has only to refer to the *Journal of Applied Behavior Analysis* to confirm this notion. This is a well-known journal, specializing in operant-based interventions and related issues. Since its inception, very few articles have carried titles involving such terms as 'fear' or 'phobia'. However, closer inspection of the content suggests that fears and phobias are being addressed in many studies (e.g. Stokes & Kennedy, 1980). Leaving aside the conflict over theoretical models and terminology, it must be stressed that operant procedures have a valuable role to play in overcoming children's phobias (Morris & Kratochwill, 1983). Positive reinforcement, shaping and extinction have been selected for more detailed discussion here.

Reinforcement

Reinforcement occurs when an event that follows a behaviour increases the likelihood of that behaviour occurring again, or the intensity with which it is performed (Deese & Hulse, 1967). The event concerned is called a 'reinforcer'. The definition is empirical in that reinforcement only occurs when there has been an increase in the frequency of the behaviour. Should the event have no impact upon a behaviour, then the particular event does not qualify as a reinforcer. The reinforcer is said to be 'contingent' upon the behaviour because the individual has to perform the behaviour before receiving the reinforcement. There are two types of reinforcement, positive and negative (Rimm & Masters, 1974). In positive reinforcement, the individual receives an event following the performance of a behaviour. A simple example is the instance of a coach praising a child for executing a correct tennis serve. Consistent with the empirical definition of reinforcement, the coach's praise must increase the probability of the good serve being performed to qualify as a positive reinforcer. In negative reinforcement, an unpleasant or aversive event is terminated following the performance of some behaviour. For example, take the behaviour of loosening one's tight shoes in order to terminate pain. Here relief from pain is the negative reinforcer. Again, consistent with the empirical definition of reinforcement, the termination of pain must increase the probability of the person loosening his shoes when his feet hurt. Positive and negative reinforcement both have the same impact upon behaviour in that they increase the likelihood of the behaviour occurring again. The terms 'positive' and 'negative' indicate whether the reinforcer is added (positive) or subtracted (negative). Parenthetically, negative reinforcement and punishment should not be confused. Reinforcement, positive or negative, increases the probability of a behaviour being performed, while punishment decreases its probability.

In overcoming childhood phobias, positive reinforcement is the most relevant. The basic problem is seen to be one of low-frequency behaviour with respect to how often the child engages in the desired behaviour. In the case of an animal-phobic child, the difficulty is seen as the low frequency with which the child appropriately encounters a dog or cat. For the test-anxious child, the problem is the low frequency of sitting tests and examinations. The challenge is to increase the likelihood of the child encountering the feared object or situation using positive reinforcement. After an appropriate encounter with an animal or sitting a test, the child might be given a special reward and praise. Of course, it could be argued that positive reinforcement is an integral part of most therapeutic interventions. Consider, for example, the eye contact, smiling and verbal praise of the therapist during systematic desensitization. Whether these behaviours are positive reinforcers in the true sense can only be determined empirically. In the use of positive reinforcement, it should also be emphasized that there is a great deal more to consider than the occasional use of social reinforcement. A number of general guidelines should be observed in the administration of reinforcers. The following guidelines are adapted from several sources (Spiegler, 1983; Sulzer-Azaroff & Mayer, 1977):

(1) The target behaviour needs to be clearly specified so that there is no doubt as to when the reinforcer should be applied.
(2) The therapist should consider what is reinforcing to the child. Given individual differences as to what is reinforcing, the therapist should carefully select the reinforcer in terms of what is appropriate for the particular child. The major categories of reinforces include edible, activity, possessional and social.
(3) The reinforcer must follow the target behaviour. In other words, reinforcement must be contingent upon performing the target behaviour. Should the reinforcer be given before the target behaviour has been performed, the therapeutic purpose of the reinforcer will be lost.
(4) The child should be aware that the reinforcer is a consequence of the target behaviour. This guideline is important when the child has performed several behaviours in close succession. The child can be informed of the relationship between the reinforcer and target behaviour (e.g. 'You kept your mouth open for the dentist... that was very good.').
(5) The reinforcer should be administered immediately after the target behaviour has been performed. Immediate reinforcement is generally more effective than delayed reinforcement. Because of practical limitations, however, the reinforcer may have to be delayed. Sometimes token reinforcers are administered under these circumstances. At a later stage the tokens are exchanged for a reward chosen by the individual.
(6) Continuous reinforcement should be used first and then followed by intermittent reinforcement. Continuous reinforcement refers to those cases in which the child receives a reinforcer every time he or she performs the target behaviour. Intermittent reinforcement involves the provision of a reinforcer for some, but not all, of the instances in which the target behaviour is performed. Continuous reinforcement is superior to intermittent reinforcement in the acquisition or initial acceleration of target behaviour. However, once the target behaviour is being performed at a reasonable frequency, intermittent reinforcement keeps the child performing the target behaviour.

(7) Reinforcers should be kept potent. Numerous procedures have been tried to maintain the potency of reinforcers. One procedure is to ensure that the reinforcer is only available to the child as a direct consequence of performing the target behaviour. Another procedure is to deprive the child temporarily of the reinforcer before treatment. Administering edible reinforcers in small amounts also helps to avoid satiation. Another tactic is to use several different reinforcers.

(8) Naturally occurring reinforcers are preferable to 'contrived' reinforcers. In order to ensure long-term maintenance of target behaviours, it is desirable to employ naturally occurring reinforcers from the outset. When 'contrived' reinforcers have to be used, it is recommended that natural reinforcers be used conjointly. The contrived reinforcers can be faded from the treatment programme with the natural reinforcers taking over in the maintenance of the target behaviour.

(9) Reinforcement should be administered consistently. It is crucial that all reinforcing agents are consistent in their application of reinforcers. It can, of course, become very confusing to the child when reinforcement is forthcoming from one person but not others for the same behaviour. To ensure that reinforcers will be administered consistently and properly (i.e. following the other guidelines), the therapist needs to consult with people who will be reinforcing the child.

Shaping

Shaping is another important contingency management procedure that can be used to overcome children's phobias. When avoidance behaviour is so extreme on the part of the phobic child that the feared object/situation is never encountered or rarely encountered, it is difficult to rely on positive reinforcement. The dilemma for the practitioner is that too few opportunities present themselves for positive reinforcement to be feasible. For example, the child who hardly visits the dentist would be problematic in terms of increasing the frequency of cooperative behaviour in dental surgery. Forcing the severely phobic child into the feared situation in order to administer positive reinforcement is unsatisfactory. Such efforts usually produce uncooperative behaviour (if not panic) and social embarrassment for all concerned, thus mitigating attempts at positive reinforcement. Under these circumstances, the therapist can institute a shaping procedure. Shaping is defined as the successive reinforcement of closer approximations to the terminal behaviour. Shaping is often referred to as the 'method of successive approximations' (Martin & Pear, 1983). In overcoming children's phobias, the therapist begins with a task that elicits very little distress, and gradually works up to the desired behaviour. Because of the graduated approach, there is a good chance of cooperation on the part of the child (and reinforcing agents). In shaping a child's cooperative dental behaviour, for instance, the child might be reinforced for each of the following sequential steps—visiting the waiting room, meeting the dentist's receptionist, meeting the dentist, examining the dental surgery, handling some of the instruments, sitting in the dental chair, sitting in the dental chair and allowing the dentist to conduct an examination, and so forth. This may remind the reader of systematic desensitization because of the graduated steps in leading up to the desired behaviour. The significant procedural difference is that in systematic desensitization an anxiety inhibitor is used, while in shaping the therapist relies upon reinforcement. Shaping is an extremely valuable behavioural method, because of its clinical usefulness in establishing competencies necessary for coping with many feared objects/situations. For the test-anxious child, a shaping procedure could be used to develop good study habits and examination skills. In the case of animal-phobic children, there is immense potential for the development of verbal and non-verbal animal-handling skills via shaping.

Ollendick and Cerny (1981) lament the fact that, while shaping procedures are often employed in behavioural programmes, there is a dearth of research dealing with the systematic application of shaping procedures. In the absence of research-based guidelines, Ollendick and Cerny offer a set of tentative guidelines for the practitioner. The guidelines are consistent with those described in the use of positive reinforcement. Of particular interest are their comments on the length of training sessions, and at what stage to progress on to the next step. Ollendick and Cerny's guidelines are as follows:

(1) Clearly specify the target behavior in objectively defined terms.
(2) At each step of the program, establish response requirements small enough to assure successful performance. Gelfand and Hartmann (1975) suggest an 80% reinforcement ratio to attempts; however, some investigators report success with rates of reinforcement as low as 66% (Horner & Keilitz, 1975) whereas most studies use a 100% reinforcement ratio to attempts.
(3) Choose potent reinforcers that are easily delivered and topographically compatible with the target responses.
(4) Choose (for reinforcement) an initial behavior that has a relatively high probability of occurring and is in some way approximate to the terminal response.
(5) Arrange the shaping situation in order to maximize the probability of the target behaviors occurring and to minimize the probability of distracting stimuli or competing behaviors.
(6) Assure reinforcement delivery as close as possible to the response.
(7) Establish and use secondary reinforcers whenever possible. Secondary reinforcers are generally more convenient to use in shaping programs and would seem, logically, to enhance generalization effects.
(8) Keep training sessions short enough to avoid fatigue, reinforcer satiation, and so on, but long enough to ensure at least several approximations of the target response(s). The experimental literature is generally ambiguous on the question of massed training trials versus spaced training trials; overall, it appears that subjects learn new behaviors under both conditions of training and that other factors, for example, the amount of effort required for a response, are more important (Hulse, Deese, & Egeth, 1975). Consequently, length of training sessions and time between sessions should be determined with reference to the type of response being shaped, the attention span of the child, the availability of the trainer, the frequency of the behavior, and so on. In our experience, several shorter sessions per day are preferable to one long session.
(9) Move to the successive steps in the shaping program only when the preceding step is consistently and successfully performed. If a child is performing the component behavior on 80% to 90% of attempts, it is probably time to move on to the next

step in the program. Although 100% correct responding may seem desirable, our experience suggests that children fatigue and fail to maintain their focus on the target response if too many repetitions are performed. Since the purpose of the shaping procedure is to establish the terminal response and not the component responses, it makes sense not to have children overlearn the component responses lest they become impediments to learning the terminal response. The overall purpose of the successive approximation strategy is to help ensure success at each step of the program. (pp. 120–1); reproduced by permission of Plenum Publishing Corp.)

Extinction

Extinction is another important contingency management procedure that can be used in the management of phobic children. Extinction refers to a procedure in which the reinforcement of a behaviour is discontinued. If a response has been increased in frequency through positive reinforcement, the cessation of reinforcement will lead to a decrease in the frequency of the response. Sometimes children's phobic reactions are reinforced by parents and others. For example, children with night-time fears are dealt with in various ways, including being allowed to sleep with their parents. The latter activity can be hypothesized to be a fairly strong positive reinforcer. Following the principle of extinction, the parents would be advised to discontinue allowing the child to sleep with them. Some procedural guidelines for the use of extinction are as follows (Martin & Pear, 1983; Sulzer–Azaroff & Mayer, 1977):

(1) The use of extinction assumes that the therapist can identify the nature and source of reinforcement responsible for the maintenance of the phobic behaviour. A clinical judgement must therefore be made on this issue.
(2) In an extinction programme, care providers are being asked to change their behaviour during and after the child's phobic reaction. The therapist should explain to the care provider what is required in as concrete and precise terms as possible.
(3) Depending upon the age of the child, the conditions for extinction can be explained to the child by the care provider. In the case of a child with an excessive fear of darkness that is unintentionally reinforced by overconcerned parents, the parents might state that no attention will be given after lights out except for emergencies.
(4) During the initial stage of extinction, the phobic reaction and disruptive behaviours may get worse before an improvement is observed. Children can be very demanding and aggressive in their response to extinction. There is a danger that parents will lose their patience and give in to the child. Thus, care providers should be forewarned of this problem, and given adequate support and reassurance by the therapist.
(5) During the implementation of an extinction programme, it is essential to control alternative sources of reinforcement. In addition to controlling the identified source of reinforcement, the possibility of other people inadvertently reinforcing the child's behaviour must be considered.

Obviously, the advent of alternative reinforcement would ruin the programme.

(6) The extinction of phobic behaviour can be combined with the positive reinforcement of acceptable and/or adaptive behaviours. The use of positive reinforcement in this way should increase the rate at which the phobic behaviour is weakened. Also, parents and teachers are probably more willing to use extinction when it is combined with something 'positive' they can do to help the child.

Extinction has been found to be an extremely useful means of controlling behaviour, although there are several problems associated with its use (Sulzer–Azaroff & Mayer, 1977). First, the elimination of a response through extinction takes considerable time, which can present problems should the phobic reaction entail danger to the child. Consider, for example, the dog-phobic child who runs on to the street to escape an approaching dog. Should extinction be indicated because of inadvertent parental reinforcement, it would be desirable to employ more efficient means of phobia reduction as well (e.g. real-life desensitization and modelling). Second, the reinforcing consequences of a phobic response are not always easy to identify. At times, reinforcement can be very subtle, especially social reinforcement (e.g. eye contact, a gentle word, smiling, a giggle). Also, a fairly thin schedule of reinforcement can be involved making the identification of the reinforcer even more problematic. Parents can be informed about the subtle and intermittent nature of reinforcement with a view to gaining their full cooperation. In certain cases, it may be possible to have the parents rehearse the implementation of extinction under the supervision of the therapist. Third, there is a possibility of the phobic response reappearing after a successful period of extinction. However, the reappearance of the response is usually transitory. This phenomenon is well known in the learning theory literature, and is referred to as 'spontaneous recovery' (Skinner, 1953). Care providers should be cautioned on this point. A possible scenario is that the care provider(s) may be caught off guard and inadvertently reinforce the child's phobic reaction. In such instances, extinction should be continued with the expectation that the phobia will eventually come under control.

Clinical and research applications

Several case reports have been published on the use of contingency management procedures in overcoming children's phobias. In the treatment of a maladaptive fear of riding a school bus, Luiselli (1978) employed exposure and reinforcement. The subject was a 7-year-old child (Bobby) who also displayed several behaviours characteristic of autism, including stereotyped hand movements, screaming, bizarre vocalizations and echolalia. Except for being toilet trained, Bobby lacked independent self-care skills. Six months prior to the programme, he began attending a public school special education classroom. This required transportation on a bus. Bobby exhibited an intense fear of riding on the school bus.

When his parents asked him to board the bus he cried frantically, fell on the sidewalk, tantrumed excessively, and attempted to run in the house. Providing the bus driver with edibles to give Bobby for getting on the bus proved futile. Consequently, the mother had to drive him to and from school. Fear of attending school was ruled out as no problems were encountered when he was driven to school by his mother.

The early part of treatment aimed at familiarizing Bobby with the physical stimulus of the bus. On day 1, the mother brought Bobby to school several minutes ahead of the bus. When the bus arrived, the therapist, Bobby and his mother sat in the bus for two minutes. In this time, Bobby received praise and edibles for 'riding on the bus'. On day 2, the procedure was repeated. Half-way through the session, the mother left the bus and stood directly beneath Bobby's window. On day 3, Bobby was placed on the bus with the mother remaining outside for the entire session. On day 4, Bobby's mother remained in the car while he was taken on to the bus by the therapist. Half-way through the session, the therapist stood outside the doorway of the bus. At the command 'come to school', Bobby got off the bus and walked into school. In view of the Bobby's good progress, it was felt that Bobby might be capable of riding the bus route from home to school. Initially, his mother boarded the bus at the house, with Bobby and the therapist boarding afterwards. Bobby was immediately given an edible treat by his mother. All three rode the bus to school. Bobby appeared very relaxed over the journey. On day 6, Bobby and the therapist rode the bus without his mother. On the final day of treatment, Bobby was placed on the bus by his mother. He rode the entire distance to school alone. From that point, Bobby was able to board the bus and ride without difficulty.

In a fairly short period of time Bobby's debilitating fear of riding a school bus was overcome. Treatment was actually a combination of graduated exposure and reinforcement (shaping). The mother's presence on the bus seemed to facilitate Bobby's confrontation with the fear stimulus. As Luiselli states: 'She appeared to function as both an anxiety inhibitor and a reinforcing agent' (p. 171). As is obvious, the behavioural methods were quite successful despite the diagnosis of autism. This is important since it is sometimes suggested that emotionally disturbed children do not respond to behavioural programmes.

Luiselli (1977) also reports the use of a contingency mangement programme in the treatment of toileting phobia in a 15-year-old mentally retarded boy (Marty). Marty had been institutionalized in a state school for the mentally retarded at 4 years of age. Marty resided on a ward with six other mentally retarded youths under the care of four attendants. The attendants drew attention to the fact that Marty had started wetting his pants several times a day, and avoided the use of the toilet. When the attendants coaxed Marty to use the toilet, he exhibited a variety of fearful behaviours (e.g. plugging his ears with his fingers, closing his eyes while urinating, making loud gutteral noises). In fact, the mere mention of the words 'bathroom' and 'toilet' elicited hyperventilation and plugging of the ears. After 5 months of coaxing, it became impossible to get Marty to use the toilet. The attendant staff were given special data sheets to record instances of pants wetting. Because of the visible signs of moistness around the frontal part of Marty's slacks, wettings were easily detected. Observations were made over Marty's waking hours every day of the week.

In a 3-week baseline period, attendants recorded the frequency of pants wetting. In a 28-week treatment period, going on special trips with attendants was made contingent upon appropriate use of the toilet. The management of the contingency varied across different treatment conditions. The initial four weeks of treatment involved token reinforcement. Marty was awarded a gold star for urinating in the toilet. When Marty reached a criterion level of stars (the amount of which varied as treatment progressed), he was able to participate in the special activity. Token reinforcement was discontinued for the subsequent 14 weeks, as it was becoming difficult for staff to reinforce every appropriate urination with a star. At this stage, Marty was simply praised for having dry pants. He was reminded that: 'Because you are using the bathroom, you will be able to visit. . . . (name of location)' (p. 285). The next stage of treatment involved one week of self-recording. Marty was taught to make a mark with a pencil on a daily chart whenever he successfully urinated in the toilet. The rationale was to provide Marty with a self-managed, positively conditioned consequence for appropriate toileting. However, staff found that Marty was trying to enter marks indiscriminate of toilet use. The final 10 weeks of treatment entailed intermittent token reinforcements. The stars were reintroduced but on an intermittent basis. The stars could be earned within three time intervals each day, and used to purchase two reinforcing events. A daily earning of three stars enabled Marty to visit the lobby of the building each evening to watch television with an attendant. Second, the usual special outing was contingent upon 18 stars being earned over the week, provided there were no more than three wettings per week. In addition to the aforementioned treatment procedures, whenever Marty did wet his pants he was required to sit by himself in a designated area of the ward for 40 minutes. He was completely ignored during this time. After this period of time was up, he was given dry underwear and slacks. Thus, the programme had a strong negative consequence for pants wetting, as well as the positive reinforcement components.

As can be seen from inspection of Fig. 5.1, Marty averaged nearly 16 pants wettings per week at baseline. The incidence of pants wettings decreased dramatically over treatment to an average of 2.6 per week for that stage of treatment when tokens were delivered on an intermittent basis. At a 4-month follow-up, only one wetting incident was recorded. Six-month and one-year follow ups indicated that pants wetting was absent. The programme, albeit uncontrolled, appeared to be effective in overcoming Marty's toileting phobia. Given that positive and negative treatment procedures were confounded, however, it is impossible to determine the critical treatment factor.

Leitenberg and Callahan (1973) conducted a study to assess the effectiveness of what they called 'reinforced practice' in the reduction of childhood fears. The researchers were particularly interested in whether a common training procedure would overcome these fears even though they may have different origins, course

136

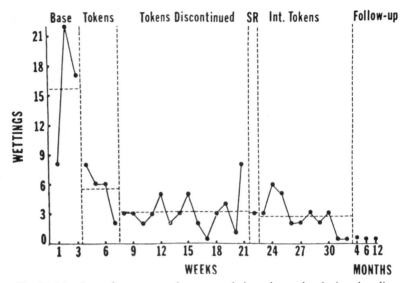

Fig. 5.1 Number of pants wettings recorded each week, during baseline treatment, and follow-up phases. Horizontal dashed lines indicate mean pants wettings. Reproduced from Luiselli (1977) by permission of Blackwell Scientific Publications.

and chronicity. Reinforced practice involved graduated and repeated practice approaching actual phobic stimuli, reinforcement for gains in performance, feedback of measurable progress, and instructions designed to arouse expectations of gradual success. The effectiveness of this procedure was evaluated against an untreated control group in the treatment of darkness fears in children.

Pre-school children served as subjects who at home insisted that some light be on at night in their bedroom, hallway or bathroom. Pre- and post-test measures were taken on how long the children were willing to remain alone in two dark rooms, referred to as the 'outer' and 'inner' rooms. Some light filtered under the door of the outer room, but the inner room was completely dark. The tests were carried out as a game involving a prize (game, trinkets, crayons) for remaining in the dark room without being afraid. Each child was allowed to select a prize after each trial regardless of their performance.

Following the pre-test, 7 pairs of subjects were matched on their pre-test performance in the outer room. One member of each pair was then randomly assigned to the treatment group, and one member to the no-treatment control group. The children in the experimental group received a maximum of 8 treatment sessions, each session consisting of 5 trials (2 sessions per week). Treatment was terminated if a child stayed in the room for 5 minutes on two consecutive trials. The training procedure was as follows:

At the start of the first session, the E explained to the S that he was to go into the outer room, shut the door and stay until he felt the least bit afraid, whereupon he was to come out. He was told he would have a chance to do this a number of times and that he would be able to choose a prize each time he came out if he had stayed in longer than his previous longest time. The concept 'longer' was explained to the Ss by saying that when they were allowed to stay up for one more TV show at night this meant that they were staying up longer.

Only the outer room was used in these training sessions. Aside from a chair which was provided for the child if he wished to sit, there was nothing in the room. Even though you could see a slight light at the bottom of the door, the room was so dark you could not see your fingers when they were approximately 10 inches away from your eyes.

Feedback of exact time spent in the room presented a special problem for this age group. Instead of telling the S his time in terms of minutes and seconds a visual 'thermometer' display was used. The thermometer was drawn on an $8\frac{1}{2} \times 11$ in sheet of paper and marked off in units of 10 sec. After each trial, increases in elapsed time were indicated by shading in with a pencil the increased degrees. The child was also praised for his improvement and allowed to choose a prize. If time decreased from the previous trial, the appropriate degrees of shading were erased, and the child was told he did not do as well this time. When the child reached the criterion of 2 consecutive trials of 5 min, or if 8 sessions had elapsed, the treatment was terminated and the experimental S and his matched control S were post-tested in both the outer room (same room as used in training) and in the inner room (not used in training). (pp. 23–4)

The results of the study are given in Table 5.1. The experimental group evinced a dramatic improvement in their ability to remain in the inner and outer rooms, compared with the control group. On the post-test, four of the seven experimental subjects stayed in the outer room for the maximum time of 5 minutes. An interesting finding was the generalization of improvement that occurred from the outer room to the inner room. Presumably, this was because of the similarity between test conditions and procedures. Unfortunately, Leitenberg and Callahan (1973) do not comment on whether any improvement occurred at home, especially in terms of coping with darkness at night. Follow-up data is also not reported.

Kohlenberg et al. (1972) conducted a study on what they called 'behaviour modification' (really contingency management) with severely mentally retarded patients who were afraid of dental procedures. Seventeen patients, aged 8 to 20, participated in the study. After the first dental appointment, the experimetal group ($n = 9$) received two 45-minute behaviour-modification sessions. Social reinforcement and tangible rewards (juice squirted into the mouth, cards of

Table 5.1 Mean time (in seconds) spent in dark rooms on pre-test and post-test

| | Pre-test | | Post-test | |
	Outer room	Inner room	Outer room	Inner room
Experimental group	34.14	21.71	190.56	198.85
No-treatment control group	33.56	22.14	27.30	27.71

SOURCE: Leitenberg and Callaham (1973). Reproduced by permission of Pergamon Press.

athletes), shaping, and fading, were used to develop good dental chair behaviour (compliance with instructions such as 'sit back in the chair', 'pay attention to the therapist', and 'open and hold your mouth open'). Reinforcement was also thinned out to ensure the maintenance of compliance. Psychology students attired in white coats conducted the behaviour modification sessions. The control group ($n = 8$) received no training but participated in two 45-minute sessions during which they were given juice and other edibles. All of the patients were then scheduled for a second dental appointment. Measures of dental chair behaviour were taken at the first and second dental sessions. Independent observers recorded the amount of time the mouth was open for each patient (forced mouth opening was excluded). The number of physical restraints employed by the dentist were also recorded on the assumption that the frequency of restraints reflects the quality of the patient's behaviour. The results of the experiment are striking in terms of the impact of the contingency management procedures. The experimental group of patients received significantly fewer physical restraining actions than controls. Also, the experimental subjects were significantly better than controls on percentage of time their mouths were open.

Discussion

Given that phobic children are often non-volunteers and do not necessarily have the commitment to change seen in adult phobics, contingency management procedures may prove helpful. Appropriate reinforcers can increase the pay-off value of approach behaviour to the phobic stimulus. However, there appears to be a definite 'public relations' problem associated with contingency management procedures. Sometimes care providers and professionals object to the use of contingency management procedures on 'humanitarian and ethical' grounds. The use of reinforcers such as edibles and stars seems to elicit the most intense reaction.

Possibly the most frequently voiced objection here is that the use of rewards is tantamount to bribery. Of course, there are points that can be made in response to such a challenge. Axelrod (1977) makes the comment that dictionary definitions of bribery incorporate the notion of people being influenced to perform illegal or immoral acts. Obviously, the use of a reinforcement system does not constitute bribery in the strict sense of the word. Rather than argue about the meaning of bribery, however, it can be agreed that the use of reinforcers is artifical and only a temporary form of intervention. With the development of 'self-control' the reinforcement system can be phased out. Of course, people may still disagree with the use of contingency management procedures even after such an explanation. Hence therapists should be sensitive to the different reactions of care providers and professionals when planning to use contingency management.

In view of the demonstratable efficacy of contingency management procedures with children in clinical and educational settings (Marholin, 1978; Ollendick &

Cerny, 1981; Ross, 1981), it is surprising that more research has not been conducted on the power of operant-based procedures with phobic children. Presumably, researchers and clinicians have viewed the phobic problems of children as essentially 'anxiety' in nature, and hence, not suitable for contingency management. However, the little research that has been conducted on the use of contingency management procedures with phobic children is encouraging.

MODELLING

Rationale and procedures

Modelling is a therapeutic procedure derived from an observational learning paradigm. By way of background, it will be appreciated that much of our everyday learning occurs on an observational basis. For example, young children often mimic the mannerisms of people around them. At school, children observe teachers work out solutions to mathematical problems. In physical education classes, children are required to attend closely as a classmate demonstrates a good dive into the pool. Given the obvious importance of observational learning in everyday life, it is not surprising that this kind of learning has been utilized in therapeutic settings. The procedure whereby an individual learns on the basis of observing another is called 'modelling'. Bandura and his associates are credited with the development of therapeutic modelling. For the purpose of the present discussion, modelling is restricted to the notion of the planned and deliberate use of observational learning in therapeutic settings.

At a general level, modelling has three important functions (Bandura, 1969; Bandura & Walters, 1963). First, modelling can have an 'acquisition' function. As a result of observing a model, a person may acquire new response patterns that did not previously exist in the individual's behavioural repertoire. For example, pre-school children develop aggressive behaviours as a result of observing other children display aggressive responses. Second, modelling can have 'inhibitory or disinhibitory effects'. The observation of models may strengthen or weaken inhibitory responses, depending upon the nature of the consequences for the model. A disinhibitory effect occurs when the observer's inhibited behaviour actually becomes more frequent, it being observed that the model has not experienced negative consequences for engaging in the behaviour. As an example of a disinhibitory effect of modelling, a child may jaywalk having witnessed another person jaywalk in the absence of immediate danger or penalty. An inhibitory effect occurs when the person's behaviour becomes less frequent, it being observerd that the model has suffered negative consequences for the action. The child contemplating whether to jaywalk would probably not do so if another person is seen to incur a fine and reprimand by a police officer for this behaviour. Third, modelling can have a 'response facilitation effect' which results in an increase in socially acceptable behaviours. For example, laughter is a response that is often facilitated by 'canned' laughter on television programmes.

Modelling occupies an extremely important place in phobia-reduction procedures because of its usefulness in teaching children various skills. In attempting to reduce the child's 'anxiety' about the fear stimulus, it can be easily overlooked that the child may have a skill deficit in handling the dog or cat, or being able to cope with darkness, water or whatever. This is particularly the case for children who have been avoiding the feared stimulus for many years or who never learned the appropriate skills displayed by non-phobic children. Thus, for many phobic children, avoidance behaviour may be a function of anxiety *and* a skills deficit. In interviewing parents on methods of overcoming fears, Jersild and Holmes (1935b) noted the importance of attempts to promote skill in dealing with the feared stimulus: 'The most effective techniques in overcoming fears are those that *help the child to become more competent and skillful and that encourage him to undertake active dealings with the thing that he fears*' (p. 102). The present authors concur that modelling is an excellent means of developing skills, and helping children overcome feared objects or situations.

From the viewpoint of clinical practice, the therapist must give careful thought to the factors which enhance modelling. An extremely useful checklist of factors

Table 5.2 Factors which enhance modelling

Factors enhancing acquisition (learning and retention)	Factors enhancing performance
Characteristics of the model	*Factors providing incentive for performance*
(1) Similarity in sex, age, race, and attitudes	(1) Vicarious reinforcement (reward to model)
(2) Prestige	(2) Vicarious extinction of fear of responding (no negative consequences to model)
(3) Competence	
(4) Warmth and nurturance	
(5) Reward value	(3) Direct reinforcement
	(4) Imitation of children
Characteristics of the observer	
(1) Capacity to process and retain information	*Factors affecting quality of performance*
(2) Uncertainty	(1) Rehearsal
(3) Level of anxiety	(2) Participant modelling
(4) Other personality factors	
	Transfer and generalization of performance
Characteristics of the modelling presentation	(1) Similarity of training setting to everyday environment
(1) Live or symbolic model	(2) Repeated practice affecting response hierarchy
(2) Multiple models	
(3) Slider model	(3) Incentives for performance in natural setting
(4) Graduated modelling procedures	
(5) Instructions	(4) Learning principles governing a class of behaviours.
(6) Commentary on features and rules	
(7) Summarization by observer	(5) Provision of variation in training situations.
(8) Rehearsal	
(9) Minimization of distracting stimuli	

SOURCE: Perry and Furukawa (1980). Reproduced by permission of Pergamon Press.

for the practitioner has been developed by Perry and Furukawa (1980). As can be seen in Table 5.2, these involve factors that enhance acquisition (learning and retention), and factors that enhance performance.

With respect to *factors that facilitate acquistion*, consideration should be given to model characteristics, observer characteristics, and modelling presentation characteristics.

Model characteristics

The choice of model is a fundamental consideration. A model who is similar to the observer in sex, age, race and attitudes is more likely to be imitated than a dissimilar model. Models who possess prestige in the eyes of the observer are generally more likely to be emulated than low-prestige models. Competence in performance is a characteristic of obvious importance. However, the discrepancy between the model's competence and the observer's perceived competence should not be so great that the observer rejects the model's behaviour. Warmth and nurturance on the part of the model also facilitate modelling effects. Practical considerations usually force the therapist to compromise on some of these characteristics. Fortunately, modelling is a robust phenomenon and does not necessitate a model with all of these characteristics (Wilson & O'Leary, 1980).

Observer characteristics

Perry and Furukawa (1980) state: 'Clinicians must attend to attributes of the observer and either alter the state of the observer in order to facilitate modelling or structure the situation in such a way as to best match its demands to the existing capabilities and state of the observer' (p. 136). Here the therapist must be aware of the child's intellectual strengths and weaknesses and alter the modelling situation accordingly. For example, a mentally retarded phobic child may need a great deal of simplification and repetition. Anxiety is another observer characteristic that may affect learning. Excessive anxiety may interfere with observation and information processing. Perry and Furukawa suggest that a relaxation technique might be tried prior to the presentation of the model, with instructions to relax during the model's actual performance. However, the effectiveness of relaxation training in this way has yet to be determined. A number of personality factors and individual characteristics (impulsivity, dependency, self-esteem, perceived level of competence, socio-economic status, racial status, and sex), are also claimed by Perry and Furukawa to exert an influence on the modelling procedure. Specific guidelines cannot be given for each of these characteristics, although the therapist should consider the possible interaction of these characteristics in a modelling programme. The present authors have found that non-compliance can be a serious problem in getting a child to attend and carryout prescribed tasks. When this is the case, firmer commands to the child and an incentive system can help.

Modelling presentation characteristics

There are several forms of model presentation. The model may be live or symbolic (e.g. film, video, cartoon, audio-tape) Perry and Furukawa (1980) point out that a live model is more interesting than a symbolic model to many people. The live model also has the advantage of allowing adjustments to performance according to the specific needs of the individual. On the other hand, there is a chance that a live model may do something unpredictable. A model that became too anxious and uncertain about the phobic object, for example, would probably serve to perpetuate the observer's anxiety and attitudes about the phobic situation. Symbolic models have a practical advantage in that they can be edited to highlight the relevant portions of the model's behaviour. Film or video-modelling is also more convenient when the treatment needs to be repeated many times, and can be more easily used in a group treatment situation. However, symbolic models may be less powerful than live models (Bandura, 1969).

Another question for the therapist is whether single or multiple models should be employed. Multiple models are to be preferred if practically feasible. Perry and Furukawa state: 'Using different models enhances the presentation by showing both the generality of the behaviour as well as its appropriateness for this particular observer' (p. 138). A greater range of coping styles may also be suggested to the observer in using multiple models.

Perry and Furukawa also advocate the use of a 'slider' model. Such a model begins performance at a level of proficiency similar to that of the observers and gradually progresses until the behaviour is modelled competently. Of relevance to this point is the distinction between coping and mastery models. The mastery model demonstrates completely fearless behaviour, while the coping model betrays some initial apprehension. Although the evidence is equivocal regarding the relative merits of coping and mastery models (Kornhaber & Schroeder, 1975; Bruch, 1975; Meichenbaum, 1971), the phobic child may be able to better identify with the coping model. Wilson and O'Leary (1980) offer several reasons for the continued use of coping models: (1) the use of coping models is compatible with the gradual shaping of behaviour emphasized by many psychologists; (2) the coping model procedure often includes the demonstration of self-control and coping techniques; and (3) children often will not look at displays of bold approach behaviour, whereas they will atttend to a model who initially shows fear but later overcomes it (Bandura *et al.*, 1967).

Graduated modelling procedures are recommended by Perry and Furukawa when complex skills are being taught. This point is highly pertinent to modelling programmes for phobic children, especially animal-phobic children, where the objective may be to teach fairly complex animal-handling skills. The initial instructions given to the observer should explain what is to be noted in the modelling display, and whether the individual is expected to reproduce the modelled behaviour. Instructions serve to 'prime' the observer to watch for particular aspects of the model's performance, thus establishing an appropriate attentional set. Therapist commentary during modelling and covert rehearsal are also advocated by Perry and Furukawa to enhance acquisition and retention.

Factors that enhance performance are crucial given that at some stage the observer must actually produce the modelled behaviour. According to Perry and Furukawa (1980), the therapist should attend to factors providing incentive for performance, factors affecting the quality of the performance, and factors that enhance transfer and generalization.

Incentive for performance

There are several possibilities with respect to incentive, i.e., vicarious reinforcement, vicarious extinction, and direct reinforcement. Vicarious reinforcement involves the observation of reinforcing consequences to the model. The source of reinforcement may be external (e.g. edible) or internal (e.g. positive self-statement). Observing that the model does not experience any negative consequences (vicarious extinction) is probably just as important in the case of overcoming phobias. In addition to vicarious reinforcement, the observer can be given direct reinforcement for actually engaging in the modelled behaviour.

Quality of performance

Given that the observer usually performs an approximation of the modelled behaviour, the therapist is concerned with the quality of the observer's performance. Having the observer actively rehearse the behaviour between modelling displays helps improve performance. This provides multiple opportunities for the observer to match the standard set by the model. A closely related procedure is called 'participant modelling'. This procedure involves direct interaction between the model and the observer. After demonstrating the desired behaviour, the model guides the observer through the steps involved, offering physical assistance if necessary. Immediate feedback and reinforcement can be provided by the model during this procedure. The powerful effects of participant modelling can be further enhanced by the use of response-induction aids (Bandura, Jeffery & Wright, 1974; Bandura, 1976). In the case of animal phobias, these may include gloves or various restraints such as a leash or playpen. For children afraid of water, response-induction aids such as floaties or water-wings might be employed.

Generalization of performance

The more similar the training setting is to the natural setting in which the behaviour is to occur, the more likely it is that the observer will be able to apply what has been learned to the natural setting. Organizing parents and teachers to ensure that the new behaviours are associated with positive consequences helps foster generalization to the natural setting. Bandura (1976) acknowledges that the subject may attribute treatments gains to the presence of the therapist. Consequently, the maintenance and generalization of treatment effects may be less than optimal if both the therapist and response-induction aids are not faded out of the programme.

Bandura (1976) also suggests that self-directed performance by the subject across relevant stimulus dimensions will strengthen maintenance and generalization. This enables the subject to practise newly acquired skills and minimizes the possibility of false attribution of treatment gains to procedural variables. Bandura's claim that self-directed performance serves to extinguish residual fears warrants discussion. The experience of the present authors indicates that whilst an initially dog-phobic child may, through observation of approach behaviours and guided participation, be able to approach and pat the dog, an avoidance response may return if the dog approaches the child. A phenomenon of clinial significance such as this should be treated directly rather than left to chance as in self-directed performance.

Clinical and research applications

Several studies attest to the effectiveness of having fearful children observe models demonstrate the appropriate behaviour. In their now classic study on vicarious extinction, Bandura et al. (1967) assigned 3- to 5-year-old dog-phobic children to one of four groups (i.e. a modelling-positive context group, a modelling-neutral context group, an exposure-positive context group, or a positive-context group). The children were matched on level of avoidance and sex. In the modelling-positive context condition, a fearless peer model displayed approach responses towards a cocker spaniel within the context of a highly enjoyable party atmosphere. In the modelling-neutral context, the children watched the same sequence of approach responses by the same peer model, except the parties were omitted. In order to control for the influence of repeated exposure to the positive atmosphere and to the dog *per se*, children in the exposure-positive context group attended the series of parties in the presence of the dog with the model absent. As a further control procedure, children in the positive-context group participated in the parties, but were never exposed to either the dog or model. Each group underwent eight 10-minute treatment sessions on four consecutive days. Assessment was by means of a graduated performance test, given before and after treatment. A 1-month follow-up was also conducted. The two groups of children who observed the model interact in a fearless manner with the dog, displayed a reduction in avoidance behaviour. They differed significantly in this respect from children in the dog-exposure and positive-context conditions (see Fig. 5.2). The reduction in avoidance behaviour was found to generalize to a white mongrel, predominantly terrier.

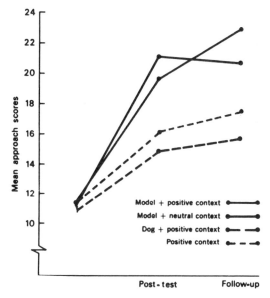

Fig. 5.2 Mean approach scores achieved by children in each of the treatment conditions on the different periods of assessment. Reproduced from Bandura, Grusec and Menlove (1967). Copyright (1967) by the American Psychological Association. Reprinted by permission of the authors.

White and Davis (1974) conducted a study on the effectiveness of modelling in overcoming excessive dental fears. The subjects were all girls (aged 4–8 years) who had previously demonstrated phobic behaviour under dental treatment. The children were randomly assigned to one of three conditions: (1) model condition (subject observed live model undergo dental treatment); (2) control condition I (subject observed dentist and assistant manipulate and name dental equipment); or (3) control condition II (subject not required to observe dental operatory). In the model condition, each subject was seated behind a one-way viewing screen in the presence of a dental student who informed the child that she was to observe a patient undergoing dental treatment. The model was an 8-year-old girl who was rehearsed in the appropriate responses. In order to maximize attentiveness in the model condition and control condition I, each child was told that a reward would be forthcoming if she could correctly answer questions on each of the sessions regarding toothbrush instruction, oral examination, prophylaxis, fluoride treatment, injection, and a restoration treatment. Six sessions of modelling were completed over a 3-week period (each session was 5 minutes in duration). All subjects in the experiment were scheduled to see the same dentist and assistant 3 days following the final experimental session for an initial assessment and 6-month follow-up examination.

Children exposed to the model, and children who viewed the dental sequence (i.e. control condition I), were able to complete significantly more steps in approach behaviour than those who were not given the opportunity to observe (i.e. control condition II). Although it appeared that modelling and observation of the dental situation were equally therapeutic, White and Davis maintain that the behaviour of children who underwent the modelling condition was far more adaptive and mature. Under treatment, these subjects never required direct support, while children who viewed the dental situation consistently demanded support in order to continue treatment.

In the previous studies the children observed the model, but were not required to participate in any interactions related to the feared situation. A significant improvement involves having the phobic child join the model in approaching the phobic stimulus. This is referred to as participant modelling. In an early study on the group desensitization of children's snake phobias, Ritter (1968) compared the effectiveness of 'vicarious' and 'contact' desensitization (i.e. participant modelling). Forty-four children, aged 5 to 11 years, served as subjects. The conditions included vicarious desensitization, contact desensitization, and no-treatment controls. Children in the vicarious desensitization condition observed the experimenter and five peer models engage in gradually bolder interactions with a tame 4 foot Gopher snake. Children in the contact desensitization condition not only observed the experimenter and peers perform as in the foregoing conditions, but also had opportunity for physical contact with model-therapists and the phobic stimulus. Initially, children in this condition placed a gloved hand on that of the experimenter during snake handling. Eventually, the children were eased into stroking with bare hands. Treatment consisted of two 35-minute sessions for both conditions. The avoidance test used for preliminary assessment was readministered to subjects the day after the final treatment session. Eighty per cent of the children who had received contact desensitization, 53% of those in the vicarious desensitization condition, and none of the control children successfully completed the terminal task of the avoidance test (i.e. sitting in chair with arms at the sides and snake on lap for 30 seconds). Thus, both treatment conditions were superior to the control condition, with contact desensitization being superior to vicarious desensitization.

Lewis (1974) conducted a well-controlled study on the relative efficacies of modelling participation, and a combination of both procedures in the treatment of children with water fears. Fifty black male children, aged 5 to 12 years, participated in the initial part of the experiment. They were attending a Boy's Club summer camp. The boys were selected from a larger group on the basis of their performance on a preliminary swimming test administered on the first day of camp. In the subsequent pre-intervention assessment, the number of subjects was reduced to 40. A behavioural test of 16 swimming related items was administered. The items ranged from getting into the pool to floating 6-feet from the side of the pool with the face in the water. The boys were matched on age and pre-test scores, and assigned to one of four groups: modelling-plus-participation, modelling, participation, or control.

In the modelling-plus-participation condition, each child was shown an 8-minute film depicting three black children (aged 7, 10 and 11 years) performing a graded series of tasks in the swimming pool that were very similar to those required in the swimming test. The models were all 'coping' models, appearing to be somewhat frightened and hesitant when they began the series of tasks and becoming more competent as they continued with the tasks. Immediately after viewing the film, another experimenter took the child to the pool for a 10-minute participation phase. The experimenter would encourage the boy to attempt the items on the assessment test. Although the experimenter entered the water and provided physical assistance and praise, the experimenter was careful not to provide any examples. Thus, modelling and participation were kept separate. In the modelling condition, the boys were shown the above film on an individual basis. This was followed by a 10-minute period at the side of the pool playing checkers with the second experimenter. Boys in the participation-only condition were shown an 8-minute cartoon film unrelated to water activities. After viewing the cartoon, the boys were taken to the pool for the participation exercise as previously described. In the control condition, the boys viewed the cartoon film and then played checkers at the side of the pool with the second experimenter.

The day after intervention had been completed, the boys were readministered the behavioural swimming test. The most effective intervention was the modelling-plus-participation condition. Interestingly, participation alone was more powerful than modelling alone. Further assessment was carried out in the study. On the day after post-assessment, all of the overnight campers ($n = 29$) participated in swimming lessons in a different pool given by another swimming instructor. After 5 consecutive days of coaching, the swimming test was administered to the available subjects ($n = 25$). The swimming instructor also rated the boys on their skill and degree of fear, as well as recording class attendance. Generally, subjects in the modelling-plus-participation condition showed more generalization of intervention-induced changes than subjects in other groups. It will be recognized, however, that not all of the boys were included in the follow-up assessment.

When normal treatment resources (model or film) for modelling are not available, covert modelling emerges as a possible treatment strategy. In this variation of modelling, the child imagines models engaging in the target behaviour. Of course, it is assumed that the child has the capacity to imagine a peer modelling a sequence of events related to his or her phobia. Given a suitable subject, a number of parameters should be considered (Kazdin, 1974a, b; 1976). First, a coping model is more effective than a mastery model (although the evidence is by no means clear-cut for live modelling on this parameter). Second, the greater the perceived similarity between the subject and the covert model, the greater the fear reduction. Third, imagining reinforcing consequences for the model appears to enhance the effectiveness of the procedure. Fourth, multiple covert models are more effective than single covert models.

Chertock and Bornstein (1979) conducted one of the first studies on the

148

efficacy of covert modelling in the treatment of children's dental fears. In this study, type of model (coping versus mastery) and number of models (single versus multiple) were examined in an attempt to develop the most efficacious treatment package. Following behavioural and self-report pre-treatment evaluation, 25 children aged 5–13 years were randomly assigned to one of five treatment groups. All children were asked to visually imagine 10 standardized scenes which were hierarchically arranged from least to most anxiety-provoking (e.g. waiting room, X-ray, prophylaxis). The five treatment conditions were as follows: (1) single-model, coping-model conditions, (2) multiple-models, coping-model conditions, (3) single-model, mastery-model condition, (4) multiple-models, mastery modelling, and (5) no-model control condition. The anxiety hierarchy provided the basis for covert modelling; upon completion of the hierarchy the procedure was repeated for a second trial. Five to fifteen days later the children underwent a standard dental examination. A behavioural checklist and three self-report measures of pre-treatment and post-treatment

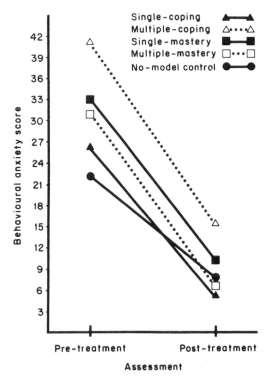

Fig. 5.3 Mean observed timed behaviour checklist scores from pre- to post-treatment. Reproduced from Chertock and Bornstein (1979) by permission of the Haworth Press.

dental fears served as dependent variables. The major dependent measure was the 'behavioural anxiety' score derived from the behavioural checklist. All groups evinced a significant decline in behavioural anxiety from pre- to post-treatment (see Fig. 5.3). However, none of the groups displayed significantly less post-treatment anxiety than controls. In contrast to previous findings using covert modelling with adults (Kazdin, 1974b; Meichenbaum, 1971), type and number of models imagined did not significantly effect behavioural anxiety reduction. At first blush, these results appear quite discouraging for the efficacy of covert modelling with children. Tearnan and Graziano (1980) have written a conceptual and methodological critique of the study, however, and identify a number of specific flaws (e.g. inadequate account of the selection of the participants, small sample size and limited statistical power, questionable design and data analysis techniques, and the possibility of regression). For the moment, however, the role of covert modelling in the treatment of children's phobias is unclear.

Discussion

Modelling has emerged as a popular method of treating children's phobias. According to Rimm and Masters (1974), a number of significant factors are at work in modelling. Modelling provides an opportunity for the vicarious extinction of a child's phobia. The child observes a model perform a feared behaviour in the absence of negative consequences, and eventually feels less fearful about the cues that usually induce avoidance behaviour. Another important factor is the acquisition of technical knowledge and information via modelling. For example, animal-phobic children learn a great deal about the habits of animals and their 'body language' in modelling programmes. With the acquisition of technical knowledge and information, the child usually becomes more skilful in coping with the feared object or situation. Following the preceding example, animal-phobic children learn how to actually handle animals. When skills acquisition is part of the rationale for the utilization of modelling, it seems prudent to develop a checklist of the specific skills and behavioural responses involved to guide intervention as systematically as possible. Should the child engage in a participation phase, the direct extinction of fear tends to occur provided negative consequences are absent. The presence of the therapist is also a significant factor in terms of physical support and social reinforcement for successful participatory acts, and minimizing the seriousness of problems (e.g. dog growls at animal-phobic child, water-phobic child stumbles at the edge of the pool) that may emerge in the participatory phase. As a general caution, severely phobic children may find the exposures and participatory exercises in a modelling programme to be too anxiety-provoking despite the efforts of a comforting therapist. In such cases, systematic desensitization can precede modelling. Modelling is a well-researched behavioural method, and has considerable clinical utility.

COGNITIVE PROCEDURES AND SELF-CONTROL

Rationale and procedures

Traditional conditioning paradigms (classical and operant) and related therapeutic procedures have tended to ignore the role of the individual's perception and active cognitive processes. In view of the fact that the 'conditioning' type of interventions are sometimes carried out in the person's imagination (consider systematic desensitization or implosion), some might consider it strange that cognitive processes were not assigned greater significance at an earlier stage. Shortly after the establishment of behavioural methods derived from learning theory, however, a number of researchers and clinicians argued persuasively that 'behaviour therapists' need to have a greater appreciation of cognitive processes in their assessment and treatment of presenting problems.

Cognitive-oriented therapists believe that emotional and behavioural problems are due to maladaptive thinking. These cognitions are referred to as 'internal dialogue', 'self-talk', 'self-statements', and 'automatic thoughts'. When using cognitive intervention procedures, the client's maladaptive thought patterns become the focus of therapeutic intervention. As people succeed in controlling their internal dialogue, and replace faulty cognitions with appropriate self-statements, it is assumed that the presenting emotional and behavioural problems will be overcome.

The cognitive approach to the conceptualization and treatment of behavioural problems does not entail a monolithic set of theoretical premises and clinical practices. There are in fact numerous forms of cognitive intervention. These include Ellis's (1970) rational-emotive therapy, Beck's (1976) cognitive therapy, Goldfried, Decenteceo and Weinberg's (1974) systematic rational restructuring, and Meichenbaum's (1977) self-instructional training. Despite the theoretical and procedural variations, all of these interventions aim at restructuring the individual's maladaptive cognitions (i.e. 'cognitive restructuring') as a means of changing behaviour. These various forms of cognitive intervention are relevant to the therapeutic management of children and adolescents as shown in the following accounts of rational-emotive therapy and self-instructional training.

Rational-emotive therapy

Ellis' rational-emotive therapy postulates that a number of irrational self-statements cause emotional upheaval. Ellis has listed 12 irrational assumptions ('dirty dozen') that are seen as the basis of most behavioural problems (Ellis & Harper, 1975); these are listed in Table 5.3. Presumably, these irrational beliefs are formed in childhood and adolescence, and are therefore seen to be relevant in working with children and adolescents. Ellis' approach is sometimes presented in terms of an A–B–C analysis. Accordingly, the A refers to the antecedent real-life event that has precipitated the problem, the B symbolizes the individual's irrational belief(s) or interpretation of the antecedent event, while C denotes the consequences (e.g. anxiety, depression) experienced by the person. The anxiety experienced by an adolescent after failing an examination serves as an illustrative example of the A–B–C analysis. In this example, failing the examination is the antecedent event that triggered his anxiety. The beliefs held by the individual in relation to this event include nagging doubts about his ability to pass further examinations, the prospect of a parental rebuke, and the thought that an examination failure is terribly humiliating. As a consequence of these beliefs, the adolescent feels extremely upset and becomes increasingly anxious about his situation.

The process of rational–emotive therapy with older children and adolescents involves three basic operations. First, the therapist and client identify the antecedent event that precipitated the problem. The antecedent event is the focus of the individual's irrational self-statements and beliefs, and must therefore be clarified. Second, the therapist helps the individual discover the specific self-statements he or she is making about the external event, and to identify

Table 5.3 Common irrational beliefs

(1) The idea that you must—yes, *must*—have sincere love and approval almost all the time from all the people you find significant.

(2) The idea that you must be thoroughly competent, adequate, and achieving; or that you must at least have real competence or talent at something important.

(3) The idea that people who harm you or commit misdeeds are generally bad, wicked or villainous individuals and that you should severely blame, damn and punish them for their sins.

(4) The idea that life is awful, terrible, horrible or catastrophic when things do not go the way you would like them to go.

(5) The idea that emotional misery comes from external pressures and that you have little ability to control your feelings or rid yourself of depression and hostility.

(6) The idea that if something seems dangerous or fearsome, you must become terribly occupied with and upset about it.

(7) The idea that you will find it easier to avoid facing many of life's difficulties and self-responsibilities than to undertake more rewarding forms of self-discipline.

(8) The idea that your past remains all-important and that because something once strongly influenced your life, it has to keep determining your feelings and behaviour today.

(9) The idea that people and things should turn out better than they do; and that you have to view it as awful and horrible if you do not quickly find good solutions to life's hassles.

(10) The idea that you can achieve happiness by inertia and inaction or by passively and uncommittedly 'enjoying yourself'.

(11) The idea that you must have a high degree of order or certainty to feel comfortable; or that you need some supernatural power on which to rely.

(12) The idea that you can give yourself a global rating as a human and that your general worth and self-acceptance depend on the goodness of your performances and the degree that people approve of you.

SOURCE: Ellis and Harper (1975). Reproduced by permission of the Institute for Rational-Emotive Therapy.

the irrational beliefs that underlie these self-statements. At this stage, it is important to catch self-statements that convey the notions of 'must' or 'should' (e.g. 'I should pass all of my tests and examinations'), that something is awful or catastrophic ('Failing this exam is about the worst thing that has ever happened to me'), that the event involved is unbearable ('I can't stand having failed the examination'), and damming or blaming oneself or others ('I am to blame... it's my fault'). Adolescents are fairly adept in identifying their 'self-talk'. At this stage, the individual may be given a homework assignment involving the identification of the self-talk that mediates the problem behaviour. Third, the therapist helps the individual analyze irrational self-statements, challenge and dispute irrational self-statements, and substitute appropriate logical statements. The therapist often models the thought process to the individual. For example, the adolescent who failed an examination might be thinking: 'I feel awful about failing my examination... may be I won't be able to complete my course... what are my parents going to say... this is really humiliating'. The therapist might model a thought process along these lines: 'I'm exaggerating the seriousness of what has happened... I pass nearly all of my exams... even if I had to repeat the subject it wouldn't be all that bad... as far as my parents are concerned I don't know that they will freak out but in any case they will get over it... it's unpleasant to fail an exam but I can cope'. A thorough account of rational emotive therapy with children and adolescents has been provided by Bernard and Joyce (1984).

Self-instructional training

Meichenbaum's (1977) self-instructional training appears to be highly pertinent to the management of children's phobias. The rationale for self-instructional training is derived from two major sources: first, Ellis' (1970) rational–emotive therapy and its emphasis upon irrational self-talk as the cause of emotional disturbance; and second, the developmental sequence according to which children develop internal speech and verbal symbolic control over their behaviour (Luria, 1961). In self-instructional training, specific self-statements are modelled by the therapist and rehearsed by the child. Thus, the major components are cognitive modelling and cognitive behaviour rehearsal. Taking Meichenbaum and Goodman's (1971) research with hyperactive children as a model, self-instructional training involves five steps:

(1) An adult performs the task while talking to himself out loud (cognitive modelling).
(2) The child performs the same talk under the direction of the model's instructions (overt, external guidance).
(3) The child performs the task while instructing himself aloud (overt self-guidance).
(4) The child whispers the instructions to himself as he goes through the task (faded overt self-guidance).

(5) The child performs the task while guiding his performance via private speech (covert self-instruction).

A number of clinical observations and practical suggestions are provided by Meichenbaum (1977) with respect to the implementation of self-instructional training with children: 'The treatment suggestions offered are *not* based upon careful empirical studies but rather represent a sort of cumulative "wisdom" culled from our own experiences and from the literature' (p. 83). We can summarize the observations and suggestions as follows:

(1) The use of play is suggested as a means by which the therapist can engage children in self-instructional training. Before embarking upon self-instructional training with an animal-phobic child, the therapist could illustrate the importance of language as a mediator of behaviour in a neutral game situation. Training can begin on a set of tasks or games in which the child is proficient, and does not have a history of failures and frustrations. Many children's games (e.g. negotiating a ball through a maze covered with plexiglass) are ideal in terms of their cognitive demands.

(2) In using self-instructional procedures, the child should make self-statements with the appropriate affect and not in a mechanical role, or automatic fashion. Attending to the affect of the self-statements is thought to enhance concentration and minimize activities that may interfere with the implementation of the programme.

(3) The rate at which the therapist proceeds with the self-instructional procedure can be tailored to the needs of the individual child. For example, some children require many trials of cognitive modelling and overt self-instructional rehearsal, whereas others may proceed directly to covert rehearsal after being exposed to a model. A major strength of the training procedure is its flexibility.

(4) Self-instructional training can be supplemented with imagery manipulations and relaxation. When the child feels he is about to lose self-control, he may employ an imagery → relaxation → self-instruction problem-solving strategy sequence to re-establish control. As an example, the adolescent who passes out in examinations could be taught imagery and relaxation as a means of enhancing self-instruction and problem-solving.

(5) The child who receives self-instructional training should be viewed as a collaborator rather than a passive recipient of the thoughts and behaviours modelled by the therapist. It is recommended that children be involved in the definition and diagnosis of the clinical problem(s), and collaborate in the development and implementation of the treatment programme.

(6) In addition to self-instructional training in the therapy setting, cognitive modelling can be carried out in other settings. In relation to overcoming children's phobias, it would seem important that people (like parents and siblings) in the natural setting say aloud positive self-statements with respect to the object or situation feared by the child. This should enhance transfer of learning from the therapy setting to the natural setting. Meichenbaum

believes there is a great need for teachers to 'think aloud' and engage in cognitive modelling in order to teach children how to solve problems.

(7) With respect to the real-life application of self-instructional training, it is important that the treatment suggestions be implemented as early as possible in the behaviour chain. Although Meichenbaum illustrates this point in relation to impulsive children, the general principle also applies to phobic children. For example, the child who has an excessive fear of water would be advised to apply self-instructions and problem-solving just prior to entering the water. Efforts at self-instruction would have less impact at the stage of panic!

(8) When modelling cognitive strategies the therapist should adopt a coping rather than a mastery style. Accordingly, failures and frustrations will be evident along with how they are dealt with by the therapist.

When negative results are obtained in self-instructional training, Meichenbaum suggests that several issues be considered. Whether the child has the requisite skills for the task is critical. This seems relevant, for example, in helping test-anxious adolescents. Self-instructional training would be of little assistance unless the individuals have the requisite knowledge and reading skills. Negative treatment results also raise concerns about the correspondence between what the child says to himself and what he does. The animal-phobic child might say 'I have to pat the dog' but not carry out the behaviour. Here, it is crucial that reinforcement be contingent upon the appropriate match between self-statement and motor responses. According to Meichenbaum: 'There is a need for a cognitive-hyphen-behavioral approach whereby reinforcements follow the appropriate correspondence between saying and doing. Focusing on only one side of the therapy equation is likely to prove less effective' (p. 81).

Self-control

In the preceding discussions of systematic desensitization, emotive imagery, flooding and implosive therapy, modelling, and contingency management, it will have been appreciated that the therapist and/or parent is usually responsible for the implementation of the therapeutic programme. The traditional behavioural approach is one in which external agents are primarily responsible for assessment, and the development and implementation of treatment. Externally administered programmes, however, suffer from a number of limitations (Kazdin, 1980b). For example, the therapeutic agent can become a discriminative stimulus for appropriate behaviour on the part of the child, as may easily happen in systematic desensitization. While behaviour change in the situation in which the problem is occurring is the goal of therapeutic intervention, the therapist must rely upon the child to integrate new ways of responding in these settings.

In recent years there has been a move towards increasing client participation in assessment, and the development and implementation of therapeutic programmes. When the person actively implements specific procedures to control his or her behaviour, 'self control' is said to have occurred. Conceptualizations and methods of enhancing self-control are heavily cognitive. As Morris and Kratochwill (1983) explain: 'In the area of fear reduction, self-control procedures focus on helping individuals develop specific thinking skills and apply them whenever they are confronted with a particular feared stimulus, event, or object' (p. 209). A general behavioural model of self-control has been proposed by Kanfer and Karoly (1972) that involves a number of sequential components. Accordingly, the major steps include (1) making a commitment to change a certain behaviour, (2) setting a specific standard of behaviour change as the goal, (3) self-monitoring and self-evaluation of the behaviour, and (4) the application of self-reinforcement or self-punishment depending upon whether the standard has been reached. Meichenbaum and Genest (1980) maintain that self-control involves helping the individual (1) become aware of the negative thinking styles that impede performance and produce emotional upsets, (2) generate a set of incompatible self-statements, strategies, and so fourth, and (3) learn specific adaptive, cognitive and behaviour skills. In addition to the cognitive component, self-control programmes can incorporate relaxation, systematic desensitization, modelling and contingency management. As numerous writers (Kanfer, 1980; Morris & Kratochwill, 1982; Thoresen & Mahoney, 1974) have commented, the child's motivation for behaviour change and sense of responsibility in treatment are enhanced with such procedures.

Clinical and research applications

Although rational–emotive therapy and self-instructional training appear to be quite popular in clinical practice, very little has been reported in the literature on their application to children's phobias. The use of self-instructional training with phobic children is illustrated in a case reported by Richards and Siegel (1978). The subject was a 10-year-old girl (Susan) with a debilitating dog phobia. She was initially treated through a sequence consisting primarily of (a) systematic desensitization, (b) discrimination training for recognizing friendly dogs versus unfriendly dogs, and (c) *in vivo* participant modelling with successively more threatening dogs. Towards the end of the treatment programme, Susan was taught in self-instruction which involved five steps. According to Richards and Siegel's description:

(1) We modeled adaptive self-verbalization by talking out loud and administering task-relevant instructions to ourselves while we performed the task (e.g. saying 'Relax; take a slow, deep breath, I'm doing fine; this dog is obviously friendly; notice his wagging tail; pet him softly; nothing to worry about,' while petting the dog appropriately.

(2) We then asked Susan to perform the task while we instructed her aloud.

(3) Susan then performed the task and instructed herself out loud.

(4) Susan then performed the task and whispered the instructions to herself.

(5) And finally, Susan interacted with dogs while using entirely covert self-instructions. (p. 316)

With extensive feedback and reinforcement from the therapist, Susan progressed through the programme very well.

Cognitive restructuring was also prominent in a case reported by Ollendick (1979a). The case involved a 16-year-old anorexic male (Rick) who was initially treated by systematic desensitization. However, the effects of systematic desensitization could not be maintained after intervention even with informational feedback on his weight. Additional assessment focused upon Rick's cognitive processes. He was frequently observed saying 'I can't eat...I'll get fat again'. It was hypothesized that these kind of irrational, self-defeating statements served to maintain poor eating habits, increased anxiety, and kept his body weight low. Consequently, the weight-relevant thoughts proposed by Mahoney and Mahoney (1975) were applied to Rick:

(1) thoughts about pounds gained ('I've tried to eat that food but haven't gained a pound');
(2) thoughts about capabilities ('There is no way I can gain weight again');
(3) excuses about not gaining weight (If those other kids liked me, I could gain weight');
(4) inappropriate standard setting ('I threw up this morning, there's no use to try. I may as well quit');
(5) thoughts about how peers would perceive him ('Nobody will like me if I gain weight').

Rick was instructed to record his 'self-talk' related to weight gain and peer criticism between treatment sessions. At treatment sessions, his homework was reviewed with adaptive thoughts being developed ('If I gain weight, it may be the case that some kids will not like me. Other kids will like me. Besides, what difference does it make whether they will like it or not? I will feel better.') Gradually, Rick's weight increased to an acceptable level.

Kanfer et al. (1975) have reported a study on the effectiveness of training children in the use of 'verbal controlling responses' for darkness tolerance. The main objective of the study was to compare the effectiveness of verbal responses that focus on the individual's competence and personal control against verbal responses that aim at reducing the aversive aspect to the threatening stimulus. A second concern was to develop a method of treatment for anxiety problems in the absence of threat-provoking cues. Consequently, any 'therapeutic effects' have to be attributed to the action of verbal–mediational responses rather than to direct counter-conditioning of fear-arousing stimuli. The subjects were 5 to 6-year-old children who could remain alone in the dark for only a very brief period (their mean baseline tolerance was less than 27 seconds). The study was conducted in a schoolroom that could be totally darkened via a rheostat.

The children were randomly assigned to one of three groups (i.e. a competence group, a stimulus group or a neutral group). During the pre-test, each child was taken to the experimental room, and shown how to operate the rheostat. The child was given a set of instructions including 'Try to keep the room as dark as you can, for as long as you can' (Kanfer et al., 1975, p. 253). If the child tolerated the dark for 180 seconds, he or she was considered to be unafraid of the dark and withdrawn from the study. Immediately after the pre-test, the child entered the training phase. Through an intercom, the child was instructed to listen and repeat the 'special words' given by the experimenter. The special words varied according to the group. In the competence group, the children were told to say 'I am a brave (girl). I can take care of myself in the dark'. In the stimulus group, the special words were 'The dark is a fun place to be. There are many good things in the dark'. In the neutral group, they were 'Mary had a little lamb. It's fleece was white as snow'. After the children had learned the special words to a criterion of three consecutive errorless repetitions, four elaborating sentences were added. The elaborating statements read to the child were as follows:

[Competence group] When you are in the dark you know that you can turn on the light when you feel like it. In your room, when it's dark, you know exactly where everything is—your bed, your dressers, your toys. When you are in the dark if you felt like talking to someone you could always talk to your parents and they could hear you. Even though you are in the dark, when the door is closed you know that nobody can come in that you would not know.

[Stimulus group] The dark is the best place to go to sleep and have good dreams. The dark is a special place where you can play games. It is more fun to watch a movie or TV in the dark because you can see the picture better. When it's dark it is nice to cuddle up with stuffed animals.

[Neutral group] Mary took a lamb to school with her one morning. That day, when she was finished with school, Mary played with the lamb in the garden behind her house. Mary was very careful and made sure that she fed the lamb every day. Sometimes Mary would run with the lamb up to the top of the hill. (p. 253)

Each subject had to repeat the special words after each sentence, with the procedure being repeated on a second trial. After the training phase, each child was post-tested for darkness tolerance. Two post-test trials were given to determine how long the child could remain in the dark. The trials were terminated after the child turned the light on, or after being in the dark for 180 seconds. A further post-test was given to determine whether training effects would generalize to a different tolerance situation. In this post-test, the lights were turned on in the experimental room. The child was instructed to turn the dial down to make the room as dark as possible and stay in the room for a long time. The trial was terminated when the child moved to a higher illumination or called for the experimenter, or after 90 seconds had elapsed.

The major dependent variables in the study were duration of tolerance of darkness and terminal light intensity. With respect to duration of toleration, children in the competence group and stimulus group were able to tolerate the dark for significantly longer times than children in the neutral group (see Fig. 5.4). Although the competence group did better than the stimulus group, the differences were not significant. On the final post-test, each child was required to reduce the light intensity and remain in the room. Tolerance times did not differ for the three groups. With respect to light intensity, all groups began by

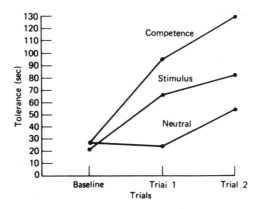

Fig. 5.4 Mean time for tolerance of the dark for
the competence, stimulus and neutral verbaliz-
ation groups during pre-test and the two test
trials. Reproduced from Kanfer, Karoly and
Newman (1975). Copyright (1975) by the American Psychological Association. Reprinted by
permission of the authors.

turning up the illumination to equally high intensity levels. On the first post-test
trial, the groups set lower levels of illumination but there were no significant
differences. However, on the second post-test, the competence group tolerated
significantly lower illumination levels than did the other two groups. On
the final post-test, the competence and stimulus groups turned down the
room illumination to a significantly lower level than children given neutral
verbalizations.

A number of comments can be made about Kanfer *et al.*'s study. In terms of
the theoretical issues of interest to the researchers, it is apparent that verbal
controlling responses that aim at reducing the aversive aspects of the threatening
stimuli (competence group) are more effective than verbal controlling responses
that address individual's competence and personal control (stimulus). However,
the process by which verbal training differentially affected the child's behaviour
in the dark is not clear. Kanfer *et al.* suggest that the children may have quietly
rehearsed their verbal controlling responses during the post-tests. As noted by
them: 'The competence group may have shown greater tolerance because of
the verbal controlling responses represented by self-instructions to behave like a
brave boy or girl with the expectation of social approval and self-reinforcements
based upon past encouragements to act competently (like a brave boy or girl)'
(p. 257). The exposures entailed in the pre-test and post-test, being in control
of the light source, plus praise from the experimenter, could account for some
improvement. Nevertheless, since these factors applied to all groups in the
study, they cannot be held to account for the superiority of the competence
group. A remarkable feature of the study concerns the extremely brief training
phase that the children underwent. The effectiveness of intervention is quite

surprising in view of the fact that the children only underwent one training phase. The study has also been criticized with respect to its unrepresentative sample in relation to clinical populations, whether fear behaviour existed outside the laboratory, and the unknown extent to which laboratory improvement reflects behaviour change in other settings (e.g. at home) (Ross, 1981).

Graziano, Mooney, Huber and Ignasiak (1979) used 'self-control instruction' in the treatment of 5 boys and 2 girls (8–12 years) with severe night-time fears. In each family, going to bed had become a highly emotional and disruptive nightly event, characterized by crying, calling-out, crawling into bed with other family members, and insisting upon bright lights being kept turned on in their room. The families were seen once a week for 5 weeks, with children and parents being seen in separate groups. The first and fifth meetings addressed assessment while the middle meetings were devoted to instruction and discussion. The children were instructed in relaxation, pleasant imagery and special words (adapted from Kanfer et al., 1975)—'I am brave. I can take care of myself when I am alone. I can take care of myself when I am in the dark'. The children were told to practise the exercises every night with their parents and whenever they started to become afraid. The children were also given 'bravery tokens' for how well they did each exercise and for being brave both going to bed and through the night. The bravery tokens could be cashed for a MacDonald's party. Each child was given a booklet which contained written instructions for daily practice and space to record the number of tokens earned each night in order to keep a self-monitoring record of progress. The rationale of the programme was explained to parents, it being emphasized that family cooperation was crucial to the success of the programme. Hence, a verbal contract was agreed to between the experimenters and parents and between parents and their children. At the child's bedtime, the parents were instructed to prompt and supervize the home practice of the self-control exercises (5 minutes), and apply the bravery tokens plus verbal praise. The most important finding was that all children reached the behavioural criteria of 10 consecutive fearless nights. The number of weeks of training required to reach criteria ranged from 3 to 19, with a mean of 8.7 weeks. Although the criterion of 10 consecutive fearless nights had been achieved, some of the children continued to show occasional night-time fearful behaviour, which is reflected in 3-, 6- and 12-month follow-ups.

Graziano and Mooney (1980) have tested the effectiveness of the afore-mentioned procedures in a more extensive investigation. Thirty-three volunteer families of 6 to 12-year-old children with severe and highly disruptive night-time fears of long duration, were randomly assigned to experimental or waiting-list control groups. The families attended three training meetings. Children practised and self-monitored nightly self-control exercises at home while parents superviz-ed, monitored and rewarded their efforts with praise and 'bravery tokens'. As in the pilot study, the nightly exercises consisted of (a) muscle relaxation, (b) imagining a pleasant scene, and (c) reciting 'self-statements'. After 3 weeks of training the experimental group had significantly less night-time fear than did the control group, as measured by the retrospective reports of the parents and their direct nightly observations of the children's fear behaviour. Follow-ups at 2, 6 and 12 months were conducted by telephone with the parents of the children in the experimental group. At the time of the 12-month follow-up, 15 of the experimental group children had met the behavioural criterion of 10 consecutive 'fearless' and 'perfect' nights. Following the post-treatment assessment period, the control group was provided with the same programme. A similar improvement occurred with nearly all children reaching the behavioural criterion. None of the experimental or control group children were reported to have developed any new problems or symptoms since the beginning of their fear behaviour change. It was also found that the two groups did not differ on post-treatment measures of school and social adjustment and total number of fears. However, family tensions about bedtime issues were virtually eliminated. Graziano and Mooney conclude that their data suggest the power of 'direct and specific instructions on a rational level to parents and children' (p. 212). As Graziano and Mooney recognize, further research is required to determine which of the several variables in the treatment programme (relaxation, imagery, self-statements, contingency management and demand characteristics) accounted for the therapeutic changes.

Discussion

The role of cognitions in the maintenance of behavioural problems and their resolution is a complex issue. Authorities disagree over the significance of cognitive processes in the cause and maintenance of behavioural problems, and whether cognitive restructuring can produce behaviour changes (Ledwidge, 1978; Locke, 1979; Mahoney and Kazdin, 1979; Rachlin, 1977; Wolpe, 1976b, 1978). The debate is beyond the scope of this book, although several cautionary comments should be made of relevance to clinical practice.

An important theoretical and practical issue is the identification of self-talk presumed to underpin or mediate the presenting problem. It appears that some clients are able to identify their self-statements and expectations fairly confidently, while many others have difficulty with this task. This is of particular concern to cognitive-oriented therapists working with children and adolescents. Enthusiasts of cognitive approaches, however, tend to emphasize that it is more important for the individual to view their behaviour as if it were affected by self-statements and work at developing positive self-statements (Meichenbaum, 1977). Encouraging the child to employ positive self-statements may still be useful in helping the child cope with stressful situations even when the cause and/or maintenance of the problem may not be directly related to cognitive processes. On the other hand, a very real danger of therapy aimed at cognitive restructuring is the assumption that a change in cognitions (inferred from the person's statements) will necessarily be accompanied by an appropriate change in behaviour.

The therapeutic viability of cognitive restructuring must be weighed up against the individual's learning history, skill competencies, environmental contingencies, and the physiological intensity of the phobic reaction. Intervention that addresses only cognitive processes is usually inadequate in view of the multiplicity of factors that operate in most cases. As an illustrative example, coaching a child to engage in positive self-statements to overcome a phobia of darkness would be futile in the face of an overwhelming physiological reaction and environmental contingencies (e.g. easy access to parents at night/ sleeping with parents) geared to the strengthening of the phobia. From the viewpoint of the child and parents, efforts restricted to cognitive restructuring would have little credibility under these circumstances. For such a clinical scenario, we believe that a combination of behavioural techniques should be used in order to satisfactorily address the multiplicity of factors.

As Meichenbaum (1977) has commented, both sides of the cognitive-behavioural equation must be addressed. It will also be recalled that in the successful programme developed by Graziano and colleagues (Graziano, Mooney, Huber & Ignasiak, 1979; Graziano & Mooney, 1980), for children with clinical fears of the dark, muscle relaxation and contingency management were included as well as positive self-statements. To reiterate it is dubious that cognitive restructuring alone is effective in overcoming specific phobic reactions. Therefore, it is strongly recommended that when cognitive procedures are employed, that they be used in combination with behavioural methods in order to optimize treatment effects (Eifert, 1984; Ellis, 1979).

SUMMARY

Contingency management, modelling and cognitive restructuring have been reviewed in relation to the treatment of children's phobias. Operant conditioning is the theoretical basis of contingency management. Hence, emphasis has been placed on environmental regulation in contingency management. From the viewpoint of this paradigm, anxiety as a mediating event is not a relevant treatment consideration. Contingency management covers many principles and procedures; positive reinforcement, shaping, and extinction were seen as the most relevant. Positive reinforcement entails the strengthening of a behaviour through the delivery of a stimulus event that is contingent upon the behaviour (e.g. an animal-phobic child being praised by parents after the child pats a dog). Shaping is defined as the successive reinforcement of closer approximations to a terminal behaviour (e.g. the manner in which a dentist prompts and reinforces a child's cooperative behaviour from entry into the surgery to mouth opening and examination). Extinction refers to the discontinuation of reinforcement of a behaviour (e.g. a mother refusing to have her child sleep in her bed any more nights despite protestations from the child about being afraid of the dark).

Operant-based procedures are sometimes resisted by care providers on the grounds that they are tantamount to bribery, or are inhumane; hence they require sensitivity on the part of the clinician.

As a therapeutic procedure. modelling capitalizes on the power of observational learning. The factors that enhance modelling have been discussed. With respect to factors that facilitate response acquisition, consideration should be given to model characteristics (especially the competence of the model), observer characteristics (e.g. general level of intellectual functioning), and modelling presentation characteristics (live versus symbolic models, single versus multiple models, mastery versus coping models). To enhance performance, the therapist needs to consider incentives for performance (vicarious and direct reinforcement), quality of performance (response induction aids, participant modelling), and factors that enhance transfer and generalization (fading out of aids, self-directed performance). When the normal resources (live model, video) are not available for modelling, covert modelling may be a possible treatment option. In view of the many experimental investigations that have been reported on the efficacy of modelling, it seems a particularly useful technique for the transmission of information and building up coping skills in children.

Consistent with the emphasis upon cognition in the contemporary behavioural approach, several cognitive therapies have been examined in relation to children's phobias. Rational–emotive therapy involves a challenging and disputation of the irrational beliefs that underpin anxiety and phobias. Ellis's A–B–C model has been presented, together with 12 common irrational beliefs. The basic operations in rational–emotional therapy have been illustrated in relation to test anxiety. In self-instructional training, the child learns the importance of private speech in the regulation of behaviour. This is accomplished over a series of steps, beginning with the modelling of self-instructions and culminating in covert self-instruction. Meichenbaum's practical suggestions on the use of self-instructional training were also summarized. Cognitive restructuring has been used in the treatment of children's night fears, for example, but empirical support is somewhat limited at this time. In clinical practice, it is advisable to employ traditional behavioural procedures in conjunction with cognitive techniques in order to cover the full range of antecedent and consequent events that maintain the child's phobic reaction.

CHAPTER 6

School phobia

INTRODUCTION

Persistent non-attendance at school is a serious problem, especially when the child's social and educational development is considered. According to Hersov (1960a): 'Long-continued absence may lead to educational backwardness, with far-reaching effects upon social and educational adjustment in later school life and adulthood' (p. 130). Bearing in mind that most children live in a society in which education is compulsory, the legal implications of persistent absenteeism must also be considered. There are, of course, many reasons why children do not attend school. Physical illness and health matters account for a high proportion of absenteeism. Sometimes children do not attend school because of an excessive amount of anxiety about the school situation. This problem has been recognized by clinicians for many decades. Consider, for example, the detailed description provided by Broadwin (1932):

> The child is absent from school for periods varying from several months to a year. The absence is consistent. At times the parents know where the child is. It is with the mother or near the home. The reason for the truancy is incomprehensible to the parents and the school. The child may say that it is afraid to go to school, afraid of the teacher, or say that it does not know why it will not go to school. When at home it is happy and apparently care-free. When dragged to school it is miserable, fearful, and at the first opportunity runs home despite the certainty of corporal punishment. The onset is generally sudden. The previous school work and conduct had been fair. (p. 254)

Typically, the above child remains at home over the school day. Johnson, Falstein, Szurek and Svendsen (1941) were the first authors to use the term 'school phobia' in reference to this problem. The diagnostic criteria for school phobia have been developed over the years, with those offered by Berg, Nichols and Pritchard (1969) being the most widely adopted. Following Berg *et al.*, the diagnostic criteria for school phobia include:

(1) severe difficulty attending school, often resulting in prolonged absence;
(2) severe emotional upset, including excessive fearfulness, temper outbursts, or complaints of feeling ill when faced with the prospect of going to school;

(3) staying at home with the knowledge of the parent when the youngster should be at school;

(4) absence of antisocial characteristics such as stealing, lying and destructiveness.

The term 'separation anxiety' is often used in clinical settings as a means of describing what is seen as the 'real' pathology, (i.e. the anxiety about leaving mother). This has been the prevailing viewpoint within the psychoanalytic school (Estes, Haylett & Johnson, 1956), although the notion has been incorporated within behavioural formulations as well (Yates, 1970). From a diagnostic viewpoint, we believe that separation anxiety should be seen as a different problem. In the DSM-III-R, separation anxiety disorder is one of the disorders within the sub-class 'anxiety disorders of childhood and adolescence'. The diagnostic criteria for separation anxiety disorder can be found in Table 6.1. Another group of children refuse to attend school for reasons unrelated to anxiety about school. These children are usually not at home throughout the school day and may in fact engage in lying, stealing, cheating and destructive

Table 6.1 Diagnostic criteria for separation anxiety disorder in the DSM-III-R

A. Excessive anxiety concerning separation from those to whom the child is attached, as evidenced by at least three of the following:

(1) unrealistic and persistent worry about possible harm befalling major attachment figures or fear that they will leave and not return

(2) unrealistic and persistent worry that an untoward calamitous event will separate the child from a major attachment figure (e.g. the child will be lost, kidnapped, killed or be the victim of an accident)

(3) persistent reluctance or refusal to go to school in order to stay with major attachment figures or at home

(4) persistent reluctance or refusal to go to sleep without being near a major attachment figure or to go to sleep away from home

(5) persistent avoidance of being alone, including "clinging" to and "shadowing" major attachment figures

(6) repeated nightmares involving the theme of separation

(7) complaints of physical symptoms, e.g., headaches, stomachaches, nausea, or vomiting, on many school days or on other occasions when anticipating separation from major attachment figures

(8) recurrent signs or complaints of excessive distress in anticipation of separation from home or major attachment figures, e.g., temper tantrums or crying, pleading with parents not to leave

(9) recurrent signs of complaints of excessive distress when separated from home or major attachment figures, e.g., wants to return home, needs to call parents when they are absent or when child is away from home

B. Duration of disturbance of at least two weeks.

C. Onset before the age of 18.

D. Occurrence not exclusively during the course of a Pervasive Developmental Disorder, Schizophrenia, or any other psychotic disorder.

behaviours. This problem is usually referred to as 'truancy'. In DSM-III-R this notion is included in the diagnostic category of 'conduct disorder'; it will not be elaborated upon further here (see Hersov & Berg, 1980).

As has been suggested by Ollendick and Mayer (1984), the diagnostic criteria for school phobia developed by Berg et al. (1969) maintain the distinction between school phobia, which is frequently associated with phobic and anxiety disorders, and school truancy, which is often associated with conduct disorders. The criteria do not prejudge aetiology (a major problem in the literature on school phobia), but implicitly allow for many causal and maintenance factors. Ollendick and Mayer have elaborated upon these criteria by operationalizing prolonged absence as at least 2 weeks in duration, and by employing self-report, other-report, and behavioural indices of fear.

The incidence of school phobia has proved difficult to estimate, as is the case with children's phobias in general. In the Isle of Wight study of 2193 children aged 10–11 years, 3 children were found with a clinically significant school phobia while another 4 children had moderate fears related to school (Rutter, Tizard & Whitmore, 1970); thus about 0.3% of children at that age would be expected to be school-phobic. Leton (1962) claimed that about 3 per 1000 primary-grade children and approximately 10 per 1000 high-school students have school phobia during any one year. Based on a survey conducted in south-western Virginia, Ollendick and Mayer (1984) found an incidence rate of 0.4% in school-aged children utilizing Berg et al.'s criteria of school phobia. Although Kennedy (1971) has reported a higher incidence of 17 per 1000 school-age children per year, it appears that school phobia occurs in less than 1% of school-aged children in most studies. However, a somewhat greater proportion of children with school phobia are seen in child-guidance clinics and psychiatric clinics. According to Hersov (1977), school refusers account for 1% to 8% of children who attend child guidance clinics. It has also been suggested that the incidence of school phobia may be increasing. For example, Eisenberg (1958) noted the incidence to have risen in his clinic from 3 cases per 1000 to 17 cases per 1000 over an 8-year period. In view of the potential stress of leaving home and the possible traumas experienced at school, it is surprising that more children with this diagnosis are not referred to child-guidance clinics. This is probably due to the fact that most parents and teachers are quite firm about school attendance at the time of school entry and the primary–secondary school transition. Because of the somatic complaints involved in school phobia, parents are also more likely to take their children to family practitioners than seek other forms of professional assistance. As well, it may be that family practitioners are able to manage many cases of school phobia (Shepherd, Cooper, Brown & Kalton, 1966).

SUB-TYPES OF SCHOOL PHOBIA

Numerous sub-types of school phobia have been proposed, as can be seen in Table 6.2. Coolidge, Hahn and Peck (1957) differentiated 'neurotic' and 'characterological' types of school phobics. The first group is thought to possess

Table 6.2 Classification within school phobia

Author(s)	Types	Personality	Prognosis
Coolidge et al. (1957)	Neurotic	Basically sound	Good
	Characterological	Chronic, complex disorders	Guarded
Kennedy (1965)	Type 1	Basically stable	Good
	Type 2	Chronic, complex disorders	Guarded
Nichols and Berg (1970)	Acute	Basically sound	Good
	Chronic	Chronic neuroticism and isolationism	Guarded
Marine (1968)	Simple separation anxiety	Sound	Excellent
	Mild acute school refusal	Basically stable	Good
	Chronic severe school refusal	Chronic maladaptive disorders	Guarded
	Childhood psychosis with school-refusal symptoms	Psychoses: depressive and compulsive reactions	Poor

SOURCE: McDonald and Sheperd (1976).

a generally sound personality, while the second group display symptoms indicating a chronic and pervasive personality disorder. The prognosis for the 'characterological' type is believed to be considerably poorer than for the 'neurotic' type. Kennedy (1965) attempted to operationalize these sub-types in terms of behavioural criteria (see Table 6.3). Again, it is claimed that the Type 1 (neurotic) school-phobic child has a better prognosis than the Type 2 (characterological) school-phobic.

Following the classification of Berg and his colleagues (Berg *et al.*, 1969; Nichols & Berg, 1970), school-phobic children may be divided into acute or chronic types. The classification of the child depends upon the child's history before the onset of the phobia. The child with at least 3 years of trouble-free attendance before the school phobia began is classified as 'acute', regardless of how long the condition has continued subsequently. All other children with school phobia are classified as 'chronic'. Berg *et al.* (1969) maintain that chronic cases show more neuroticism, more maladjustment, more attachment to mothers, less interest in other young people, a greater tendency to stay at home and less freedom of movement away from home than the acute cases. In a follow-up study of school-phobic adolescents that had been admitted to an inpatient psychiatric unit, Berg (1970) concluded that the chronic cases were more disturbed and less amenable to treatment than acute cases. In many respects, Nichols and Berg's categories parallel those of Kennedy.

Marine (1968) has proposed a broader set of diagnostic categories of school phobia that incorporates change agents and treatment methods. Her four types are (1) simple separation anxiety; (2) mild acute school refusal; (3) severe chronic

Table 6.3 Type 1 and Type 2 school phobia

Type 1	Type 2
(1) The present illness is the first episode	(1) Second, third or fourth episode
(2) Monday onset, following an illness on the previous Thursday or Friday	(2) Monday onset following minor illness, not a prevalent antecedent
(3) An acute onset	(3) Incipient onset
(4) Lower grades most prevalent	(4) Upper grades most prevalent
(5) Expressed concern about death	(5) Death theme not present
(6) Mother's physical health in question: actually ill or child thinks so	(6) Health of mother not an issue
(7) Good communication between parents	(7) Poor communication between parents
(8) Mother and father well adjusted in most areas	(8) Mother shows neurotic behaviour; father a character disorder
(9) Father competitive with mother in household management	(9) Father shows little interest in household or children
(10) Parents achieve understanding of dynamics easily	(10) Parents very difficult to work with

SOURCE: Kennedy (1962). Copyright (1962) by the American Psychological Association. Reproduced by permission of the author.

school refusal, and (4) childhood psychosis with school-refusal symptoms. Simple separation anxiety is seen in young children undergoing their first major separation from parents at the time of school entry. After about one week, the symptoms usually dissipate. Because of its transient nature, it is questionable as to whether this is a form of school phobia. Nevertheless, the problem is disconcerting to the child, and can be prevented or treated by parents and school personnel. Children with mild acute school phobia experience an acute and dramatic onset of symptoms. This type of school phobia corresponds to Kennedy's (1965) Type 1 school phobia. The children are unresponsive to parental reasoning and discipline in relation to school attendance. Marine recommends treatment involving parents and school personnel for this type of school refusal, and that a mental health professional be responsible for the coordination of home and school. Severe chronic school refusal corresponds to Kennedy's Type 2 school phobia. The children are older, and the onset is usually incipient. The attitudes of the parents towards school and achievement are usually problematic. School refusal is seen to be part of a more general picture of maladjustment and personality disorder. Individual therapy, family counselling and close coordination with school personnel is recommended by Marine. Childhood psychosis with school-refusal symptoms is rare in comparison with the other types of school phobia. Residential-based treatment is advocated by Marine for children in this category. The child is also expected to attend some form of school class over the period of residential treatment.

The empirical validity of these prognostic statements and the selection of treatment technique on the basis of diagnostic classification is unknown. As Ollendick and Mayer (1984) have noted: 'Clearly, more research is required before the reliability and validity of "subtyping" can be established and before such conceptual distinctions can be meaningfully used in clinical practice. Certainly, our own experience would suggest that these children and their parents do not present themselves as neat and packaged "subtypes"' (p. 372). Ollendick and Mayer believe that continued research is warranted, and with a sharper behavioural focus: 'It may well be the case that subtyping based on primary etiology (e.g. separation anxiety, school situations, absence following illness) and/or topographic characteristics of the phobia (e.g. frequency, intensity, and duration) will be more fruitful' (p. 372). From the viewpoint of clinical practice, it would appear that individual differences in the factors which precipitate and maintain school-avoidance behaviour are so diverse that interventions based on a thorough behavioural assessment may be more successful than those based on global diagnostic categories offered to date. The prognosis of the case will likely vary depending on the particular child, family and school.

AETIOLOGY OF SCHOOL PHOBIA

From a behavioural perspective, school phobia is viewed as a learned maladaptive behaviour pattern. A general account of the aetiology of children's phobias has already been given in Chapter 2. However, further comments in relation to school phobia are warranted. In the traditional view, school phobia is the result of an unresolved mother–child dependency relationship that produces anxiety in the child and mother at the time of separation (hence 'separation anxiety'). As will become apparent, behavioural accounts of school phobia have not completely rejected this interpretation. Prima facie, it might be assumed that school-related factors (e.g. difficulties relating to teachers, academic failure, peer rejection) would also be significant in theoretical accounts of school phobia. Surprisingly this is not totally the case (Gordon & Young, 1976), although the behavioural analysis of school phobia readily accommodates school-related factors as well home-related events.

Following a case report on a 10-year-old school-phobic boy, Garvey and Hegrenes (1966) propose a parsimonious stimulus–response conditioning model of school phobia. Accordingly the child fears loss of the mother as a result of comments about leaving and separation. This fear becomes verbally conditioned to ideas about going to school, where the child would 'lose' his or her mother. As the fear of school intensifies, the child finally refuses to attend school. Staying at home has a reinforcing influence in that it reduces fear and usually offers other rewards, such as toys and affection. A major criticism of this account is that insufficient attention is given to school-related factors.

A more comprehensive behavioural account of school phobia has been provided by Yates (1970). While he emphasizes the importance of mother–child relationships in determining school phobia, he argues that they can be accounted for within a learning-theory framework. Since parents act as strong reinforcers for children during the pre-school years, the children see them as a refuge to which they may return when they feel frightened or uncertain. Feelings of anxiety about separation may be both prompted and reinforced by a mother (or father) who is overly concerned about the safety of her child. Consequently, many children will feel some anxiety in separation from the mother when first attending school. Whether or not this anxiety develops into a fear of school will depend on the availability of reinforcers in the school, which effectively compete with anxiety reactions, and on the response of the mother to the fears of the child: 'Hence, the genesis of a school phobia may be complexly determined by one or more of the following factors: separation anxiety leading to overdependence on the home as a safe refuge; insufficient rewards or actual anxiety-arousing experiences at school; and possibly, of course, actual traumatic events at school' (p. 152). This account is a more balanced interpretation of school phobia because of its emphasis upon school-related factors (i.e. insufficient rewards and traumatic events within the school setting) as well as important home-related factors.

Although separation anxiety is frequently seen as the cause of school phobia, the significance of separation anxiety has been overstated. Smith (1970) examined the files of 63 cases of school refusal referred to the Children's Department of the Maudsley Hospital in London, between the years 1958 and 1964. Among the variables examined were precipitants and types of symptomatic behaviour. In 27 of the 63 cases examined, change of school was reported to be the event which precipitated the school-avoidance behaviour. The majority of these cases involved the transition from primary to secondary school. A further nine cases indicated that a school-related traumatic event had occurred prior to the onset of school phobia. Eight children refused to attend school after an absence due to illness; seven after a family event of an upsetting kind; one developed a fear after watching a film; three were starting school for the first time; and for the remaining eight children, no precipitant could be identified.

Smith's analyses of symptomatic behaviours described in the case notes showed that 12 children (less than 20% of the school refusers) were marked either by anxiety which occurred when the child was separated from the parent or by dependency on the mother. An additional 4 children were attached to the parents in that they expressed concern that some harm may come to the parent if separation occurred. Smith draws a distinction between refusal to leave the parent and fear of leaving the parent. In 10 cases the symptomatology was less that of fear and more that of manipulation and over-indulgence. The case notes indicated that 21 children displayed a general fearfulness that could not be allayed by the presence of the parents. Additional fears were evident for these particular children, including fears of violence, social situations, illness and going out even when accompanied by a parent. The other cases were categorized as fear of failure, depression or schizoid withdrawal, with a number of cases not having any comments with regard to general symptomatology. The reliability of the determinations is questionable, however, particularly for those cases involving failure of separation. Nevertheless, Smith concludes that of the children referred for treatment of school refusal, those suffering from separation anxiety are a distinct group. From the data presented, they appear to be a minority, more than two-thirds of whom are 8 years of age or under. Similar findings have been reported by Miller et al. (1972a): 'Fear of separation, which is often reported to be the core problem in school phobias, was listed as the target fear when separation was primary and fear was manifested in many situations. Fourteen of our 46 school phobics showed such generalized separation fear' (p. 270).

The aetiology and maintenance of school phobia can be understood in terms of learning principles, without necessary reference to separation anxiety, as shown in the behavioural analysis of school phobia provided by Ollendick and Mayer (1984). Accordingly, some children make negative statements about school and how bad they feel at school, and subsequently opt to stay home instead of going to school. Parents and significant others in the child's environment may inadvertently reinforce such statements and behaviours, thereby contributing to the child's desire to avoid school. Under these circumstances, the child probably does not possess an excessive 'fear' of school but has found it simply more reinforcing at home (parental attention and affection). Of course, the child's reluctance to go to school may be genuine and reflect what the child perceives as a punishing environment (perceived criticism, academic failure). The child who is continuously subject to ridicule and criticism from peers or teachers may have legitimate problems. On the other hand, the child's complaints can be exaggerated. In such cases, the child learns that parents are overly sensitive to such complaints and that they respond with much attention. Thus a little 'fear' leads to intense and frequent responses from significant others. The more fear and avoidance behaviour the child displays, the more attention he or she receives. An analysis of this kind is supported by several case investigations (e.g. Ayllon *et al.*, 1970; Hersen, 1970).

The behaviour analysis of school phobia provided by Ollendick and Mayer (1984) can be taken further with respect to the child's academic and social functioning. Our clinical experience suggests that school-phobic children find it difficult to cope at school, with many worries about classwork and social interactions. Aversive experiences at school can be a function of the child not having the requisite skills to cope with the demands placed upon him or her. Ross (1981) illustrates how academic skill deficits contribute to school refusal:

> Afraid of school and therefore avoiding it, a girl falls behind in the school work and then fears returning even more because in going back to school she might encounter academic failure. Conversely, a boy who is not doing well academically may find school so aversive that he refuses to go there, whereupon the extended absence results in even greater academic retardation. (p. 252)

Whereas Ross discusses academic skill deficits as a crucial factor in school phobia, social skill deficits must also be taken into consideration. Sometimes school-phobic children lack the necessary social skills and self-confidence in order to mix with other children, and approach their teacher(s) in an appropriate manner. A child with these difficulties must inevitably suffer many negative consequences given that social skills are necessary to most aspects of school life. The notion of academic and/or social problems being partly or fully responsible for school phobia is a fairly sensitive issue, since it can be construed that schools are remiss in meeting the needs of the individual child. Interestingly, Hersov (1960b) found that many school-phobic children were afraid of a strict and sarcastic teacher or of academic failure. Since many children with academic and/or social problems continue to attend school, these factors cannot be held to be fully responsible for school phobia. Nevertheless, they should be considered in an individual assessment. Even though such factors may not have been significant in the aetiology of the phobia, they can be quite profound in the maintenance of the problem.

BEHAVIOURAL MANAGEMENT

The behavioural management of school phobia is primarily based upon techniques derived from classical and/or operant conditioning. Lazarus *et al.* (1965) were the first to recognize the existence of both operant and respondent components in the maintenance of school-phobic behaviour, and developed the following guidelines for effective treatment:

> When avoidance behaviour is motivated by high levels of anxiety, classical counterconditioning techniques are called for; when anxiety is minimal, and avoidance behaviour is seemingly maintained by various secondary reinforcers, operant strategies should be applied. (p. 225)

However, it would appear that some child and adolescent school-phobics, who report experiencing high subjective anxiety levels, can be treated successfully using operant strategies alone. The same is probably true of young children who are entering school for the first time. While Lazarus et al. strongly advise that attention be paid to both respondent (conditioned anxiety) and operant components in treating school refusal, most studies have given heavy emphasis to either one or the other. This is particularly the case where contingency management is the major therapeutic intervention (Ayllon et al., 1970; Cooper, 1973; Tahmisian & McReynolds, 1971; Vaal, 1973).

As Ollendick and Mayer (1984) note, treatment procedures based on vicarious conditioning principles have yet to make a significant impact upon the behavioural management of school phobia. However, it may be argued that modelling is an integral part of behavioural interventions. Siblings, parents, therapist, or therapist–assistant frequently accompany the child to school in contingency management and in vivo desensitization programmes (Ayllon et al., 1970; Garvey & Hegrenes, 1966; Tahmisian & McReynolds, 1971). In these situations the accompanying individual is competent with respect to approaching the school and school entry. Presumably the phobic child pays at the least some attention to what the person concerned says and does. Thus a strong modelling effect is probably at work in these interventions. Further consideration should be given to the use of live modelling with respect to school approach, school entry, classroom interactions, and other problematic aspects of school life. In fact, on the basis of the success of modelling with the other fears and phobias of childhood (Graziano, DeGiovanni & Garcia, 1979), modelling would seem to have considerable potential in the behavioural management of school phobia.

The behavioural management of school phobia shall now be reviewed in terms of classical- and operant-conditioning-based treatment procedures. Subsequently, a comprehensive assessment and rapid treatment strategy will be presented.

Classical-conditioning-based procedures

Several intervention methods related to the principles of classical conditioning have been applied to school phobia. These include systematic desensitization, emotive imagery, flooding and implosion. The use of these procedures is predicated upon the assumption that anxiety of some kind is responsible for school phobia. Using systematic desensitization, the school-phobic child is required to imagine a series of anxiety-provoking scenes, while in a state of deep muscular relaxation. Three steps are involved: (1) training in relaxation, (2) construction of the anxiety hierarchy, and (3) imagining each scene while relaxed (Wolpe, 1958). Experienced behavioural practitioners state that school-phobic children often have difficulty identifying the source(s) of the anxiety. This is a fairly critical issue from the viewpoint of anxiety-reduction procedures like systematic desensitization. A good clinical tip has been offered by Yule (1979): 'The child often cannot put into words what he is afraid of, so it can be helpful to walk with him to school and observe closely the circumstances under which anxiety is shown' (p. 62). Another possibility is to have the child describe and visualize the events that occur over a school day, while the clinician pays careful attention to physiological changes and their critical antecedents (Smith & Sharpe, 1970).

Systematic desensitization in imagination has been successfully applied in the management of school-phobic children, as illustrated by the following case reports. In an early study, Lazarus (1960) described the case of a $9\frac{1}{2}$- year-old girl whose major problem was thought to be difficulty in separating from her mother. Refusal to attend school was seen as a consequence of separation problems. The girl developed multiple symptoms after experiencing a number of traumatic events over a short period of time. In quick succession she had three traumatic experiences of death (a school friend drowned, a playmate died suddenly of meningitis, and she witnessed a man killed in a motorbike accident). She was afraid of being separated from her mother, had nightmares and was enuretic. Using a 7-item hierarchy of fears relating to separation from the mother, a systematic desensitization procedure was successfully implemented over five treatment sessions. All problematic behaviours were reduced 10 days after the commencement of treatment, and a 15-month follow-up revealed normal school attendance. Similarly, Chapel (1967) reported the case of an 11-year-old boy with moderately severe school phobia. Separation anxiety was seen as the main component of this phobic reaction as well. The boy had received conventional one-to-one therapy on an outpatient basis but without success. He was admitted on to a ward as a day-patient, and trained in hypnosis to help induce relaxation. Systematic desensitization was then applied to his fear of separation. After 18 sessions of systematic desensitization, over a period of 6 weeks, the boy returned to school. However, difficulty in attending school occurred after the summer vacation when he had to go back to a new class. An additional 15 sessions of systematic desensitization were given, to which the boy responded fairly well.

Systematic desensitization in real life can also been utilized in the treatment of school phobia. Garvey and Hegrenes (1966) reported the successful treatment of a 10-year-old school-phobic boy using *in vivo* desensitization. A month prior to the referral, he had suffered a bronchial infection, following which were the Christmas holidays. When he thought about going to school in the morning he became frightened and often vomited. He was described as being highly strung, sensitive and preoccupied with high-level performance. Secondary factors began to arise, consisting of avoidance of friends and peers. Concerns about his mother, and prospect of losing her, were also expressed. After 6 months of traditional psychotherapy he felt more confident but unable to return to school. The desensitization procedure in this case was carried out in the school environment. School officials were informed of the procedure, and were very cooperative. Since it was known that the child could tolerate going by the school in a car, the first step consisted of sitting in the car in front of the school with the therapist. The remaining 11 steps in the anxiety hierarchy were as follows: (2) getting out of the car and approaching the curb; (3) going to the footpath; (4) going to the top of the steps; (5) going to the top of the steps; (6) going to the door of the school; (7) entering the school; (8) approaching the classroom with the teacher present; (9) entering the classroom; (10) sitting in the classroom with the teacher present; (11) sitting in the classroom with the teacher and one or two classmates; (12) sitting in the classroom with the full class present. This procedure was carried out over 20 consecutive days, including Saturdays and Sundays. The amount of time spent each day ranged from 20 to 40 minutes. Following desensitization, the child resumed a normal school routine with no return of the symptoms noted during a 2-year follow-up.

A combination of imaginal and real-life systematic desensitization is also possible in the treatment of school phobia. Miller (1972) presented the case of a 10-year-old boy with multiple fears that responded to imaginal and *in vivo* desensitization. He was afraid of separation from his mother, his own death, and the school situation. Approximately 8 weeks before treatment he had been criticized by a teacher and subsequently refused to attend school. The subject's fears were treated separately using systematic desensitization. He was trained in muscular relaxation over three 20-minute sessions, with candy and verbal praise being used to reinforce the relaxation response. Separation anxiety was successfully treated by working through a hierarchy of imaginal scenes related to distance from his mother. Desensitization to imagined scenes of dying was unsuccessful, as the subject was unable to experience the anxiety in relation to these scenes. For this problem, the child was instructed to phone the therapist at night when he experienced anxiety. Each time the subject called, instructions to relax were given over the telephone. After about 6 weeks the boy no longer reported fears of dying. The subject's fear of the school situation was then tackled. A hierarchy of scenes was constructed involving a distance continuum (being a block from school, standing in front of school, walking into the classroom and so on). After desensitization to these scenes in imagination, the subject reported less school-related anxiety and agreed to gradually return to the classroom. For the next week he was required to walk to school, stand at the front door, and then return home. He was instructed to apply muscle relaxation if he experienced anxiety. The length of time the subject spent near school (and subsequently in the classroom) was gradually increased. By the fifth week after initial re-entry, complete normal school attendance was achieved. Three-month and 18-month follow-ups revealed the maintenance of all behaviour changes. In a similar vein, Eysenck and Rachman (1965) reported a case of a 13-year-old boy who had been off school for a year. School refusal was precipitated by a tooth infection and sport's injury at the time he started secondary school. The behavioural programme that was eventually developed for him involved a graded reintroduction to school in the mornings, paralleled by relaxation training and imaginal desensitization in the afternoons. The programme was administered on an inpatient basis. After 2 weeks of treatment he was discharged as his school attendance was very good. Prior to the start of the new school term, he was admitted for a 1-week 'booster' treatment. Further difficulties were encountered that required more treatment, but after 3 months his attendance was satisfactory.

As noted in Chapter 4, emotive imagery is a variation of systematic desensitization (Lazarus & Abramovitz, 1962). Rather than muscular relaxation being used as the anxiety inhibitor, however, feelings of 'positive effect' are employed to counter anxiety. An exciting story involving the child's hero images might be told, with school-related scenes being interwoven at various points in hierarchical order. An example of the approach can be found in Lazarus and Abramovitz (1962). They presented the case of an 8-year-old girl referred for treatment because of nocturnal enuresis and school phobia, which had been precipitated by a series of emotional upsets in the classroom. Avoidance mechanisms concerning school attendance included temper tantrums, complaints of pain, and an episode of truancy. Emotive imagery was introduced and featured Noddy as the child's hero image. Noddy was a truant who responded fearfully to the school setting. The girl's imagery role was to protect Noddy by issuing reassuring statements or by modelling appropriate behaviour. A hierarchy of assertion problems in the school setting was encountered in emotive imagery. The school-phobia symptoms were extinguished after four sessions, with the bedwetting disappearing within 2 months. The child continued to improve over an unspecified follow-up period, despite an 'unsympathetic teacher'.

In addition to emotive imagery and systematic desensitization, flooding and implosion procedures in which the child is required to confront the feared situation have also been used. Flooding is usually an *in vivo* procedure, and would involve the school-phobic child being forced to attend school despite protests and tantrums. Implosion is carried out in the individual's imagination, and can involve extremely intense (exaggerated) scenes of a psychodynamic nature. Smith and Sharpe (1970) employed implosive therapy with a 13-year-old school-phobic boy. He had been absent from school for 60 days prior to treatment. The school-phobic symptoms included extreme anxiety, inability to eat breakfast, chest pains, and trembling and crying when at school. His phobic symptoms developed after a 3-week absence from school due to illness. Neither tranquilizers, force, punishment nor bribes could induce the boy to return to school. He insisted that he was unaware of the reasons for his intense fear, despite attempts to understand why he was afraid. Thus, he was asked to describe minutely and visualize a typical school day. Physiological changes such as flushing of the skin, vocal tremors, bodily movements and muscular tension were carefully noted at various points of the description. This assessment procedure indicated that mathematics and literature classes were the probable sources of intense anxiety, especially when being called on in class or unable to answer the teacher's questions. Consequently, nine scenes were constructed around the hypothetical anxiety-arousing cues. The boy was seen for six consecutive daily sessions of implosive therapy. Each scene was presented until a visible reduction in anxiety was observed. The seventh scene involving the literature class entailed the following description:

> The patient is ordered to his literature classroom by the principal. The room is dark and strange, and the chairs have been pushed to the sides of the room. Students begin silently filing into the room. It is too dark to identify them. Tension grows as Billy wonders what will happen. The students encircle him, pressing ever closer, and begin

to murmur 'Crazy Billy' and 'stupid, stupid, stupid'. They then begin to jostle and strike him. (p. 241)

The first session was extremely anxiety-provoking and physically exhausting. At the conclusion of the first implosive therapy session, the boy was directed to attend his anxiety-provoking mathematics class the next day. Following the second and third sessions, he was told to attend half-day sessions of school. After the fourth session, he was directed to school on a full-time basis. A 13-week follow-up indicated that he continued to attend school regularly with no reported anxiety. Despite the fact that implosive therapy is less time-consuming than desensitization treatments, it has not become popular amongst behavioural practitioners (see Chapter 4).

Kennedy (1965) developed a rapid-treatment programme for school-phobic children, entailing forced return to school (flooding). Because of the impact this programme has had on the behavioural management of school phobia it will be reported in some detail. According to Kennedy (1965): 'The treatment involved the application of broad learning theory concepts by blocking the escape of the child and preventing secondary gains from occurring. In addition, the child was reinforced for going to school without complaint' (pp. 286–7). Kennedy's rapid-treatment programme for Type-1 school phobia involves six essential components: good professional public relations, avoidance of emphasis on somatic complaints, forced school attendance, structured interview with parents, brief interview with child, and follow-ups. The components are fairly self-evident, although several deserve emphasis. Kennedy urges that parents should not become preoccupied with the somatic complaints of their children. Nevertheless, a medical examination is advised. According to Kennedy:

...the child's somatic complaints should be handled matter-of-factly, with an appointment to see the pediatrician after school hours. Abdominal pains will probably require the pediatrician to make a prompt physical examination, but this can be probably done on the way to school. (p. 287)

The critical aspect of the programme is forced school attendance:

It is essential to be able to require the child to go to school and to be willing to use any force necessary. In all of the present cases, simply convincing the parents of this necessity and having them come to a firm decision, has generally been enough. (p. 288)

It is advocated that the father take the child to school, where the principal or other staff take an active part in keeping the child in the classroom. Interestingly, Kennedy(s) rapid treatment programme was by no means a completely new innovation, as it is very similar to the early work of Rodriguez, Rodriguez and Eisenberg (1959).

Kennedy (1965) carried out his rapid-treatment programme with 50 Type-1 school-phobic cases over an 8-year period. The age range of the children was 4 to 16 years, although only 10 children were older than 12 years. The symptomatology of these children is shown in Table 6.3. Of the 50 Type-1 school-phobic cases, Kennedy reports that five might be considered semicontrols.

They were untreated Type-1 cases of considerable duration, or were Type-1 cases that had been unsuccessfully treated elsewhere. All of the 50 cases responded to the rapid-treatment programme with a complete remission of the school-phobia symptoms. The families were followed up 2 weeks and 6 weeks after intervention, and then on an annual basis for 2 to 8 years. In discussing these results, which are quite outstanding, Kennedy comments: 'perhaps what is called Type-1 School Phobia is not really a severe phobic attack at all, but borders on malingering of a transient nature which would spontaneously remit in a few days anyway' (p. 289). Taking into account these considerations, Kennedy concludes that the treatment programme may accelerate a facilitated remission of what is a serious problem despite its possible transient nature. In the absence of no-treatment controls, however, it is difficult to gauge the effectiveness of Kennedy's rapid-treatment programme. As we shall see later in the chapter, Kennedy's ideas are still a major influence on the behavioural management of school phobia (Blagg, 1977; Blagg & Yule, 1984).

Operant-conditioning-based procedures

From an operant perspective, school phobia can be treated without reference to classical conditioning principles. Ollendick and Mayer (1984) have summarized the essence of the operant approach:

> Essentially, strategies based on the operant model attempt to increase the reinforcement value of school attendance (e.g. increased peer acceptance; teacher and parental approval) as well as decrease the reinforcement value of staying at home (e.g. withdrawal of parental attention, prohibiting the watching of television). Until 'natural' consequences (i.e., good grades, improved peer relations) associated with the regular school attendance are realized by the school-phobic child, material or social reinforcers in the form of preferred objects and social praise may be required. (p. 391)

Thus an operant-based programme should involve the school and home with respect to the management of contingencies (positive reinforcement and extinction). Following a shaping procedure, full-time school attendance can be established via a series of graduated approximations. Usually the therapist has the child carry out a tolerable school-related morning task (e.g. visit school at normal starting time without going into school), and builds up from this point until satisfactory school attendance is achieved. On the other hand, the therapist can have the child start with a school-related afternoon task (e.g. sitting in on the last class) and work backwards in increasing the amount of time spent at school until full-time school attendance occurs. The operant approach does not make any assumptions regarding the presence or absence of anxiety, regardless of physiological changes that are observed in the child. Several illustrative case reports will be presented on the operant approach to the treatment of school refusal.

The now classic study on the operant approach to school phobia is that reported by Allyon et al. (1970). The case involved an 8-year-old girl who had gradually stopped attending school in the second grade, with this refusal continuing on into the third grade. Whenever the mother attempted to take her to school, she threw such violent temper tantrums, screamed and cried, that it was impossible to take her to school. A 10-day baseline was taken in which behavioural observations were made in the child's home and a neighbours home. The child's principal and teachers were also interviewed. Table 6.4 shows the procedural and behavioural effects of intervention. Four distinct procedures were used in treatment. The first procedure entailed the prompting–shaping of school attendance. The subject was taken to school by the therapist's assistant towards the end of the school day. Each day she was taken to school progressively earlier. Although progress was made to the stage where she would remain in school all day without the presence of the assistant, she still refused to get dressed in the morning and walk to school with her three siblings. Thus, the problem was how to provide sufficient motivation to ensure her leaving for school. The second procedure entailed withdrawal of social reinforcers upon failure to leave for school. As the subject was able to spend one hour with her mother then left for work at the designated time, the subject still refused to go for work at the same time the children were to go to school. Although the mother than left for work at the designated time, the subject still refused to go to school. For 10 days she refused to attend school, and each day was taken to her neighbour's apartment. The subject also started to follow her mother to work. The third procedure entailed prompting school attendance combined with a home-based motivational system. This time the mother, rather than the assistant, was responsible for the prompting. A large chart with each child's

Table 6.4 Procedural and behavioural progression during the treatment of school phobia

Temporal sequence	Procedure	Valerie's behaviour
(1) Baseline observations, days 1–10	Observations taken at home and at the neighbour's apartment where Val spent her day	Valerie stayed at home when siblings left for school; mother took Val to neighbour's apartment as she left for work
(2) Behavioural assessment, days 11–13	Assistant showed school materials to Val and prompted academic work	Val reacted well to books; she coloured pictures and copied numbers and letters
(3) Behavioural assessment, day 13	Assistant invited Val for a car ride after completing academic work at neighbour's apartment	Val readily accepted car ride and on way back to neighbour's apartment she also accepted hamburger offered her
(4) Procedure 1, days 14–20	Taken by assistant to school; assistant stayed with her in classroom; attendance made progressively earlier while assistant's stay in classroom progressively lessens	Val attended school with assistant; performed school work; left school with siblings at closing time

Table 6.4 (*Contd.*)

Temporal sequence	Procedure	Valerie's behaviour
(5) Day 21	Assistant did not take Val to school	Val and siblings attended school on their own
(6) Procedure 1, day 22	Val taken by assistant to school	Val attended school with assistant; performed school work; left with siblings at school closing time
(7) Return to baseline observations, days 23–27	Observations taken at home	Val stayed at home when siblings left for school; mother took Val to neighbour's apartment as she left for work
(8) Procedure 2, days 28–29	Mother left for work when children left for school	Val stayed at home when children left for school; mother took her to neighbour's apartment as she left for work
(9) Procedure 3, days 40–49	Taken by mother to school; home-based motivational system	Val stayed at home when siblings left for school; followed mother quietly when taken to school
(10) Procedure 4, days 50–59	On day 50, mother left for school *before* children left home; home-based motivational system	Siblings met mother at school door; Val stayed at home
	After 15 minutes of waiting in school, mother returned home and took Val to school	Val weekly followed her mother
	On day 51, mother left for school *before* children left home	Val and siblings met mother at school door
	On day 52, mother left for school before children left home	Siblings met mother at school door; Valerie stayed at home
	After 15 minutes of waiting in school, mother returned home and physically hit and dragged Valerie to school	Valerie cried and pleaded with her mother note to hit her; cried all the way to school
	On days 53–59, mother left for school before children left home	Val and siblings met mother at school door
(11) Fading procedure, days 60–69	Mother discontinued going to school before children; mother maintained home-based motivational system	Val and siblings attended school on their own
(12) Fading procedure, day 70	Mother discontinued home-based motivational system	Val and siblings attended school on their own

SOURCE: Allyon, Smith and Rogers (1970). Reprinted with permission by Pergamon Press.

name and the days of the week was given to the mother. The placement of a star signified one day of going to school on a voluntary basis; five stars indicated perfect attendance for the week and would result in a special treat or outing. Candy was also dispensed for going to school. Under these conditions school attendance improved. The fourth procedure was designed to prompt voluntary school attendance and introduced a mild aversive element for the mother if the subject failed to attend school. The mother now left 10 minutes before the children left for school, and met the children at school with a reward. If the subject did not arrive at school with her siblings, the mother had to return home and escort her to school. It was hoped that this inconvenience would prompt the mother into becoming firmer with the subject. The motivational system employed in the third procedure was maintained. Only twice was the mother inconvenienced by school refusal under these conditions. The second incident was very significant: 'As it was raining, it was a considerable inconvenience for Val's mother to have to go back home. Once she reached home she scolded Val and pushed her out of the house and literally all the way to school. As Val tried to give some explanation the mother hit her with a switch. By the time they arrived at school, both were soaking wet' (pp. 134–5). The home-based motivational system was withdrawn after one month, with all of the children continuing to attend school. The subject was successfully treated in 45 days. Academic and social skills improvements were also noted on 6-month and 9-month follow-ups (see Fig. 6.1).

The outstanding feature of this case report is the way in which intervention strategies were determined on an empirical basis and systematically evaluated. Another significant aspect is that school refusal was finally brought under control by the mother's use of punishment for staying at home. The use of punishment is rarely reported in the behavioural management of school phobia.

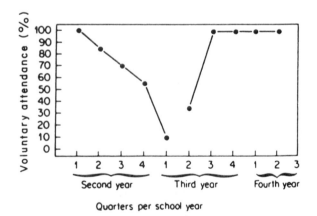

Fig. 6.1 Valerie's voluntary school attendance. Reproduced from Allyon, Smith and Rogers (1970) by permission of Pergamon Press.

Nevertheless, it is a treatment option that can be adopted in conjunction with positive treatment procedures, as this case illustrates.

The importance of changing parental reinforcement contingencies has been demonstrated in numerous case reports. For example, Cooper (1973) described the case of Lisa, who cried at kindergarten, complained of being ill and wanted to go home. An interview with her mother revealed that Lisa had been reinforced since infancy, by much attention from the mother, for being ill. When Lisa arrived home from school, her mother usually asked her if she had been sick or if she had cried. It seemed that Lisa's negative comments about school were being reinforced by the mother's attention. The mother was instructed to prompt and reinforce positive comments about school, and to ignore negative comments and complaints of illness. After 18 days Lisa was happily attending school. Similarly, Hersen (1970) treated a $12\frac{1}{2}$-year-old school-phobic boy by a programme consisting of three components: (1) restructuring familial reinforcement contingencies, such that appropriate behaviour was reinforced and inappropriate behaviour ignored; (2) advising school personnel on how to reverse reinforcement contingencies; and (3) seeing the boy for 15-hour sessions to reinforce positive comments about school. Follow-ups at 6 and 8 months revealed normal school attendance, plus above-average grades, and other interests. These case reports illustrate how illness complaints and negative comments about school, which can be very upsetting or annoying to parents and teachers, can be brought under operant control, as well as school attendance.

Vaal (1973) reported the implementation of an operant-based programme for a case of school refusal that is noteworthy because of its simplicity and effectiveness. A 13-year-old boy began attending classes for the first 3 days of the school year. At the end of the third day he arrived home in tears, and refused to go back to school. Any attempt to force him to return to school were met with crying, yelling and clinging to the parents and furniture. During the first 6 months of that school year he was absent on an average of 94% of days. A contingency contract was developed between the subject, parents and school. The following target behaviours were identified: (1) attending school on time without tantrum behaviour; (2) attending all classes; and (3) remaining at school until dismissed at the end of each day. If the subject met these contingencies, he was allowed to engage in various activities when he returned home. These included: (1) going to professional basketball games; (2) bowling on Saturdays; (3) visiting a neighbour who was a professional basketball player (4) playing basketball with friends after school; and (5) going home for a short period after lunch and then returning for afternoon classes. If he failed to meet any of these criteria, the privileges were withheld. For the following 3 months the boy did not miss a single day of school. Further, the subject came on time, attended all classes, and did not engage in temper tantrums. After a $2\frac{1}{2}$-month summer holiday, he returned tò school without experiencing any problems. Furthermore, the formal contract procedures were only in effect for the first 6 weeks, after which the treatment was terminated. A notable feature of the contract was that the rewards to be received contingent on normal school attendance had all been freely available to the boy before the contract was introduced. Thus a clear statement of the rewards for attending school, in the form of a simple contract, can be very helpful. A critical consideration is the extent to which the parents are able to enforce the contract in a reliable manner.

An interesting case that calls into question the comparative effectiveness of systematic desensitization and operant-based procedures was reported by Tahmisian and McReynolds (1971). Carol, a 13-year-old girl, was referred for treatment when she developed a fear of school after attending a summer camp. At school she reported being very frightened and unable to stop crying. Her only explanation for this was that she felt left out of class activities. Systematic desensitization was attempted and Carol was able to complete a 12-step anxiety hierarchy. However, she continued to refuse to attend school. It became apparent that Carol was somewhat overindulged by her parents. They tended to give in to her whenever she became upset. A second treatment phase was thus implemented whereby Carol's behaviour was shaped, following a school approach hierarchy. Her parents were instructed not to give in to emotional outbursts and to reward cooperation with verbal praise and special privileges. Carol was able to attend school normally by the third week of treatment, and had begun to show renewed interest in peer relationships. The authors describe this programme as an 'instrumental behaviour shaping procedure' (p. 225). It is worth noting that in shaping procedures such as this, a significant feature of the treatment is graded exposure to the school situation. Even though an anxiety inhibitor was not used, the results may still be accounted for within the classical conditioning paradigm. Tahmisian and McReynolds do not state whether imaginal or *in vivo* desensitization was used in the first treatment phase. If the former, then the lack of success of this procedure could be explained in terms of failure to generalize to the real-life situation. The success of the second phase could be due to the superiority of *in vivo* over imaginal graded exposure with children. Although not often acknowledged in the literature, a confounding problem concerns the training and expertise of the behavioural practitioner. Some therapists are, of course, very good with desensitization techniques, while other therapists are excellent with operant-based procedures. Unfortunately, very few behavioural practitioners have high degrees of competence with each of the major conditioning paradigms and their therapeutic strategies. Whatever the correct interpretation may be, this case illustrates the difficulties involved when one attempts to interpret the effects of a treatment procedure that may involve both operant and respondent components.

The operant approach to the management of school phobia has so far stressed consequential control (i.e. reinforcement of appropriate behaviour and the extinction of inappropriate behaviour). Antecedent stimulus control has not been considered, especially as it relates to events in the home. To a certain extent, school phobia can be seen as non-compliant behaviour with parental instructions about going to school. Hence, the quality of parent instructions should be considered. With respect to parent instructions, Forehand and McMahon (1981) outline five general types of command that can lower child compliance. These include long chains of commands, vague commands, question commands, 'let's...' commands, and commands followed by a rationale or other verbalizations. Training parents in antecedent stimulus-control procedures like command-giving would seem a valuable service in many cases. Forehand's and McMahon's model of helping parents manage non-compliant children seems particularly useful here. An important part of their programme involves training parents to give clear and direct commands to their children. Emphasis is placed upon getting the child's attention, firmness of voice, specific and direct commands, and giving only one command at a time. Parents can be taught to improve their command-giving via modelling and behaviour rehearsal in a structured learning situation. Helping parents establish rules and organizational procedures related to 'getting ready for school' might also be of assistance, especially in families that seem very disorganized with respect to school matters. It is to be hoped that more attention will be given to antecedent stimulus control in the behavioural management of school phobia.

Comprehensive behavioural management

From the preceding account it will be appreciated that numerous behavioural methods, derived from classical- and operant-conditioning principles, have been employed in the management of school phobia. Given the multiplicity of aetiological and maintenance factors in school phobia, it appears that comprehensive behavioural programmes may be required. A detailed strategy for the rapid treatment of school phobia that draws upon classical and operant conditioning has been developed by Blagg (1977). Blagg's treatment plan stresses early return to school and incorporates:

(1) desensitization of the stimulus through humour and emotive imagery;
(2) blocking the avoidance response through forced school attendance;
(3) maximizing positive reinforcement for school attendance both at home and at school;
(4) extinction of protests, fear reactions and psychosomatic complaints through contingency management.

Blagg (1977) suggests that the child and parents be interviewed in the school with the onus on the parents to get the child to school (by force if necessary) for the interview. A number of practical advantages are seen to be associated with this tactic. For example, it minimizes parent and child collusion from the beginning, demonstrates the parent's desire to get the child to school under protest and ability to act as an escort, and gives information on whether the child's problem is largely that of separation from mother and leaving home or a phobic avoidance of school. As Blagg explains, a change of school may be necessary in certain cases. A range of factors should be considered, including the child's level of intellectural functioning and need for special services, insurmountable peer-group difficulties (e.g. bullying or excessive teasing), major conflicts between the child and school staff, a long and unpleasant journey to school, and excessive antagonism on the part of parents towards the current school. At this stage Blagg believes that the harsh realities of the situation should be impressed upon parents (the legal requirements, the complications of prolonged absenteeism, and the fact that life requires people to face frightening and unpleasant situations).

Within the treatment plan outlined by Blagg (1977) the child's parents play a crucial role in returning the child to school. Consequently, the therapist needs to secure their trust and confidence. Blagg emphasizes that the 'successful application of these techniques is dependent upon establishing good relationships, reducing anxiety, rationalizing guilt feelings and inspiring confidence' (p. 70). Usually the parents are responsible for escorting the child to school. Blagg suggests that a special effort be made to involve the father who very often is ineffectual and avoids taking responsibility. When it is apparent the parents will not be able to force the child to attend school because of their anxiety and/or lack of firmness, other escorts have to be considered (close relatives, school teacher, social worker, psychologist). The escort must be able to handle the child's temper tantrums, be supportive but firm with parents, and continue to take the child to school until protest and/or psychosomatic symptoms have passed even if this takes several weeks. When the child arrives at school: 'Supervising staff should be warm but firm, ignoring the child's tears and protests but attending to the child when he shows signs of recovering. The child should be integrated into the normal school routine as quickly as possible' (p. 74). Teachers are required to look for ways of reinforcing the child for being at school; by, for example, giving the child responsibilities, building success into the child's work, and praising the child for improvements. As far as the child is concerned, Blagg advocates a frank discussion of the reality of the situation, the use of emotive imagery, and information on what can be expected (e.g. escort procedure, special arrangements at school, initial feelings of distress).

There are several treatment options that Blagg has not covered in his plan, that may be worthy of inclusion. Encouraging parents to set household routines and rules with respect to preparation for school, and helping parents in the way in which they issue instructions to their children, are simple antecedent stimulus-control measures that have already been noted. A common anxiety on the part of the child in returning to school is how to explain his absence and/or distress to peers who are prone to ask questions and possibly tease the child. Blagg recommends that the child be 'allowed to recover quietly in a supervised situation away from other children. This should minimize the chance of the child being teased by other pupils over being distressed in the mornings' (p. 74). Some very focused social skills training may help the child cope with peers. This would require the child rehearsing responses in relation to peer enquiries and teasing. Whether this is possible will depend upon the time constraints and the child's willingness to cooperate. Overall, Blagg's rapid treatment plan is similar to the forced-attendance programme advocated by Kennedy (1965). There are, however, several important differences. Blagg's approach takes into account the expressed anxieties of the child, and considers whether the child is correctly placed in his present school. Although not acknowledged by Blagg, his programme has a stronger operant component (consider emphasis upon reinforcement at school). Whereas Kennedy restricted his programme to Type-1 school phobics, Blagg points out that his approach is advocated for a wide range of school-refusal cases (i.e. Type-1 and Type-2 school-phobia).

In addition to providing comprehensive guidelines on the behavioural management of school phobia, Blagg and Yule (1984) have evaluated the effectiveness of their behavioural prescription. As would be appreciated, the general management of school phobia varies according to the orientation of the individual professional and clinic. Rather than insist upon an early return to school, some professionals prefer the child to remain off school but receive psychotherapy and some kind of home-based instruction. Another approach is to have the child referred to an inpatient psychiatric unit. Here the child is likely to participate in eclectic treatment, and be required to attend a hospital school. In their research investigation, Blagg and Yule compared the effectiveness of behavioural treatment with these more traditional forms of treatment.

The behavioural treatment approach (BTA) was systematically applied to a series of 30 school-refusal cases referred over a 3-year period. These 30 cases were compared with 16 hospitalized school refusers (HU), and 20 who received home instruction and psychotherapy (HT). The 66 cases that were involved in the study met diagnostic criteria of school refusal similar to those proposed by Berg *et al.* (1969). Although there was no random allocation to treatment groups, the groups were systematically compared on a range of variables. Most of the children were in the 11 to 16 year age range. There were no statistically significant differences on sex, social-class distribution, intelligence, or reading age. They were very similar with respect to associated symptoms, school and home-related anxieties, family size, parent attitudes, and employment. Applying Kennedy's criteria, half of the children in the BTA groups, three-quarters of the HU group, and one-quarter of the HT groups were classified as Type-2 school-refusal. Thus the three groups were reasonably similar at the start of treatment.

The BTA entailed: (1) a detailed clarification of the child's problems; (2) a realistic discussion of child, parental and teacher worries; (3) contingency plans to ensure maintenance; (4) *in vivo* flooding (return to school); and (5) follow-up for at least 6 weeks, plus care at times of illness, on long weekends, at the start of a new academic year, etc. The HU treatment involved: (1) physical separation of the child and parents; (2) therapeutic mileu (daily group psychotherapy); (3) educational and occupational therapy (attendance at hospital school); (4) drug therapy (tranquillizers); and (5) management of discharge (child contracting to attend school). Each of the children in the HT group was allowed to remain off school. They received instruction (at the tutor's house) and psychotherapy on a fortnightly basis at a child-guidance clinic.

Operational criteria were employed to compare treatment results. A child was judged a treatment 'success' if he returned to full-time schooling without any further problems. Here, one attendance breakdown was allowed provided that the child quickly responded to booster treatment. A child was classified as a 'partial success' if he returned to school for at least one year but then had attendance breakdowns culminating in school refusal. A child was judged a treatment 'failure' if he did not return to normal school or returned for less than 3 months but was unresponsive to further treatment. After one year of treatment, 93.3% of the BAT group were judged to be successful compared with 37.5% of the HU group and 10% of the HT group. Attendance rates were also compared for the year prior to follow-up. While 83% of the BTA group were attending school on more than 80% of occasions, this occurred for only 31% of the HU group and for none of the HT group. Five girls in the BTA group did not meet the criterion attendance rate between the end of treatment and follow-up. The girls concerned were over 13 years of age, had low scores on the WISC-R (Verbal), and were classified as Kennedy Type-2 cases. According to Blagg and Yule (1984): 'Four of the girls had siblings who also had attendance problems, and most of the parents were far from co-operative during treatment' (p. 127).

The findings of the study highlight a number of points of clinical significance. Despite frequent objections about the behavioural management of school phobia (consider stress upon the child), the behavioural approach was very effective. Furthermore, it was more effective than hospitalization or home instruction and psychotherapy. With all of the concern about separation anxiety, it is interesting to note that there was less separation anxiety in children who had been treated behaviourally. The results also indicate that so-called 'disturbed' cases of school phobia can respond to behavioural treatment. This is quite important as it has become part of behavioural mythology that only simple cases of school phobia respond to behavioural intervention. However, it must be acknowledged that the treatment failures of the behavioural approach were classified as Kennedy Type-2 cases. Thus greater difficulty is likely to be encountered with these cases. As well as being effective, it must be emphasized that behavioural treatment was the most economical form of intervention. The average length of behavioural treatment was 2.53 weeks, compared with 45.3 weeks of hospitalization, and 72.1 weeks for home instruction. As emphasized by the researchers, this is to say nothing of salary costs which would be extremely high for those cases involving hospitalization. Of course, the study is by no means immune to criticism. Although quite understandable in terms of obligation to provide a clinical service, a no-treatment control condition was not included. Thus the extent to which spontaneous remission accounts for the results can be queried. Given the differences in outcome between the three groups, however, it does not seem likely that spontaneous remission is the operative variable in so far as behavioural treatment is concerned. Another possible criticism is that subjects were not randomly allocated to the treatment conditions. Thus it can be argued that easier cases were dealt with in behavioural treatment. This does not appear to be so in view of the fact that no significant differences were found between the groups on major subject characteristics. In conclusion, Blagg's work is a significant development in the behavioural management of school phobia. Although methodological problems are present, it represents the type of clinical–research study that must be undertaken to verify our treatment procedures (see also Blagg, 1987).

USE OF PSYCHIATRIC DRUGS

Whether the use of psychiatric drugs improves the effectiveness of behavioural methods in the treatment of school phobia is an intriguing question. Gittelman-Klein and Klein (1971) conducted a study on the use of an antidepressant in conjunction with a semi-behavioural programme. The rationale for the use of the antidepressant was based upon the observation that imipramine regularly blocks the spontaneous panic attacks of adult agoraphobic patients (Klein, 1964). It was postulated that these patients suffered from a disruption of biological processes that regulate anxiety triggered by separation. On the basis that separation anxiety is the major cause of school phobia, it was hypothesized that imipramine should be effective in the treatment of school phobia.

Children between the ages of 6 and 14 years who had been absent from school for at least 2 weeks, or had been attending intermittently under extreme distress, were considered for the study. Forty-five children (24 girls and 21 boys), were randomly assigned to placebo or imipramine groups in double-blind fashion for a 6-week period. Twenty-five children received the placebo, while 20 children received imipramine. Seven children dropped out of the study; five children were on imipramine, and two children were on placebo. Dosage was fixed for the first 2 weeks, and adjusted thereafter with a maximum of 200 mg/day being set. Medication was administered in the morning and in the evening. At the end of the study, the dosage ranged from 100 to 200 mg/day. Over this time the child and family were seen weekly. In many ways the non-pharmacological aspects of the programme were consistent with behavioural principles. The case worker instructed the family to maintain a firm attitude with respect to school attendance, and in most cases a family member was advised to accompany the child to school. If the child could not tolerate being forced back into the classroom, a graded approach was instituted. Treatment recommendations varied according to the severity of the child's anticipatory anxiety and the mother's ability to set and enforce limits. After 6 weeks of treatment, 44% of the placebo group and 70% of the imipramine group were back at school. Interesting data emerged on the children's report of improvement. Of the 25 children in the placebo condition, six reported feeling much better. However, of the 19 children on imipramine 17 reported a similar degree of symptomatic relief.

On the clinical use of imipramine, Gittelman-Klein and Klein (1980) have noted that children usually respond within 6–8 weeks. They recommend that medication should be continued for at least 4 weeks after remission, and then gradually withdrawn in order to minimize withdrawal effects (nausea, abdominal pain and vomiting). According to these researchers, imipramine-associated side effects are not a significant problem. Dry mouth is the most common side effect. Orthostatic hypotension, sweating and mild tremor are fairly rare. Although the therapeutic benefits of the antidepressant are largely attributed to the modification of separation anxiety, many other factors come into play, including anxiety-reduction with forced school attendance, and the significance of parent and school management. Nevertheless, their findings suggest that antidepressant medication is of therapeutic value in certain cases of school phobia.

Placing the role of antidepressants into perspective, Gittelman-Klein and Klein point out that most school-phobic children respond to the simple environmental manoeuvre of forcing the child back to school. Thus medication is reserved for the minority of recalcitrant cases, as in the above study. Of particular interest are Gittelman-Klein and Klein's comments on the use of these agents. According to these authorities: 'Even when pharmacotherapy is indicated, it is almost always necessary to use other treatments as well' (p. 338). Despite their theoretical rationale for the use of imipramine, they are quite emphatic that behavioural methods be adopted: 'We are emphasizing therapeutic tactics that provide child and family with firm guidance and support in the framework of a behavioural approach' (p. 338).

In a recent study on the effectiveness of antidepressant medication in the treatment of school phobia, Berney *et al.* (1981) failed to demonstrate any significant short-term effects over a 12-week double-blind trial comparing clomipramine (antidepressant) and placebo conditions. Individual psychotherapy for the child and casework with parents was a concurrent feature of treatment. Furthermore, there was pressure on children to attend school but only when it was felt that the child and family could cope. (However, it should be noted that less than half the amount of medication was used than in the Gittelman-Klein and Klein (1971) study.) In light of the literature and our clinical experience, we do not advocate the use of pharmacological agents like antidepressants in the management of school phobia, except under those conditions specified by Gittelman-Klein and Klein (1980).

SUMMARY

Persistent non-attendance at school is a serious threat to a child's educational and social development, quite apart from the legal statutes on school attendance. Slightly less than 1% of children become extremely frightened of school and avoid attendance by crying, tantrums, somatic complaints and so forth. The diagnostic criteria for school phobia developed by Berg *et al.* maintain the distinction between school phobia (frequently associated with phobic and anxiety disorders) and school truancy (often associated with conduct disorders). Various sub-types of school phobia have been offered in the literature; the best known is Kennedy's Type-1 (neurotic) and Type-2 (characterological) classification in which the former sub-type is supposed to have a better prognosis. Because of the diversity of factors in school phobia, we argue here that interventions based on a thorough behavioural assessment are more likely to be successful than those based on global diagnostic categories.

The common precipitants of school phobia include a change of school, parent death or illness and hospitalization, or staying at home due to an accident or illness. School-phobic children sometimes express fears of harm to mother, strict and sarcastic teachers, ridicule or bullying from other children, and academic failure. We have presented a learning-theory explanation of school phobia, highlighting the importance of events within the home and school. Although separation anxiety is often seen as the cause of school phobia, its significance has been overstated. In fact, separation anxiety should be regarded as a different problem.

The behavioural management of school phobia is primarily based on techniques derived from classical and/or operant conditioning. When avoidance behaviour is motivated by high levels of anxiety, classical-conditioning-based techniques like systematic desensitization are warranted. For those cases in which secondary reinforcement is responsible for the maintenance of avoidance behaviour, operant-based strategies should be applied. Here we attempt to make the school experience as positive as possible while making the home experience through the day somewhat aversive. Contracting with the child might also be a useful treatment option. As well as consequential control, it has been suggested that antecedent stimulus control (household organization, parent commands) might be considered in certain cases. We advise a combination of operant- and classical-conditioning treatment principles to cover anxiety reduction and environmental contingencies. Of note here is the detailed strategy for the rapid treatment of school phobia developed by Blagg, in which forced school attendance is a major feature. Although not generally recommended, anti-depressant medication has been used in the treatment of school-phobic children. When used in the treatment of school phobia, antidepressant medication should be an adjunct to behavioural management.

Section 3
Conceptual Issues

CHAPTER 7

Prevention of children's phobias and negative reactions to stressful events*

INTRODUCTION

Interest in the prevention of children's phobias is of relatively recent origin. Such concern is related to a more general trend in the behavioural literature to focus attention on the prevention of behavioural and educational problems in children (Gelfand & Hartmann, 1977; Peterson, Hartmann & Gelfand, 1980). Such interest is also consistent with the general trend in human service delivery programmes towards enhanced provision for preventive efforts. However, the actual allocation of resources to these programmes has increased less rapidly (Demone & Harshbarger, 1974; Attkisson, Hargreaves, Horowitz & Sorensen, 1978). Nonetheless, these developments are important ones and reminiscent of Sarason and Ganzer's (1969) admonition that 'prevention must always be an important goal of the clinician'.

When discussing preventive intervention it is customary to distinguish among primary, secondary and tertiary efforts. Caplan (1964) states:

> ...the term 'preventive psychiatry' refers to the body of professional knowledge, both theoretical and practical, which may be utilized to plan and carry out programs for reducing (1) the incidence of mental disorders of all types in a community ('primary prevention'), (2) the duration of a significant number of those disorders which do occur ('secondary prevention'), and (3) the impairment which may result from those disorders ('tertiary prevention') (pp. 16–17)

Bolman (1969) elaborates upon these three levels of intervention in the following way:

> Primary prevention attempts to prevent a disorder from occurring. Secondary prevention attempts to identify and treat at the earliest possible moment so as to reduce the length and severity of disorder. Tertiary prevention attempts to reduce to a minimum the degree of handicap or impairment that results from a disorder that has

---

*This chapter is an adaptation of King et al. (1983) first published in *Child and Family Behaviour Therapy* 5, 43–57, and is reproduced by kind permission of the Haworth Press.

> already occurred. From the standpoint of the community, these distinctions are equivalent to reducing incidence, prevalence and extent of disability respectively. (p. 208)

Although there has been much dissatisfaction with the use of these terms, particularly the distinction between secondary and tertiary prevention, they continue to be used in the literature (Kessler & Albee, 1975; Poser & Hartman, 1979).

Undoubtedly much of the enthusiasm for preventive intervention is inspired by breakthroughs in medical research and the efficacy of certain public health practices. Programmes of inoculation and sanitation and various kinds of environmental interventions have effectively removed the threat of, for example, typhoid and polio. The preventive measures that succeeded in combating major diseases suggest that a preventive approach might be considered with children's fears and phobias. In addition to sparing children and their families needless suffering, the preventive approach might be recommended on additional grounds. First, the prevention of behavioural problems should ease the long-term burden on existing clinical and educational services. Second, it is likely that a preventive approach would reach (and hopefully help) more children than the 'curative' approach that relies upon referral. Third, the preventive approach is to be recommended because it is related more closely to the natural environment where the problems occur. Such programmes might be directed at individual persons or social systems such as schools and communities (Cowen, 1973). Resistance to preventive programmes often stems from the view that such programmes entail massive change to the social system (Bower, 1969). The fact that many preventive programmes can be aimed at the individual or relatively restricted social systems (e.g. the family, the pre-school) in the absence of disruption or threat to the wider social structure is particularly important in the light of this concern (Barrios & Shigetomi, 1980).

Looking at the preventive challenge from a behavioural perspective, the principles of behavioural assessment employed in the treatment of child and adult problems prove useful. Poser and Hartmann (1979) maintain that 'behavioral prophylaxis seeks to apply the methods and principles of behavior modification to the preventive enterprise' (p. 2). For these authors, three steps are implicit in such an endeavour:

(1) Identification of target behaviour to be prevented.
(2) A behavioral analysis of these problems for the purpose of pin-pointing the most appropriate intervention and also the dependent variables whereby outcome can be assessed.
(3) Evaluation of outcome in terms of differential incidence of target problems in the experimental and control groups at the post-intervention stage when new crisis situations, natural or experimentally induced, have been encountered by both groups (p. 2)

Consistent with these guidelines, Peterson et al. (1980) have explored some of the major parameters in mounting a preventive programme. First, the preventionist must select an appropriate problem behaviour for prevention. According to Peterson *et al.*: 'The choice of problem behavior will depend upon the availability of a cost-effective and otherwise suitable (e.g. politically acceptable) prevention techniques as well as upon the prevalence and seriousness of the problem' (p. 198). Second, the preventionist must select a general strategy. Bloom (1968) distinguished three general strategies or approaches: community-wide, milestone, and high-risk. The prevention of children's phobias would seem to entail milestone (e.g. school-entry children) and high-risk populations (e.g. children undergoing surgery). Third, the preventionist must decide upon a specific intervention technique and a route for implementing the technique. Behavioural-oriented preventionists may employ a variety of intervention techniques (e.g. systematic desensitization and modelling). Programmes may be implemented directly with the child, or through their caregivers (parents, teachers, health-care personnel). Fourth, each programme should be evaluated to establish its effectiveness and to monitor its adverse side effects.

PREPARING CHILDREN FOR STRESSFUL EVENTS

Preparing children for stressful events like elective surgery and school entry should enhance cooperative behaviour and reduce the risk of conditioned fear reactions. Typically, care providers rely on verbal explanation and reassurance in preparing children for stressful events.

A limited amount of information is usually given by care providers about the necessity to go to school, the hospital, and so forth. Sometimes the child is told a story about children who are at school or have undergone an operation in hospital. Rewards may be promised for cooperative behaviour up to and during the stressful event. Even in health-care settings, verbal explanation and reassurance is the mainstay of preparing children for dental treatment, tonsillectomies, hernia, eye and urogenital surgery. This standard method of preparing children for stress has been reinforced by the medical and nursing literature (Heller, 1967; Mellish, 1969). Additional procedures have at times been recommended. For example, Vernon, Foley, Sipowicz & Schulman (1965) have suggested that the major purpose of preoperative preparation is to provide information to the child, encourage emotional expression, and establish a trusting relationship with the hospital staff. Puppet therapy and play therapy have also been used as preoperative preparation techniques (Cassell, 1965; Impallaria, 1955). Cherches and Blackman (1963) emphasized the importance of home preparation for the dental visit; friendly greetings from the dentist and assistants, the use of books, movies and slides as distracting entertainment; use of 'tell, show, do method', and premedication if necessary. Some degree of success would be expected to be produced by these techniques as they are partially consistent with learning-theory principles (e.g. reciprocal inhibition).

It must also be recognized that children prepare themselves for stressful events, with various degress of success. In his classic text, Janis (1958) posited a curvilinear relationship between preoperative anxiety level and the patient's adjustment to surgery. Janis reported that a moderate level of anxiety prior to surgery was predictive of satisfactory post-surgical adjustment. It was surmized that a moderate level of anxiety stimulated thought and fantasy about the forthcoming operation. In experiencing these surgery-related thoughts and images, the patient developed coping mechanisms that could be used during stress. This process was seen as the 'work of worrying' (Marmor, 1958). Janis's model of coping with psychological stress has been investigated by Burstein and Meichenbaum (1979) in relation to children undergoing surgery. In this study, two groups of children were identified. One group of children distinguished themselves in terms of their disposition to engage in the 'work of worrying'. They were 'low defensive' prior to hospitalization, actively played with stress-related toys prior to hospitalization, and reported minimal stress and anxiety following surgery. The other group of children were 'high defensive', avoided playing with stress-related toys, and reported more anxiety following surgery. However, the notion that preoperative anxiety level and its associated features are related directly to postoperative adjustment has not gone unchallenged (Johnson, Leventhal & Dabbs, 1971; Levy, 1959). Accordingly, many questions remain as to the most effective means of helping children cope with stressful procedures.

Procedures based on classical, operant and vicarious conditioning paradigms can be used for primary prevention as well as secondary and tertiary prevention (Jason, 1980). Thus, systematic desensitization, emotive imagery, contingency management, modelling and cognitive-verbal training may have valuable prophylactic as well as therapeutic roles (Graziano, DeGiovanni & Garcia, 1979; Ollendick, 1979b; Ollendick & Cerny, 1981; Richards & Siegel, 1978). The use of behavioural methods in the prevention of phobic reactions is predicated upon the assumption that one is best prepared for stressful events by undertaking direct or indirect exposure that serves to reduce anxiety and/or increase coping skills. As Epstein (1967) explains

> ...the ability to tolerate stress is acquired, not through previous security, but through 'inoculations' with increasing amounts of stress. More specifically, our theory suggests that a child who is to enter a world where he must deal with anger, frustration and uncontrolled emotion should have some exposure to such experiences in the home, where they can be handled at levels that are not devastating, if he is not to be devastated when he experiences them in the outside world. (p. 74)

The notion of stimulus pre-exposure in phobia prevention has been articulated most forcefully by Poser (Poser, 1970; 1976; Poser & King, 1975). Poser maintains that this principle is supported by a host of animal and human conditioning studies that entail stimulus pre-exposure ('latent inhibition') (e.g. Carlton & Vogel, 1967; Lubow, 1965; MacDonald, 1946). The behavioural prophylaxis of children's maladaptive fears or phobias can be examined in terms of research developments in health-care settings, in the home and at school (King, Hamilton & Murphy, 1983).

PREVENTIVE EFFORTS IN HEALTH-CARE SETTINGS

A great deal of prophylactic work has been carried out in health-care settings, especially in the preparation of children for hospitalization and surgery (see reviews by Horne & King, 1986; King et al., 1983; Melamed, 1982; Melamed, Robbins & Graves, 1982; Melamed & Siegel, 1980; Siegel, 1976; Varni, 1983). Experiencing physical pain, maternal separation, and a strange environment are very stressful for hospitalized children. When the need for psychological preparation for surgery is recognized in a hospital, it is invariably the nursing staff who are assigned this responsibility. Presumably this is because nurses have significantly more contact with patients on a daily basis than other health professionals. In most hospitals the preparation of children for surgery is not standardized, with considerable variation in relation to the timing of preparation, the number of personnel, the kind of materials, continued support, and parental involvement.

A study by Visintainer and Wolfer (1975) is of particular interest because of the manipulations to the preparation and supportive care given by nurses to children. The subjects were children 3 to 12 years old admitted to hospital for tonsillectomies. The children were randomly assigned to one of four conditions: (1) a combination of systematic preparation, rehearsal (e.g. holding arm still for a blood test), and supportive care were conducted prior to each stressful procedure (therefore called 'stress-point nursing'); (2) a single 45-minute session of preparation conducted after admission; (3) consistent supportive care given by one nurse at the same points as in the first condition, but including no systematic preparation or rehearsal; and (4) a control condition that involved routine nursing care without systematic preparation. On a variety of measures of coping and adjustment, children who underwent the first treatment condition showed significantly less emotional distress and more cooperation in the hospital and better post-hospital adjustment than did children in the other groups. Also, the parents of children in the first condition indicated significantly less anxiety and more satisfaction with care and information than the other parents.

Within the broad framework of psychological preparation undertaken by nurses, it is apparent that there is considerable potential for the application of behavioural techniques. Film-modelling has emerged as the most researched behavioural technique in the psychological preparation of children for hospitalization and surgery (Faust & Melamed, 1984; Ferguson, 1979; Melamed, Meyer, Gee & Soule, 1976; Melamed & Siegel, 1975; Peterson, Schultheis, Ridley-Johnson, Miller & Tracy, 1984; Vernon & Bailey, 1974) and dental treatment (Green, Meilman, Routh & McIver, 1977; Klingman, Melamed, Cuthbert & Hermecz, 1984; Klorman, Hilpert, Michael, LaGana & Sveen, 1980; Machen & Johnson, 1974; Melamed, Weinstein, Hawes & Katin-Borland, 1975; Melamed, Yurcheson, Fleece, Hutcherson & Hawes, 1978; Sawtell, Simon & Simeonsson, 1974). In recent years, however, the possibility of teaching children active coping skills has been investigated more thoroughly (Peterson & Shigetomi, 1981; Siegel & Peterson, 1980). The main studies and issues will now be addressed.

Film-modelling is a convenient method of preparing children for elective surgery and other operative procedures. Compared with other forms of behavioural intervention, such as systematic desensitization, film-modelling is a straightforward and simple procedure, and not too demanding on staff time. In an initial study, Melamed and Siegel (1975) showed 60 children about to undergo elective surgery for hernias, tonsillectomies, or urogenital difficulties, either a relevant peer-modelling film or an unrelated control film. The children were between 4 and 12 years of age and had no prior history of hospitalization. The children were in hospital from 2–3 days; all received the same standard preoperative preparation once admitted to the hospital (talks with the surgeon and/or anethesiologist, demonstration of equipment). The experimental film, *Ethan Has an Operation*, was developed for the project. Considerable attention was given to the variables thought to enhance modelling in the production of the film. As a result, the film has become quite well known as an aid in the preparation of children for surgery. The length and content of the film can be appreciated from the following account.

> The ...film... depicts a 7-year-old white male who has been hospitalized for a hernia operation. This film, which is 16 minutes in length, consists of 15 scenes showing various events that most children encounter when hospitalized for elective surgery from the time of admission to time of discharge including the child's orientation to the hospital ward and medical personnel such as the surgeon and anesthesiologist; having a blood test and exposure to standard hospital equipment; separation from the mother; and scenes in the operating and recovery rooms. In addition to explanations of the hospital procedures provided by the medical staff, various scenes are narrated by the child, who describes his feelings and concerns that he had at each stage of the hospital experience. Both the child's behavior and verbal remarks exemplify the behavior of a coping model so that while he exhibits some anxiety and apprehension, he is able to overcome his initial fears and complete each event in a successful and nonanxious manner. Meichenbaum (1971) has shown that film models who are initially anxious and overcome their anxiety (coping models) result in greater reduction in anxiety than models who exhibit no fear (mastery models). (pp. 514–515).

Self-report, behavioural and physiological measures were employed, thus reflecting the multi-dimensional nature of anxiety. The distinction between state and trait anxiety was also observed. Measures of state or situational anxiety included the Palmar Sweat Index (a measure of transitory physiological arousal), Hospital Fears Rating Scale, and the Observer Rating Scale of Anxiety. Three measures were used to assess trait anxiety: an anxiety scale derived from the Personality Inventory for Children (Wirt & Broen, 1958), Children's Manifest Anxiety Scale, and the Human Figure Drawing Test. The situational measures were taken at four points: before the film, after the film, the night before surgery, and postoperatively (3 to 4 weeks after discharge). The trait measures of anxiety (and Behavior Problems Checklist) were taken only at the first and last measurement periods on the grounds that these measures do not reflect change over short intervals. The efficacy of preoperative modelling was demonstrated on all measures of transitory anxiety. The experimental subjects who had viewed the hospital peer-modelling film showed lower sweat-gland activity, fewer self-reported medical concerns, and fewer anxiety-related behaviours than the control subjects at both the preoperative and postoperative assessments. The parents of children who did not view *Ethan Has an Operation* reported a post-hospital increase in the frequency of behaviour problems. However, the impact of the hospital experience was not reflected in the trait measures of anxiety. It should also be noted that the children who viewed the experimental film demonstrated an increase in arousal level immediately after it was observed. According to the researchers, this finding supports Janis's (1958) contention that a moderate amount of arousal might help people adjust to the stress of impending surgery. From this well-controlled experiment it appears that film modelling adds to the potency of more standard methods of preparing children for surgery.

While the results of the above study are encouraging, many questions arise in relation to the use of film-modelling in preparing children for surgery. The stage at which the preparation should be undertaken along with the age and prior experience of the child are important issues. In a subsequent experiment on children undergoing elective surgery, Melamed et al. (1976) varied the time prior to actual hospital admission during which the children viewed the film *Ethan Has an Operation*. One group of children viewed the film 5–9 days prior to surgery, while a second group was shown the film on the day of admission. Both groups of subjects viewed the film in a research laboratory near the hospital, thus minimizing the possibility of desensitization to anxiety-eliciting cues in the hospital. Again the groups were matched for age, sex, race and type of operation. None of the children had been hospitalized before the study. Since many hospitals do not have the resources to engage in preoperative education, a film of this nature might have a sensitizing effect upon the child. In order to examine this issue, 50% of the children received the standard hospital preparation while the others were given minimal preparation. The results replicated the previous research findings concerning the general effectiveness of film-modelling, but highlight the need to consider the age of the child as well as the time of preparation. Children who were 7 years and older appeared to benefit from seeing the film one week in advance of actual hospitalization; younger children needed more immediate preparation. There were no significant differences between children receiving additional hospital preparation and children receiving minimal preparation. As the quality of hospital preparation depends on the particular staff and hospital, care should be taken in concluding that film-modelling alone will always be the most potent influence (Melamed & Siegel, 1980). Whether the child has had a previous hospitalization for surgery seems to be an important factor in determining the effectiveness of film-modelling. Melamed and Siegel report that showing *Ethan Has an Operation* to children immediately prior to subsequent hospitalizations failed to produce a significant effect on the measures of state anxiety. The researchers emphasize that children in this category were more anxious prior to surgery than children experiencing their first hospitalization. The use of a film entailing a child that has undergone one or more hospitalizations is recommended along with repeated exposures to ensure habituation or extinction. Although not suggested by Melamed and Siegel, systematic desensitization and contingency management (possibly a contract between staff or parent and child) might also prove useful.

Confirmation of the above findings on the general effectiveness of film-modelling can be found in a study conducted by Ferguson (1979). In this study, nurses were responsible for the preparation and showing of a peer-modelling film. The study also examined whether preparation for surgery should begin in the child's home prior to the hospital admission. The rationale for this is that preparatory efforts in a safe and comfortable environment ought to be of more benefit to the child and parents. The children who participated in the experiment were undergoing elective tonsillectomies. The children were 3 to 7 years of age; none had previous hospitalization experience. All subjects in the study were given admission information (general rules and routines) by the same nurse in the hospital or home. Each child was assigned to one of four groups:

(1) those who experienced a regular hospital-admission procedure and viewed a film unrelated to hospital;
(2) those who experienced a regular hospital-admission procedure and viewed a hospital-related peer-modelling film;
(3) those who experienced a pre-admission visit from a nurse in their home prior to their hospital admission and viewed a film unrelated to hospitals;
(4) those who experienced a pre-admission visit from a nurse in their home prior to their hospital admission and viewed a hospital-related peer-modelling film.

The experimental film entitled *Yolando and David Have Their Tonsils Out* runs for 15 minutes and involves two children describing their experiences at each stage of hospitalization for tonsillectomies. The control film of the same duration was about a futuristic spaceship. A number of evaluation measures were employed, including self-report (Hospital Fears Rating Scale and Mood Adjective Checklist), physiological measures (EMG readings of the trapezius and masseter muscles), and behavioural measures (Observer Rating Scale of Anxiety and Post-Hospital Behaviour Rating Scale). The pre-admission home visit contributed to a lessening of maternal anxiety during and after the child's hospitalization, and reduced the incidence of negative post-hospital behaviour, particularly with the 6- and 7-year-olds. Children who viewed a peer-modelling film displayed a significantly lowered incidence of undesirable post-hospital behaviour. Further, the older age group (6- and 7-year-olds) seemed to benefit more from the pre-admission home film viewing than the younger age group. The results of the experiment are consistent with those of Melamed and her colleagues (Melamed & Siegel, 1975; Melamed et al., 1976), including the finding that younger children do not benefit as much as older children from an early preparation. While the notion of a home visit by a nurse to prepare the child and parent for hospitalization is laudable in a humanitarian sense, it does not seem to be a feasible nor practical option given the economics and staffing levels at most hospitals.

Attention is now turned to active training in coping skills for children prior to hospitalization. Peterson and Shigetomi (1981) make the sound observation that, although seeing a film of a model coping with similar hospitalization/ medical procedures the child is about to undergo undoubtedly helps the child to cope better, the viewing of the modelling film does not provide instruction in acquiring coping skills, nor does it provide a means of ensuring emotional support throughout the hospitalization experience. These researchers conducted an experiment on coping skills training with children $2\frac{1}{2}$ to $10\frac{1}{2}$ years old presenting for elective tonsillectomies. The children and their parents were treated in small groups using one of the following procedures: information only, coping, film-modelling, or coping-plus-film-modelling. There were no significant differences in age and sex between the groups, and none of the children had experienced previous surgery or hospitalization during the last year. The preoperative information procedure included an ice-cream party attended by a 'Big Bird puppet' at the hospital, 4 days before admission, where Big Bird told the children about typical hospital experiences of a child having a tonsillectomy. The coping procedures entailed three techniques: cue-controlled relaxation, distracting mental imagery, and comforting self-talk. In the film-modelling procedure the children viewed *Ethan Has an Operation*. Every group of children was also taken on a hospital tour by a nurse at the beginning of the study. A variety of measures were used to assess the effects of these preparation procedures, including direct behavioural and observational measures. The results were complex and the differences between the groups were not very large. However, there were some statistically significant findings that highlight the complexity of preparing a child for surgery. In general, children receiving coping-plus-modelling were more calm and cooperative during invasive procedures than children receiving coping or modelling alone. The most consistent group differences were found in the data provided by parents.

Parents of children with coping training tended to rate these procedures as being very helpful, whereas the parents of children undergoing modelling saw the procedure as less useful. In fact the children in the modelling-alone group were perceived by their parents as more anxious and less cooperative immediately after surgery than the other groups. There was some confirmation of these effects from non-parent measures as well. Peterson and Shigetomi also mentioned that younger children were probably not capable of implementing the coping procedures themselves and probably relied on parental guidance. In view of the small differences between the procedures it is difficult to draw firm conclusions about the clinical usefulness of combining cognitive and behavioural techniques in preparing children for surgery. The information procedure—which all subjects underwent—with the Big Bird puppet pantomiming (modelling) hospital activities may have diluted the effects of the other interventions. Probably the most critical point is that the researchers only partially controlled for previous hospitalization and that some of the children may have been too young to benefit from any of the procedures (e.g. those under 4 years of age).

A significant factor in the child's adjustment to hospitalization is the parent–

child interaction. Some parents cope very well with their child's hospitalization, while other parents become extremely upset and distressed. The danger, of course, is that parent anxiety will make the child's adjustment far more difficult. Consequently, joint preparation of child and parent is an important consideration for health professionals. The pragmatics of this issue have been cogently expressed by Melamed *et al.* (1982):

> It is a question of great concern to doctors and medical staff whether participation of parents should be encouraged or whether parental presence is more of a burden on the staff and not likely to contribute to the welfare of the child. This question is answered in several ways, depending on the parental response to stress and on the hospitals' beliefs about the deleterious effects of separating children from their families, particularly their mothers, during times of great pain, discomfort, and stress. In either case, parents must be 'prepared' for their role in their child's hospitalization.
>
> Theoretically, one could posit a range of possible points on a continuum that express the degree of parental involvement in the child's hospitalization. The parent may be the agent who delivers and retrieves the child from the hospital. The parent may be the noninvolved visitor who arrives periodically and remains uninvolved with the ongoing treatment or care of the child. The parent may dutifully visit during the prescribed hours and entertain the child, but still remain separate from the care of the child. Or the parent may become an intricate and involved member of the care team, becoming involved in and responsible for the nonmedical care of the child.
>
> The degree of parental involvement may depend on a variety of factors, not the least of which is the policy, both implicit and explicit, of the hospital or clinic toward that involvement. (p. 246)

A research investigation by Zabin and Melamed (1980) addressed the relationship between parental discipline and children's ability to cope with stress. To assess each child's reinforcement history, the Child Development Questionnaire was designed and administered to parents through the mail. The questionnaire consisted of 14 items (e.g. having a haircut, injection, operation, tooth drilled) believed to represent hypothetical situations in which children often become fearful and refuse to engage in the feared act. For each of the 14 items, the parents were asked individually to respond in the way that he or she would deal with the situation if it arose at the present time with their child. Five coded categories (i.e. positive reinforcement, punishment, force, reinforcement of dependency, modelling and reassurance) plus 'another' category were represented in each item. The predictive validity of the questionnaire was evaluated by correlational analyses with the assessment of fear (behavioural, subjective and physiological) in the children during hospitalizations for surgery. Parents who reported use of positive reinforcement, modelling and persuasion as ways of encouraging the child to deal with fearful situations had children who were low in anxiety during the actual stressful life experience. The reported use of punishment, force or reinforcement of dependency was correlated with higher anxiety. Differences in the use of these methods by mothers and fathers were reported. For example, fathers who employed punishment when their children faced fearful situations had children who were high scorers on several measures of anxiety. However, a similar finding was not found in the maternal use of the technique. As Zabin and Melamed stated: 'The study of parental discipline is crucial not only for the better understanding of how children cope with stress but also for the understanding of how children develop specific behavior patterns, in addition to how they deal with various environmental situations' (pp. 35–6).

As several authors (e.g. Horne & King, 1986; Varni, 1983) point out, most research on the psychological preparation of children for surgery involves children admitted to hospital for elective surgery. The preparation of children for emergency and paediatric intensive care is a comparatively neglected area. Horne and King (1986) suggest that whenever possible the health professional might still ensure that appropriate information is given to the patient. Informing children of what can be expected may help to reduce anxiety and enhance the patient's cooperation and recovery. It should also be emphasized that the aversive nature of intensive care units for children frequently produces 'neutral affect' and 'non-interaction'. These reactions can be mitigated to a certain extent by efforts aimed at positive stimulation and interactions (Cataldo, Bessman, Parker, Pearson & Rogers, 1979; Pearson, Cataldo, Tureman, Bessman & Rogers, 1980). Finally, long-term preventive programmes may be helpful. Television already provides much information about hospitalization through popular medical programmes, but whether these types of programme are effective in reducing anxiety and enhancing coping in the event of a hospital admission is highly debatable and certainly untested. However, with video-tapes becoming ubiquitous it ought to be possible to develop appropriate modelling tapes like *Ethan Has an Operation* for use at home and in schools. The results of two studies (Penticuff, 1977; Roberts, Wurtele, Boone, Ginther & Elkins, 1981) indicate that children's attitudes towards doctors and medical procedures can be improved through the use of film presentations in schools. More research is needed on the preparation of children for emergency hospitalization and their management in paediatric intensive-care units.

PREVENTIVE EFFORTS IN THE HOME AND SCHOOL

The home is obviously a crucial setting in the context of the prevention and management of children's problems. Although parents may automatically engage in prevention actions in their everyday childrearing practices, little research has addressed the precise nature of these techniques and their effectiveness. Of note is Jersild and Holme's (1935b) early investigation on the prevention of childhood fears and phobias in the home. In interviewing parents of young children, Jersild and Holmes collected data on both their methods of overcoming fears and common preventive measures. The methods used to 'forestall fear' developed largely with methods used in overcoming fears, and included:

(1) previous explanation and reassurance, including direct or indirect forewarning;

(2) explanation combined with a partial introductory experience, or a demonstration, or an example of fearlessness;

(3) casual attitude with or without explanation (actually a reference to the use of modelling as a preventive aid);

(4) promotion of skill;

(5) anticipating the effects of maturation (e.g. accustoming the child to the dark during early infancy in anticipation of the age when the fear of darkness is likely to emerge);

(6) prevention of fear stimulation, in which parents refrain from telling the child frightening stories and making frightening gestures, and refrain from playing upon the child's fears for disciplinary purposes.

Jersild and Holmes concluded that teaching the child how to cope with potential fear objects or situations is probably the most crucial factor in preventing fears. The researchers made an interesting comment regarding the need for parents to be fairly natural and unobtrusive: 'Steps taken to forestall fear are likely to be more effective if introduced unobtrusively and as a functional part of other projects and topics than if an abrupt or direct approach is employed' (p. 102). However, the reliability and validity of the parent reports and the relative efficacies of these preventive measures are unknown at this time.

Accompanying the clinical and research developments in behavioural psychology, many 'behaviour-modification' training manuals and self-help books have been written for parents on the management of normal, mentally retarded, and physically handicapped children. The preventive value of this material in the home setting should be considered. In terms of the primary prevention of children's negative reactions and phobias such material has focused almost exclusively on preparing children for school. For example, Freeman (1979) suggests that parents can prepare their children for school by talking to their child about positive school experiences, taking the child on a visit to the school, encouraging independence through outings with friends and overnight stays with friends. Similar suggestions are made by Mitchell (1973) who encourages parents to develop independence in their child, convey the idea that school is an enjoyable place, and make some visits to the school with their child prior to the first official school day. Drawing on the early work of Jersild and Holmes (1935b), Herbert (1975) listed the most effective, sometimes effective, and practically useless techniques that parents and teachers employ to overcome children's excessive fears. McMurray (1979) described an extensive list of specific suggestions the parent can use in the management of children's phobias. These included providing knowledge about the fear stimulus, changing the environment, changing environmental expectancies, skill training, desensitization, and positive self-statements for coping. In a book written for the parent of the handicapped child, Carr (1980) advises the parent to use guided practice, flooding and modelling in overcoming the phobias of their children. Thus, a diverse range of suggestions have been offered to the parent on the prevention and treatment of children's phobias.

Generally, the aforementioned specific suggestions for parents on the prevention and treatment of children's phobias are consistent with behavioural principles, and it does not seem unreasonable that such material has some preventive value in the home setting. However, many crucial questions remain unanswered about the use of such manuals and self-help books for parents. On the consumer side, there is no published data on the characterisitics of the parent population that purchases such material and how well the parent is able to understand the principles and recommendations. In assessing the readability of behaviour modification training manuals and primers, Andrasik and Murphy (1977) and O'Farrell and Keuthen (1983) found a vast range in the grade reading level of these texts. Without doubt, many of these books have a grade reading level well beyond the average consumer. Even for the parent who is able to understand the material, no research has been conducted on the short- and long-term efficacy of behavioural strategies presented in this format.

Entering school and the primary–secondary school transition are very stressful experiences for many children, creating marked academic and social adjustment problems (Chazan & Jackson, 1971; Coleman, Wolkind & Ashley, 1977; Cox, 1978; Hughes, Pinkerton & Plewis, 1979). For some children these negative reactions involve intense anxiety and school avoidance. Perhaps surprisingly, little research has been reported on school-orientation programmes derived from behavioural principles. Nevertheless, a number of suggestions can be made with respect to the preparation of children for school from a behavioural perspective. The initial discussion will focus on school entry. A fundamental point is that children need many competencies in order to cope with the demands of the school environment. It is generally agreed that when starting school, children should know their name, address and telephone number, travel arrangements to and from school, safety rules (especially in relation to road traffic), how to use and flush the toilet, be able to put on and take off jumpers and coats, and so on. Also, being able to mix with other children and cope with maternal separations are critical entry skills to the school situation. Of course, it can be argued that many of these competencies are taught to children by parents without formal assistance. Yet, this is not always the case and it would appear sensible to help parents in developing these skills in children. Educational authorities sometimes provide parents with brochures or booklets setting out what children should know and what they should be able to do independently (usually such material does not explain how these skills are to be taught). Preparation for school in terms of knowledge and skills acquisition is a long-term endeavour on the part of parents, however. This fact needs to be recognized by schools that emphasize the desirability of new children having requisite skills.

As far as more immediate preparation for school entry is concerned, modelling and systematic desensitization have much potential as preparatory strategies. In view of the success of film-modelling in preparing children for hospitalization and surgery, there would seem to be a great deal of merit in the development of equivalent peer-modelling films or videos for use with children about to start school. Taking the film *Ethan Has an Operation* (Melamed & Siegel, 1975) as a model, the film should be about 15 minutes in duration and depict a young child being taken to school by his or her parents, the child engaging in school-related activities involving teachers and other children, and returning home after school. A salient point is that the film or video be based upon what is known about the factors which enhance modelling. Such a film could be shown to small groups of children and parents at the school to be attended, and also include a tour of the school, and discussion of school activities and rules (perhaps in the context of a party atmosphere). Given the research findings of Melamed *et al.* (1976) and Ferguson (1979) on the timing of film-modelling preparation for children undergoing elective surgery, it may be that a film-modelling package of the kind just outlined should be introduced fairly close to the first day of school.

Children who appear very anxious about starting school may be helped by a more graduated exposure to the school and related activities. Real-life systematic desensitization—entailing parent and child visits to the school in which the child is introduced to his future teacher, classroom, school routines and play activities—should serve to attenuate the impact of the 'official' entry to school. The role of the parents is critical on the first day of the child's attendance at school. In the behaviour chain of events associated with going to school, the parents are the most important external influence and a great deal of valuable prophylactic work can be done by increasing the child-management skills of these agents (consider the need for parents to establish a routine for getting ready for school, travel arrangements, handing the child over to the teacher, and coping with resistance and crying). It can be argued, of course, that schools already attend to these issues albeit informally. Thus the effectiveness of behavioural methods in preparing children for school should be compared with the informal procedures of teachers and parents. The variables that might be anticipated to affect 'settling in' include previous symptomatology, parent–child interactions, amount of pre-school involvement, class size, and stage of entry within the school year.

The transition from primary to secondary school may be a stressful aspect of a child's school years. Even for children with average academic and social skills, the move from primary to secondary school may be anxiety-provoking because of the changes involved (e.g. a different route and mode of transport, a new set of peers, new teachers, unknown routines). For children of this age (11 to 12 years), training in appropriate coping skills is a possible preventive solution. In such a programme the child could be given information, perhaps in the form of a brochure about the organization and rules of the secondary school and an opportunity to learn assertive responses related to threatening aspects of the new school. Given the age of the children, cognitive restructuring and relaxation training may add to the repertoire of skills that could be applied at the time of the transition. Film-modelling would also seem to have a valuable role to play in preparing children for the transition to secondary school. As shown in the following study, a valuable resource for school-orientation programmes are students enrolled at the new school. Students can be selected to act as guides and leaders for the new children.

Bogat, Jones and Jason (1980) evaluated a peer-led preventive orientation programme aimed at allaying the detrimental effects of a forced school closing. Students transferring into a public elementary school were matched by grade and sex with students currently enrolled at the public school. The group of transfer students were then randomly assigned to either the orientation programme or no programme. Four children were selected from the new school to act as guides and discussion leaders; they were given a 2-hour training session consisting of an outline of their responsibilities and behaviour rehearsal (role plays). A 2-day orientation programme was conducted in the week prior to the commencement of the school year. A 2-hour orientation session was held each day. The first day featured juices and cookies, booklets containing school information, a school tour by the peer guides and peer-led discussion. The second day involved a two-team treasure hunt competition which provided the children with an opportunity to explore all the rooms in the school, a game which emphasized school rules and regulations, discussion of feelings about the transition, being shown their home room, and where morning line-up occurred. Following the intervention, the experimental group was superior to the control condition in terms of self-esteem related to peer difficulties, knowledge of school rules, and teacher conduct ratings. The success of the orientation programme was explained in terms of desensitization, modelling and information. It appears that Bogat *et al.* have developed a cost-effective orientation programme for children undergoing a transition to a new school. Obviously the choice of peer leaders and support of the school administration are crucial to the outcome of the orientation programme.

BARRIERS TO PREVENTION

The behavioural approach to primary prevention holds considerable promise in relation to preparation for stressful events. Although the research findings are very encouraging, particularly for health-care and school settings, it would be naive to assume that prophylactic intervention will always be successful. A number of variables may be anticipated to affect the outcome of preventive programmes for children encountering stressful situations. These include the child's prior experience and information regarding the stressor; the suitability of the programme in view of the child's age, cognitive development and coping style predisposition; the degree of support given by the parent; the timing of the intervention; and unanticipated trauma at the time of the stressful event (Melamed *et al.*, 1982). Furthermore, individual differences may occur across subjective, physiological and overt–behavioural measures of coping (Hodgson & Rachman, 1974; Melamed & Siegel, 1980). In other words, behavioural prevention does not appear to produce uniform results in children, which suggests the need for more individualized programmes. In addition to this concern, the professional committed to preventive intervention must contend with broader issues.

Despite the humanitarian and economic appeal of prevention programmes being established for children, the professional interested in the promotion of such programmes must overcome a number of organizational problems. First, there is the problem of access to the setting. The home setting may be difficult to infiltrate, but so also may be the school or hospital even for the professional employed in service-related organizations. In practical terms, the professional needs to be employed in the particular setting or have close association with its services and staff. Second, there is the problem of assessing the extent of the problem within the setting and making a cost/benefit analysis of the preventive programme. The organization that maintains a careful data-gathering system facilitates this primary investigation. Third, there is the question of the target population. The programme may involve all children undertaking the service, volunteer children, or 'high-risk' children. The latter may be the most economical but the reliability and validity of selection remains to be determined. Fourth, there remains the problem of convincing the administration and staff of the merits of prevention and that the proposed programme deserves support. Fifth, the suspicion and barriers that exist between professional groups is a serious impediment, especially when the professional mounting the programme is moving into another professional's area of responsibility. A prime example of this problem would be the psychologist developing preparatory strategies for children undergoing painful surgery, an area of responsibility that is traditionally regarded as that of the 'doctor and nurse'. Assuming the aforementioned problems can be overcome, it is conceivable that even the most carefully formulated preventive programme may lose support during implementation. This is especially the case for a behavioural programme which may be operating in an organization unsympathetic to the principles of behavioural programming (Murphy & Remenyi, 1979).

In sum, although the development of learning-based strategies for the prevention of childhood fears and worries is on the increase, many problems remain. Further, whether these programmes actually *prevent* behavioural problems from occurring is not at all clear and remain to be empirically demonstrated. As noted by Ollendick and Cerny (1981)

> claims of prevention have been based more on the intuitive appeal of the model than on actual demonstrable effects. Considerably more research is needed to evaluate both the short- and long-term effects of such interventions. Until such time, primary prevention remains on admirable goal in need of empirical verification. (p. 296)

SUMMARY

In this chapter we have addressed the prevention of childhood fears and phobias. By way of background information we identified three levels of prevention, primary, secondary and tertiary. Preparing children for stressful events like school entry and elective surgery may help in the prevention of conditioned fear reactions. Following a discussion of the standard methods of preparing children for stressful events, we pointed out that the use of behavioural procedures is predicated on the assumption that children are best prepared for stressful events through stimulus pre-exposure. The behavioural prophylaxis of childhood fears and phobias has been examined in relation to health-care settings, the home and school.

There is considerable scope for preventive efforts in health-care settings, especially in relation to the preparation of children for hospitalization and elective surgery. Of all the behavioural techniques that can be employed, video-modelling has proved the most popular in combination with the customary methods of preparation. Naturally, video-modelling is attractive because of its low cost and practical feasibility. However, the age of the child, the timing of preparation, and previous hospitalization, need to be considered in use of video-modelling. In recent years, active training in coping skills for children prior to hospitalization has been espoused. Here children are taught muscular relaxation, distracting mental imagery and comforting self-talk, as a means of coping in hospital. When using cognitive–behavioural procedures with children, the role of parents in the child's adjustment to hospital should not be overlooked.

Turning to preventive effects in the home, Jersild and Holmes identified six methods used by parents to 'forestall fear' in their children. Skills promotion was considered to be the most potent intervention by parents. We noted that self-help books for parents often contain advice of a behavioural nature on the management and prevention of children's anxieties and fears. In addition to their limited appeal and the question of readability, the preventive value of self-help books has yet to be demonstrated. The school setting is also an area in which valuable preventive work may be undertaken. It has been suggested that a video-modelling package could be very helpful in preparing children for school entry. Furthermore, peer-led orientation programmes may be the most cost-effective means of handling the primary–secondary school transition and other forms of school transition. Before engaging in preventive intervention, however, the professional should consider many individual variables and organizational matters. Finally, at least at the moment, preventive programmes are in need of sound empirical verification before their routine use can be endorsed.

CHAPTER 8

Integrative issues

INTRODUCTION

In previous chapters we examined the nature, aetiology, asessment, treatment and prevention of children's fears and phobias. Particular attention was given to behavioural techniques, including systematic desensitization, emotive imagery, flooding and implosion, contingency management, modelling and cognitive procedures. The need for behavioural assessment and interventions to be developmentally sensitive has been emphasized at various stages. In this chapter we discuss a number of integrative issues related to the behavioural management of childhood fears and phobias. First, we examine the role of care providers in phobia-reduction programmes. While there is little doubt as to the value of care providers, several important questions are raised with respect to their level of knowledge and expertise and preparedness for such a role. Second, we examine the actual effectiveness of behavioural procedures. It is emphasized that the various behavioural methods have different amounts of support for their use. Also, the methodological problems associated with research on phobia-reduction methods are outlined. Third, we examine the issue of 'symptom substitution' in relation to the use of behavioural procedures with phobic children. Although symptom substitution is not the general rule, new problems occasionally emerge during or after behaviour therapy. Fourth, we examine the underlying mechanisms shared by behavioural procedures in overcoming children's phobias. Although acknowledged as the common mechanism in previous chapters, we examine exposure in greater detail along with social learning theory (self-efficacy theory). Fifth, we examine the desynchrony of cognitive, physiological and overt behavioural measures. Of particular concern is the fact that desynchronous changes may occur over treatment and at follow-up. Sixth, we examine the need for comprehensive behavioural treatment in clinical practice. Drawing upon the conditioning paradigms, we propose a model for optimal phobia reduction with children. In this context, we discuss the sequencing of behavioural techniques. Finally, the issue of social validation is highlighted. The social acceptability of behavioural interventions is viewed as just as important as hard data on therapeutic outcome and experimental control.

THE ROLE OF CARE PROVIDERS

Care providers play a significant role in the aetiology, assessment and treatment of children's phobias. As previously explained, parents can be important influences in the development and maintenance of children's phobias. Parents can emit 'fear messages', act as poor models, and inadvertently (or deliberately) reinforce maladaptive fear behaviour. During behavioural assessment, the therapist usually relies upon the care provider(s) for much of the information about the problem. Care providers may also be given data-collection sheets for the dual purposes of measuring the target behaviour, and collecting vital clinical information about antecedent and consequent events. At the point of intervention, care providers are given varying degrees of responsibility. Typically, parents are given homework assignments (e.g. *in vivo* exposures) and required to act as good coping models in overcoming the child's phobia. Sometimes the treatment focus is the parent, especially in those cases where the phobic behaviour of the child is seen to be a function of the parent's behaviour. With respect to maintenance and generalization, what happens in the natural environment is far more important than the immediate potency of 'therapy' sessions. Should difficulties be encountered in the implementation of a behavioural programme, they are often care-provider-related problems (e.g. inadequate data collection, change of mind on problems, misunderstanding about homework, deliberate effort to sabotage programme). Prior to termination of therapeutic intervention, the therapist requests the care provider's opinion as to the usefulness of the programme. There are, in fact, many reasons why care providers should be utilized in behavioural programmes. As Yule (1977) has explained: (1) it is potentially more economical; (2) it is potentially more efficient; (3) it reduces the problems of generalization; (4) it reduces the problems of maintenance of change; and (5) if parents learn both principles and skills, they are in a position to prevent further problems arising. Accordingly, it is desirable that the therapist should consult with the care provider(s) at every possible step in the assessment, development and implementation of the behavioural programme.

The literature on children's phobias is replete with studies involving care providers as agents of behaviour change. Therapists who view children's phobias as conditioned emotional responses, frequently have care providers take responsibility for *in vivo* desensitization. For example, Stableford (1979) describes the case of a 3-year-old girl who had developed a fear of sudden loud noises following on automobile accident. She was successfully treated by an *in vivo* deconditioning programme carried out by her parents. Similarly, Pomerantz Peterson, Marholin and Stern (1977) present the case of a 4-year-old child's water phobia that was eliminated through a programme of *in vivo* desensitization combined with participant modelling. The mother was trained by a 'para-professional' behaviour therapist participating in a community-based intervention project. There are many reports on the operant-based management of children's phobias (especially school phobia) entailing the services of care providers. For example, Brown, Copeland and Hall (1974) described how a school principal modified an 11-year-old boy's intense fear of the classroom by systematic reinforcement and shaping. A changing criterion design was used to demonstrate that the operant procedures applied by the principal were, in fact, responsible for the improvement in daily attendance. Hersen (1970) coordinated the efforts of mother, school counsellor and individual therapist in the treatment of a 12-year-old school-phobic boy. The combined efforts were designed to reinforce appropriate school-related behaviour and extinguish deviant behaviour. Care providers have also been instrumental in the implementation of behavioural programmes in institutional and health settings. For example, Luiselli (1977) presented a case report on an attendant-administered contingency management programme for a 15-year-old boy with a toilet phobia, while Stokes and Kennedy (1980) give an illustration of the application of behavioural methods to dentistry. Modelling and reinforcement were instigated fairly naturally by a dental nurse and her assistant to reduce the uncooperative behaviour of eight children undergoing dental treatment.

Although there are good reasons for the continued involvement of care providers in behavioural programmes for phobic children, a number of issues need to be highlighted. First, the degree of sophistication or level of skill that can be expected of care providers in the use of behavioural principles and methods needs to be clarified. In the resolution of children's phobias, care providers operate very much as applicators, to use Gardner's (1976) terminology. The parent is required to apply a certain behavioural procedure or complete a specific homework assignment. Usually the parent carries out the procedure independently and reports back to the therapist (Allyon et al., 1970, Jackson & King, 1982; Kennedy, 1965; Pomerantz et al., 1977; Sellick & Peck, 1981; Vaal, 1973; Waye, 1979), although sometimes the therapist or therapist's assistant is with the parent when the programme is implemented in the natural environment (Luiselli, 1978; Obler & Terwilliger, 1970). For multiple problem cases the care provider may have to be trained in several methods to be effective, thus necessitating a higher level of training. Although parents and other care providers appreciate an overview of the programme and it's rationale, it is essential that their input be well-defined and structured.

Second, the means by which care providers can become proficient in the use of behavioural techniques is of vital concern. Typically, the consultative approach is taken in which an individual care provider presents with a specific problem and is instructed to carry out a particular intervention with a given child. The use of groups with parents of children with similar problems is an alternative to the consultative approach. Graziano and Mooney (1980) had parents meet in small groups in the treatment of their children's night-time fears. Three-weekly training classes were held for parents, with children's meetings being held separately. Organizing the parents and children in groups was cost-effective in reducing the children's night-time fears and parent–child battles. Regardless of whether training is done on an individual or group basis, methods that directly shape the desired behaviours of care givers have been reported to be the most effective in the parent-training literature (Griffin & Hudson, 1980; O'Dell, 1974). Such methods include written material, modelling, behaviour rehearsal, cueing and feedback. So far these training procedures have been largely ignored in the preparation of care providers in the treatment of children's phobias. It is to be hoped that the above training procedures will be applied more systematically to parents of phobic children in future years. Video-modelling should be of great value in training care providers for their role in phobia-reduction programmes (consider demonstrations of *in vivo* exposures, prompting and reinforcement, and participant modelling exercises).

A parent-training manual for reducing children's fear of the dark has been evaluated by Giebenhain and O'Dell (1984). The primary components of the package included desensitization, reinforcement, and verbal self-control coping skills. Employing a multiple baseline design, the four-part manual was given to the parents of four boys and two girls aged 3 to 11 years. Part I instructed parents on baseline; Part II contained the rationale of the treatment procedures; Part III described the actual treatment procedures; and Part IV explained the fading of reinforcement procedures and how to deal with the recurrence of fear. Following an initial interview, contact with parents was maintained via phone calls and a minimal number of home visits for data collection purposes. The intervention was successful in terms of the level of night-time illumination (voluntarily set by the child on a rheostat) and the child's subjective rating of his or her fear level during the night. Follow-up measures at 3, 6 and 12 months showed treatment gains. While the findings can only be considered preliminary, they are nevertheless encouraging in so far as the development of parent-training manuals for childhood phobias is concerned.

Written instructions and manuals can be extremely valuable aids in helping care providers overcome children's phobias. However, several important practical points should be noted by the clinician wishing to develop such material:

(1) The material should be well-organized (with headings and subheadings), straightforward (using a point form where possible) and specific (precise statements).
(2) The length of sentences, sentence structure, and choice of words, need to be at a level that can be understood by parents.
(3) The overall length of the material should be manageable to the parent (the material might be organized in sections that can be sequentially introduced to parents).
(4) The therapist needs to go over the content of the material with the parent in order to clarify any points of confusion or concern.
(5) In terms of good clinical practice, the therapist should maintain contact with the parent over the course of intervention in case further explanations are necessary or unforeseen problems arise.

(6) The therapist should be willing to recognize the efforts of parents in reading the material, attempting to understand the content, and actual compliance in relation to data gathering and the specific suggestions.

Third, the issue of how well care providers are able to execute the recommendations and skills they have been taught is fundamental. There are, in fact, many questions that can be raised in relation to this issue. Will the care provider be able to implement the procedure in different settings (i.e. setting generality)? Will the care provider be able to apply the techniques to other children with similar problems (i.e. child generality)? Will the care provider's behaviour be maintained over time in order to overcome the problem and prevent its reappearance (i.e. temporal generality)? Because of the many successful studies on children's phobias that involve care providers, it might be argued that care providers must display some degree of temporal and setting generality in relation to their behavioural skills. However, there is a dearth of hard data on these aspects of care-provider behaviour in phobia-reduction programmes for children.

These general issues are of concern to the therapist wishing to make the best possible use of care providers in the management of phobic children. As has become clear, the literature on children's phobias is fairly weak on these issues. In recent decades, however, a large body of literature has developed on the training of paraprofessionals in the use of behavioural techniques. The reader looking for more information on these general issues should consult this literature (reviews by Berkowitz & Graziano, 1972; Forehand and Atkeson, 1977; Graziano and Katz, 1982; Griffin and Hudson, 1980; Moreland, Schwebel, Beck & Well's, 1982; O'Dell, 1974; Reisinger, Ora & Frangia, 1976; Sanders & James, 1983).

THE EFFECTIVENESS OF BEHAVIOURAL METHODS

The scientific basis of behavioural methods used in the treatment of children's fears and phobias has been of concern to several authors over the years (Ollendick, 1986). In an early review, Berecz (1968) stated: 'there is presently too little empirical evidence in the area of childhood phobias to allow many meaningful generalizations' (pp. 714–15). Miller *et al.* (1974) implied an inadequate amount of hard evidence on treatment effectiveness in a chapter they cleverly entitled 'Phobias of childhood in a prescientific era'. At the moment the behavioural methods of interest have uneven research foundations. Thus, a general statement on the efficacy of behavioural methods with phobic children is not possible. As we found in Chapter 4, systematic desensitization has empirical support as a fear and phobia-reduction method for children (e.g. Deffenbacher & Kemper, 1974a, b; Kondas, 1967; Laxer *et al.*, 1969; Miller *et al.*, 1972a) with *in vivo* exposures enhancing the effectiveness of desensitization. (Ultee *et al.*, 1982). Emotive imagery has very weak research foundations, along with flooding and implosive therapy. Well-controlled research is definitely needed on the effectiveness of these procedures with phobic children, although many clinical researchers are concerned about the ethics of flooding and implosion with children. As we noted in Chapter 5, modelling is a well-researched behavioural method with childhood fears and phobias (e.g. Bandura *et al.*, 1967; Melamed & Siegel, 1975; Melamed *et al.*, 1976; White & Davis, 1974). Participant modelling appears to be an especially powerful technique (Lewis, 1974; Ritter, 1968). Operant-based procedures show considerable promise (Kohlenberg *et al.*, 1972; Leitenberg & Callahan, 1973) but have not been extensively researched with phobic children. The cognitive self-control approach to children's fears and phobias has captured a great deal of interest, but very few studies have examined its effectiveness (Graziano & Mooney, 1980; Kanfer *et al.*, 1975). When the behavioural methods utilized with phobic children are considered in terms of their empirical support, it appears that systematic desensitization and modelling are the only procedures that have been shown to be reasonably effective.

There are a number of methodological problems associated with research endeavours aimed at demonstrating the effectiveness of behavioural methods with phobic children. These problems are commonly encountered in research of a clinical nature. The first problem is that of sampling bias. Because of the difficulty of obtaining a sufficient number of clinically referred phobic children, researchers are often forced to work with non-referred subjects obtained as a result of advertising or approaching schools and agencies. The problem behaviours that are frequently targeted in evaluation studies include animal fears, darkness fears and dental fears, as these are very common among normal children (Bandura *et al.*, 1967; Kanfer *et al.*, 1975; Lewis, 1974; Leitenberg & Callahan, 1973; Ritter, 1968; Ultee *et al.*, 1982). The objection is that the severity and complexity of these fears is not representative of those seen in clinical populations. Thus, doubt is cast on the real effectiveness of the behavioural method in question. On the other hand, research should not be hastily dismissed because of this problem. The fears/phobias of children obtained through advertising and approaching schools can be quite disruptive or severe, as is the case in a number of studies (e.g. Graziano, Mooney, Huber & Ignasiak, 1979; Graziano & Mooney, 1980; Matson, 1981). Also, children from clinical populations have been included in between-group evaluations (Blagg & Yule, 1984; Obler & Terwilliger, 1970). More importantly, the advent of single-subject or time-series designs has allowed for the effectiveness of behavioural methods to be empirically demonstrated with individual phobic children in clinical settings (e.g. Luiselli, 1977; Matson, 1983; Ollendick, 1979a; Van Hasselt *et al.*, 1979).

The second problem concerns the measurement of children's phobias. The major categories of measures include self-report, physiological and behavioural. These broad categories are consistent with the view that phobic reactions involve cognitive–verbal, physiological and overt behavioural response systems. Although a variety of measures have been developed it is unfortunate that their scientific status has not been given greater attention; the reliability and validity of these measures are in need of more thorough research (see Chapter 3). As

Johnson and Melamed (1979) state:

> In our desire to treat children, it seems we have often prematurely accepted a particular test or method as an adequate measure for a child's fears, anxieties, or avoidance behavior. Efforts to develop empirically validated assessment measures need to be at least as extensive as the efforts to develop successful treatment procedures. After all, without adequate measurement, we can never be sure whether our treatment really 'worked'. (p. 121)

A useful challenge concerns ways by which the fear thermometer can be made more reliable and age-appropriate. The use of mechanical aids to make the exercise as concrete as possible seems beneficial and deserves further exploration (Kelley, 1976; Matson, 1981). A positive step in terms of more valid measures has been the development of behaviour observation checklists and rating scales that can be used to assess the child's behavioural reaction in the real fear-inducing situation (e.g. a dental surgery or medical clinic). Examples of these instruments include the Behavior Profile Rating Scale (Melamed, Weinstein, Hawes & Katin-Borland, 1975) and the Procedure Behavioral Rating Scale (Katz et al., 1980). Once reliable and valid measures have been developed for the subjective, physiological and overt behavioural components of children's phobias, researchers will be in a more confident position to appraise the effectiveness of behavioural methods on several criteria.

The third problem concerns the maintenance of therapeutic gains. When a behavioural programme is implemented it is assumed that the benefits will be fairly durable, and that the child will be able to cope with similar fear/phobia-inducing situations. Because of the difficulties in maintaining contact with parents, it is possible to be left with a biased sample upon which the long-term effectiveness of behavioural intervention is evaluated. Generally speaking, the decision about the long-term success of the behavioural programme is based upon a clinical interview, home visit, telephone check-up, or mail questionnaire. The literature on the behavioural treatment of children's phobias involves various follow-up periods. Most case reports (e.g. Ayllon et al., 1970; Bentler, 1962; Lazarus, 1960; Lazarus & Abramovitz, 1962; Ollendick & Gruen, 1972; Pomernatz et al., 1977; Stableford, 1979; Walker & Werstlein, 1980) entail follow-ups of 6–18 months. Longer follow-ups in the range of 19–26 months have been reported in several cases (e.g. Screenivasan et al., 1979; Waye, 1979; Yule et al., 1974) and up to 3 years in at least on study (Ollendick, 1979a). Generally speaking, therapeutic gains have been maintained at follow-up.

Moreover, several between-group experimental investigations have entailed follow-ups of 12 months or more. Hampe et al. (1973) reported 1- and 2-year follow-up studies of 67 phobic children who participated in a comparative evaluation of reciprocal inhibition therapy, psychotherapy, and waiting-list control. Clinical ratings, parent ratings, a fear scale, and a Total Disability Scale (of the Louisville Behaviour Check List) were employed. Successfully treated children tended to remain symptom-free, and to be free of other problems as well. Of 30 school-refusal cases that had received behavioural treatment, Blagg and Yule (1984) classified five as treatment failures on follow-up. The average follow-up was 1.71 years. All five of the treatment failures were described as Kennedy Type-2 cases. Most of the parents in these cases were uncooperative during treatment.

The most extensive follow-up reported in the behavioural literature is that by Graziano and Mooney (1982). These researchers conducted a $2\frac{1}{2}$- to 3-year follow-up of children who participated in a behaviourally oriented self-control programme for their night-time fears. Thirty-four of the 40 families were contacted using a mail questionnaire and telephone to determine if (a) significant improvements had been maintained, (b) new, related problems had developed, and (c) generalization of effects had occurred. Nineteen of the children also responded to telephone and mail questionnaires. Of the 34 follow-up children, 31 had maintained significant behavioural improvements. New problems were reported for 9 of the 34 children. These included academic, psychological, social and somatic difficulties. According to the parents, however, these problems were not related to the behavioural programme. In relation to generalization of treatment effects beyond night-time fears, most children (24 out of 34) had limited their new skills to the initial problem. Overall, the follow-up data that have been reported are fairly encouraging.

The manner in which follow-ups are conducted needs to be improved by clinicians and researchers. In the main, there is excessive reliance upon subjective impressions, which of course are in danger of overestimating the child's improvement. Ensuring that follow-up entails hard data of some kind will increase confidence in the maintenance of behavioural treatment effects. School phobia is an area in which this is readily possible given access to attendance records (Blagg & Yule, 1984). However, a period of data gathering at follow-up is possible for other problems such as animal phobias and night-time fears. Also it would be extremely useful to have more information on the circumstances under which therapeutic failures occur. Of significance here is the extent to which care providers can implement behavioural programmes. For a variety of reasons, some parents are not able to implement behavioural programmes. For example, the phobic child may be only one child in a large family, the parent may have emotional or psychiatric problems, the parent may feel harassed and cannot be consistent in the desired manner, and the spouse may not give support or may actively undermine the problem. Further aversive experiences for the child can also precipitate a return of the phobia (Rachman, 1979). Having undergone successful behavioural treatment for an animal phobia, for example, the child could relapse if attacked by dogs. It is generally agreed that further research is required into why therapeutic failures occur in behavioural programmes (Foa & Emmelkamp, 1983).

SYMPTOM SUBSTITUTION

The possibility of 'symptom substitution' is often raised by clinicians concerned about the use of behavioural methods. Treatment success is thought to be superficial as the underlying problem has not been resolved and will therefore break out in the form of another symptom. Thus a child's animal phobia might be removed through systematic desensitization and participant modelling, but bedwetting could take its place. While this line of argument is forthcoming from psychoanalysts, it is also voiced by many non-Freudian clinicians as well. In the evaluation of behavioural methods with phobic children, researchers have been alert to the possible emergence of other 'symptoms'. Generally, the empirical evidence in fear- and phobia-reduction studies does not favour symptom substitution. In their follow-up of 67 phobic children referred because of excessive or unrealistic fears, Hampe *et al.* (1973) concluded:

> Only one of our subjects developed a new symptom (obesity) over the three-year period. Further, we found that as primary fear reduced, so did a host of other deviant behaviors. Thus, there is little evidence in our data to support the concept of symptom substitution. Indeed, there is evidence that the child responds as a whole. When disturbance is observed in a specific area, general disturbance is also observed (Miller, Hampe, Barrett & Noble, 1973), and conversely, when distress in a specific area is diminished, a general reduction in deviancy also occurs. (p. 451)

The breadth of changes that can occur as a result of a behavioural programme should not be played down. Non-targeted improvements regarding social and family relationships, academic performance, self-concept, and general adjustment, are frequently reported (e.g. Lazarus & Abramovitz, 1962; MacDonald, 1975; Ollendick & Gruen, 1972; Tasto, 1969). Response covariation of this nature is an important outcome of behavioural interventions with phobic children.

On the other hand, it would be naive to insist that further problems never arise during or following the course of behavioural intervention. An unusual case reported by Waye (1979) raises the issue of 'symptom substitution' and its behavioural management. The subject was a 5 year-old girl who believed her hands were shrinking. A behavioural analysis indicated that her fear was due to a number of factors, including what she had been taught at Sunday School ('Neglect your bible and refuse to pray and you will shrink, shrink, shrink'). Parental attention to emotional outbursts about shrinking also seemed to reinforce the child's fear of shrinking hands. Treatment involved an attempt to dispel the belief that the child's thumbs were shrinking. A cardboard model of her hands was used to demonstrate that her hands were not shrinking. Appropriate play behaviours were immediately reinforced with parental attention. The amount of time spent with the child was gradually reduced once an improvement was evident. As the child improved in terms of the frequency of hand-shrinking reports, she began to complain that her ears were shrinking. Cardboard ear forms were made for comparison with her ears, but she refused to use these devices. Complaints that ears were shrinking decreased, but were followed by reports of nose and mouth shrinkage. The parents were instructed to ignore these protestations (extinction), with parental attention being diverted to appropriate play activities. This become problematic as the child became even more demanding of the parents. However, parental participation in play activities was gradually reduced and complaints about anatomical shrinkage

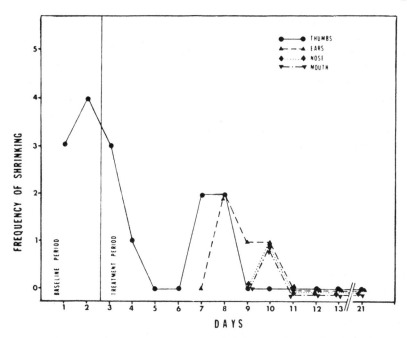

Fig. 8.1 Frequency of reported anatomical shrinkage during the programme. Reproduced from Waye (1979) by permission of Plenum Publishing Corp.

were brought under control (see Fig. 8.1). It should also be pointed out that the child was withdrawn from Sunday School. In this particular case the additional fears that emerged were conceptualized within a learning-theory framework rather than a psychoanalytic one. Treatment was given on the assumption that the fears were a means of obtaining parental attention. An important clinical issue here appears to be the functional significance of children's phobias; maybe there is a danger of relapse or 'symptom substitution' when the social significance of the child's phobia is neglected in therapy. Under these circumstances greater attention should be given to building up the individual's repertoire of coping skills and positive interactions if treatment is to be fully satisfactory.

UNDERLYING MECHANISMS

Behavioural methods have been reasonably successful in the treatment of children's phobias, although it is recognized that the procedures concerned have uneven research foundations and supportive evidence. Assuming the effectiveness of behavioural methods in phobia reduction, an intriguing question is the underlying mechanism by which these treatment methods overcome children's phobias. Traditionally, there has been a tendency to account for successful behavioural interventions in terms of a particular conditioning paradigm.

Perhaps the final common pathway is reciprocal inhibition, with the deliberate or inadvertent application of anti-anxiety states. On the other hand, reinforcement—planned or unplanned—might be the key to all successful behavioural programmes. As noted in our introduction to behavioural procedures (Chapter 4), the general consensus of opinion is that exposure is the critical factor in phobia reduction. Consider the manner in which behavioural methods bring the child in contact, imaginal or real-life, with the phobic stimulus. Systematic desensitization has the child gradually approach the phobic situation in imagination or real life. Emotive imagery brings the child into imaginal contact with the phobia through an exciting story or fantasy. Flooding and implosive therapy entail a rapid approach to the phobic situation. With operant procedures like shaping, a reward is used to bring the child into closer proximity and contact with the frightening object or situation. In modelling the child is required to observe a live or video model, with the additional possibility of having to match the modelled behaviour. Cognitive procedures can involve the rehearsal of positive coping statements in imaginal or real-life situations. Furthermore, cognitive procedures usually entail some degree of exposure. Thus all behavioural methods require the child to confront the phobic stimulus.

However, the manner in which the term 'exposure' is used is in need of clarification. Any form of exposure is not enough to overcome phobias. de Silva and Rachman (1981) specify some of the essential conditions:

> It refers to the exposure of the subject to the fear-evoking stimulus, either in real life (*in vivo* exposure) or in fantasy (imaginal exposure). Imaginal exposure, as carried out for example in systematic desensitization (Wolpe, 1958, 1973; Paul, 1966) consists in planned, sustained and repetitive evocations of images/image sequences of the stimuli in question. Mere thoughts or fleeting images do not constitute imaginal exposure in this sense. (p. 227)

Thus exposure may be real-life or imaginal, and involves prolonged rather than brief or momentary encounters. Obviously exposure should not be traumatic lest it reinforces the phobia. Usually care is taken by clinicians in the planning of exposures to ensure that nothing of an aversive or frightening nature occurs. de Silva and Rachman (1981) make a distinction between passive and active exposure (sometimes called 'engaged exposure'). Passive observation of the phobic stimulus is perhaps less likely to produce success as some kind of active interaction with the feared object, as in participant modelling (Bandura, Blanchard & Ritter, 1969; Ritter, 1968). In a similar vein, the 'cognitive set' (positive attitude) adopted by the individual during exposure might also be significant (Marks, 1975).

A crucial question is whether exposure is always necessary in overcoming phobias. The clinician using behavioural methods is likely to conclude that carefully organized exposure is necessary since exposure is part and parcel of behavioural intervention for phobias. However, whether exposure must be present in the treatment of phobia's is another question. de Silva and Rachman (1981) argue that, while there is little doubt about the clinical usefulness of exposure-based treatment methods, it should not be assumed that exposure is a necessary condition to fear reduction. These authorities maintain that fear reduction can take place in the absence of exposure to the fear stimulus. Several examples of fear reduction of the non-exposure type are given by de Silva and Rachman:

(a) the common clinical and experimental observation that imparting information about the harmlessness of the stimulus can lead to a reduction of fear; (b) suggestive evidence that cognitive therapy produces fear reduction; (c) spontaneous remissions of neurotic, including anxiety, reactions in a proportion of patients; (d) improvement observed after administration of placebos; (e) experimental results showing improvements in some patients after non-exposure types of therapy; (f) improvements shown by patients in the phobia(s) other than the treated one; and (g) indirect experimental evidence from the success of non-exposure therapy with obsessional neurotics. (p. 230)

If these kind of observations are correct, then it would have to be conceded that exposure is not the basic mechanism in phobic reduction.

The purported evidence for non-exposure-based fear reduction needs to be considered carefully. In a critical reply to de Silva and Rachman's (1981) argument, Boyd and Levis (1983) criticize the examples of non-exposure-based fear reduction. Boyd and Levis's handling of the claim that there is suggestive evidence that cognitive therapy produces fear reduction is of particular interest. While accepting that fear reduction occurs in cognitive therapy, Boyd and Levis point out that exposure to external stimuli via desensitization and other procedures is often part of cognitive intervention. Even when external stimuli are not directly addressed, this does not mean that exposure is not at work. Fear-relevant internal cues (thoughts and images) are subject to direct or indirect exposure (self-verbalization, discussion and relabelling of past experience). In a subsequent article, de Silva and Rachman (1983) emphasize that the evidence for non-exposure reductions of fear is not yet satisfactory. Nevertheless, the literature on non-exposure fear reduction is growing, which in the opinion of de Silva and Rachman demands greater investigation of non-exposure method of reducing fears.

The implications of the above controversy are fairly important in terms of therapeutic intervention with children and the advice that is given to parents. A comparison of exposure and non-exposure treatments would seem pertinent in resolving this issue. Sheslow et al. (1982) reported a study on the relative efficacies of graduated exposure, verbal coping skills, and their combined effects, in the treatment of children's fear of the dark. Thirty-two children with minimal dark tolerance served as subjects. The children were attending a private day-care centre and were not clinically referred. The BAT was administered as a pre-test, and re-administered twice following intervention under low and high instructional-demand conditions. Following the BAT administrations, each child was asked to indicate a fear rating on a manipulable fear thermometer. The subjects were matched for sex and duration of dark tolerance on the pre-test BAT and were randomly assigned to one of four groups: a graduated-exposure group; a verbal-coping-skills group; coping-skills/graduated-exposure group;

or a contact-control group. Children in the graduated-exposure group were exposed to a 9-step hierarchy of decreasing illuminations. During treatment sessions the experimenter and child talked, sang songs, played with toys and games and so on (this positive context occurred in all conditions). Children in the verbal-coping-skills group were given three training phases culminating in the practising of 'special words' during 'pretend (imaginal) games'. Training procedures in the coping-skills/graduated-exposure group were similar to those in the verbal-coping-skills group, except that in the last session the children practised the coping phrases at each of the nine graduated exposures. Children in the contact-control group were taught to recite part of nursery rhymes in the same positive context utilized for the other treatment groups. Only children in the two treatment conditions that included *in vivo* exposure to the dark demonstrated significant increases in dark tolerance (subjective fear ratings were of questionable validity in the experiment). Examination of Fig. 8.2 shows that the graduated-exposure group did better on both post-tests than the coping-skills/graduated-exposure group. The latter finding is possibly due to the fact that the graduated-exposure group involved more dark exposure than the coping-skills/graduated-exposure group. The outcome of this particular

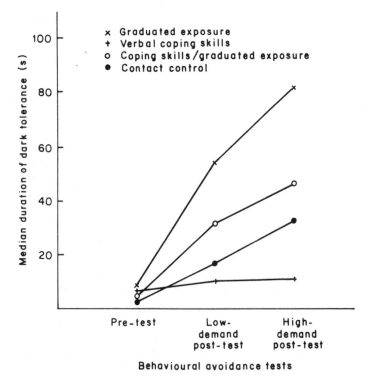

Fig. 8.2 Medians of dark tolerance for pre-test, high-demand post-test and low-demand post-test. Reproduced from Sheslow, Bondy and Nelson (1982) by permission of the Haworth Press.

study suggests that exposure is desirable in overcoming children's fears and phobias. To completely dismiss the therapeutic value of non-exposure methods like verbal-coping-skills training is premature, however. The children in the experiment were 4 and 5 years old. Older children with more advanced cognitive and verbal skills may have responded much better to non-exposure methods.

So far the discussion of theoretical mechanisms has focused mainly on the clinician's efforts at overcoming children's phobias. The notion that exposure is common to all behavioural methods (if not cognitive procedures) appears to be a reasonable account of the essence of behavioural intervention. Such an assertion is of course a *description* of external events controlled by the clinician, rather than an explanation of the *process* of behaviour change. As Emmelkamp (1982) has written: 'While it is obvious that almost all procedures contain elements of exposure to phobic stimuli, this fact does not elucidate the therapeutic process involved. Exposure is merely a description of what is going on during treatment and not an explanation of its processes' (p. 376).

Relevant to an explanation of the therapeutic action of exposure are two closely related processes, habituation and extinction (Barlow & Mavissakalian, 1981). Both processes involve the repeated presentation of the phobic stimulus and response decrement. Habituation refers to the decline of unlearned responses after repeated presentations of the stimulus; low arousal is presumed to facilitate the habituation of phobias in therapy (Lader & Wing, 1966; Lader & Mathews, 1968). Extinction entails the repeated presentation of the phobic stimulus (conditioned stimulus) in the absence of the aversive stimulus (unconditioned stimulus) with a decrement in the strength of the conditioned response. Rachman (1978) has pointed out the major differences between habituation and extinction:

> Habituation refers to decrements in the strength of unlearned responses, whereas extinction refer to decrements in the strength of learned responses. Habituation is said to be a temporary decrement whereas extinction tends to be stable. Only one condition is required for habituation to occur—the repeated presentation of the relevant stimulus. But for extinction two conditions are necessary: the repeated presentation of the relevant stimulus and an absence of reinforcement. In extinction one has to break a link (which has been learned). (p. 273)

Rachman believes that the latter distinction is probably the most useful in differentiating the two processes experimentally. Although it is difficult to disentangle the two processes, Rachman suggests that the three components of phobia reactions—cognitive, physiological and overt behavioural—may be subject to different decremental processes. Habituation may be the most pertinent for the physiological component; extinction may be the most significant process for avoidance behaviours; and perhaps both processes operate on the subjective component. This, of course, is speculation and experimental research remains to be undertaken in which habituation and extinction are compared in the context of the three response systems.

A cognitive explanation of phobia-reduction methods has been advanced by Bandura (1977). The principal assumption is that psychological procedures, whatever their form (behavioural, psychoanalytic, etc.) serve as a means of creating and strengthening expectations of personal efficacy (hence 'self-efficacy' theory). In other words, psychological interventions serve to develop a firm belief or sense of confidence in one's ability to handle a particular situation. In relation to the behavioural treatment of children's phobias, the various techniques—systematic desensitization, flooding, modelling, and contingency management, etc.—exert their influence through the development of efficacy expectations. Bandura makes a distinction between efficacy expectations and outcome expectations. An efficacy expectation refers to a person's conviction or confidence that he or she can execute a behaviour, while an outcome expectancy is the individual's estimate that a given behaviour will lead to certain outcomes. Efficacy expectations are believed to be situation-specific. Thus an adolescent may have confidence in his ability to mix in party gatherings, but lacks confidence in his ability to handle a formal dinner situation. Efficacy expectations are seen to depend very much on one's coping skills. In Bandura's conceptualization, a child is not likely to develop a strong sense of self-efficacy or mastery in relation to examinations unless the requisite knowledge and examination techniques are present. Given appropriate skills and incentives, Bandura maintains that: 'efficacy expectations are a major determinant of people's choice of activities, how much effort they will expend, and how long they will sustain effort in dealing with stressful situations' (p. 194).

Bandura (1977) has identified several dimensions of efficacy expectations that have important performance implications. First, efficacy expectations differ in *magnitude*. For example, children's efficacy expectations in being able to cope at school will vary from those limited to very simple tasks (e.g. sitting at a desk, having appropriate books) to those that include quite taxing performances (e.g. calculus). Second, efficacy expectations differ in *generality*. Some experiences create well-defined or narrow mastery expectations while others result in a more generalized sense of efficacy. In the treatment of dog-phobic children, the efficacy expectations that are instilled may be restricted to dogs (even a certain breed of dog). For other children the efficacy expectations may take in insects and animals, in general. Third, efficacy expectations vary in *strength*. The child with weak efficacy expectations is likely to give up in threatening situations, while the child with strong efficacy expectations will persevere despite unpleasant experiences. The reader will probably recognize that these dimensions bear on what is usually referred to as maintenance and generalization in the behavioural literature.

Following Bandura's (1977) analysis, the child's expectations of personal efficacy are based on four major sources: performance accomplishments, vicarious experience, verbal persuasion, and physiological states. For each of these sources there are many modes of induction, as displayed in Fig. 8.3. Performance accomplishments entail direct experience with phobia stimuli and are therefore especially influential. Successful engagement in an *in vivo* desensitization and participant-modelling programme raise mastery expectations in the child. Repeated failures on the part of the child will lower mastery expectations.

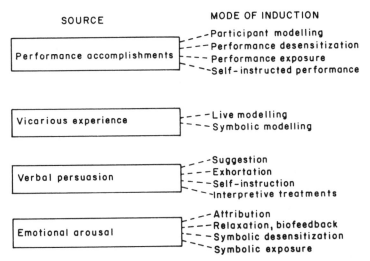

SOURCE   MODE OF INDUCTION

Fig. 8.3 Major sources of self-efficacy with different modes of treatment. Reproduced from Bandura (1977). Copyright (1977) by the American Psychological Association.

Once strong expectations have been developed through repeated success, the child can tolerate the negative impact of the occasional failure. Vicarious exposure in the form of modelling (observing a live or video model) can instil efficacy expectations in children. Verbal persuasion is another factor in the development of efficacy expectations. However, Bandura warns of the dangers inherent in verbal persuasion:

> Efficacy expectations induced in this manner are also likely to be weaker than those arising from one's own accomplishments because they do not provide an authentic experiential base for them. In the face of distressing threats and a long history of failure in coping with them, whatever mastery expectations are induced by suggestion can be readily extinguished by disconfirming experiences. (p. 198)

Verbal persuasion can contribute to the enduring sense of personal mastery in the phobic child provided the therapist attends to the conditions that facilitate effective performance, thus giving credibility to verbal messages. Emotional arousal is also a source of information concerning efficacy expectations. The physiological arousal experienced in a phobic reaction is aversive and debilitating to the child. This state can be elicited by an external stimulus or sometimes by the child's own thoughts and images. As the child's level of physiological arousal diminishes in therapy, a positive expectation is built up around being able to perform appropriate behaviour.

Self-efficacy theory has important implications for the clinical management of children's phobias in terms of both assessment and treatment. Self-efficacy theory demands an assessment of the child's efficacy expectations. A simple means by which efficacy expectations can be measured is to have children rate the degree of confidence they have in their ability to perform the fear-related tasks in question. Using a variety of fear-related tasks, the magnitude, generality and strength of efficacy expectations can be measured (Bandura, Adams, Hardy & Howells, 1980). Furthermore, from the viewpoint of self-efficacy theory, a therapeutic programme should emphasize performance accomplishments as a means of instilling a strong sense of personal mastery. The child's efficacy expectations should be checked at various stages of intervention as a means of deciding when to terminate therapy. In addition to the acquisition of behavioural skills, the objective is to have the child leaving therapy actually believing in his or her ability to perform the behaviour in question, thus minimizing the chances of relapse. At this point efficacy expectations are seen to be a better predictor of the child's future behaviour than current behavioural observations. Follow-up assessments would again examine the child's efficacy expectations with a view to taking remedial action if the child expresses less certainty about handling the threatening situation.

Self-efficacy theory has had a major impact on applied behavioural psychology with much research addressing self-efficacy as a predictor of behaviour and therapeutic outcome. Although a number of studies have examined self-efficacy in adult phobics (e.g. Bandura & Adams, 1977; Bandura, Adams & Beyer, 1977; Bandura et al., 1980), research has yet to be undertaken with phobic children. An obvious concern in working with children is the reliability of self-efficacy ratings. It is anticipated that reliability would be a problem with young children; more reliable measures are likely to be provided by older children and adolescents. A full account of the methodological and conceptual issues of self-efficacy theory is not possible here. Wilson (1978) believes that self-efficacy theory integrates the known facts, generates specific predictions concerning the initiation, generalization and maintenance of behaviour change, and is extremely heuristic. According to Wilson: 'self-efficacy theory promises to help sustain and nourish this impetus towards a better understanding and more effective treatment of psychological disorders' (p. 227). On the other hand, self-efficacy theory has been severely criticized. Borkovec (1978) believes it to be less parsimonious than traditional learning theory, and offers a view that many share: 'It is perhaps heuristic to view self-efficacy as a potentially important *reflection* of behavioral change mechanisms rather than as the mediator of such change' (p. 163). In a similar vein, Eysenck (1978) argues:

> Bandura's paper begins with the paradox that modern theories of behaviour change tend to be cognitive in nature, while the methods which actually produce such behaviour changes are performance-based. His theory does not succeed in solving this paradox, the proper answer to which must surely be that cognitive theories stress epiphenomenal concepts, leaving out the truly causal elements in the chain of events which mediates changes in behaviour. (pp. 174–5)

Thus, while the theory has considerable appeal, it is by no means widely accepted as the mechanism operative in fear-reduction procedures. As with other accounts, it is in need of greater empirical verification.

DESYNCHRONY

An important theoretical and practical issue concerns the impact of exposure-based treatments on the cognitive, physiological and overt behavioural response systems in children. In early years it was presumed that in the behavioural treatment of phobias, changes of an attitudinal and cognitive nature followed an improvement in overt behavioural functioning. This, of course, is in contrast to the view of more traditional psychotherapists who believe that behavioural and physiological changes follow the development of insight and attitudinal changes (Barlow & Mavissakalian, 1981). Common to both positions is the assumption that eventually all of the response systems evince significant changes. In the behavioural treatment of children's phobias, clinicians have assumed that a therapeutic improvement involves changes in all the response systems. However, the relationship between the response systems is far more complex and variable. While there may be improvements in all three response systems for some children, it is not the case for other children. This raises the issue of 'desynchrony' in measures of phobic reactions.

Contemporary theory regarding desynchrony is indebted to the writings of Rachman and Hodgson (1974), and Hodgson and Rachman (1974). In their first article, Rachman and Hodgson defined the basic terms—concordance, discordance, synchrony and desynchrony—used to describe the relationships between fear and avoidance. Extending their definitions to cover the three response systems, concordance occurs when there is a high correlation between two or more systems, while discordance involves a low correlation. Synchrony and desynchrony refer to the relative changes among the response systems; the response systems might covary (synchrony) or vary inversely or independently (desynchrony). In their second article, Hodgson and Rachman formulated five hypotheses regarding desynchronous measures of fears and phobias derived from an examination of the behaviour therapy literature. They suggested that 'desynchrony is a function of the intensity of emotional arousal, level of demand, therapeutic technique, length of follow-up and choice of physiological measure' (p. 319). The hypotheses are given in full in Table 8.1. Hodgson and Rachman emphasize that there are a number of artifacts which could contaminate attempts to measure concordance and desynchrony. The law of initial values, different levels of threat across the response systems, and the unreliability of measures could reduce intercorrelations and hence the apparent synchrony between measures. It should be emphasized that the research studies examined by Hodgson and Rachman entail work with adult subjects (mainly agoraphobics and obsessive–compulsive patients'. Presumably the hypotheses regarding desynchronous changes were thought to apply to children, although this is not explicitly stated. Seven years later, Barlow and Mavissakalian (1981) confirmed desynchrony and the priority it should be given: 'desynchrony seems an established fact in the treatment of fear, and the implications of this desynchrony will be a major concern of theorists and clinical researchers in the next decade' (p. 213).

Table 8.1 Hypotheses pertaining to desynchrony

Hypothesis 1
(a) Concordance between response systems is likely to be high during strong emotional arousel.
(b) Discordance will be more evident when emotional responses are relatively mild.

Hypothesis 2
(a) Concordance between response systems will be greater under low levels of demand.
(b) High levels of demand will produce discordance.

Hypothesis 3
The degree of synchrony resulting from a therapeutic intervention will be a function of the particular therapeutic technique employed.

Hypothesis 4
The degree of concordance between measures in different response systems after treatment intervention will increase during the follow-up period.

Hypothesis 5
In the treatment of phobic behaviour, the desynchrony between physiological and other measures will be greater for skin-conductance than for heart-rate.

SOURCE: Hodgson and Rachman (1974).

Van Hasselt *et al.* (1979) have reported a case which illustrates desynchrony in children. The case entailed an 11-year-old boy with three phobias (heights, blood and test anxiety). Using a multiple-baseline design, the three phobias were treated via relaxation and systematic desensitiation. Probes were administered over baseline, treatment (although independent of therapy sessions), and follow-up in order to gather data on the various components of the phobias—motor (performance on analogue test and BAT), physiological (pulse rate, heart rate, finger pulse volume), and cognitive (fear thermometer ratings). In terms of the hypotheses pertaining to desynchrony, some interesting findings emerged. The most impressive changes were obtained on the motor and cognitive measures, with improvement in subjective fear ratings generally following motor changes. Except for hear-rate-change scores on the ladder climb test (height phobia), the subject did not exhibit much change on physiological measures. Thus desynchronization was evident in the probe sessions (consistent with Hypothesis 2 in Table 8.1). Generally, systematic desensitization produced greater improvements than relaxation training, especially in relation to subjective fear ratings. The results were maintained over 1-, 4- and 6-month follow-up assessments. Thus the desynchronization pattern was not affected by the length of follow-up (contrary to Hypothesis 4 in Table 8.1). Despite the persistent uncoupling of the response systems, relapse did not occur.

Certainly, more intensive research is required on desynchrony in children. A problem for researchers concerns the fact that a response system can be measured in different ways. For example, physiological activity may be measured using heart rate and GSR, but these measures may not correlate very well. As far the overt behavioural response system is concerned, it may be questioned whether we should rely on an avoidance test or another source of data such as observations in the natural setting. Nevertheless, taking multiple measures at baseline, treatment, post-treatment and follow-up should help identify desynchronous patterns. Perhaps a number of children are resistant to therapy on physiological indices, despite making good progress in terms of their overt behaviour and subjective fear levels (Van Hasselt *et al.*, 1979). Other children may retain fear at a subjective level, while they do quite well physiologically and behaviourally. Of course, the crucial question is whether children who evince uneven improvements within the three responses systems are more prone to relapse. Follow-up assessments that entail measures of the three response systems would be of particular interest in relation to the question of desynchrony as a predictor of relapse.

COMPREHENSIVE BEHAVIOURAL TREATMENT

Given the low intercorrelation between the three response systems, and that empirical support for the efficacy of any one behavioural method with children's phobias is limited, it seems logical to develop comprehensive treatment programmes, thus enhancing the likelihood of good therapeutic outcomes. Ollendick (1979b) has argued for an 'integrated' treatment model derived from the principles of classical, operant and vicarious conditioning. According to Ollendick:

> Such a treatment might provide the following therapeutic agents, in addition to graduated exposure: (1) counterconditioning to reduce the intensity of the fear, (2) participant modelling to demonstrate interactive skills with the feared object, and (3) reinforcement to praise the child for non-fearful and approach behaviours. The comibination of these techniques might result in optimal fear reduction. (p. 162)

At the present time we advocate a slightly more elaborate and comprehensive behavioural programme that is highly individualized. It consists of:

(1) education to cover the possibility of ignorance and misinformation about the feared situation;
(2) systematic desensitization or emotive imagery as a means of dealing with the physiological anxiety experienced by the child;
(3) participant modelling in order to build up any necessary coping skills and overcome residual anxiety;
(4) reinforced to increase the incentive for approach/interaction behaviour on the part of the child;
(5) cognitive procedures for the enhancement of positive self-statements when age-appropriate.

Alongside these intervention procedures, parent counselling is required when there is evidence of overprotection and inadvertent reinforcement of the child's phobic behaviour. In our clinical experience the model has been useful in the treatment of separation anxiety, night-time fears, animal phobias, excessive fears of dental and medical procedures, test anxiety, and many other maladaptive fears seen in children. The model could be applied to school phobia, although it must be remembered that forced school attendance (flooding) seems both effective and acceptable here (Blagg & Yule, 1984).

Of course, the combination of behavioural methods in the treatment of children's phobias is by no means new in clinical practice. For example, MacDonald (1975) reported the treatment of a long-standing dog phobia in an 11-year-old boy using 'multiple impact' behaviour therapy. The major elements of the programme included abbreviated progressive relaxation, imaginal desensitization, the use of desensitization adjuncts (e.g. photographs of dogs, tape recordings of a barking dog), dog-interaction skill training, modelling, programmed outdoor activity, and social environmental structuring (parent management). The programme was successful in dealing with the child's conditioned anxiety, inadequate dog-handling skills, and parental expectations that he would be fearful. There were 16 treatment sessions with considerable overlap between the above components, although relaxation was commenced ahead of the other procedures. Somewhat similarly, Stokes and Kennedy (1980) found a combination of modelling and reinforcement to be effective in reducing the uncooperative behaviour of 8 children during dental treatment. At a certain stage in their dental treatment, each child was invited to observe the prior child being treated for about 10 to 15 minutes. The child received a small trinket (capsule for mixing silver alloy amalgam) and was allowed to raise the next child in the pneumatic chair, if a low level of uncooperative behaviour was displayed. As far as the operative variable is concerned, some children appeared very interested in observing a peer undergo dental treatment, while others seemed to be more influenced by the rewards. It should not be concluded, however, that a combination of behavioural methods automatically guarantees a positive outcome. In her research on 4 and 5 year old children who were afraid of darkness, Kelley (1976) found play desensitization to be quite ineffective. Moreover, the addition of M & Ms did not improve the potency of the therapeutic condition. Presumably, individual needs were not being met in this experimental research. In clinical practice this is of paramount significance, even with a comprehensive behavioural programme. There are of course many other instances in which a combination of behavioural methods has been successful in phobia reduction with children.

From the above illustrations of comprehensive behavioural programmes, it will be evident that behavioural procedures can be applied sequentially or concurrently depending upon the complexity of the problem and the available resources. The behavioural treatment of children's phobias is frequently characterized by a 'natural mix' of education, desensitization, modelling, reinforcement and cognitive restructuring, thus reflecting the concurrent approach. This may be justified on cost-efficient grounds as well as the differences between procedures being somewhat blurred in clinical practice. However, for children with severe phobias attention should be given to the sequencing of behavioural procedures, especially, systematic desentization and participant modelling. It is recommended that systematic desensitization and/or emotive imagery should be undertaken prior to participant modelling, otherwise the latter could be too anxiety-provoking for the child. Should intense anxiety be experienced, the highly avoidant child may not benefit from participant modelling. In fact, it is conceivable that such an aversive experience could reinforce the child's phobia. In a critical review of desensitization procedures employed with children, Hatzenbuehler and Schroeder (1978) state:

> ...with severely phobic subjects, a treatment involving initial passive association with subsequent active participation should prove more effective than passive association alone. This hypothesis is based on the notion that active participation techniques afford subjects the opportunity for actual rehearsal of new coping behaviors. With severely phobic individuals, such active rehearsal would be meaningful only if their fear was no longer grossly debilitating and allowed some voluntary behavior. (p. 842)

While the above hypotheses concerning the desensitization–participant-modelling sequence appear quite sensible from the viewpoint of clinical practice, research should be undertaken to establish the merits of this advice.

SOCIAL VALIDATION

Social validation refers to the social acceptability of behavioural interventions and their outcomes. Traditionally, behavioural programmes have been evaluated on the basis of hard data and controlled experimental designs. The perception of clients and others was secondary to 'scientific' issues. On the other hand, social acceptability of behavioural intervention could not be avoided if client needs were to be addressed on a clinical service basis. Behavioural practitioners also became aware of the 'public relations' problem associated with their approach. The language of 'behaviour modification' sometimes elicited negative reactions, and it was suggested that softer terms be adopted by therapists (Woolfolk, Woolfolk & Wilson, 1977). Apart from choice of language, not all people (clients and professionals) saw the need for data-collection and data-based decision making which constitute the heart of the behavioural approach (Murphy, 1980). Thus, it is not surprising in the historical sense that much concern is now voiced about social validation.

According to Wolf (1978), society needs to evaluate behavioural endeavours on at least three levels:

(1) The social significance of the *goals*. Are the specific behavioral goals really what society wants?
(2) The social appropriateness of the *procedures*. Do the ends justify the means? That is, do the participants, caregivers and other consumers consider the treatment procedures acceptable?
(3) The social importance of the *effects*. Are consumers satisfied with the results? *All* the results, including any unpredictable ones? (p. 207)

In a discussion of the above three facets of social validation, Kazdin (1977) draws attention to the social validation of clinical change. As a means of evaluating whether behaviour change achieved during treament has clinical or social importance, Kazdin outlines two methods of assessment, i.e. social comparison and subjective evaluation. With the social-comprison methods, the behaviour of the client before and after treatment is compared with the behaviour of non-problem peers. With the subjective-evaluation method, the client's behaviour is evaluated by individuals who have contact with the client in the natural setting.

Generally, researchers interested in phobia reduction with children have not considered the issue of social validation in an empirical manner. A notable exception is a study conducted by Matson (1981) on the behavioural treatment of clinical fears in mentally retarded children. As Matson comments: 'the current study is the first to attempt to conduct a social validation study comparing fearful children to children judged to be functioning normally on these same behaviors and who were matched to the participants on the variables of age, race, and sex' (p. 288). Three moderately retarded white females between 8 to 10 years old participated in the study. All of the girls had been referred to a community mental-health centre for debilitating fears. They had few friends and complained of being fearful of strangers and acquaintances. To establish the children's fearful behaviour before the study, an assessment was conducted at school. This involved approaching a male stranger and rating how 'afraid' the encounter had made them. As a means of obtaining a criterion for treatment success, the teacher and teacher's aide were asked to rank-order the same sex peers from their class in order to socially appropriate fear level. The child with the lowest total score was taken as the most normal on fear of strangers. Participants and peers were matched for age, sex and level of mental retardation. The child selected for a normal amount of fear was run through the same assessment given to the participants in the study. Their scores were then used as a 'clinical' criterion for successful treatment. The children's fears were assessed in the clinic on three dependent measures (i.e. approaching a strange adult, speaking with a strange adult, and a self-report of fear). Four adult strangers (2 males and 2 females) were involved in the assessment. One approach trial was run with each adult under standardized conditions with respect to the involvement of the mother and adult strangers.

A multiple-baseline design across subjects was employed. Treatment involved participant modelling, with the mother of the afflicted child serving as the therapist. The treatment sessions were carried out in the clinic. The mother was equipped with a bug in the ear device and took instructions from the experimenter who observed the mother and child through a one-way mirror. In the first training session, the child was required to practise the greeting procedure, with prompting and reinforcement from the mother, in the absence of a strange adult. As homework the mother was to practise with the child twice a day on making a greeting with the father or another family member who served as the 'strange adult'. After the completion of the first phase of training, the child was exposed to a series of strange adults. Initially, the mother went through the greeting response practice with the child in the absence of a

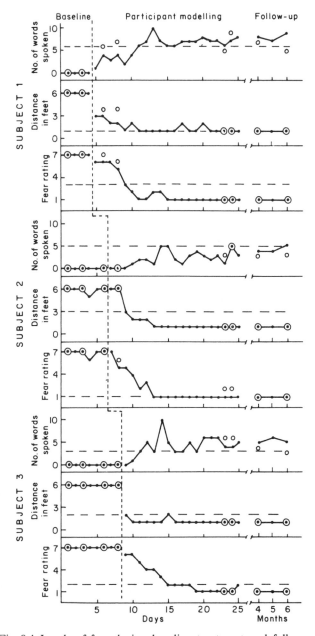

Fig. 8.4 Levels of fear during baseline treatment and follow-up
sessions. The open circles represent a measure of generalization at
the children's homes. Dependent measures are represented for all
three children in a multiple baseline design. The dotted horizontal
lines represent scores of non-fearful children. Reproduced from
Matson (1981) by permission of the Society for the Experimental
Analysis of Behaviour, Inc.

stranger. For the first trial involving a stranger, the mother walked up to the person while holding the child's hand. Prompts to speak and/or what to say were employed when necessary. After a successful response, the mother would praise her child with a tangible reward being given in another room. The same procedure was followed with a second strange adult. No session was terminated unless some approximation of a successful response was completed. The mother gradually faded her verbal prompts, physical proximity and contact with the child.

As can be seen in Fig. 8.4, all of the dependent variables changed in the desired direction with the introduction of treatment. The changes were maintained over 6 months. In order to assess the generalization of treatment effects, participants were assessed periodically throughout the study on their willingness to interact with friends or their parents. These probe sessions were identical to the clinic assessment sessions, except that the location was the child's home. The father of the child was responsible for the probe sessions. From the viewpoint of social validation of clinical changes it will be noted that the changes put the children in the normal range based on the response of their 'matched' normal peer. Consumer satisfaction was also evident, with children and parents expressing satisfaction about the programme.

Further research needs to be conducted on the social validation of behavioural intervention for children's phobias. In addition to the social validation of clinical change, it is also important to examine the social validation of the goals and therapeutic procedures employed in phobia-reduction programmes for children. Research on social validation is likely to gain momentum for several reasons. First, when a range of treatment options are suspected to be about equally effective, it would seem important to know what techniques are preferred and what techniques are unacceptable to clients. It can also be argued that on ethical grounds, behavioural intervention should not only be effective, but also acceptable to the consumer (Wolf, 1978). Second, having data on the consumer satisfaction regarding behavioural intervention can help influence administrative (and possibly legal) decisions on the use of behavioural methods in organizations like schools and hospitals (Budd & Baer, 1976; Martin, 1975). Third, the examination of social acceptance should serve to identify variables that enhance the client's positive perception of behavioural intervention (Kazdin, 1980a). Consider the 'artificiality' of the behavioural avoidance test versus naturalistic observations of the child's phobic behaviour (possibly the latter are more acceptable to parents). Fourth, it would be expected that when social validation of goals and treatment procedures is positive, the client or care provider will be more likely to comply with the advice and recommendations issued by the clinician.

SUMMARY

We have examined a number of issues related to the behavioural treatment and prevention of childhood phobias, and have pointed out the significant role of parents and other care providers in behavioural interventions. Parents need to have a well-defined and structured input, along with some preparation for their role as agents of behaviour change. Therapy may actually begin with a parent if he or she has the same fear as the child. As to the effectiveness of behavioural techniques with phobic children, systematic desensitization and modelling have the strongest empirical support. We have noted that treatment evaluations have been impeded by a number of methodological problems (biased samples, inadequate measures, and insufficient follow-up). Generally, symptom substitution is not a concern in the use of behavioural methods with phobic children. In fact, we noted improvements in addition to the targeted gains.

Exposure is thought to be the mechanism shared by behavioural interventions with children. The exposures may be real-life or imaginal, and involve prolonged rather than brief or momentary encounters. Exposure can be understood in terms of two closely related processes, habituation and extinction. Social learning theory posits that the common mechanism is of a cognitive nature. Accordingly, children develop a belief in their ability to cope with the frightening object or situation (efficacy expectations) over the course of intervention. Performance accomplishments through systematic desensitization and participant modelling are the most powerful means of instilling feelings of mastery in children.

The desynchrony of subjective fear, physiological reactivity and overt behaviour has been subject to little research with children. Of clinical significance is whether children who evince uneven improvements across the three response systems are more prone to relapse. In clinical practice, the optimal phobia-reduction programme should be highly individualized and might incorporate the principles of classical, operant and vicarious conditioning. The sequencing of behavioural methods is an important consideration; clinical wisdom has it that systematic desensitization precedes participant modelling, especially for children with severe phobias. As well as being concerned about the effectiveness of behavioural procedures, the underlying mechanism, and so forth, we should also address the social acceptability of behavioural interventions and their outcome (social validation). Specifically, the social acceptability of our goals, procedures, and effectiveness need to be evaluated in phobia-reduction programmes with children.

References

Achenbach, T. M. (1966). The classification of children's psychiatric symptoms: a factor analytic study. *Psychological Monographs*, **80**, 1–37.

Achenbach, T. M., & Edelbrock, C. S. (1978). The classification of child psychopathology: a review and analysis of empirical efforts. *Psychological Bulletin*, **85**, 1275–301.

Achenbach, T. M., & Lewis, M. (1971). A proposed model for clinical research and its application to encopresis and enuresis. *Journal of the American Academy of Child Psychiatry*, **10**, 535–54.

Agras, W. S., Chapin, N. H., & Oliveau, D. C. (1972). The natural history of phobias: course and prognosis. *Archives of General Psychiatry*, **26**, 315–7.

Agras, W. S., Sylvester, D., & Oliveau, D. (1969). The epidemiology of common fears and phobias. *Comprehensive Psychiatry*, **10**, 151–6.

Allyon, T., Smith, D., & Rogers, M. (1970). Behavioral management of school phobia. *Journal of Behavior Therapy & Experimental Psychiatry*, **1**, 125–38.

American Psychiatric Association (1968). *Diagnostic and Statistical Manual of Mental Disorders* (2nd ed.). Washington, DC: American Psychiatric Association.

American Psychiatric Association (1987). *Diagnostic and Statistical Manual of Mental Disorders* (3rd ed.—Rev.). Washington, DC: American Psychiatric Association.

Andrasik, F., & Murphy, W. D. (1977). Assessing the readability of thirty-nine behavior-modification training manuals and primers. *Journal of Applied Behavior Analysis*, **10**, 341–4.

Angelino, H., Dollins, J., & Mech, E. V. (1956). Trends in the 'fears and worries' of school children as related to socio-economic status and age. *Journal of Genetic Psychology*, **89**, 263–76.

Attkisson, C. C., Hargreaves, W. A., Horowitz, M. J., & Sorensen, M. J. (Eds.) (1978). *Evaluation of Human Service Programs*. New York: Academic Press.

Axelrod, S. (1977). *Behavior Modification for the Classroom Teacher*. New York: McGraw-Hill.

Bamber, J. H. (1974). The fears of adolescents. *Journal of Genetic Psychology*, **125**, 127–40.

Bamber, J. H. (1979). *The Fears of Adolescents*. London: Academic Press.

Bandura, A. (1969). *Principles of behavior modification*. New York: Holt, Rinehart & Winston.

Bandura, A. (1976). Effecting change through participant modeling. In J. D. Krumboltz & C. E. Thoresen (Eds.), *Counseling methods* (pp. 248–65). New York: Holt, Rinehart & Winston.

Bandura, A. (1977). Self-efficacy: towards a unifying theory of behavioral change. *Psychological Review*, **84**, 191–215.

Bandura, A., & Adams, N. E. (1977). Analysis of self-efficacy theory of behavioral change. *Cognitive Therapy & Research*, **1**, 287–310.

Bandura, A., Adams, N. E., & Beyer, J. (1977). Cognitive processes mediating behavioral change. *Journal of Personality & Social Psychology*, **35**, 125–39.

Bandura, A., Adams, N. E., Hardy, A. B., & Howells, G. N. (1980). Tests of the generality of self-efficacy theory. *Cognitive Therapy & Research*, **4**, 39–66.

Bandura, A., Blanchard, E. B., & Ritter, B. (1969). Relative efficacy of desensitization and modeling approaches for inducing behavioral, affective, and attitudinal changes. *Journal of Personality & Social Psychology*, **13**, 173–99.

Bandura, A., Grusec, J. E., & Menlove, F. L. (1967). Vicarious extinction of avoidance behavior. *Journal of Personality & Social Psychology*, **5**, 16–23.

Bandura, A., Jeffery, R. W., & Wright, C. A. (1974). Efficacy of participant modeling as a function of response induction aids. *Journal of Abnormal Psychology*, **83**, 56–64.

Bandura, A., & Menlove, F. L. (1968). Factors determining vicarious extinction of avoidance behavior through symbolic modeling. *Journal of Personality & Social Psychology*, **8**, 99–108.

Bandura, A., & Walters, R. H. (1963). *Social Learning and Personality Development*. New York: Holt, Rinehart & Winston.

Barlow, D. H., Hayes, S. C., & Nelson, R. O. (1984). *The Scientist Practitioner: Research and Accountability in Clinical and Educational Settings*. New York: Pergamon Press.

Barlow, D. H., & Mavissakalian, M. (1981). Directions in the assessment and treatment of phobia: the next decade. In M. Mavissakalian & D. H. Barlow (Eds.), *Phobia: Psychological and Pharmacological Treatment* (pp. 199–245). New York: Guilford Press.

Barrios, B. A., Hartmann, D. P., & Shigetomi, C. (1981). Fears and anxieties in children. In E. J. Mash & L. G. Terdal (Eds.), *Behavioral Assessment of Childhood Disorders* (pp. 259–304). New York: Guilford Press.

Barrios, B. A., & Shigetomi, C. C. (1980). Coping skills training: potential for prevention of fears and anxieties. *Behavior Therapy*, **11**, 431–9.

Bauer, D. H. (1976). An exploratory study of developmental changes in children's fears. *Journal of Child Psychology & Psychiatry*, **17**, 69–74.

Bayley, N. (1969). *Bayley Scales of Infant Developmental Manual*. New York: Psychological Corporation.

Beck, A. T. (1976). *Cognitive Therapy and the Emotional Disorders*. New York: International Universities Press.

Begelman, D. H., & Hersen, M. (1971). Critique of Obler and Terwilliger's 'Systematic desensitization with neurologically impaired children with phobic disorders'. *Journal of Consulting & Clinical Psychology*, **37**, 10–13.

Bentler, P. M. (1962). An infant's phobia treated with reciprocal inhibition therapy. *Journal of Child Psychology & Psychiatry*, **3**, 185–189.

Berecz, J. M. (1968). Phobias of childhood: aetiology and treatment. *Psychological Bulletin*, **70**, 694–720.

Berg, I. (1970). A follow-up study of school phobic adolescents admitted to an in-patient unit. *Journal of Child Psychology & Psychiatry*, **11**, 37–47.

Berg, I., Nichols, K., & Pritchard, C. (1969). School-phobia—its classification and relationship to dependency. *Journal of Child Psychology & Psychiatry*, **10**, 123–41.

Berger, S. M. (1962). Conditioning through vicarious instigation. *Psychological Review*, **69**, 450–66.

Berkowitz, B. P., & Graziano, A. M. (1972). Training parents as behavior therapists: a review. *Behaviour Research & Therapy*, **10**, 297–317.

Bernard, M. E., & Joyce, M. R. (1984). *Rational–Emotive Therapy with Children and Adolescents: Theory, Treatment Strategies, Preventative Methods*. New York: Wiley.

Berney, T., Kolvin, I., Bhate, S. R., Garside, R. F., Jeans, J., Kay, B., & Scarth, L. (1981). School phobia: a therapeutic trial with clomipramine and short-term outcome. *British Journal of Psychiatry*, **138**, 110–18.

Bernstein, D. A. (1973). Behavioral fear assessment: anxiety or artifact? In H. E. Adams & I. P. Unikel (Eds.), *Issues and Trends in Behavior Therapy* (pp. 225–67). Springfield, Ill.: Charles C. Thomas.

Bernstein, D. A., & Borkovec, T. D. (1973). *Progressive Relaxation Training: A Manual for the Helping Professions*. Champaign, Ill.: Research Press.

238

Bersh, P. J. (1980). Eysenck's theory of incubation: a critical analysis. *Behaviour Research & Therapy*, **18**, 11–17.

Betts, G. H. (1969). The distribution and functions of mental images. In A. Richardson (Ed.), *Mental imagery*. New York: Springer (Original work published in 1909).

Blagg, N. (1977). A detailed strategy for the rapid treatment of school phobics. *Behavioural Psychotherapy*, **5**, 70–5.

Blagg, N. (1987). *School Phobia and Its Treatment*. London: Croom Helm.

Blagg, N. R., & Yule, W. (1984). The behavioural treatment of school refusal—a comparative study. *Behaviour Research & Therapy*, **22**, 119–27.

Blanchard, E. B. (1970). Relative contributions of modeling, informational influences and physical contact in extinction of phobic behavior. *Journal of Abnormal Psychology*, **76**, 55–61.

Bloom, B. L. (1968). The evaluation of primary prevention programs. In L. M. Roberts, N. S. Greenfeld & M. H. Miller (Eds.), *Comprehensive Mental Health: The Challenge of Evaluation* (pp. 117–35). Madison: University of Wisconsin Press.

Bogat, G. A. Jones, J. W. & Jason, L. A. (1980). School transitions: preventive intervention following an elementary school closing. *Journal of Community Psychology*, **8**, 343–52.

Bolman, W. M. (1969). Toward realizing the prevention of mental illness. In L. Bellak & H. H. Barten (Eds.), *Progress in Community Mental Health*, Vol. 1. New York: Grune & Stratton.

Bondy, A., Sheslow, D., & Garcia, L. T. (1985). An investigation of children's fears and their mothers' fears. *Journal of Psychopathology & Behavioral Assessment*, **7**, 1–12.

Borkovec, T. D. (1978). Self-efficacy: cause or reflection on behavioral change. *Advances in Behaviour Research & Therapy*, **1**, 163–70.

Borkovec, T. D., Weerts, T. C., & Bernstein, D. A. (1977). Assessment of anxiety. In A. R. Ciminero, K. A. Calhoun and H. E. Adams (Eds.), *Handbook of behavioural assessment* (pp. 367–428). New York: Wiley.

Bower, E. M. (1969). Primary prevention of mental and emotional disorders: a conceptual framework and action possibilities. In A. J. Bindman & A. D. Spiegel (Eds.), *Perspective in Community Mental Health* (pp. 231–49). Chicago: Aldine.

Bowlby, J. (1973). *Attachment and Loss*, Vol. 2. New York: Basic Books.

Boyd, T. L., & Levis, D. L. (1983). Exposure is a necessary condition for fear-reduction: a reply to de Silva and Rachman. *Behaviour Research & Therapy*, **21**, 143–9.

Bregman, E. (1934). An attempt to modify the emotional attitudes of infants by the conditioned response technique. *Journal of Genetic Psychology*, **45**, 169–96.

Broadwin, I. T. (1932). A contribution to the study of truancy. *American Journal of Orthopsychiatry*, **2**, 253–9.

Bronson, G. W. (1968). The development of fear in man and other animals. *Child Development*, **39**, 409–31.

Brown, J. A. C. (1961). *Freud and the Post-Freudians*. Harmondsworth: Penguin.

Brown, R. E., Copeland, R. E. & Hall, R. V. (1974). School phobia: effects of behavior modification treatment applied by an elementary school principal. *Child Study Journal*, **4**, 125–33.

Bruch, M. A. (1975). Influence of model characteristics on psychiatric inpatients' interview anxiety. *Journal of Abnormal Psychology*, **84**, 290–4.

Budd, K. S., & Baer, D. M. (1976). Behavior modification and the law: implications of recent judicial decisions. *Journal of Psychiatry & Law*, **4**, 171–244.

Burstein, S., & Meichenbaum, D. (1979). The work of worrying in children undergoing surgery. *Journal of Abnormal Child Psychology*, **7**, 121–32.

Buss, A. H. (1966). *Psychopathology* New York: Wiley.

Campbell, D., Sanderson, R. E., & Laverty, S. G. (1964). Characteristics of a conditioned response in human subjects during extinction trials following a sample traumatic conditioning trial. *Journal of Abnormal & Social Psychology*, **68**, 627–39.

Caplan, G. (1964). *Principles of Preventive Psychiatry*, New York: Basic Books.

239

Carlton, P. L., & Vogel, J. R. (1967). Habituation and conditioning. *Journal of Comparative & Physiological Psychology*, **63**, 348–51.

Carr, A. T. (1979). The psychopathology of fear. In W. Sluckin (Ed.), *Fear in Animals and Man* (pp. 199–235). New York: Van Nostrand Reinhold.

Carr, J. (1980). *Helping your Handicapped Child*. Harmondsworth: Penguin.

Cassell, S. (1965). Effects of brief puppet therapy upon the emotional responses of children undergoing cardiac catheterization. *Journal of Consulting Psychology*, **29**, 1–8.

Castaneda, A., McCandless, B. R., & Palermo, D. S. (1956). The children's form of the Manifest Anxiety Scale. *Child Development*, **27**, 317–26.

Cataldo, M. F., Bessman, C. A., Parker, L. H., Pearson, J. E., & Rogers, M. C. (1979). Behavioral assessment for pediatric intensive care units. *Journal of Applied Behavior Analysis*, **12**, 83–97.

Cattell, R. B., & Scheier, I. H. (1958). The nature of anxiety: a review of thirteen multivariate analyses comparing 814 variables. *Psychological Reports*, (Monograph Supplement, 5), 4, 315–88.

Cattell, R. B., & Scheier, I. H. (1961). *The Meaning and Measurement of Neuroticism and Anxiety*. New York: Ronald.

Cautela, J. R., & Groden, J. (1978). *Relaxation: A Comprehensive Manual for Adults, Children, and Children with Special Needs*. Champaign, Ill.: Research Press.

Cautela, J. R., & Upper, D. (1977). Behavioral analysis, assessment and diagnosis. In D. Upper (Ed.), *Perspectives in Behavior Therapy* (pp. 3–27). Kalamazoo, MI: Behaviordelia.

Chapel, J. L. (1967). Treatment of a case of school phobia by reciprocal inhibition. *Canadian Psychiatric Association Journal*, **12**, 25–8.

Chazan, M., & Jackson, S. (1971). Behaviour problems in the infant school. *Journal of Child Psychology & Psychiatry*, **12**, 191–210.

Cherches, M. L., & Blackman, S. (1963). Alleviating the anxiety of children in dental treatment. *Journal of the American Dental Association*, **66**, 824–6.

Chertock, S. L., & Bornstein, P. H. (1979). Covert modeling treatment of children's dental fears. *Child Behavior Therapy*, **1**, 249–55.

Cheshire, N. M. (1979). A big hand for Little Hans. *Bulletin of the British Psychological Society*, **32**, 320–3.

Cheshire, N. M. (1980). Hands off Little Hans. *Bulletin of the British Psychological Society*, **33**, 69–70.

Chudy, J. F., Jones, G. E., & Dickson, A. L. (1983). Modified desensitization approach for the treatment of phobic behavior in children: a quasi-experimental case study. *Journal of Clinical Child Psychology*, **12**, 189–201.

Ciminero, A. R., Calhoun, K. S., Adams, H. E. (Eds.) (1977). *Handbook of Behavioral Assessment*. New York: Wiley.

Clowes-Hollins, V., & King, N. J. (1981, May). Survey data on the acquisition and parent management of children's phobias. Paper presented at the Annual Conference of the Australian Behaviour Modification Association, Sydney, N.S.W.

Coleman, J., Wolkind, S., & Ashley, L. (1977). Symptoms of behaviour disturbance and adjustment to school. *Journal of Child Psychology & Psychiatry*, **18**, 201–9.

Cone, J. D., & Hawkins, R. P. (Eds.) (1977). *Behavioral Assessment: New Directions in Clinical Psychology*. New York: Brunner/Mazel.

Conway, A. V. (1978). Little Hans: misrepresentation of the evidence? *Bulletin of the British Psychological Society*, **31**, 285–7.

Cooke, G. (1966). The efficacy of two desensitization procedures: an analogue study. *Behaviour Research & Therapy*, **4**, 17–24.

Cooke, G. (1968). Evaluation of the efficacy of the components of reciprocal inhibition psychotherapy. *Journal of Abnormal Psychology*, **73**, 464–7.

Coolidge, J. C., Hahn, P. B., & Peck, A. L. (1957). School phobia: neurotic crisis or way of life. *American Journal of Orthopsychiatry*, **27**, 296–306.

Cooper, J. A. (1973). Application of the consultant role to parent–teacher management of school avoidance behavior. *Psychology in the Schools*, **10**, 259–62.

Costin, F. (1976). *Abnormal Psychology*. Homewood, Ill.: Learning Systems Company.

Cotler, S. B. (1970). Sex differences and generalization of anxiety reduction with automated desensitization and minimal therapist interaction. *Behaviour Research & Therapy*, **8**, 273–85.

Cowen, E. L. (1973). Social and community interventions. *Annual Review of Psychology*, **24**, 423–472.

Cox, T. (1978). Children's adjustment of school over six years. *Journal of Child Psychology & Psychiatry*, **19**, 363–71.

Cradock, C., Cotler, S., & Jason, L. A. (1978). Primary prevention: immunization of children for speech anxiety. *Cognitive Therapy & Research*, **2**, 389–96.

Croake, J. W. (1969). Fears of children. *Human Development*, **12**, 239–47.

Croake, J. W., & Knox, F. H. (1973). The changing nature of children's fears. *Child Study Journal*, **3**, 91–105.

Croghan, L., & Musante, G. J. (1975). The elimination of a boy's high-building phobia by *in vivo* desensitization and game playing. *Journal of Behavior Therapy & Experimental Psychiatry*, **6**, 87–8.

Cummings, J. D. (1944). The incidence of emotional symptoms in school children. *British Journal of Educational Psychology*, **14**, 151–61.

Cummings, J. D. (1946). A follow-up study of emotional symptoms in school children. *British Journal of Educational Psychology*, **16**, 163–77.

Danquah, S. J. (1974). The treatment of monosymptomatic phobia by systematic desensitization. *Psychopathologie Africaine*, **10**, 115–20.

Davidson, S. (1960). School phobia as a manifestation of family disturbance: its structure and treatment. *Journal of Child Psychology & Psychiatry*, **1**, 270–87.

Davison, G. C., & Neale, J. M. (1974). *Abnormal Psychology: An Experimental Clinical Approach*. New York: John Wiley.

Deese, J., & Hulse, S. H. (1967). *The Psychology of Learning*. New York: McGraw-Hill.

Deffenbacher, J. L., & Kemper, C. C. (1974a). Counseling test-anxious sixth graders. *Elementary School Guidance & Counseling*, **7**, 22–9.

Deffenbacher, J. L., & Kemper, C. C. (1974b). Systematic desensitization of test anxiety in junior high school students. *School Counselor*, **22**, 216–22.

Delprato, D. J. (1980). Hereditary determinants of fears and phobias: a critical review. *Behavior Therapy*, **11**, 79–103.

Demone, H. W. & Harshbarger, D. (1974). *A Handbook of Human-Service Organizations*. New York: Behavioral Publications.

Derevensky, J. L. (1979). Children's fears: a developmental comparison of normal and exceptional children. *Journal of Genetic Psychology*, **135**, 11–21.

de Silva, P., & Rachman, S. (1981). Is exposure a necessary condition for fear-reduction? *Behaviour Research & Therapy*, **19**, 227–32.

de Silva, P., Rachman, S., & Seligman, M. E. P. (1977). Prepared phobias and obsessions: therapeutic outcome. *Behaviour Research & Therapy*, **15**, 65–77.

de Silva, P., & Rachman, S. (1983). Exposure and fear-reduction. *Behaviour Research & Therapy*, **21**, 151–2.

Dixon, J. J., Monchaux, C., & Sandler, J. (1957). Patterns of anxiety: The phobias. *British Journal of Medical Psychology*, **30**, 34–40.

Dykman, R. A., Mack, R. L., & Ackerman, P. T. (1965). The evaluation of autonomic and motor components of the unavoidance conditioned response in the dog. *Psychophysiology*, **1**, 209–230.

Eccles, J. C. (1953). *The Neurophysiological Basis of Mind*. Oxford: Clarendon.

Eifert, G. H. (1984). Cognitive behaviour therapy: a critical evaluation of its theoretical–empirical bases and therapeutic efficacy. *Australian Psychologist*, **19**, 179–91.

Eisenberg, L. (1958). School phobia: diagnosis, genesis and clinical management. *Pediatric Clinics of North America*, **5**, 645–66.

Eisenberg, L. (1959). The pediatric management of school phobia. *Journal of Pediatrics*, **55**, 758–66.

Ellis, A. (1970). *The Essence of Rational Psychotherapy: A Comprehensive Approach to Treatment*. New York: Institute for Rational Living.

Ellis, A. (1979). A note on the treatment of agoraphobics with cognitive modification versus prolonged exposure *in vivo*. *Behaviour Research & Therapy*, **17**, 162–4.

Ellis, A., & Harper, R. A. (1975). *A New Guide to Rational Living*. Englewood Cliffs, N.J.: Prentice-Hall.

Eme, R., & Schmidt, D. (1978). The stability of children's fears. *Child Development*, **49**, 1277–9.

Emmelkamp, P. M. G. (1982). Anxiety and fear. In A. S. Bellack, M. Hersen, & A. E. Kazdin (Eds.), *International Handbook of Behavior Modification and Therapy* (pp. 349–95). New York: Plenum Press.

English, H. B. (1929). Three cases of the 'conditioned fear response'. *Journal of Abnormal and Social Psychology*, **24**, 221–5.

Epstein, S. (1967). Toward a unified theory of anxiety. In B. A. Maher (Ed.), *Progress in Experimental Research*, Vol. 4 (pp. 1–89). New York: Academic Press.

Estes, H. R., Haylett, C. H., & Johnson, A. M. (1956). Separation anxiety. *American Journal of Orthopsychiatry*, **10**, 682–95.

Evans, I. M. (1982). Review of *Multimethod clinical assessment* by W. R. Nay. *Behavioral Assessment*, **4**, 121–4.

Eysenck, H. J. (1957). *The Dynamics of Anxiety and Hysteria*. London: Routledge & Kegan Paul.

Eysenck, H. J. (1965). *Fact and Fiction in Psychology*. Harmondsworth: Penguin.

Eysenck, H. J. (1967a). Single-trial conditioning, neurosis and the Napalkov phenomenon. *Behaviour Research & Therapy*, **5**, 63–5.

Eysenck, H. J. (1967b). *The Biological Basis of Personality*. Springfield, Ill.: Charles C. Thomas.

Eysenck, H. J. (1968). A theory of the incubation of anxiety/fear responses. *Behaviour Research & Therapy*, **6**, 309–21.

Eysenck, H. J. (1971) (Ed.). *Readings in Extraversion–Introversion 3: Bearings on Basic Psychological Processes*. London: Staples Press.

Eysenck, H. J. (1976). The learning theory model of neurosis—a new approach. *Behaviour Research & Therapy*, **14**, 251–67.

Eysenck, H. J. (1978). Expectations as causal elements in behavioural change. *Advances in Behaviour Research & Therapy*, **1**, 171–5.

Eysenck, H. J. (1979). The conditioning model of neurosis. *Behavioural & Brain Sciences*, **2**, 155–99.

Eysenck, H. J., & Rachman, S. (1965). *The Causes and Cures of Neurosis*. San Diego: Knapp.

Farmer, R. G. (1971, August). The role of disinhibition in the etiology and maintenance of phobias: implications for behaviour therapy. Paper presented at the Annual Conference of the Australian Psychological Society, Melbourne, Victoria.

Faust, J., & Melamed, B. G. (1984). Influence of arousal, previous experience, and age on surgery preparation of same day of surgery and in-hospital pediatric patients. *Journal of Consulting & Clinical Psychology*, **52**, 359–65.

Ferguson, B. F. (1979). Preparing young children for hospitalization: a comparison of two methods. *Pediatrics*, **64**, 656–64.

Finch, A. J., & Rogers, T. (1984). Self-report instruments. In T. H. Ollendick & M. Hersen (Eds.), *Child Behavioral Assessment: Principles and Procedures* (pp. 106–23). New York: Pergamon Press.

Foa, E. B., & Emmelkamp, P. M. G. (Eds.) (1983). *Failures in behavior therapy*. New York: Wiley.

Forehand, R., & Atkeson, B. M. (1977). Generality of treatment effects with parents as therapists: a review of assessment and implementation procedures. *Behavior Therapy*, **8**, 575–93.

Forehand, R. L., & McMahon, R. J. (1981). *Helping the Non compliant Child: A Clinician's Guide to Parent Training*. New York: Guilford Press.

Franks, C. M. (1982). Behavior therapy: an overview. *Annual Review of Behavior Therapy: Theory and Practice*, **8**, 1–38.

Freeling, N. W., & Shemberg, K. M. (1970). The alleviation of test anxiety by systematic desensitization. *Behaviour Research & Therapy*, **8**, 293–9.

Freeman, L. (1979). School refusal. In M. Griffin & A. Hudson (Eds.), *Children's Problems: A Guide for Parents* (pp. 151–68). Melbourne: Circus Books.

Freeman, B. J., Roy, R. R., & Hemmick, S. (1976). Extinction of a phobia of physical examination in a seven-year-old mentally retarded boy—a case study. *Behaviour Research & Therapy*, **14**, 63–4.

Freud, S. (1959). Turnings in the ways of psychoanalytic therapy. In *Collected Papers*, Vol. 3. New York: Basic Books (Original work published 1919).

Freud, S. (1963). The analysis of a phobia in a five-year-old boy. *Standard Edition of the Complete Psychological Works of Sigmund Freud*, Vol. 10. London: Hogarth Press (Original work published in 1909).

Gantt, W. H. (1944). Experimental basis for neurotic behavior. *Psychosomatic Medicine Monographs 3*, Nos. 3 and 4.

Gardner, J. M. (1976). Training parents as behavior modifiers. In S. Yen & R. McIntire (Eds.). *Teaching behavior modification* (pp. 17–53). Kalamazoo, MI: Behaviordelia.

Garvey, W. P., & Hegrenes, J. R. (1966). Desensitization techniques in the treatment of school phobia. *American Journal of Orthopsychiatry*, **36**, 147–52.

Gelfand, D. M. (1978). Social withdrawal and negative emotional states: behavior therapy. In B. B. Wolman, J. Egan, & A. O. Ross (Eds.), *Handbook of Treatment of Mental Disorders in Childhood and Adolescence* (pp. 330–53). Englewood Cliffs, NJ: Prentice-Hall.

Gelfand, D. M., & Hartman, D. P. (1977). The prevention of childhood behavior disorders. In B. Lahey & A. E. Kazdin (Eds.), *Advances in Clinical Child Phychology*, Vol. 1. New York: Plenum Press.

Gelfand, D. M., & Hartmann, D. P. (1984). *Child Behavior Analysis and Therapy* (2nd ed.), New York: Pergamon Press.

Giebenhain, J. E., & O'Dell, S. L. (1984). Evaluation of a parent-training manual for reducing children's fear of the dark. *Journal of Applied Behavior Analysis*, **17**, 121–125.

Gittelman-Klein, R., & Klein, D. F. (1971). Controlled imipramine treatment of school phobia. *Archives of General Psychiatry*, **25**, 204–7.

Gittelman-Klein, R., & Klein, D. F. (1980). Separation anxiety in school refusal and its treatment with drugs. In L. Hersov & I. Berg (Eds.), *Out of School* (pp. 321–41). Chichester: Wiley.

Glennon, B., & Weisz, J. R. (1978). An observational approach to the assessment of anxiety in young children. *Journal of Consulting & Clinical Psychology*, **46**, 1246–57.

Goldfried, M. R. (1971). Systematic desensitization as training in self-control. *Journal of Consulting and Clinical Psychology*, **37**, 228–34.

Goldfried, M. R., Decenteceo, E. T., & Weinberg, L. (1974). Systematic rational restructuring as a self-control technique. *Behavior Therapy*, **5**, 247–54.

Gordon, D. A., & Young, R. D. (1976). School phobia: a discussion of aetiology, treatment and evaluation. *Psychological Reports*, **39**, 783–804.

Graziano, A. M. (1975). Reduction of children's fears. In A. M. Graziano (Ed.), *Behavior Therapy with Children* vol. 2. (pp. 283–90). Chicago: Aldine.

Graziano, A. M., & DeGiovanni, I. S. (1979). The clinical significance of childhood phobias: a note on the proportion of child-clinical referrals for the treatment of children's fears. *Behaviour Research & Therapy*, **17**, 161–2.

Graziano, A. M., DeGiovanni, I. S., & Garcia, K. A. (1979). Behavioral treatment of children's fears: a review. *Psychological Bulletin*, **86**, 804–30.

Graziano, A. M., & Katz, J. N. (1982). Training paraprofessionals. In A. S. Bellack, M. Hersen, & A. E. Kazdin (Eds.), *International Handbook of Behavior Modification and Therapy* (pp. 207–29). New York: Plenum Press.

Graziano, A. M., & Mooney, K. C. (1980). Family self-control instruction for children's nighttime fear reduction. *Journal of Consulting & Clinical Psychology*, **48**, 206–13.

Graziano, A. M., & Mooney, K. C. (1982). Behavioral treatment of 'nightfears' in children: maintenance of improvement at $2\frac{1}{2}$ to 3-year follow-up. *Journal of Consulting & Clinical Psychology*, **50**, 598–599.

Graziano, A. M., Mooney, K. C., Huber, C., & Ignasiak, D. (1979). Self-control instructions for children's fear reduction. *Journal of Behavior Therapy & Experimental Psychiatry*, **10**, 221–7.

Green, R. V., Meilman, P., Routh, D. K., & McIver, F. T. (1977). Preparing the preschool child for a visit to the dentist. *Journal of Dentistry*, **5**, 231–6.

Griffin, M. W., & Hudson, A. M. (1980). Parent training. In Hudson, A. M. & Griffin, M. W. (Eds.), *Behaviour analysis and the problems of childhood* (pp. 201–20). Bundoora, Victoria: PIT Publishing.

Gross, A. M. (1984). Behavioral interviewing. In T. H. Ollendick & M. Hersen (Eds.), *Child Behavioral Assessment: Principles and Procedures* (pp. 61–79). New York: Pergamon Press.

Hagman, E. R. (1932). A study of fears of children of pre-school age. *Journal of Experimental Education*, **1**, 110–30.

Hall, G. S. (1954). *A Primer of Freudian Psychology*. New York: Mentor.

Hall, G. S. (1897). A study of fears. *American Journal of Psychology*, **8**, 147–249.

Hall, G. S., & Allin, A. (1897). The psychology of tickling, laughing, and the comic. *American Journal of Psychology*, **9**, 1–41.

Hallam, R. S., & Rachman, S. (1976). Current status of aversion therapy. In M. Hersen, R. M. Eisler & P. M. Miller (Eds.), *Progress in Behavior Modification*, Vol. 2. New York: Academic Press.

Hampe, E., Noble, H., Miller, L. C., & Barrett, C. L. (1973). Phobic children one and two years posttreatment. *Journal of Abnormal Psychology*, **82**, 446–53.

Harris, S. L. (1979). DSM-III—its implications for children. *Child Behavior Therapy*, **1**, 37–46.

Harris, S. L., & Ferrari, M. (1983). Developmental factors in child behavior therapy. *Behavior Therapy*, **14**, 54–72.

Hatzenbuehler, L. C., & Schroeder, H. E. (1978). Desensitization procedures in the treatment of childhood disorders. *Psychological Bulletin*, **85**, 831–44.

Haynes, S. N. (1978). *Principles of Behavioral Assessment*. New York: Gardner Press.

Haynes, S. N., & Horn, W. F. (1982). Reactivity in behavioral observation: a review. *Behavioral Assessment*, **4**, 369–85.

Haynes, S. N., & Wilson, C. C. (1979). *Behavioral Assessment*. San Francisco: Jossey Bass.

Heller, J. A. (1967). *The Hospitalized Child and his Family*. Baltimore: John Hopkins Press.

Herbert, M. (1975). *Problems of Childhood: A Complete Guide for All Concerned*. London: Pan Books.

Hersen, M. (1970). Behavior modification approach to a school-phobia case. *Journal of Clinical Psychology*, **26**, 128–32.

Hersen, M., & Barlow, D. H. (1976). *Single-Case Experimental Designs: Strategies for Studying Behavior Change*. New York: Pergamon Press.

Hersen, M., & Bellack, A. S. (Eds.) (1976). *Behavioral Assessment: A Practical Handbook*. New York: Pergamon Press.

Hersov, L. A. (1960a). Persistent non-attendance at school. *Journal of Child Psychology & Psychiatry*, 1, 130–6.

Hersov, L. A. (1960b). Refusal to go to school. *Journal of Child Psychology & Psychiatry*, 1, 137–45.

Hersov, L. (1977). School refusal. In M. Rutter & L. Hersov (Eds.), *Child Psychiatry. Modern Approaches* (pp. 455–86). Oxford: Blackwell.

Hersov, L., & Berg, I. (Eds.) (1980). *Out of School. Modern Perspectives in Truancy and School Refusal*. Chichester: John Wiley.

Higa, W. R., Tharp, R. G., & Calkins, R. P. (1978). Developmental verbal control of behavior: implications for self-instructional training. *Journal of Experimental Child-Psychology*, 26, 489–97.

Hodgson, R., & Rachman, S. (1974). II. Desynchrony in measures of fear. *Behaviour Research & Therapy*, 12, 319–26.

Holmes, F. B. (1936). An experimental investigation of a method of overcoming children's fears. *Child Development*, 7, 6–30.

Horne, D. J. de L., & King, N. J. (1986). Preparation for surgery. In N. J. King & A. G. Remenyi (Eds.), *Health Care: A Behavioural Approach* (pp. 167–73). Sydney: Grune & Stratton.

Horner, R. D., & Keilitz, I. (1975). Training mentally retarded adolescents to brush their teeth. *Journal of Applied Behavior Analysis*, 8, 301–9.

Horner, T. M. (1980). Two methods of studying stranger reactivity in infants: a review. *Journal of Child Psychology & Psychiatry*, 21, 203–19.

Hugdahl, K. (1981). The Three-Systems-Model of fear and emotion—a critical examination. *Behaviour Research & Therapy*, 19, 75–85.

Hughes, M., Pinkerton, G., & Plewis, I. (1979). Children's difficulties on starting infant school. *Journal of Child Psychology & Psychiatry*, 20, 187–96.

Impallaria, C. (1955). The contribution of social group work: the hospitalized child. *American Journal of Orthopsychiatry*, 25, 293–318.

Jackson, H. J., & King, N. J. (1981). The emotive imagery treatment of a child's trauma-induced phobia. *Journal of Behavior Therapy & Experimental Psychiatry*, 12, 325–8.

Jackson, H. J., & King, N. J. (1982). The therapeutic management of an autistic child's phobia using laughter as the anxiety inhibitor. *Behavioural Psychotherapy*, 10, 364–9.

Janis, I. L. (1951). *Air War and Emotional Stress*. New York: McGraw-Hill.

Janis, I. L. (1958). *Psychological Stress*. New York: John Wiley.

Jason, L. A. (1980). Prevention in the schools. Behavioral approaches. In R. H. Price, R. F. Ketterer, B. C. Bader, & J. Monahan (Eds.), *Prevention in Mental Health: Research, Policy and Practice* (pp. 109–34). Beverley Hills, CA: Sage Publications.

Jersild, A. T., & Holmes, F. B. (1935a). *Children's fears*. New York: Teachers College, Columbia University.

Jersild, A. T., & Holmes, F. B. (1935b). Methods of overcoming children's fears. *Journal of Psychology*, 1, 75–104.

Jersild, A. T., Markey, F. U., & Jersild, C. L. (1933). Children's fears, dreams, wishes, daydreams, likes, dislikes, pleasant and unpleasant memories. *Child Development Monographs*, No. 12.

Johnson, A. M., Falstein, E. I., Szurek, S. A., & Svendsen, M. (1941). School phobia. *American Journal of Orthopsychiatry*, 11, 702–11.

Johnson, J. E., Leventhal, H., & Dabbs, J. M. (1971). Contribution of emotional and instrumental response processes in adaptation to surgery. *Journal of Personality & Social Psychology*, 20, 55–64.

Johnson, S. B., & Melamed, B. G. (1979). The assessment and treatment of children's fear. In B. B. Lahey, & A. E. Kazdin (Eds.), *Advances in Clinical Child Psychology*, Vol. 2. New York: Plenum Press.

Johnson, T., Tyler, V., Thompson, R., & Jones, E. (1971). Systematic desensitization and assertive training in the treatment of speech anxiety in middle-school students. *Psychology in the Schools*, 8, 263–7.

Jones, H. E. (1931). The conditioning of overt emotional responses. *Journal of Educational Psychology*, **22**, 127–30.

Jones, M. C. (1924a). A laboratory study of fear: the case of Peter. *Journal of Genetic Psychology*, **31**, 308–15.

Jones, M. C. (1924b). Elimination of children's fears. *Journal of Experimental Psychology*, **7**, 382–90.

Jones, M. C. (1974). Albert, Peter, and John B. Watson. *American Psychologist*, **29**, 581–3.

Jones, M. C. (1975). A 1924 pioneer looks at behavior therapy. *Journal of Behavior Therapy & Experimental Psychiatry*, **6**, 181–7.

Kanfer, F. H. (1980). Self-management methods. In F. H. Kanfer & A. P. Goldstein (Eds.), *Helping People Change* (2nd ed.) (pp. 334–89). New York: Pergamon Press.

Kanfer, F. H., & Karoly, P. (1972). Self control: a behavioristic excursion into the lion's den. *Behavior Therapy*, **3**, 398–416.

Kanfer, F. H., Karoly, P., & Newman, A. (1975). Reduction of children's fear of the dark by competence-related and situational threat-related verbal cues. *Journal of Consulting & Clinical Psychology*, **43**, 251–8.

Kanfer, F. H., & Phillips, J. S. (1970). *Learning Foundations of Behavior Therapy*. New York: Wiley.

Kanfer, R., Eyberg, S. M., & Krahn, G. L. (1983). Interviewing strategies in child assessment. In C. E. Walker & M. C. Roberts (Eds.), *Handbook of Clinical Child Psychology* (pp. 95–108). New York: Wiley.

Katz, E. R., Kellerman, J., & Siegel, S. E. (1980). Behavioral distress in children with cancer undergoing medical procedures: developmental considerations. *Journal of Consulting & Clinical Psychology*, **48**, 356–65.

Kauffman, J. M. (1985). *Characteristic of Children's Behavior Disorders* (3rd ed.). Columbus: Merrill.

Kazdin, A. E. (1974a). Covert modeling, model similarity, and reduction of avoidance behavior. *Behavior Therapy*, **5**, 325–40.

Kazdin, A. E. (1974b). The effect of model identity and fear-relevant similarity on covert modeling. *Behavior Therapy*, **5**, 624–35.

Kazdin, A. E. (1976). Effects of covert modeling, multiple models, and model reinforcement on assertive behavior. *Behavior Therapy*, **7**, 211–22.

Kazdin, A. E. (1977). Assessing the clinical or applied importance of behavior change through social validation. *Behavior Modification*, **1**, 427–52.

Kazdin, A. E. (1980a). Acceptability of time out from reinforcement procedures for disruptive child behavior. *Behavior Therapy*, **11**, 329–44.

Kazdin, A. E. (1980b). *Behavior Modification in Applied Settings* (revised ed.). Homewood, Ill.: Dorsey Press.

Kazdin, A. E. (1983). Psychiatric diagnosis, dimensions of dysfunction and child behavior therapy. *Behavior Therapy*, **14**, 73–99.

Keefe, F. J., Kopel, S. A., & Gordon, S. B. (1978). *A Practical Guide to Behavioral Assessment*. New York: Springer.

Kelley, C. K. (1976). Play desensitization of fear of darkness in preschool children. *Behaviour Research & Therapy*, **14**, 79–81.

Kennedy, W. A. (1965). School phobia: rapid treatment of fifty cases. *Journal of Abnormal Psychology*, **70**, 285–9.

Kennedy, W. A. (1971). A behavioristic, community-oriented approach to school phobia and other disorders. In H. C. Rickard (Ed.), *Behavioral Intervention in Human Problems* (pp. 37–60). New York: Pergamon Press.

Kennedy, W. A. (1983). Obsessive–compulsive and phobic reactions. In T. O. Ollendick & M. Hersen (Eds.), *Handbook of Child Psychopathology* (pp. 277–91). New York: Plenum Press.

Kessler, M., & Albee, G. W. (1975). Primary prevention. *Annual Review of Psychology*, **26**, 557–91.

Kimble, G. (1961). *Hilgard and Marquis' Conditioning and Learning* (2nd ed.). New York: Appleton Century-Crofts.

King, N. J. (1980). The therapeutic utility of abbreviated progressive relaxation: a critical review with implications for clinical practice. In M. Hersen, R. E. Eisler & P. M. Miller (Eds.), *Progress in Behavior Modification*, Vol. 10. New York: Academic Press.

King, N. J., Hamilton, D. I., & Murphy, G. C. (1983). The prevention of children's maladaptive fears. *Child & Family Behavior Therapy*, **5**, 43–57.

Kissel, S. (1972). Systematic desensitization therapy with children: a case study and some suggested modifications. *Professional Psychology*, **3**, 164–8.

Klein, D. F. (1964). Delineation of two-drug-responsive anxiety syndromes. *Psychopharmacologica*, **5**, 397–408.

Kleinknecht, R. A., Klepac, R. K., & Alexander, L. D. (1973). Origins and characteristics of fear of dentistry. *Journal of the American Dental Association*, **86**, 842–8.

Klesges, R. C., Malott, J. M., & Ugland, M. (1984). The effects of graded exposure and parental modeling on the dental phobias of a four-year-old girl and her mother. *Journal of Behavior Therapy & Experimental Psychiatry*, **15**, 161–4.

Klingman, A., Melamed, B. G., Cuthbert, M. I., & Hermecz, D. A. (1984). Effects of participant modeling on information acquisition and skill utilization. *Journal of Consulting & Clinical Psychology*, **52**, 414–22.

Klorman, R., Hilpert, P. L., Michael, R., LaGana, C., & Sveen, O. B. (1980). Effects of coping and mastery modeling on experiences and inexperienced pedodontic patients' disruptiveness. *Behavior Therapy*, **11**, 156–68.

Koeppen, A. S. (1974). Relaxation training for children. *Elementary School Guidance & Counseling*, **9**, 14–21.

Kohlenberg, R., Greenberg, D., Reymore, L., & Hass, G. (1972). Behavior modification and the management of mentally retarded dental patients. *Journal of Denistry for Children*, **39**(1), 61–7.

Kondas, O. (1967). Reduction of examination anxiety and 'stage-fright' by group desensitization and relaxation. *Behaviour Research & Therapy*, **5**, 275–81.

Kornhaber, R. C., & Schroeder, H. E. (1975). Importance of model similarity on extinction of avoidance behavior in children. *Journal of Consulting & Clinical Psychology*, **43**, 601–7.

Krapfl, J. E., & Nawas, M. M. (1970). Differential ordering of stimulus presentation in systematic desensitization. *Journal of Abnormal Psychology*, **75**, 333–7.

Kurtz, K. H., & Walters, G. C. (1962). The effects of prior fear experiences on an approach–avoidance conflict. *Journal of Comparative & Physiological Psychology*, **55**, 1075–8.

Lacey, J. I., Bateman, D. E., & Van Lehn, R. (1953). Autonomic response specificity: an experimental study. *Psychosomatic Medicine*, **15**, 8–21.

Lacey, J. I., & Lacey, B. C. (1958). Verification and extension of the principle of autonomic-response stereotypy. *American Journal of Psychology*, **71**, 50–73.

Lader, M., & Marks, I. (1971). *Clinical Anxiety*. New York: Grune & Stratton.

Lader, M., & Mathews, A. M. (1968). A physiological model of phobic anxiety and desensitization. *Behaviour Research & Therapy*, **6**, 411–21.

Lader, M. H., & Wing, L. (1966). *Physiological Measures, Sedative Drugs, and Morbid Anxiety*. Maudsley Monograph. London: Oxford University Press.

Lang, P. J., & Lazovik, A. D. (1963). Experimental desensitization of a phobia. *Journal of Abnormal & Social Psychology*, **66**, 519–25.

Lapouse, R., & Monk, N. (1959). Fears and worries in a representative sample of children. *American Journal of Orthopsychiatry*, **29**, 803–18.

Last, C. G., Francis, G., Hersen, M., Kazdin, A. E., & Strauss, C. C. (1987). Separation anxiety and school phobia: a comparison using DSM-III criteria. *American Journal of Psychiatry*, **144**, 653–7.

Lautch, H. (1971). Dental phobia. *British Journal of Psychiatry*, **119**, 151–8.

Laxer, R. M., Quarter, J., Kooman, A., & Walker, K. (1969). Systematic desensitization and relaxation of high-test-anxious secondary school students. *Journal of Counseling Psychology*, **16**, 446–51.

Lazarus, A. A. (1960). The elimination of children's phobias by deconditioning. In H. J. Eysenck (Ed.), *Behaviour Therapy and the Neuroses* (pp. 114–22). Oxford: Pergamon.

Lazarus, A. A. (1971). *Behavior Therapy and Beyond*. New York: McGraw-Hill.

Lazarus, A. A., & Abramovitz, A. (1962). The use of emotive imagery in the treatment of children's phobias. *Journal of Mental Science*, **108**, 191–5.

Lazarus, A. A., Davison, G. C., & Polefka, D. A. (1965). Classical and operant factors in the treatment of a school phobia. *Journal of Abnormal Psychology*, **70**, 225–9.

Ledwidge, B. (1978). Cognitive behavior modification: a step in the wrong direction.? *Psychological Bulletin*, **85**, 353–75.

Leitenberg, H., & Callahan, E. J. (1973). Reinforced practice and reduction of different kinds of fears in adults and children. *Behaviour Research & Therapy*, **11**, 19–30.

Leton, D. A. (1962). Assessment of school phobia. *Mental Hygiene*, **46**, 256–64.

Levis, D. J. (1974). Implosive therapy: a critical analysis of Morganstern's review. *Psychological Bulletin*, **81**, 155–8.

Levy, D. (1951). Observations of attitudes and behaviors in the child health center: sample studies of maternal feelings, dependency, resistant behavior, and inoculation fears. *American Journal of Public Health*, **41**, 182–90.

Levy, E. (1959). Children's behavior under stress and its relation to training by parents to respond to stress functions. *Child Development*, **30**, 307–24.

Lewis, S. (1974). A comparison of behavior therapy techniques in the reduction of fearful avoidance behavior. *Behavior Therapy*, **5**, 648–55.

Lichtenstein, P. E. (1950). Studies of anxiety: I. The production of a feeding inhibition in dogs. *Journal of Comparative & Physiological Psychology*, **43**, 16–29.

Lick, J. R., & Unger, T. E. (1977). The external validity of behavioral fear assessment. *Behavior Modification*, **1**, 283–306.

Liddell, H. S. (1944). Conditioned reflex method and experimental neurosis. In J. McV. Hunt (Ed.), *Personality and the Behavior Disorders*, Vol. 1. New York: Ronald Press.

Locke, E. A. (1979). Behavior modification is not cognitive—and other myths: a reply to Ledwidge. *Cognitive Therapy & Research*, **3**, 119–25.

Lomont, J. F. (1965). Reciprocal inhibition or extinction? *Behaviour Research & Therapy*, **3**, 209–19.

Lovibond, S. H. (1966). The current status of behavior therapy. *Canadian Psychologist*, **7**, 93–101.

Lubow, R. E. (1965). Latent inhibition: effects of frequency of nonreinforced preexposure of the CS. *Journal of Comparative & Physiological Psychology*, **60**, 454–7.

Luiselli, J. K. (1977). Case report: an attendant-administered contingency management program for the treatment of a toileting phobia. *Journal of Mental Deficiency Research*, **21**, 283–8.

Luiselli, J. K. (1978). Treatment of an autistic child's fear of riding a school bus through exposure and reinforcement. *Journal of Behavior Therapy & Experimental Psychiatry*, **9**, 169–72.

Luria, A. R. (1961). *The Role of Speech in the Regulation of Normal and Abnormal Behavior.* New York: Liveright.

MacCoby, E. E., & Jacklin, C. N. (1974). *The Psychology of Sex Differences*. Stanford: Stanford University Press.

MacDonald, A. (1975). Multiple impact behavior therapy in a child's dog phobia. *Journal* formation of conditioned avoidance responses. *Journal of Experimental Psychology*, **36**, 1–12.

MacDonald, A. (1975). Multiple impact behavior therapy in a child's dog phobia. *Journal of Behavior Therapy & Experimental Psychiatry*, **6**, 317–22.

MacFarlane, J. W., Allen, L., & Honzik, M. P. (1954). *A Developmental Study of the Behavior Problems of Normal Children Between Twenty-One Months and Fourteen Years.* Berkeley: University of California Press.

Machen, J. B., & Johnson, R. (1974). Desensitization, model learning, and the dental behavior of children. *Journal of Dental Research,* 53, 83–7.

Mackintosh, N. J. (1974). *The Psychology of Animal Learning.* London: Academic Press.

Mahoney, M. J., & Kazdin, A. E. (1979). Cognitive behavior modification: Misconceptions and premature evacuation. *Psychological Bulletin,* 86, 1044–9.

Mahoney, M. J., & Mahoney, K. (1975). Treatment of obesity: a clinical exploration. In B. J. Williams, S. Martin, & J. P. Foregt (Eds.), *Obesity: Behavioral Approaches to Dietary Management* (pp. 30–9). New York: Brunner/Mazel.

Marholin, D. (Ed.) (1978), *Child Behavior Therapy.* New York: Gardner Press.

Marine, E. (1968–69). School refusal—who should intervene? (diagnostic and treatment categories). *Journal of School Psychology,* 7, 63–70.

Marks, I. M. (1969). *Fears and Phobias.* New York: Academic Press.

Marks, I. M. (1975). Behavioral treatments of phobic and obsessive–compulsive disorders: a critical appraisal. In M. Hersen, R. M. Eisler, & P. M. Miller (Eds.), *Progress in Behavior Modification,* Vol. 1. New York: Academic Press.

Marks, I. M. (1981). *Cure and Care of Neuroses.* New York: John Wiley.

Marks, I. M., & Gelder, M. G. (1966). Different ages of onset in varieties of phobia. *American Journal of Psychiatry,* 123, 218–21.

Marks, I. M., & Gelder, M. G. (1967). Transvestism and festishism: clinical and psychological changes during faradic aversion. *British Journal of Psychiatry,* 117, 173–85.

Marmor, J. (1958). The psychodynamics of realistic worry. *Psychoanalysis & Social Science,* 5, 155–63.

Marshall, W. L., Gauthier, J., Christie, M. M., Currie, D. W., & Gordon, A. (1977). Flooding therapy: effectiveness, stimulus characteristics, and the value of brief *in vivo* exposure. *Behaviour Research & Therapy,* 15, 79–87.

Marshall, W. L., Gauthier, J., & Gordon, A. (1979). The current status of flooding therapy. In M. Hersen, R. E. Eisler & P. M. Miller (Eds.), *Progress in Behavior Modification,* Vol. 7. New York: Academic Press.

Martin, G., & Pear, J. (1983). *Behavior Modification: What It Is and How To Do It* (2nd ed.). Englewood Cliffs, NJ: Prentice-Hall.

Martin, R. (1975). *Legal Challenges to Behavior Modification: Trends in Schools, Corrections and Mental Health.* Champaign, Ill.: Research Press.

Mash, E. J., & Terdal, L. G. (1981). Behavioral assessment of childhood disturbance. In E. J. Mash, & L. G. Terdal (Eds.), *Behavioral Assessment of Childhood Disorders* (pp. 3–76). New York: Guilford Press.

Maserman, J. H. (1943). *Behavior and Neurosis.* Chicago: University of Chicago Press.

Matson, J. L. (1981). Assessment and treatment of clinical fears in mentally retarded children. *Journal of Applied Behavior Analysis,* 14, 287–94.

Matson, J. L. (1983). Exploration of phobic behavior in a small child. *Journal of Behavior Therapy & Experimental Psychiatry,* 14, 257–9.

Maurer, A. (1965). What children fear. *Journal of Genetic Psychology,* 106, 265–77.

McAllister, D. E. & McAllister, W. R. (1967). Incubation of fear: an examination of the concept. *Journal of Experimental Research in Personality,* 2, 180–90.

McDonald, J. E., & Sheperd, G. (1976). School phobia: An overview. *Journal of School Psychology,* 14, 291–306.

McGlynn, F. D. (1971). Individual versus standardized hierarchies in the systematic desensitization of snake-avoidance. *Behavior Research & Therapy,* 9, 1–5.

McGlynn, F. D., & Williams, C. W. (1970). Systematic desensitization of snake-avoidance under three conditions of suggestion. *Journal of Behavior Therapy & Experimental Psychiatry,* 1, 97–101.

McMurray, N. E. (1979). Childhood fears and phobias. In M. Griffin & A. Hudson, (Eds.), *Children's Problems: A Guide for the Parent* (pp. 169–79). Melbourne, Victoria: Circus Books.

Meichenbaum, D. H. (1971). Examination of model characteristics in reducing avoidance behavior. *Journal of Personality & Social Psychology,* **17,** 298–307.

Meichenbaum, D. H. (1976). A cognitive-behavior modification approach to assessment. In M. Hersen & A. S. Bellack (Eds.), *Behavioral Assessment: A Practical Handbook* (pp. 143–71). New York: Pergamon Press.

Meichenbaum, D. H. (1977). *Cognitive-behavior Modification.* New York: Plenum Press.

Meichenbaum, D. H., & Genest, M. (1980). Cognitive behavior modification: an integration of cognitive and behavioral methods. In F. H. Kanfer & A. P. Goldstein (Eds.), *Helping People Change: A Textbook of Methods* (2nd ed., pp. 390–442). New York: Pergamon Press.

Meichenbaum, D. H., & Goodman, J. (1971). Training impulsive children to talk to themselves: a means of developing self-control. *Journal of Abnormal Psychology,* **77,** 115–26.

Melamed, B. G. (1979). Behavioral approaches to fear in dental settings. In M. Hersen, R. E. Eisler, & P. Miller (Eds.), *Progress in Behavior Modification,* Vol. 7. New York: Academic Press.

Melamed, B. (1982). Reduction of medical fears: an information processing analysis. In J. C. Boulougouris (Ed.), *Learning Theory Approaches to Psychiatry* (pp. 205–18). Chicester: John Wiley.

Melamed, B., Hawes, R. R., Heiby, E., & Glick, J. (1975). Use of filmed modeling to reduce uncooperative behavior of children during dental treatment. *Journal of Dental Research,* **54,** 797–801.

Melamed, B. G., Meyer, R., Gee, C., & Soule, L. (1976). The influence of time and type of preparation on children's adjustment to hospitalization. *Journal of Pediatric Psychology,* **1,** 31–7.

Melamed, B. G., Robbins, R. L., & Graves, S. (1982). Preparation for surgery and medical procedures. In D. C. Russo & J. W. Varni (Eds.), *Behavioral Pediatrics: Research and Practice* (pp. 225–67). New York: Plenum.

Melamed, B. G., & Siegel, L. J. (1975). Reduction of anxiety in children facing hospitalization and surgery by use of filmed modeling. *Journal of Consulting & Clinical Psychology,* **43,** 511–21.

Melamed, B. G., & Siegel, L. J. (1980). *Behavioral Medicine: Practical Applications in Health Care.* New York: Springer.

Melamed, B. G., Weinstein, D., Hawes, R., & Katin-Borland, M. (1975). Reduction of fear-related dental management problems with use of film modeling. *Journal of the American Dental Association,* **90,** 822–6.

Melamed, B. G., Yurcheson, R., Fleece, E. L., Hutcherson, S., & Hawes, R. (1978). Effects of film modeling on the reduction of anxiety-related behaviors in individuals varying in levels of previous experience in the stress situation. *Journal of Consulting & Clinical Psychology,* **46,** 1357–67.

Mellish, R. W. P. (1969). Preparation of a child for hospitalization and surgery. *Pediatric Clinic of North America,* **16,** 543–53.

Miller, L. C. (1967). Louisville Behavior Check list for males, 6–12 years of age. *Psychological Reports,* **21,** 885–96.

Miller, L. C. (1983). Fears and anxiety in children. In C. E. Walker & M. C. Roberts (Eds.), *Handbook of Clinical Child Psychology* (pp. 337–80). New York: John Wiley.

Miller, L. C., Barrett, C. L., & Hampe, E. (1974). Phobias of childhood in a prescientific era. In A. Davids (Ed.), *Child Personality and Psychopathology: Current Topics,* Vol. 1 (pp. 89–134). New York: John Wiley.

Miller, L. C., Barrett, C. L., Hampe, E., & Noble, H. (1971). Revised anxiety scales for the Louisville Behavior Check list. *Psychological Reports,* **29,** 503–11.

250

Miller, L. C., Barrett, C. L., Hampe, E., & Noble, H. (1972a). Comparison of reciprocal inhibition, psychotherapy and waiting list control for phobic children. *Journal of Abnormal Psychology*, **79**, 269–79.

Miller, L. C., Barrett, C. L., Hampe, E., & Noble, H. (1972b). Factor structure of childhood fears. *Journal of Consulting & Clinical Psychology*, **39**, 264–8.

Miller, L. C., Hampe, E., Barrett, C. L., & Noble, H. (1973). Method factors associated with assessment of child behavior: fact or artifact? Unpublished manuscript, Child Psychiatry Research Center, University of Louisville School of Medicine, Louisville.

Miller, N. E. (1948). Studies of fear as an acquirable drive 1: Fear as motivation and fear-reduction as reinforcement in the learning of new responses. *Journal of Experimental Psychology*, **38**, 89–101.

Miller, N. E. (1951). Learnable drives and rewards. In S. S. Stevens (Ed.), *Handbook of experimental psychology* (pp. 435–72). New York: John Wiley.

Miller, P. M. (1972). The use of visual imagery and muscle relaxation in the counter-conditioning of a phobic child: a case study. *Journal of Nervous & Mental Disease*, **154**, 457–60.

Miller, R. E., Murphy, J. V., & Mirsky, I. A. (1959). Non-verbal communication of affect. *Journal of Clinical Psychology*, **15**, 155–8.

Miller, S. R. (1979). Children's fears: a review of the literature with implications for nursing research and practice. *Nursing Research*, **28**, 217–23.

Milne, G. (1977). Cyclone Tracy: II. The effects on Darwin children. *Australian Psychologist*, **12**, 55–62.

Mitchell, C. (1973). *Time for School: A Practical Guide for Parents of Young Children.* Harmondsworth: Penguin.

Moreland, J. R., Schwebel, A. I., Beck, S., & Wells, R. (1982). Parents as therapists: a review of the behavior therapy parent training literature—1975 to 1981. *Behavior Modification*, **6**, 250–76.

Morganstern, K. P. (1973). Implosive Therapy and flooding procedures: a critical review. *Psychological Bulletin*, **79**, 318–34.

Morris, R. J., & Kratochwill, T. R. (1983). *Treating Children's Fears and Phobias. A Behavioral Approach.* New York: Pergamon Press.

Mowrer, O. H. (1939). A Stimulus-response theory of anxiety and its role as a reinforcing agent. *Psychological Review*, **46**, 553–65.

Murphy, C. M., & Bootzin, R. R. (1973). Active and passive participation in the contact desensitization of snake fear in children. *Behavior Therapy*, **4**, 203–11.

Murphy, G. C. (1980). Consulting with human-service organizations: A difficult role for behavioural psychologists. In A. M. Hudson & M. W. Griffin (Eds.), *Behaviour Analysis and the Problems of Childhood* (pp. 232–45). Bundoora, Victoria: PIT Press.

Murphy, G. C., Hudson, A. M., & King, N. J. (1982). Perceptions of child psychologists held by parents of Australian school children. *Psychological Reports*, **51**, 47–51.

Murphy, G. C., Hudson, A. M., King, N. J., & Remenyi, A. (1985). An interview schedule for use in the behavioural assessment of children's problems. *Behaviour Change*, **2**, 6–12.

Murphy, G. C., & Remenyi, A. G. (1979). Behavioral analysis and organizational reality: the need for a technology of program implementation. *Journal of Organizational Behavior Management*, **2**, 121–31.

Nalven, F. B. (1970). Manifest fears and worries of ghetto versus middle class suburban children. *Psychological Reports*, **27**, 285–6.

Napalkov, A. V. (1963). Information process of the brain. In N. Wiener & J. P. Schadé (Eds.), *Progress in Brain Research.* Vol. 2: *Nerve, Brain and Memory Models* (pp. 59–69). Amsterdam: Elsevier.

Neisworth, J. T., Madle, R. A., & Goeke, K. E. (1975). 'Errorless' elimination of separation anxiety: a case study. *Journal of Behavior Therapy & Experimental Psychiatry*, **6**, 79–82.

Newstatter, W. L. (1938). The effect of poor social conditions in the production of neurosis. *Lancet*, **234**, 1436–41.

Nichols, K., & Berg, I. (1970). School phobia and self-evaluation. *Journal of Child Psychology & Psychiatry*, **11**, 133–41.

Norton, G. R., Dinardo, P. A., & Barlow, D. H. (1983). Predicting phobics' response to therapy: a consideration of subjective, physiological, and behavioural measures. *Canadian Psychologist*, **24**, 50–9.

Obler, M., & Terwilliger, R. F. (1970). Pilot study on the effectiveness of systematic desensitization with neurologically impaired children with phobic disorders. *Journal of Consulting & Clinical Psychology*, **34**, 314–18.

O'Connor, R. D. (1969). Modification of social withdrawal through symbolic modeling. *Journal of Applied Behavior Analysis*, **2**, 15–22.

O'Dell, S. L. (1974). Training parents in behavior modification: a review. *Psychological Bulletin*, **81**, 418–33.

O'Farrell, T. J., & Keuthen, N. J. (1983). Readability of behavior therapy self-help manuals. *Behavior Therapy*, **14**, 449–54.

Öhman, A. (1979). Fear relavance, autonomic conditioning, and phobias: a laboratory model. In P. Sjödén, S. Bates, & W. S. Dockens (Eds.), *Trends in Behavior Therapy* (pp. 107–33). New York: Academic Press.

Ollendick, T. H. (1979a). Behavioral treatment of anorexia nervosa: a five-year study. *Behavior Modification*, **3**, 124–35.

Ollendick, T. H. (1979b). Fear reduction techniques with children. In M. Hersen, R. M. Eisler, & P. M. Miller (Eds.), *Progress in Behavior Modification*, Vol. 8. New York: Academic Press.

Ollendick, T. H. (1983a). Anxiety-based disorders. In M. Hersen (Ed.), *Outpatient Behavior Therapy: A Clinical Guide*. (pp. 273–305). New York: Grune & Stratton.

Ollendick, T. H. (1983b). Reliability and validity of the revised Fear Survey Schedule for Children (FSSCR-R). *Behaviour Research & Therapy*, **21**, 685–92.

Ollendick, T. H. (1986). Child and adolescent behavior therapy. In S. L. Garfield & A. E. Bergin (Eds.), *Handbook of Psychotherapy and Behavior Change, An empirical analysis* (pp. 525–64). (3rd ed.), New York: John Wiley.

Ollendick, T. H., & Cerny, J. A. (1981). *Clinical Behavior Therapy with Children*. New York: Plenum Press.

Ollendick, T. H., & Francis, G. (in press). Assessment and treatment of childhood phobias. *Behavior Modification*.

Ollendick, T. H., & Gruen, G. E. (1972). Treatment of a bodily injury phobia with implosive therapy. *Journal of Consulting & Clinical Psychology*, **38**, 389–93.

Ollendick, T. H., & Hersen, M. (1984). An overview of child behavioral assessment. In T. H. Ollendick & M. Hersen (Eds.), *Child Behavioral Assessment: Principles and Procedures* (pp. 3–19). New York: Pergamon Press.

Ollendick, T. H., Huntzinger, R. M., & King, N. J. (1987, November). Fears in children and adolescents: Gender, developmental and cultural differences. Paper presented at the convention of the Association for the Advancement of Behavior Therapy. Boston, Massachusetts.

Ollendick, T. H., & Mayer, J. A. (1984). School phobia. In S. M. Turner (Ed.), *Behavioral Theories and Treatment of Anxiety*. (pp. 367–411). New York: Plenum Press.

Ollendick, T. H., Matson, J. L., & Helsel, W. J. (1985a). Fears in children and adolescents: Normative data. *Behaviour Research & Therapy*, **23**, 465–7.

Ollendick, T. H., Matson, J. L., & Helsel, W. J. (1985b). Fears in visually-impaired and normally-sighted youths. *Behaviour Research & Therapy*, **23**, 375–8.

Öst, L., & Hugdahl, K. (1981). Acquisition of phobias and anxiety response patterns in clinical patients. *Behaviour Research & Therapy*, **19**, 439–47.

Paul, G. L. (1966). *Insight versus Desensitization in Psychotherapy*. Stanford, CA: Stanford University Press.

Pavlov, I. P. (1927). *Conditional Reflexes* (Translation by G. V. Annep). London: Oxford University Press.

Pearson, J. E., Cataldo, M. F., Tureman, A., Bessman, C. H., & Rogers, M. C. (1980). Pediatric intensive care unit patients: effects of play intervention on behavior. *Critical Care Medicine*, **8**, 64–7.

Penticuff, J. H. (1976). The effect of filmed peer modelling, cognitive appraisal, and autonomic reactivity in changing children's attitudes about health care procedures and personnel. Unpublished doctoral dissertation, Case Western Reserve University.

Perry, M. A., & Furukawa, M. J. (1980). Modeling methods. In F. H. Kanfer, & A. P. Goldstein (Eds.), *Helping People Change* (2nd ed.) (pp. 131–71). New York: Pergamon Press.

Peterson, L., Hartmann, D. P., & Gelfand, D. M. (1980). Prevention of child behavior disorders: a lifestyle change for child psychologists. In P. O. Davidson & S. M. Davidson (Eds.), *Behavioral Medicine: Changing Health Lifestyle* (pp. 195–221). New York: Brunner/Mazel.

Peterson, L., & Shigetomi, C. (1981). The use of coping techniques in minimizing anxiety in hospitalized children. *Behavior Therapy*, **12**, 1–14.

Peterson, L., Schultheis, K., Ridley-Johnson, R., Miller, D. J., & Tracy, K. (1984). Comparison of three modeling procedures on the presurgical and postsurgical reactions of children. *Behavior Therapy*, **15**, 197–203.

Pomerantz, P. B., Peterson, N. T., Marholin, D., & Stern, S. (1977). The *in vivo* elimination of a child's water phobia by a paraprofessional at home. *Journal of Behavior Therapy & Experimental Psychiatry*, **8**, 417–21.

Poser, E. G. (1970). Toward a theory of 'Behavioral Prophylasis'. *Journal of Behavior Therapy & Experimental Psychiatry*, **1**, 39–43.

Poser, E. G. (1976). Strategies for behavioral prevention. In P. O. Davidson (Ed.), *The Behavioral Management of Anxiety, Depression and Pain* (pp. 35–53). New York: Brunner/Mazel.

Poser, E. G., & Hartman, L. M. (1979). Issues in behavioral prevention: empirical findings. *Advances in Behaviour Research & Therapy*, **2**, 1–25.

Poser, E. G., & Hartman, L. M. (1979). Issues in behavioral prevention: empirical responses. *Canadian Journal of Behavioral Science*, **7**, 279–94.

Poznanski, E. O. (1973). Children with excessive fears. *American Journal of Orthopsychiatry*, **43**, 428–38.

Pratt, K. C. (1945). The study of the 'fears' of rural children. *Journal of Genetic Psychology*, **67**, 179–94.

Quay, H. C. (1975). Classification in the treatment of deliquency and antisocial behavior. In N. Hobbs (Ed.), *Issues in the Classification of Children*, Vol. 1. San Francisco: Jossey-Bass.

Quay, H. C. (1979). Classification. In H. C. Quay, & J. S. Werry (Eds.), *Psychopathological Disorders of Childhood* (2nd ed.). New York: John Wiley.

Rachlin, H. (1976). *Introduction to Modern Behaviorism* (2nd ed.). San Francisco: Freeman.

Rachlin, H. (1977). Reinforcing and punishing thoughts. *Behavior Therapy*, **8**, 659–65.

Rachman, S. (1962). Disinhibition and the reminiscence effect in a motor learning task. *British Journal of Psychology*, **53**, 149–57.

Rachman, S. (1968). *Phobias: their nature and control*. Springfield, Ill.: Charles C. Thomas.

Rachman, S. (1969). Treatment by prolonged exposure to high intensity stimulation. *Behaviour Research & Therapy*, **7**, 295–302.

Rachman, S. (1974). *The Meanings of Fear*. Harmondsworth: Penguin.

Rachman, S. (1976). The passing of the two-stage theory of fear and avoidance: fresh possibilities. *Behaviour Research & Therapy*, **14**, 125–34.

Rachman, S. (1977). The conditioning theory of fear acquisition: a critical examination. *Behaviour Research & Therapy*, **15**, 375–87.

Rachman, S. (1978). *Fear and Courage*. San Francisco: Freeman.

Rachman, S. (1979). The return of fear. *Behaviour Research & Therapy*, **17**, 164–5.

Rachman, S., & Costello, C. G. (1961). The aetiology and treatment of children's phobias: a review. *American Journal of Psychiatry*, **118**, 97–105.

Rachman, S., & Hodgson, R. (1974). 1: Synchrony and desynchrony in fear and avoidance. *Behaviour Research & Therapy*, **12**, 311–18.

Rachman, S., & Seligman, M. E. P. (1976). Unprepared phobias: 'Be prepared'. *Behaviour Research & Therapy*, **14**, 333–8.

Radaker, L. D. (1961). The visual imagery of retarded children and the relationship to memory for word forms. *Exceptional Children*, **27**, 524–30.

Razran, G. H. S. (1939). Decremental and incremental effects of distracting stimuli upon the salivary CRs of 24 adult human subjects (inhibition and disinhibition). *Journal of Experimental Psychology*, **24**, 647–52.

Reisinger, J. J., Ora, J. P., & Frangia, G. W. (1976). Parents as change agents for their children: a review. *Journal of Community Psychology*, **4**, 103–23.

Reynolds, C. R., & Paget, K. D. (1981). Factor analysis of the revised Children's Manifest Anxiety Scale for blacks, whites, males, and females with a National Innovative Sample. *Journal of Consulting & Clinical Psychology*, **49**, 352–9.

Reynolds, C. R., & Richmond, B. O. (1978). What I think and feel: a revised measure of children's manifest anxiety. *Journal of Abnormal Child Psychology*, **6**, 271–80.

Reynolds, C. R., & Richmond, B. O. (1979). Factor structure and construct validity of 'What I think and feel': the Revised Children's Manifest Anxiety Scale. *Journal of Personality Assessment*, **43**, 281–3.

Rheingold, H. L., & Eckerman, C. O. (1973). Fear of the stranger: a critical examination. In H. W. Reese (Ed.), *Advances in Child Development and Behavior*, Vol. 8. New York: Academic Press.

Richards, C. S., & Siegel, L. J. (1978). Behavioral treatment of anxiety states and avoidance behaviors in children. In D. Marholin (Ed.), *Child Behavior Therapy* (pp. 274–338). New York: Gardner Press.

Rimm, D. C., Janda, L. H., Lancaster, D. W., Nahl, M., & Dittmar, K. (1977). An exploratory investigation of the origin and maintenance of phobias. *Behaviour Research & Therapy*, **15**, 231–8.

Rimm, D. C., & Lefebvre, R. C. (1981). Phobic disorders. In S. M. Turner, K. S. Calhoun, & H. E. Adams (Eds.), *Handbook of Clinical Behavior Therapy* (pp. 12–40). New York: John Wiley.

Rimm, D. C., & Masters, J. C. (1974). *Behavior Therapy: Techniques and Empirical Findings*. New York: Academic Press.

Ritter, B. (1968). The group desensitization of children's snake phobias using vicarious and contact desensitization procedures. *Behaviour Research & Therapy*, **6**, 1–6.

Roberts, M. C., Wurtele, S. R., Boone, R. R., Ginther, L. J., & Elkins, P. D. (1981). Reduction of medical fears by use of modeling: a preventive application in a general population of children. *Journal of Pediatric Psychology*, **6**, 293–300.

Rodriguez, A., Rodriguez, M., and Eisenberg, L. (1959). The outcome of school phobia: a follow-up study based on 41 cases. *American Journal of Psychiatry*, **116**, 540–4.

Rosenstiel, A. K., & Scott, D. S. (1977). Four considerations in using imagery techniques with children. *Journal of Behaviour Therapy & Experimental Psychiatry*, **8**, 287–90.

Ross, A. O. (1974). *Psychological Disorders of Children: A Behavioral Approach to Theory, Research and Therapy*. New York: McGraw-Hill.

Ross, A. O. (1981). *Child Behavior Therapy: Principles, Procedures and Empirical Basis*. New York: John Wiley.

Ross, D. M., Ross, S. A., & Evans, T. A. (1971). The modification of extreme social withdrawal by modeling with guided participation. *Journal of Behavior Therapy & Experimental Psychiatry*, **2**, 273–79.

Rowland, L. A., & Canavan, A. G. M. (1983). Is a B.A.T. therapeutic? *Behavioural Psychotherapy*, **11**, 139–46.

Russell, G. W. (1967). Human fears: a factor analytic study of three age levels. *Genetic Psychology Monographs*, **76**, 141–62.

Rutter, M., Tizard, J., & Whitmore, K. (1970). *Education, Health and Behavior*, New York: John Wiley.

Ryall, M. R., & Dietiker, K. E. (1979). Reliability and clinical validity of the children's fear survey schedule. *Journal of Behavior Therapy & Experimental Psychiatry*, **10**, 303–9.

Sanders, M. R., & James, J. E. (1983). The modification of parent behavior: a review of generalization and maintenance. *Behavior Modification*, **7**, 3–27.

Sanderson, R. E., Campbell, D., & Laverty, S. G. (1962). Traumatically conditioned responses acquired during respitory paralysis. *Nature*, **196**, 1235–6.

Sarason, S. B., Davidson, K. S., Lighthall, F. F., Waite, R. R., & Ruebush, B. K. (1960). *Anxiety in Elementary School Children*. New York: John Wiley.

Sarason, I. G., & Ganzer, V. J. (1969). Social influence techniques in clinical and community psychology. In C. Spielberger (Ed.), *Current Topics in Clinical and Community Psychology*, Vol. 1. New York: Academic Press.

Sawtell, R. O., Simon, J. F., & Simeonsson, R. J. (1974). The effects of five preparatory methods upon children behavior during the first dental visit. *Journal of Dentistry for Children*, **41**, 37–45.

Scarr, S., & Salapatek, P. (1970). Patterns of fear development during infancy. *Merrill–Palmer Quarterly of Behavior and Development*, **16**, 53–90.

Scherer, M. W., & Nakamura, C. Y. (1968). A Fear Survey Schedule for Children (FSS-FC): a factor analytic comparison with manifest anxiety (CMAS). *Behaviour Research & Therapy*, **6**, 173–82.

Screenivasan, U., Manocha, S. N., & Jain, V. K. (1979). Treatment of severe dog phobia in childhood by flooding: a case report. *Journal of Child Psychology & Psychiatry*, **20**, 255–60.

Seligman, M. E. P. (1971). Phobias and preparedness. *Behavior Therapy*, **2**, 307–20.

Seligman, M., & Hager, J. (1972) (Eds.), *Biological Boundaries of Learning*. New York: Appleton–Century–Crofts.

Sellick, K. J., & Peck, C. L. (1981). Behavioral treatment of fear in a child with cerebral palsy using a flooding procedure. *Archives of Physical Medicine & Rehabilitation*, **62**, 398–400.

Shapiro, A. H. (1975). Behavior of kibbutz and urban children receiving an injection. *Psychophysiology*, **12**, 79–82.

Shapiro, E. S. (1984). Self-monitoring procedures. In. T. H. Ollendick & M. Hersen (Eds.), *Child Behavioral Assessment: Principles and Procedures* (pp. 148–65). New York: Pergamon Press.

Shepherd, M., Cooper, B., Brown, A. C., & Kalton, A. A. (1966). *Psychiatric Illness in General Practice*. London: Oxford University Press.

Sherman, A. R. (1971, March). Some reflections on behavior modification: problems, issues, and possible future directions. Paper presented at the Camarillo Behavior Modification Conference, Camarillo, California.

Sherman, A. R. (1973). *Behavior Modification: Theory and Practice*. Monterey, CA: Brooks/Cole.

Sherrington, C. S. (1906). *The Integrative Action of the Nervous System*. New Haven: Yale University Press.

Sheslow, D. V., Bondy, A. S., & Nelson, R. O. (1982). A comparison of graduated exposure, verbal coping skills, and their combination in the treatment of children's fear of the dark. *Child & Family Behavior Therapy*, **4**, 33–45.

Shirley, M. M. (1933). *The First Two Years*. Vol. III: *Personality Manifestations*. Institute of Child Welfare Monograph No. 8. Minneapolis: University of Minnesota Press.

Shoben, E. J., & Borland, L. (1954). An empirical study of the etiology of dental fears. *Journal of Clinical Psychology*, **10**, 171–4.

Siegel, L. J. (1976). Preparation of children for hospitilization: a selected review of the research literature. *Journal of Pediatric Psychology*, **1**, 26–30.

Siegel, L. J., & Peterson, L. (1980). Stress reduction in young dental patients through coping skills and sensory information. *Journal of Consulting & Clinical Psychology*, **48**, 785–7.

Skinner, B. F. (1953). *Science and Human Behavior.* New York: Macmillan.

Smith, P. K. (1979). The ontogeny of fear in children. In W. Sluckin (Ed.), *Fear in Animals and Man* (pp. 164–98). New York: Van Nostrand Reinhold.

Smith, R. E., & Sharpe, T. M. (1970). Treatment of a school phobia with implosive therapy. *Journal of Consulting & Clinical Psychology,* **35,** 239–43.

Smith, S. L. (1970). School refusal with anxiety: a review of sixty-three cases. *Canadian Psychiatric Association Journal,* **15,** 257–64.

Spiegler, M. D. (1983). *Contemporary Behavioral Therapy.* Palo Alto, CA: Mayfield.

Spiegler, M. D., & Liebert, R. (1970). Some correlates of self-reported fear. *Psychological Reports,* **26,** 691–95.

Spielberger, C. D. (1972). Anxiety as an emotional state. In C. D. Speilberger (Ed.), *Anxiety: Current Trends in Theory and Research,* Vol. 1. New York: Academic Press.

Spielberger, C. (1973). *Manual for the State–Trait Anxiety Inventory for Children.* Palo Alto, CA: Consulting Psychologists Press.

Spitzer, R. L., & Cantwell, D. P. (1980). The DSM-III classification of the psychiatric disorders of infancy, childhood, and adolescence. *Journal of the American Academy of Child Psychiatry,* **19,** 356–70.

Sreenivasan, V., Manocha, S. N., & Jain, V. K. (1979). Treatment of severe dog phobia in childhood by flooding: a case report. *Journal of Child Psychology & Psychiatry,* **20,** 255–60.

Sroufe, L. A. (1977). Wariness of strangers and the study of infant development. *Child Development,* **48,** 731–46.

Stableford, W. (1979). Parental treatment of a child's noise phobia. *Journal of Behavior Therapy & Experimental Psychiatry,* **10,** 159–60.

Stafford-Clark, D. (1965). *What Freud Really Said.* Harmondsworth: Penguin.

Stampfl, T. G., & Levis, D. J. (1967). Essentials of implosive therapy: a learning-based-psychodynamic behavioral therapy. *Journal of Abnormal Psychology,* **72,** 496–503.

Stampfl, T. G., & Levis, D. J. (1968). Implosive therapy—a behavioral therapy? *Behaviour Research & Therapy,* **6,** 31–6.

Stokes, T. F., & Kennedy, S. H. (1980). Reducing child uncooperative behavior during dental treatment through modeling and reinforcement. *Journal of Applied Behavior Analysis,* **13,** 41–9.

Stone, L. J., & Church, J. (1957). *Childhood and Adolescence: A Psychology of the Growing Person.* New York: Random House.

Sulzer-Azaroff, B., & Mayer, G. R. (1977). *Applying Behavior Analysis Procedures with Children and Youth.* New York: Holt, Rinehart & Winston.

Tahmisian, J. A., & McReynolds, W. T. (1971). Use of parents as behavioral engineers in the treatment of a school phobic girl. *Journal of Counseling Psychology,* **18,** 225–8.

Tasto, D. L. (1969). Systematic desensitization, muscle relaxation and visual imagery in the counterconditioning of a four-year-old phobic child. *Behaviour Research & Therapy,* **7,** 409–11.

Taylor, J. A. (1953). A personality scale of manifest anxiety. *Journal of Abnormal & Social Psychology,* **48,** 285–90.

Tearnan, B. H., & Graziano, W. G. (1980). Covert modeling and children's fears: a methodological critique of Chertock and Bornstein. *Child Behavior Therapy,* **2,** 73–7.

Terwilliger, R. F., & Obler, M. (1971). Comment on research in behavior therapy. *Journal of Consulting & Clinical Psychology,* **37,** 14–15.

Thoresen, C. E., & Mahoney, M. J. (1974). *Behavioral Self-control,* New York: Holt, Rinehart & Winston.

Thorpe, G. L. (1979). A big hand for Neil Cheshire; but.... *Bulletin of the British Psychological Society,* **32,** 429–30.

Thorpe, G. L., & Burns, L. E. (1983). *The Agoraphobic Syndrome: Behavioural Approaches to Evaluation and Treatment.* Chichester: John Wiley.

Ultee, C. A., Griffioen, D., & Schellekens, J. (1982). The reduction of anxiety in children: a

256

comparison of the effects of 'systematic desensitization *in vito*' and 'systematic desensitization *in vivo*'. *Behaviour Research & Therapy*, **20**, 61–7.

Upper, D. (Ed.) (1977). *Perspectives in Behavior Therapy*. Kalamazoo, MI: Behaviordelia.

Vaal, J. J. (1973). Applying contingency contracting to a school phobic: a case study. *Journal of Behavior Therapy & Experimental Psychiatry*, **4**, 371–3.

Valentine, C. W. (1946). *The Psychology of Early Childhood* (3rd ed.). London: Methuen.

Van Hasselt, V. B., Hersen, M., Bellack, A. S., Rosenblum, N. D., & Lamparski, D. (1979). Tripartite assessment of the effects of systematic desensitization in a multiphobic child: an experimental analysis. *Journal of Behavior Therapy & Experimental Psychiatry*, **10**, 51–5.

Von Isser, A., Quay, H. C., & Love, C. T. (1980). Interrelationships among three measures of deviant behavior. *Exceptional Children*, **46**, 272–6.

Varni, J. W. (1983). *Clinical Behavioral Pediatrics: An Interdisciplinary Biobehavioral Approach*. New York: Pergamon Press.

Vernon, D. T. A. (1973). Use of modeling to modify children's responses to a natural, potentially stressful situation. *Journal of Applied Psychology*, **58**, 351–6.

Vernon, D. T. A., & Bailey, W. C. (1974). The use of motion pictures in the psychological preparation of children for induction of anesthesia. *Anesthesiology*, **40**, 68–72.

Vernon, D. T. A., Foley, J. M., Sipowicz, R. R., & Schulman, J. L. (1965). *The Psychological Responses of Children to Hospitalization and Illness*. Springfield, Ill.: Charles C. Thomas.

Vernon, D. T. A., Schulman, J. L., & Foley, J. M. (1966). Changes in children's behavior after hospitalization. *American Journal of the Diseases of Children*, **3**, 581–93.

Visintainer, M. A., & Wolfer, J. A. (1975). Psychological preparation for surgical pediatric patients: the effect on children's and parent's stress responses and adjustment. *Pediatrics*, **56**, 187–202.

Walk, R. D. (1956). Self-ratings of fear in a fear-invoking situation. *Journal of Abnormal & Social Psychology*, **52**, 171–8.

Walker, C. E., & Werstlein, R. (1980). Use of relaxation procedures in the treatment of toilet phobia in a 4-year-old child. *The Behavior Therapist*, **3**, 17–18.

Walters, G. C. (1963). Frequency and intensity of pre-shock experiences as determinants of fearfulness in an approach–avoidance conflict. *Canadian Journal of Psychology*, **17**, 412–9.

Waters, W. F., McDonald, D. G., & Koresko, R. L. (1972). Psychophysiological responses during analogue systematic desensitization and non-relaxation control procedures. *Behaviour Research & Therapy*, **10**, 381–93.

Watson, J. B. (1913). Psychology as the behaviourist views it. *Psychological Review*, **20**, 158–77.

Watson, J. B. (1924). *Behaviorism*. New York: People's Institute.

Watson, J. B., & Rayner, R. (1920). Conditioned emotional reactions. *Journal of Experimental Psychology*, **3**, 1–14.

Watson, J. B., & Watson, R. R. (1921). Studies in infant psychology. *Scientific Monthly*, **13**, 495–515.

Watson, J. B. (1928). *Psychological Care of Infant and Child*. New York: Norton.

Waye, M. F. (1979). Behavioral treatment of a child displaying comic-book mediated fear of hand shrinking: a case study. *Journal of Pediatric Psychology*, **4**, 43–7.

Wechsler, D. (1949). *Wechsler Intelligence Scale for Children*. New York: Psychological Corporation.

White, W. C., & Davis, M. T. (1974). Vicarious extinction of phobic behavior in early childhood. *Journal of Abnormal Child Psychology*, **2**, 25–32.

Wilson, B., & Jackson, H. J. (1980). An *in vivo* approach to the desensitization of a retarded child's toilet phobia. *Australian Journal of Developmental Disabilities*, **6**, 137–41.

Wilson, G. D. (1966). An electrodermal technique for the study of phobias. *New Zealand Medical Journal*, **65**, 696–8.

Wilson, G. T. (1978). The importance of being theoretical: a commentary on Bandura's 'Self-efficacy: towards a unifying theory of behavioral change'. *Advances in Behaviour Research & Therapy*, **1**, 217–30.

Wilson, G. T. (1982). Fear reduction methods and the treatment of anxiety disorders. *Annual Review of Behavior Therapy. Theory and Practice*, **8**, 82–119.

Wilson, G. T., & Davidson, G. C. (1971). Process of fear reduction in systematic desensitization: animal studies. *Psychological Bulletin*, **76**, 1–14.

Wilson, G. T., & O'Leary, K. D. (1980). *Principles of Behavior Therapy*. Englewood Cliffs, NJ: Prentice-Hall.

Windheuser, H. J. (1977). Anxious mothers as models for coping with anxiety. *Behavioral Analysis & Modification*, **2**, 39–58.

Wirt, R. D., & Broen, W. E. (1958). *Booklet for the Personality Inventory for Children*. Minneapolis: published by the authors.

Wish, P. A., Hasazi, J. E., & Jurgela, A. R. (1973). Automated direct deconditioning of a childhood phobia. *Journal of Behavior Therapy & Experimental Psychiatry*, **4**, 279–83.

Wolf, M. M. (1978). Social validity: the case for subjective measurement or how applied behavior analysis is finding its heart. *Journal of Applied Behavior Analysis*, **11**, 203–14.

Wolpe, J. (1958). *Psychotherapy by Reciprocal Inhibition*. Stanford, CA: Stanford University Press.

Wolpe, J. (1973). *The Practice of Behavior Therapy* (2nd ed.). New York: Pergamon Press.

Wolpe, J. (1976a). Behavior therapy and its malcontents. I: Denial of its bases and psychodynamic fusionism. *Journal of Behavior Therapy & Experimental Psychiatry*, **7**, 1–5.

Wolpe, J. (1976b). Behaviour therapy and its malcontents. II: Multimodal electicism, cognitive exclusivism and 'exposure' empiricism. *Journal of Behavior Therapy & Experimental Psychiatry*, **7**, 109–16.

Wolpe, J. (1977). Inadequate behavior analysis: the Achilles heel of outcome research in behavior therapy. *Journal of Behavior Therapy & Experimental Psychiatry*, **8**, 1–3.

Wolpe, J. (1978). Cognitive and causation in human behavior and its therapy. *American Psychologist*, **33**, 437–46.

Wolpe, J., & Rachman, S. (1960). Psychoanalytic 'evidence': a critique based on Freud's case of Little Hans. *Journal of Nervous & Mental Diseases*, **131**, 135–48.

Woodward, J. (1959). Emotional disturbances of burned children. *British Medical Journal*, **1**, 1009–13.

Woodworth, R. S. (1959). Obituary of John Broadus Watson 1878–1958. *American Journal of Psychology*, **72**, 301–10.

Woolfolk, A. E., Woolfolk, R. L., & Wilson, G. T. (1977). A rose by any other name...labeling bias and attitudes toward behavior modification. *Journal of Consulting & Clinical Psychology*, **45**, 184–91.

Yates, A. J. (1970). *Behavior Therapy*. New York: John Wiley.

Yates, A. J. (1975). *Theory and Practice in Behaviour Therapy*. New York: John Wiley.

Yule, W. (1977). The potential of behavioural treatment in preventing later childhood difficulties. *Behavioural Analysis & Modification*, **2**, 19–31.

Yule, W. (1979). Behavioural approaches to the treatment and prevention of school refusal. *Behavioural Analysis & Modification*, **3**, 55–68.

Yule, W., Sacks, B., & Hersov, L. (1974). Successful flooding treatment of noise phobia in an eleven-year-old boy. *Journal of Behavior Therapy & Experimental Psychiatry*, **5**, 209–11.

Zabin, M. A., & Melamed, B. G. (1980). Relationship between parental discipline and children's ability to cope with stress. *Journal of Behavioral Assessment*, **2**, 17–38.

Ziv, A., & Israeli, R. (1973). Effects of bombardment on the manifest anxiety level of children living in kibbutzim. *Journal of Consulting & Clinical Psychology*, **40**, 287–91.

Subject Index